Cursor Mundi

PART VII

Early English Text Society.

Original Series, No. 101

1893 (reprinted 1962)

Price 25s.

Cursor Mundi

A NORTHUMBRIAN POEM OF THE

XIVTH CENTURY

BRITISH MUSEUM MS. COTTON VESPASIAN A. III

BODLEIAN MS. FAIRFAX 14

GÖTTINGEN UNIVERSITY LIBRARY MS. THEOL. 107

TRINITY COLLEGE CAMBRIDGE MS. R. 3. 8.

BY

RICHARD MORRIS

PART VII

ESSAY ON THE MANUSCRIPTS AND DIALECT

BY

H. HUPE

Published for

THE EARLY ENGLISH TEXT SOCIETY

by the

OXFORD UNIVERSITY PRESS

LONDON   NEW YORK   TORONTO

OXFORD

UNIVERSITY PRESS

Great Clarendon Street, Oxford OX2 6DP
United Kingdom

Oxford University Press is a department of the University of Oxford.
It furthers the University's objective of excellence in research, scholarship,
and education by publishing worldwide. Oxford is a registered trade mark of
Oxford University Press in the UK and in certain other countries

First Edition published in 1893
Reprinted 1962

Published in the United States of America by Oxford University Press
198 Madison Avenue, New York, NY 10016, United States of America

British Library Cataloguing in Publication Data
Data available

Library of Congress Cataloging in Publication Data
Data available

Original Series, 101

ISBN 978-0-19-722101-3

ON THE FILIATION AND THE TEXT
OF THE MSS. OF THE MIDDLE-ENGLISH POEM
CURSOR MUNDI
BY
H. HUPE

THE FILIATION AND TEXT OF THE MSS.

THE ' *Cursor Mundi*,' named by its author ' Cursur o werld,' a well-known compilation of Scriptural history, to which legendary and allegorical tales and reminiscences of secular, Oriental and Occidental, history are added, was edited by Dr. Richard Morris for the Early English Text Society during the years 1874-78. In its five volumes it treats of the ' 7 eldis of þe werld,'[1] and is fore-worded by a prologue of 270 lines, in which the author speaks of the motives which induced him to undertake his work, and gives a brief sketch of the whole of it, and finally declares that he has not made use of French in order that the common folk may the better understand him.

The I. age, ll. 271—1626, treats of the Creation, the Fall of Lucifer, Para-dise, Adam's sin, Cain's curse, Adam's death, and the corruption of the world by man's sin (*Gen.* i.—vi.).[2]

---

[1] Compare Part IV. Morris, Contents of *C. M.* of Parts I., II., III., IV., and Tables of Contents in the Fairfax, Göttingen, and Laud MSS. in Part V. The above statement is not a mere repetition.

[2] Compare 'An Inquiry into the Sources of the Cursor Mundi, by Dr. Haenisch. 1885,' published by the E. E. T. Soc. Haenisch's very able essay is not quite exhaustive. I should have liked first to have seen what the *Cursor* has in common with Scripture. In the above enumeration I have stated what it owes to the Old Testament. That the Old Testament was the direct source of the compiler is still. questionable ; for we may some day find some earlier Southern-English poem which treated the same subject, and likewise made use of the *Historia Scholastica*. just as, in another part of *C. M.*, the ' Assumption ' is found to be from a Southern-English source. Besides, there is no doubt that, as Haenisch clearly proves, the compiler knew, and availed himself of, Wace and Grosseteste. The parallel passages of *Cursor* and *Historia Scholastica* cited by Dr. Haenisch may often be explained otherwise than he has done it. Only compare l. 3214 (Haenisch, page 7), which contains a common tradition of the Hebrews ; ll. 3481-82, and the previous lines may as well refer to *Gen.* xxv. 22 ; l. 3864 ('Jacob was master hird of his fee ') is not to be com-pared with *Historia Scholastica*—' Tandem curam gregis eum habere decrevit ' ; l. 4204 will easily be inferred from *Gen.* xxxvii. 29, 30, ff. ; ll. 5604-6 (Haenisch, page 8—'Aram [it must be 'Amram '] had three children, Moses, Aaron, and Mary ') were surely known to every 'clerk,' and he would also have known Amram's wife, Jochebeth. As to l. 9197, about which Haenisch makes bold to say, ' In the Bible the name of Jechonias is not to be found,' cf. *St. Matth.* i. 11, where the genealogy of Joseph (ll. 9233-47) is also found. I will just mention some other lines, 19509-10 (Philip þat was o dekens an þe neist fra Steuen was slan), about which Haenisch remarks: " The latter line in *C.* is not to be found in the *Historia Scholastica*. I assume (Haenisch is of opinion that Philip was

The II. age, ll. 1627—2314, treats of the ark and flood, Noah and his three sons, the family of Shem, ancestor of ' leuedi Mari,' and the tower of Babylon (*Gen.* vii.—xi.).

The III. age, ll. 2315—7860, treats of Abraham, Lot and Sarah, Isaac and Ishmael, Sarah's death, Isaac's marriage, Jacob and Esau, Jacob's wooing, Joseph, Moses, and Pharaoh, the twelve plagues, the passage of the Red Sea, the tree of life and Moses' wands, the golden calf, the laws of Moses, the Jews' entrance into Canaan under Joshua, the Judges, Samson, Samuel, Saul, David and Goliath, and Saul's jealousy of David (*Gen.* xii.—xxxiii., xxxvii., xxxix.—l. ; *Exod.* i.—xviii., xix. 20—25, xxi.—xxiii., xxiv. 18, xxxii. ; *Num.* xvii. ; *Deut.* xxxiv. 5—7 ; *Joshua* i., iii., xxiv. 32 ; *Judges* i. 12, 13, iii. 9—11, 15, 31, iv. 4, 6, vi. 11, vii. 7, 25, viii. 10, x. 1—3, xi. 1, 6, xii. 8, 11—14, xiv.—xvi. ; 1 *Samuel* vii. 6, viii., ix. 16, x. 1, xvi.—xviii.).

The IV. age, ll. 7861—9228, treats of David's reign, his purpose to build a temple, and his successor (2 *Sam.* vii., xi., xii.).

' The Story of the Three Holy Rods, or Trees,' ll. 7973—8262,[1] which is a legend, I have not found any correspondency to in the Bible, nor have I to the ' Choice of David's Successor,' ll. 8331—8434 [1] (which in the Bible is quite differently related), nor to ' The Wonderful Childhood of Solomon,' ll. 8435—8508,[1] nor to ' The Story of David is finished,' ll. 8509—8538.[1]

Then there is an account of Solomon's choice of wisdom, and his judgment between the two harlots (1 *Kings* iii.).

In what follows, the text relates Solomon's building of the Temple. Compare the rather legendary substance with 1 *Kings* v., vi., which is quite at variance with our text, especially the insertion of the ' Master Spar,' which the tree in the garden of the King is to furnish; and the tale of the first martyr, Maximilla, ll. 8890—8978,[1] cannot be found in Holy Writ.

At last it tells us of Solomon's death (1 *Kings* xii. 42, 43), and of his successors, which enumeration may have easily been put together from the Bible.

The V. age, ll. 9229—12740, treats of the family of Joseph and Mary (*St. Matth.* i.), Isaiah's prophecy (*Is.* vii., ix. 6, 7, xi. ; *Jerem.* xxiii.), Adam's fall, and the scheme to save mankind.

---

slain next to Stephen), a misreading here, especially as the three other manuscripts differ." That is a gross mistake ; for the omission of the relative pronoun, nominative case, which is rather frequent in M. E., is not paid attention to ; we must therefore take it as : " Steuen þat was slan " !

[1] Haenisch, cf. page 9, has omitted these lines in his comparison.

Then we find the insertion of the parable of a King and his four Daughters. Again we hear of prophecies of Jesus, ll. 9817—9876, which first correspond again with *Is.* ix. 6, 7, to which a paraphrase is added. There follows the parable of the Castle of Love and Grace.

Then the poem treats of a prayer to Mary, her birth, childhood, and marriage, Gabriel, John the Baptist, the birth of Christ, the Three Kings, Christ's childhood, His miracles, His stay in Egypt, how the son of a priest was killed by Him, and another who had struck Him a 'scou'; His first school-life, the resuscitation of a boy fallen out of a loft, and other wonders; how Jesus carried the water in His lap when the pot was broken; how He sowed a grain of wheat which in one day grew, so that they reaped a hundred measures; how the lions fawned on Him; how He pulled the short tree long; how He was brought again and again to school, and how He put His masters to shame by His great learning; how He restored to life the burgess Joseph of Capernaum; how He slew the adder; how the light of heaven shone on Jesus asleep; His disputes with the Doctors in the Temple; Joachim's wife Anne, who, after Joachim's death, married Cleophas, and after his death, Salomas.

The *VI. age*, ll. 12752—21846, treats of John the Baptist and Jesus, Christ's baptism, His temptation, John's death, Christ's ministry and the choice of the apostles, the miracle at the Bridal at Cana, and other wonders according to St. John, as the feeding of 5000 men with five loaves and two fishes; how He restored to sight the man who was born blind, how He delivered the woman taken in adultery, how, on the Sabbath day, He cured a man who had been diseased thirty-eight years, how He raised Lazarus four days buried; the obstinacy of the Jews and their plot against Christ's life, Christ's entry into Jerusalem, the last supper (*in long lines*), the betrayal and last hours of Christ (*long lines*), the trial before Caiaphas and Pilate (*long lines*), the Crucifixion and Burial (*long lines*); a discourse between Christ and Man, Joseph of Arimathea, the Resurrection of Christ, the Resurrection of Simeon's two sons, Carius and Lenthius, and their story of Christ's entry into Hell; Pilate's letter to Rome; our Lord's life after He had risen, the Ascension; the description of the person of Christ, the acts of the apostles, the descent of the Holy Ghost, the falsehood of Ananias and Sapphira, the imprisonment of the apostles, and their deliverance by an angel; the stoning of Stephen, the persecution of the Christians, and Saul's hand in it; Simon Magus, the conversion of Saint Paul, Peter's vision and preaching to the Heathen, the assumption

of our Lady, and her burial; the works and death of each of the apostles, the
finding of the Holy Cross, and the bond-story,[1] the virtues of the cross.

The VII. age, ll. 21847—24968, treats of the arrival of Christ, of Ante-
christ, the Fifteen Signs before Doomsday, of Doomsday itself, the description of
Hell and its nine pains; Heaven, and the seven gifts of the blessed; the state
of the world after Doomsday; the author's exhortation to his fellow-men, a
prayer to our Lady, the sorrows of Mary (de lamentacione Marie, in six-lined
ryme couee); the story of Elsey, and the Festival of the Conception.

Of these varying contents I am able to compare 10 MSS., four of which are
completely, and five in certain fragments, published by R. Morris,[2] and one by
J. R. Lumby. I enumerate them according to their age, such as I take it
to be.

1. Gg = MS. Gg. 4. 27. 2, in the Cambridge University Library, published
by J. R. Lumby, for the E. E. Text Soc. 'King Horn, with Fragments of
Floris and Blauncheflur, and of the Assumption of Our Lady, from a MS.
(Gg. 4. 27. 2) in the Camb. Lib., etc., London, 1866.' This MS. of 14 folios,
which, according to Lumby's preface, appears to be of about the latter half of
the 13th century, contains, on leaves 13b—14b, a fragment, written in double
columns of 40 lines each, and occasionally, as the lines are short, with two
lines joined into one. The initial letters of the lines are written a little
apart from the rest, and coloured. This fragment of 240 lines treats of the
"Assumption of our Lady,"[3] and corresponds to ll. 20065—20848 of Cursor
Mundi, of which ll. 20065—20304 are = ll. 11—240 Gg.

2. E = Edinburgh Fragment, in the Library of the Royal College of
Physicians, in a thin quarto, vellum, of 50 leaves closely written in double
columns, each of about 40—50 lines. This volume, on account of its 3

---

[1] The attention of the Shakspere student was called to this—the widely-known story
being in Shakspere's Merchant of Venice—by Miss L. T. Smith's paper in the New Sh.
Soc.'s Trans., 1875-6, p. 181. Here it is a goldsmith who had borrowed from a Jew
a sum he could not repay. The Jew demanded a pound of flesh for the debt. Two
messengers of Constantine's mother, Ellen, were to give judgment, and said that he
might take the Christian's flesh, but not his blood. The Jew, outwitted, curses them for
their judgment, but must pay for his abusive words. So he said he would show where
the cross lay, and the queen gave him respite.

[2] In the following lines I shall not call the attention of the reader to every mistake,
or omission in the remarks, or the numbering of lines of our printed text. Only when it
is quite indispensable, or I am at a loss, shall I make a remark.

[3] Compare F. Gierth's Ueber die älteste mittelenglische Version der Assumptio
Mariæ (Kölbing, Engl. Stud., vii. 1—33). Gierth compares Gg with A, and other MSS.,
but not with Morris' texts. My results are therefore different; cf. Gierth. p. 22, 30.

different handwritings, may be divided into 3 parts, the first and third of which contain parts of the *Cursor*. The 3 handwritings belong to the latter half of the 13th century, or to the first quarter of the 14th century,[1] though the orthography is not alike[2] in them.

C. M., ll. 18989—22417 = leaf 37a, col. 1—50b, col. 2.

Remarks. l. 19226 is inserted in a different hand, a blank being originally left here; after l. 19476 we find a blank space of 14 lines' width; after l. 19656 such a one of 13 lines, but no lines are omitted; after l. 20149 four leaves are lost, so that, between the leaves 43 and 44, ll. 20150-800 are omitted; at the end of ll. 19717 and 19718, ll. 20849, 50, 54, ll. 20902-23, ll. 22373-8, some letters cut off by the book-binder are wanting; leaves 44 and 45 are much injured; of lines 21024, 28, 32-48, 21073-88, 21135-41, more than half of each line is wanting; ll. 21142-258 and ll. 21259-600 are wanting, only of ll. 21257-64 some letters or words at the end of the lines are preserved. Morris remarks that between leaves 45 and 46 two leaves are wanting, and without calling the attention to the gap of ll. 21142-258, adds that 337 lines are thus wanting, so that he counts from ll. 21264-600. Can the injured lines 21259-64 be on leaf 45b, col. 2, on which 48 lines already are? l. 22040 is in the margin, and therefore partly cut off. There are some Latin headings in a later hand.

C. M., ll. 22418—24968 = leaf 1a, col. 1—15b, col. 2.

Remark. ll. 24360—24520 (of the latter line only 'Sa fersli to fall' is preserved) are wanting between leaves 12 and 13, so that one leaf is lost. Morris only says: 'A gap in the MS.'

3. C = Cotton Vespas. A iii. MS. in the Library of the British Museum. The MS. is a folio-volume, vellum, which contains the completest version of the *Cursor Mundi* on 138 leaves, closely written in double columns, each of about 45 lines, in 3 different hands of the first half of the 14th century, and, in some passages, in a fourth hand of a later time. On 23 other leaves there are several 'Additions.'

C. M., ll. 1—16748 = leaf 2—91b, col. 2 written in one hand.

„ ll. 16749—16762, then 149 extra lines, and

„ ll. 16803—814, then 72 extra lines = leaf 92a, col. 1—93b, col. 1. l. 8 in a second hand and a different (midland) dialect.

---

[1] Compare *Engl. Metrical Homilies* from MSS. of the Fourteenth Century, etc., by John Small, Edinburgh, 1862, Introd. XI.

[2] Observe in part 1 of the MS. f. i. 'you, ye,' etc., and in part 3 'gie, giu,' etc.

C. M. ll. 16849—17288 = leaf 93*b*, col. 1, l. 9—95*b*, col. 2, l. 19 in the first hand. The insertion 'Of the Resurrection,' 466 extra lines, and

,, ll. 17289—17316 = leaf 95*b*, col. 2, l. 20—98*b*, col. 2 are in the second hand again.

,, ll. 17317—17852 = leaf 99*a*, col. 1—101*b*, col. 2 are in the first hand.

,, ll. 17853—18028 are wanting. 'The Cotton MS. seems to have lost a leaf here, as the catchwords "þou late us" are not on the next page.'

,, ll. 18029—20064 = leaf 102*a*, col. 1—112*b*, col. 2 in the first hand.

,, ll. 20065—21172 = leaf 113*a*, col. 1—119*a*, col. 1 in a third hand.

,, ll. 21173—23450 = leaf 119*a*, col. 2—131*a*, col. 2, and

,, ll. 23451—23542 = leaf 132*a*, then

,, ll. 23543—23634 = leaf 131*b*, and

,, ll. 23635—24968 = leaf 132*b*, col. 1—139*b*, col. 1, l. 36 in the first hand.

The pages of leaves 131*b* and 132*a* are misplaced in the MS.

Remarks. In ll. 1037 and 38 the words 'gyon,' 'eufrates & fison,' are in a different hand and ink. l. 6779 and half of l. 6780 do not correspond to the other MSS., and are written in a later hand. In l. 7222 the later hand will read 'hoo' instead of 'þou,' in l. 7252 'hore' instead of 'hare,' in l. 7286 'enoynted' instead of 'smerld'; compare also ll. 7328, 7376, 7399. In l. 7304 'nise' at the end does not correspond to the other MSS., and is in a later hand. In l. 7408 the MS. corrected 'wit his gleu' to 'wit gleu wald.' In the ll. 24306-10 the MS. is torn, so that the beginning of the lines is wanting. In l. 24383 the ryming word 'sare' is to be added.

After l. 24968 come the 'Additions.'

1. An Exposition of the Creed, ll. 24973—25102 = leaf 139*b*, col. 1, l. 37—140*a*, col. 2, l. 26.

2. The Lord's Prayer and its Exposition, ll. 25103—25402 = leaf 140*a*, col. 2, l. 27—141*b*, col. 2, l. 18.

3. A Prayer to the Trinity, ll. 25403—25486 = leaf 142*b*, col. 1, l. 12 [1]— 143*a*, col. 1, ll. 1—3.

---

[1] Morris has made the following remark as to l. 25403 : 'This prayer comes after l. 25474, page 1458, in the Cotton MS.,' which seems to be a mistake. In the Cotton MS. 'A Prayer to the Trinity' comes after 'A Prayer for the Hours of the Passion,' which does not correspond to the Göttingen and Fairfax MSS.

4. A Prayer for the Hours of the Passion, ll. 25487—25618 = leaf 141*b*, col. 2, l. 19—142*b*, col. 1, l. 11.[1]

5. The 'Boke of Penance,' ll. 25684—29547 = leaf 143*a*, col. 1—163*a*, col. 1, l. 20.

Remarks. In the ll. 25151-54 some words are defaced. The ll. 25619 —83, ' A Song of the Five Joys of our Lady,' are only in the Göttingen MS.

4. A = Additional MS. 10,036 in the Library of the British Museum. It is a nice little small 8vo. MS., early 14th century, which, on leaves 62—80 in one column of regularly 24 lines, contains in 904 lines (cf. ll. 20065—20848 of the main text) an extract, viz. the Assumption of our Lady. It has a beginning of 12 lines of its own, and the end quite differs from the 84 last lines of the main text, so that it contains about 200 lines of fresh matter.

5. G = MS. Theol. 107r. in the Göttingen University Library. The MS. is a quarto, vellum, written in a nice hand of the first half of the 14th century. On 164 leaves and part of leaf 165, written in double columns (but with two exceptions) each of about 38 lines, it contains the completest version next to C. The 'Contents' on the front of leaf 1 of the MS. are in 4 columns, in red. No. 96, ' Of þe purgatori of saint patrick,' is the last mentioned among the ' Additions,' but is no longer in the MS., which ends in the prologue to the Book of Penance, l. 25766. At the foot of the Table of Contents we see a shield in 4 quarters, much rubbed. In Part V., 1 a Morris remarks : ' A fly-leaf has the book-plate (with arms, and motto " prudenter et sincere ") of C. T. Sullow, and a note that the MS. was bought at auction, in Hanover, on June 14, 1786.'

C. M. ll. 1—974 = leaf 1*b*, col. 1—7*b*, col. 2.

„ ll. 975—988 are wanting ; 'no gap.'

„ ll. 989—14933 = leaf 8*a*, col. 1—100*b*, col. 1, l. 22 and col. 2, l. 16.

„ ll. 14937—17110 in one column of long lines = leaf 100*b*, l. 23— 114*b*, l. 34. ll. 14934—6 are the heading for the Passion in T.

„ ll. 17111—23944 in double columns again = leaf 114*b*, col. 1, l. 34/8 + col. 2, l. 34/8—159*a*, col. 2, l. 8.

„ ll. 23945—24049 in six-lined ryme couee = leaf 159*a*, col. 2, l. 8— 159*b*, col. 2.

„ ll. 24050—24201 are wanting ; one leaf is lost here, as the MS. breaks off in the midst of a stanza, and again begins on leaf 160 with a sixth line.

„ ll. 24202—24968 = leaf 160*a*, col 1—165*a*, col. 1, l. 6.

[1] See foot-note on p. 64*.

Now follow the 'Additions' 1, 2, 3, 4, as in C.:

    ll. 24973—25618 = leaf 165*a*, col. 1, l. 7—169*a*, col. 1, l. 12.

    ll. 25619—25683 ('A Song of the Five Joys of our Lady,' in five-lined stanzas, only in the Göttingen MS.) = leaf 169*a*, col. 1, l. 13—169*a*, l. 6 from foot.

    ll. 25684—25766 (Beginning of 'Addition' 5 in C.) = leaf 169*a*, l. 5 from foot—169*b*, col. 2.

    6. F = Fairfax MS. 14 in the Bodleian Library, Oxford.   This folio-volume, vellum, contains the *Cursor*, on 103 leaves, in double columns, each of about 50 lines, in one hand of the second half of the 14th century, and has a great many gaps.   Originally (cf. Part V., 1 a) it was of the same contents as C., but now it has about 6000 lines less than C., though, beside small gaps of 2—10 lines, there are a great many additional lines compared with C. or G.

Mr. W. H. Allnutt, Bodl. Libr., Oxford, tells me that the MS. is only described in the old catalogue of 1697, where it is called "A Book of old English Poetry drawn from the Scripture."

In Part V., 1 a we find the Table of Contents, divided into 90 chapters, but as instead of chapter 79 there is miswritten 69, we see at the end LXXX.

Leaf 1 has some scribbling, and some Latin, English, and French lines; at foot there are some notes and words, and on leaf 3 back some Latin lines in a later (16th cent.) hand.

Leaves 2 and 3 contain the Table of Contents.

    C. M. ll. 1—9324 = leaf 4*a*—51*b*.[1]

      „   ll. 9325—11614 are wanting; about 11 leaves are lost here, one leaf of which seems to be torn out, so that l. 11615 is on leaf 53.

      „   ll. 11615—16226 = leaf 53*a*—75*b*.

      „   ll. 16227—18512 are wanting, so that about 11 leaves are lost here.

      „   ll. 18513—18894 = leaf 76*a*—77*b*.

      „   ll. 18895—19084 are wanting, so that about 6 leaves are lost here.[2]

      „   ll. 19085—20248 = leaf 78*a*—83*b*.

      „   ll. 20249—20436 are wanting, so that one leaf is lost here.

      „   ll. 20437—24972 = leaf 84*a*—107*b*, l. 2.

Remarks.   In some lines, letters wanting are added in the text.   I do not think it worth while to name all these passages.   ll. 11917-20, 11925-34, 11937-54, 12015-18 are almost erased.   In ll. 24385-8 and ll. 24433-6 the MS. is torn.

---

[1] In the Text of the Fairfax MS. I seldom found the addition 'col 1' or 'col 2.'

[2] Morris' foot-note on page 1082 seems to be a mistake.

The next leaves give the ' Additions,' 1, 2, 3, 4, as in C. :

   ll. 24973—25618 = leaf 107b, l. 3—110b, col. 2, 41st line from foot.

   ll. 25684—27899 (Part of ' Addition' 5) = leaf 110b, 40th line from foot—121b.

Leaf 121b, foot, has the catchwords ' and hit is.'

ll. 25619—25683, only in G., and ll. 27900—29547, according to C., are wanting, as well as part of Chapter lxxxx, which is divided into ' Catoun litil,' and ' Catoun mykil.'

Leaves 122 and 123 have only 378 lines of *Cato's Morals*, but in several lines, f. i. ll. 280-8, the MS. is torn, and after l. 327 ' 9 lines 1½ stanzas torn off.' It is signed at foot: ' Stokynbrig scripsit istum librum Wilhelmo Kervour de Lancastre.' Two blank leaves follow, partly scribbled on in different hands. On the 2nd leaf there are two Latin lines in a modern hand, the rest, some Latin ryming proverbs, are in a hand of 15th century.

7. T. = MS. R. 3. 8. in the Library of Trinity College, Cambridge. It is a folio-volume, vellum, containing 144 leaves, two of which are blank. It is written in double columns (except as noted below), each of about 40 lines, in a hand of the first quarter of the 15th century. When compared with G., it is an almost complete, nice copy of *Cursor Mundi*.

The MS. is signed at foot by a later hand : John Digby.

As to the handwriting Dr. W. Aldis Wright, Trinity College, Cambridge, had the kindness to tell me that it is not unlike the MS. of Chaucer in the Brit. Mus., Harl. 7334.

C. M. ll. 1—974 = leaf 1a, col. 1—7a, col. 1, l. 10.

   ,, ll. 975—988 are wanting, but ' no gap.'

   ,, ll. 989—14915 = leaf 7a, col. 1, l. 11—92b, l. 42.

   ,, ll. 14916-33 are wanting, but ' no gap.'

   ,, ll. 14934-36 are the heading for the ' Passion.'

   ,, ll. 14937—16966 = leaf 92b, l. 19 from foot—105a, l. 10, and

   ,, ll. 16967—17008 at the end of the Passion, according to G., are omitted, but ' no gap.'

   ,, ll. 17009—17082 = leaf 105a, l. 11—105b, l. 7 are written, in one column, across the page.

   ,, ll. 17083—17110 omitted ; ' no gap.'

   ,, ll. 17111—17270 (Discourse between Christ and Man) and

C. M. ll. 17271-88 (Beginning of 'Joseph of Arimathea,' according to G.)
    omitted, 'no gap'; before l. 17289 T. has a heading of its own:
    'Of Joseph of Aramathi: To speke now spede wol I.'

  „ ll. 17289—21344 = leaf 105*b*, col. 1, l. 8—130*a*, col. 1, l. 24.

  „ ll. 21345—6, according to C., are neither in G. nor in T.

  „ ll. 21347—846 (The Finding of the Holy Cross) omitted; 'no
    gap.'[1]

  „ ll. 21847—23892 and, with a conclusion of its own,

  „ ll. 23893—23898 = leaf 130*a*, col. 1, l. 25—142*b*, l. 8.

8. H. = Herald's College MS., Arundel press, 57, in the British Museum.
It is a folio-volume in a handwriting of about the middle of the 15th century,
containing 132 leaves written in double columns, each of 40 lines.

It begins with l. 153 on leaf 1, sign. A. ii, col. 1, and ends with l. 23898,
as T., on leaf 132*b*.

In the printed text H. has been used for filling up gaps in F. (cf. ll.
18895—992 etc.), and in C. (cf. ll. 17853—18028); besides, the Editor
has given a specimen at the end of Part V.

9. B. = Bedford MS., in the Town Library, Bedford. This MS. (cf. Part
V, 1164, at foot), a paper one, bearing the date 1442 on one of the leaves,
contains 175 leaves in quarto, written in double columns, each of 30 lines.
When compared with T., it is a nearly complete copy. It begins with l. 1,
and suddenly stops at l. 22004, giving a conclusion of its own of two lines.

Miss L. Toulmin Smith was kind enough to tell me that it is notable as
containing, instead of certain parts of Cursor, the translation of Bonaventura's
Meditations, supposed to be Robert of Brunne's.

In the printed text we find only some specimens of this MS.

10. L. = Laud MS. 416, in the Bodleian Library, Oxford. It is a folio-
volume, containing on leaves 66—181*b* (written in double columns, each of
about 45 lines), when compared with T., a rather incomplete [2] copy of *C. M.*
It begins with l. 1, and ends, like T., with l. 23898.

Leaf 65 (old paging C xvj), 'the only leaf left' (cf. Part V, p. 5), contains
a Calendarium de Cursor Mundi.

Mr. Allnutt, Oxford, had the kindness to tell me that Laud MS. 416 is
described in Mr. Coxe's catalogue as 'sec. xv. anno scilicet 1459 scriptus,' and

---

[1] The above lines are likewise omitted in H. B. L.

[2] Cf. ll. 14782—14960 which are wanting in L., two leaves torn out, and ll. 18633—
18990 (?).

containing *a metrical paraphrase of the ten commandments, a tretyce of the vii dedly synnys*,[1] *Cursor Mundi*, a short tretyce by Vigesyus, the destruction of Thebes, the gouernaunce of kynggis and pryncis, of the assemble of the byrdis on Seint Volantins day.

In the printed text L. has been used for filling up gaps, especially in F. The Editor has also given at the end of Part V a specimen of 270 lines by the side of B. and H. specimens.

§ 1. In considering these 10 MSS. with regard to their filiation, we cannot help seeing a parentage in C. E. (= x) when compared with F. G. (= y). The arguments are not very easily found, for E. in its extract of ll. 18989—24968, as well as F. and G. in their part, have several gaps. On account of this deficiency of the materials to be compared, I have taken leave to make a comparison between x and y even where of y only G. or F. exists, and that on the principle that such a proof may be admitted, when the variations of G. or F. from x seem to be original. There is no doubt, of course, that the latter way will often lead to mere suppositions, but the reader is requested at once to compare § 2.

Orthographic peculiarities, or expressions which are owing to the dialects[2] or to the age of the respective MSS., are not taken into consideration.

1. There are the same mistakes in C. E. (= x): F. G. (y)—

    l. 20058, giuis tuenti x; fourti y.

    l. 23373, in bodi suetnes (suecnes, E.) and fairhede x; in bodi suiftnes and fairhede y. cf. l. 23381.

2. There are the same expressions or rymes in C. E.—

    (*a*) when compared with y :

        l. 19640, lere / x ; here / y (cf. l. 19654).

        l. 22633, þe erth þai sal do for to rift x ; þe erd þan sal it do to rift y.

        l. 23734, for-þi we agh be bun at bide x ; for-þi we au ai him abide y.

        l. 24305, wordes quone / x; wordis sone / y. cf. 24685, where G. has 'quon.'

    (*b*) when compared with G. (where F. is wanting) :

        ll. 19013—14, gan turne : murne x ; gan tru : þai ru.

        l. 23766, þe ture (E. has the mistake 'turne') x ; þe land.

---

[1] Cf. Part V, p. 6, foot: 'The rest of the page (*i.e.* 65*b*) is blank, the MS. not (?!) being intended to contain any of the Additions in other MSS.'

[2] Cf. l. 19648 smitte x, stime (blenke) y, or l. 20932 of chesing fetil x, vessel of chesing, G.

(c) When compared with F. (where G. is wanting):

x :	F. :
ll. 21029-30 sted : bred (E. has 'bed' f. bred)	stede : rede.
ll. 24059-61 I moder murnand, wep cod þu	our ladi saide allas þis quile
þis soru seand apon Iesu?	wa worþ him þat wroȝt þis gile
min soru I ne can noht sai.	mi sone þus-gatis betray.
l. 24088 þat wroȝt me out of witte	þai ware wode out of witte.
l. 24092 Quen sli lett (sett, E.) did him me forlete	was þer nane his bale to bete.
l. 24110 lune wald i spak, might me wit-stode	and þus my sorou mi speche wiþ-stode.
l. 24112 þar nagat es to gamen	me liste ful litil gammen.
l. 24157 Quat wise na force i-wiss	hit is na force I-wisse.
l. 24164 hu sal i liue wit-uten lijf	how salle I liue þis waful life.
l. 24184 sa heind was neuer child	and þou art my childe.
l. 24198 mi sun me renis care sa crus	I haue na keper of my hous.
(Cf. l. 14740 where F. has used 'crus'.)	

I cannot forbear emphatically repeating here that the comparison between x and F. alone is most difficult, especially as we shall afterwards see that F. shows a great many alterations and additional lines, and has evidently made use of other English sources which treated of the same subject.

3. x has additional lines when compared with G. (where F. is wanting).

     ll. 19061—19064 are only in x. These lines seem to me to be a rather useless insertion. Peter and John found a paralyzed cripple begging. Peter and John answered to him:

> "Bihald on us," þai said, "þou man."
> Qua sai, "behald on hus and se,
> And understand ur priuete,
> Als sua sai þou sal se ur wan
> For giftes ha we to þe nan."

Now ll. 19061—19064 have:

> "He þan beheild, bot wel wend he
> Þai suld him giue sum charite.
> Petre said til him onan,
> Gold ne siluer ha we nan."

I do not think it very likely that the scribe of G. made a mistake here on account of the same endings in ll. 19060 and 19064.

§ 2. The results of § 1 will be made more evident by comparing F. G. with C.:

1. Where C. has a gap, and y (= F. G.) seems to have an addition of its own:
ll. 3429-30:

> Of seint John (þe, G.) Baptist
> Þat til man sende (scheud, G.) Ihesu Christ.

As to the substance, these lines may be disregarded as being quite useless ; for the scribe of y only tells us of whom Elizabeth "come noȝt ethe to haue hir birthe." The rhythm, too, is not fluent at all.

ll. 12733-8, which contain a genealogical tree of Mary's family, seem to be given for the squares only drawn in C., and do not agree with l. 12732, which in C. is followed by ll. 12739-40 :

> " Jesus bring us til þat ending
> Þar godd lauerd es of all thing ! "

ll. 14932-33 :

> To louing of god and hali kirk
> And to mannis note to wirk

seem to be useless, when they are compared with the concluding lines in C. :

ll. 14930-31 :

> Þat i it rede wit sli louing
> I mai it wel to ending bring.

2. Where y has omitted lines, and C. seems to be original :

ll. 2755-56 :

> Our lauerd said til Abraham :—
> " Wenis þou i wil sua for-do man "

are necessary for the contents, for from the words of Abraham there must be a transition to those of our Lord.

ll. 4143-44 :

> Ful fellik þai again answard,
> " Quar-for suld we of oght be ferd ? "

are necessary as being the transition to the words of the brothers.

ll. 15431-32 :

> " And yee him sal haf at your will, if i mai rede "

cannot be disregarded, on account of the corresponding ryme of rede : spede in the preceding line.

The same must be said of :

ll. 15439-40, wit suerd and ax and wepend wel, and als wit staf and stang (: strang).

ll. 21345-46 :

> Þir four for us ai prai to dright
> Þat we mai folu þair lares sight

seem on account of their rhythm as well as their contents to be rather necessary for concluding the preceding lines.

3. Where y shows mistakes or alterations, and C. seems to be original.

ll. 3051-52 :

y : Now gase ho forth þat wil of wane
Wandrande in wilderness allane.

C : Now gas sco for (f. forth) þat wreche
allane
Wandrand in wildernes hir an.

Can it be that the scribe of y has misunderstood, or not understood O., the common source of x and y? Is it really strange that the text of C. has not Paran f. hiran = 'hir an'? No matter; but I think it a matter of question that C. should have altered O. As to 'wil of wane,' cf. 1. 980.

1. 3114:

G. : to lere na gode giue þai na tent.   C. : to lere o godd gif þai na tent.
F. : to lere ne god men giues nan entant.

It is evident that the words 'lere na' or 'lere ne' must be joined together to form the verb 'to lerne.'

In making use of the 'Additions,' cf. 1. 25319 : wit þat ilk sal yow be mett, C., where y has 'þu,' though, in the preceding line, y has 'ȝe,' as C. has.

Of little or no consequence, there are in C.

> (a) such concluding lines as ll. 1447-8, 2137-8, 2313-4, 7971-2, 12739-40, 13188-91, 13450-51, 15715-6, 15891-2, which seem to be rather useless, and among which ll. 7971-2 and ll. 12739-40 easily account for their origin and use.

> (b) lines omitted, where y seems to be original :

> ll. 5635-6 in y cannot be disregarded on account of their contents. Moses's sister fetched her mother to nurse the child. Pharaoh's daughter (cf. ll. 5637-8) 'taght it hir to fede' and 'heȝt hir mede.' The latter lines want the former.

> ll. 9238-9 in y cannot be done without in the genealogy of our lady.

> ll. 12872-3 in y

>> þe fader steuen þar thoru it brast
>> Right als it war a thonir blast.

> are rather necessary for the understanding of the following lines :

>> 'þis is my sone, etc.'

As to the 'Additions,' cf. 1. 25515, which is by mistake omitted in C., for the line is necessary for the corresponding ryme in 1. 25514.

γ. evident mistakes :

C. :	y :
1. 299 erth	hete
1. 524 men sen	men eyen
1. 2482 to seit his fee	to sette his see.

Long s is in C. mistaken for f.

| 1. 3850 cald | tald |

1. 4846 'es ur fader nam' is wrongly repeated by the scribe in C.

| 1. 5715 þar fare (cf. 1. 2482) | þar sare |
| 1. 7013 Manigath | Samgath (Samigath G.). |

The right reading is ' Samgar.'

l. 7017 Sarach　　　　　　　　　　　Barach (Barath F.)
l. 23738 Bot if we here ha made us　and if we here haue made na frende.
freind

δ. a difference in the expression, or the succession of lines, where y is to
be preferred.

C.:　　　　　　　　　　　　　　　　　　y:
l. 314 þat haldes stat　　　　　　　　he haldes in state.
l. 413 and sette þam in haly palais　and sett ham in his hey pales.
l. 1009 þar neuer neghes nede ne night　þar euer es day widuten night G.
(nede = ne dai?)　　　　　　　　þar euer ys day and neuer niȝt F.
l. 2527 deliuerd prisuns al, and loth　deliuered þaire prayes (= prey; paas G
　　　　　　　　　　　　　　　　　　= faas?) al and lote.
l. 2758 fifty or fourte　　　　　　　forti or þritty.

ll. 16059-62 y are in C. in the succession 16061, 62, 59, 60.

l. 24381 to thirl þoru þin aun hert　þorou and þorou þin awen hert.

It would be easy to put most of these passages to γ.

§ 3. This relationship of C. E. : y cannot be separated by passages where—
in consequence of mistakes, or omissions, or additions in C.—an apparent connection of y with E. seems to exist, when compared with C.

1. C. has mistakes, or is not original.

C.:　　　　　　　　　　　　　　　　　E. y:
l. 19074 þou hame　　　　　　　　　þou lame

The alteration (hame) is perhaps owing to a remembrance of the Scripture
words.

l. 19185 bald　　　　　　　　　　　calde. In G. the wanting ' C' is marked
　　　　　　　　　　　　　　　　　　by the Editor by [T].
l. 19211 Til him said petre : þi wijf and　Till his wijf he (viz. Ananias) said: ic
þou　　　　　　　　　　　　　　　and þu, y
(The scribe of C. must have mis-　Ic, he saide his wiue, and þu, E.
taken the preceding words which Ana-
nias puts to himself.)
l. 19427 puruaid　　　　　　　　　　proued.
l. 19452 eien　　　　　　　　　　　　eren (erin, eres).
ll. 19717-8 be keped : thrette　　　　beget : þrette.

' be keped ' seems to have been misheard.

l. 21118 o leui cald & chosin & cald o　o leui cald and cosin of crist.
crist
l. 22001 oiþer land of　　　　　　　of lawid or of religiun.
l. 22089 maidenhede　　　　　　　　manhede.

' maidenhede ' is of no consequence ; cf. ll. 24678 and 24683.

l. 22391 hight　　　　　　　　　　　light.
l. 22398 wit driten　　　　　　　　　wid dred.

' wit driten ' reminds us of ' be-seeten ' in the preceding line

l. 22620 þat þou utewandre us suffers sua	þat þu of fire us suffers sua.
ll. 22726-7 E. y are inverted in C.	
l. 23114 þe hali	þe help.
l. 23199 Alsua þe pine of hell pine	alsua þe pitte of helle pine.
l. 23704 þe werld þat es ai lastand	þat (or == our) lauerd þat es ai lastand.

The scribe has misheard, and in consequence of the ending words of the line he may have remembered the common words 'world without end'?!

l. 23964 schain (== sclain?)	slain.
l. 24056 þar born	þar droch.
l. 24540 in sterin stanging	unsterin stakid (staking).
ll. 24650-1 hale of light: sight	of hight: sight.
For 'light' cf. l. 24647.	
l. 24670 na mai certes nan	nai, nai! certis nane.
	E. has 'nan nai,' and F. 'and ellis certan nane.'
ll. 24683/4 maiden-hede es less: angels.	is lele: angele.
l. 24722 creand	I þe biseke ur errand be.
l. 24890 won	vou (vow).
l. 24891 con	don (do).
l. 24913 to knau þat dai	to knau, he said.

2. C. has by mistake omitted lines, when compared with E. y.

> ll. 19422-3, which are necessary for the contents, are wanting in C., but in E., ll. 19421-4, there is a different succession of lines from y.

> ll. 19971-2, 23961, 23842, 23851, the latter two of which are necessary for the corresponding ryme, are likewise omitted in C. Besides, cf. l. 24104, where C. has omitted 'a word,' and l. 24342 where C. has left out 'satt.'

3. C. shows additional lines:

> ll. 19279-80 are an amplification of the preceding lines.

> ll. 20819-20 serve to conclude the preceding thought; F. has a different addition which is of no consequence.

This § seems to me clearly to prove that, whatever may be inferred from the archaic forms of E., such as 'gie, giu, giur, giuor, hauid, hauis, ande, gia, giet,' E. *does not depend upon C.*, and that *C. is not its original.*

§ 4. A frequent conformity of C. with y, when compared with E., will not take us by surprise, when we are considering the incorrect readings of E. The gap after l. 20149, where four leaves are lost, and the injury done to the leaves 44 and 45 in E. are not taken into account.

1. E. shows clear mistakes, or is not original.

E.:	C. y:
ll. 19039-40 ilke dai: þoȝte	it broght: thoght.

The scribe got into a wrong line, cf. l. 19041.

l. 19108 niȝte	might
l. 19203 he	hete
l. 19330 hiȝte	might
l. 19356 & gremli on þair corsis dang	& scurged sare, þai let þam gang.

ll. 19395-6 :

And archidenis þai þaim made   And athes þai þam made
    O þaim þare-of þai toke þe hade   O þam þar-of þai tok þe lade.
ll. 19407-8 wiþ : hiȝte   wiþ : kyth.

ll. 19695-8 in C. y are drawn together into two in E. :

to christen men some wa he cuþe
in sinagoge spel biguþe (on ' biguþe ' cf. l. 24580).

l. 19752 aȝte gier	seuen ȝeire.
l. 19947 aske	all
l. 19948 lake	lau (lagh)

(Is ' lake ' dialectical ?)

l. 19965 he	we
l. 20049 perile	peris
l. 20825 tuenti gier	þritti ȝere
l. 21131 leuedis broþir	lauerd broþer.
l. 21134 halines and hiȝte	halines and light.
l. 21634 de grant vertu	o gret vertu.
l. 21754 o vi	o seuen
l. 21918 sald	l. 21916 tald.
l. 22029 bereme & baer bald	breme and bald
l. 22432 þrau	sothsau, F. has altered for the sake of the ryme.
l. 22478 faadli.	saddli (radli, F.). (' radli ' is the right reading, so that we have here the common mistaking of the initials.)
l. 22492 and þar of wil we neuir blin	& als we wonden war þam in (þer-in)
l. 22525 to the erthe	right unto þe air

E.'s reading is a correction, which T. has also found.

l. 22534 þe wallis, touris, þe felles to falle	þe dals up-rise, þe fells dun fell
ll. 22551-2 quak : quak	quak : scak
l. 22664 sal kerel	sal knele.
l. 22688 þai sal habide	þai sal þam hide.
l. 22832 norising	uprising
l. 23046 arlik	anerli
ll. 23091-2 rest : rest	rest : gest
ll. 23149-50 weld : in elde	on bred : in lede.
l. 23153 schilke /	slik /
l. 23180 fra wake	fra wrak
ll. 23209-10 hate : hate	hatte : wate.
l. 23259 al þair lim es	al þair limes ar
l. 23279-80 hete : hite	hete : ete.
l. 23377 strensip	frenscip
l. 23386 him bem	his (' hir ' is the right reading of G.) lem.
	ll. 22385-6 are wanting in F.

l. 23749 to flihtis fus — to filthes fus.
l. 23762 þaim haf — þai haf
l. 23765 eie — eth (ll. 23765-6 are wanting in F.)
l. 24012 his mane — hir mane.
l. 24024 swaipe / — snaipe /
l. 24031 we folud him þaim — we folud þam
l. 24032 I staker — I stakerd
l. 24106 it brastin — it brast in
l. 24145 : 48 dey : end — wend : end (ll. 24050—24201 are wanting in G.).

l. 24534 and ein and chek — and eien eke
l. 24764 rais / — sais / (long s again mistaken for r)
ll. 24789-90 her & tar : he & tar — here & þare : euer ai quar
l. 24836 abute — aboue
l. 24852 perlir ar — perel mare
l. 24928 sai ye — sal be
l. 24965 him — hir.

2. E., when compared with C. y, shows an inversion of

ll. 19577-8, 19739-40, 19855-6, 22689-90 (only the ryming words 'il', 'gril' are inverted in E.), 22795-6, 22866 = 22865, but l. 22865 is not = l. 22866, which in E. is different, 23324-5.

3. E., when compared with C. y, shows this omission of

ll. 19226 ('inserted in a different hand'), 19735-6, 19865-6, 20843-4, 20846-8, 21702, 22107-10, 22651-2, 22992-3, 23719-20, 23743-4, 24351, 24931-4.

A word or two are wanting in ll. 19543, 'þam' after 'for', 19555 'ay' /, 19812 'radd', 23125 'demd', 24137 'pay'.

4. E. has additional lines when compared with C. y :

Between l. 20834 and l. 20835 E. has two lines inserted :

'and ten mone & dais seuin
Qua wel can caste sal finde it euin,'

which are quite useless, and ll. 21916-7, which are wanting in C. y :

'alle sal we dei, baþe ginge and alde,
Es nan hauis of him seluin walde,'

are at least not necessary.

So I hope I have proved that E. is not a fragment of the Original; nor can it be the source of C. y.

§ 5. Some conformity of x G. with F. cannot take us by surprise.

1. F. shows a great many mistakes or alterations :

F. :
l. 20845 xxi — fourteen ȝere.
l. 23970 synnis — finis
l. 24214 I note quidde to wende — ne wit þe sal weind

x G. :

ll. 24215-7 þen sais þe clerk þat made þis boke   Sin suilk it war þi cares kidd

    lauedi for þe sorou þou toke   þou dreied dule, leuedi? þou did

    a þing þou me neiuen   ful god it was þin euen.

l. 24220 quen he herde þi steiuen   if him stode ani steuen

ll. 24029-30 sling: ȝinge   steng: ȝeng

> ll. 24224-5 and ll. 24227-8 are inverted in F.

l. 24226 tel me quat hit is   wit-uten ani mis

l. 24311 our lauedi & John þat I of mene   þir martirs tuin þat i of mene

l. 24314 ful stille he spac al sulde noȝt here   Sa waik þat vnethes most þai here

ll. 24323-5 our lauedi saide quat vs is wa   Vr spirit was als fled us fra

    childer ho saide haue I na ma   For we ne wist o naþing bot wa

    mi hert na-þing is paide   þof we herd quat he said

ll. 24329-30 þe penaunce þat we on him seye   Als suith þar com a uord

    muȝt na creature hit dreye   Fra þe croice o crist suord

l. 24358 myself I muȝt noȝt welde   and hyed me til held.

ll. 24470-2 þi bodi is wanne as þou ware dede   þi saul es molten al to ded

    quere is þi faire blode was rede   þi face es wan as ros vnrede

    and in þi bodi graide   Als forwit þat he was said C. G., wanting in E.

l. 24593 I for ' it.'

ll. 24595-6 bot forþ ho lete him lede   Als freindes bath and fede

    & þus shortli wiþ-outen mare   Quat did yee þan, leuedi sai mar?

ll. 24677-8 dide: maydenhede   madd: maiden-hed.

ll. 24871-2 to ihesu crist þai lift þair hande   Apon þair brestes fast þai beft

    þaire sinful praier to understand   Al in god self þai þam bileft

ll. 24967-8 þe quilk seruise I rede we neyuen   sco dos us her to serue hir sua

    þat we come to þe joy of heyuen   þat we be wit hir euer & A.   Amen.

    (which are followed by four concluding lines).

2. F. has the following omissions of lines, when compared with x G. :

    ll. 19277-8, 23931-2, 24587-92 (one stanza), 24839-40 (cf. ll. 24871-2, where the scribe also avoided ' beft ').

3. F., when compared with x G., has the following additional lines:

    ll. 20897-900, cf. on Simon Magus, ll. 20899-900 :

> qua wille haue mare of þis matere
> rede þe legende and ȝe mai here.

    ll. 20919-20, 20922-23 Peter is buried in Rome :

> þer now a faire mynster dos stande
> suche a-noþer is in na lande.

ll. 21007-8, 21889-90, 22939-40, 23033-4, 23941-2, 24873-4, 24969-72, all of which are not original.

It may easily be inferred from this paragraph that F. is not the source of G., or even of x, and that, when compared with x G., it differs most of all from the Original.

§ 6. The result found in § 5 is still confirmed by a comparison of F. with C. or C. G. :

 1. F. shows mistakes or alterations :

  ll. 31-34 are inverted in F. in this succession : 33, 34, 31, 32.

 F. : l. 94 rimes lyte   C. G. : rimes fele (mani).

  ll. 113-14 are inverted, and slightly altered in F.

ll. 223-4 now I will be-gynne in dede	schortly rimand on þe dede (renand G.)
Ihesu leue me wele to spede	for mani er þai her-of to spede (ar þar for G.)
l. 226 to wyte how he first began	to knaw him self how he began.
l. 272 for mirþ he merkis mon to mede	þat mirþes mettes (settes)
l. 322 tyte	bath
l. 378 craftely wroȝt wit myche wonder	in þese he sounded al wit wonder
ll. 413-14 pales : sese	palais : unpais.
l. 574 miȝtful lorde in trinite	wit nankyn creature mai be
ll. 585-6 as I you talde : riȝt as ihesus	o mans eild : als he moght welle him
crist walde	self weild
l. 828 al was wrath þat er was blithe	alle blurdid (lourid þan) þat was forwit
	(ar) bliþe
l. 927 þou sal wen þi life ys gane	bituix & þou again began
l. 1008 wit joy & blis & mirþis best	wit blis & beild (bote G.) broiden best
	(cf. on 'beild' l. 23653 in G.).
l. 1255 þe gresse ys falow on þe grene	foluand thoru þat gresse gren
l. 1517 stoer of fe he dalt wiþ	was first loger, and fee delt wit
l. 1609 quen he hanged on rode tree	for his choslinges on rod-tre.
ll. 1844-5 are inverted in F.	
l. 2264 & neuer an wiste quat oþer ment	als þai had sare þar fra ben beft C.
(cf. on 'beft'—ll. 24871 & 24840 in C.).	& went away, sua sais þe bok G.
ll. 2275-6 are inverted in F.	
ll. 2375-6 wysse : blisse	blisse : misse
ll. 2447-8 sprede : brede	sprede : knede C., sprede, nedede G.
ll. 2463-4 take : forsake	loft : left
ll. 2467-8 a lefe to se : sa faire to se	a leue (faire) cuntre : ful fair to se.
l. 2576 & thonked our lorde, I wyte him	ur lauerd to serue forgat he noght (was
noght	all his thoght G., the preceding line
	ends in 'forgat he noght.')
ll. 2681-2 do him out of ȝour company	for-qui þe werk of circumcising
& lete him stande to his foly.	Bers in itself gret for-biseying.
l. 2697 xiij	thritti
ll. 2718-9 and sayde þai hardly soþ to Myn	þan said þat lauerd 'i wil yow min
at salt gaine come if I haue	At mi gain-com, if i haue lijf.
life	
ll. 2783-4 þe þeues þat him be niȝt come	þe gestes him com wit nighter tale
for-til bringe ham til þaire	for-soth, þai said, knaw tham we sale
dome	

ll. 3055-7 are inverted in F. in this succession : 3056, 3057, 3055.

l. 3077 & he þat xij ȝere war gane   for quen he throded was (was waxyn) to yoman (man)

ll. 3105-6 show inverted endings in F.

l. 3426 I mai noȝt telle ȝet of þa   Rebecca, Rachel & Anna alsua.

l. 3809 shows indirect discourse in F., and l. 3810 has the mistake 'me'.   direct discourse.

l. 4962 als wisely as wrange ys on us broȝt   on (in) oþer helpe yeit hope (ne trast) i noght

l. 5009 is altered, and has indirect discourse, whereas there is the direct one in C. G.

ll. 5387-8 are changed into a contrary sense, so that ll. 5389-90 are added to give the right understanding.

l. 5406 is altered for an easier understanding.

Besides, the wording is changed in ll. 5511, 5517 (: C. and G.), 5539, 5656 (in the ending), 5763, 5789-90, 5792 (in the ending), 5802, 5852, 5867, 5893 (þai F., he C. G.), 6001-2 (in the ending), 6026, 6091, 6103, 6200, 6386, 6524, 6568, 6608, 6639, 7114, and 7272 (in the sense), 7304 (in the ending), 7332, 7630, 7858 (in the ending), 7917, 8152 (G. T. have mistakes), 8600, 9018 (besides, a mistake 'ham' for 'hir'), 9026, 9091 (strife f. scrift, the same in l. 9094), 9095/6 ('his eyen .. shent he' for his sin sceud he, C. G.), 12008-10, 12136 (VII F., fiue C. G.), 12634-6, 12730, 12860-1, 13118-21 (shortened), 13186-7 (: C.), 13446-51, 13507, 13779 (28 ȝere F., 38 ȝere C. G.), 13794, 13806-9 (in the sense), 13836-7, 14004, 14119, 14166 (: G.), 14287, 14359, 14647, 14655, 15096, 15740, 15811-2, 15838, 18552, 18563, 18652, 19145-6 (in the ending, too), 19153 (sone f. fader), 19619-20, 19674, 19864, 20042, 20050, 20533-4, 20824, 20847, 20985-6, 21315, 21593-4, 21891, 21911, 21924, 23383 (: C. and G.), 23940, 24096 (: C.), 24311, 24358, 24814, 24871-2.

When compared with the 'Additions,' cf. ll. 25301 (first f. fifth), 25366, 26762-3, 27671, 27830-1.

There may still be added these inversions of lines : 5569-70, 5585-6, 6482-3, 8469-70, 13448-9 C .G. = 13444-5 F., so that ll. 13444-5 in C. G. are wanting in F., 13988-9, 14210-1, 14415-6, 14470-1, 14726-7, 20945-6, 21077-8, C. G. = 21075-6 F., but ll. 21075-6 C. G. are different from ll. 21077-8 F., 21579-80, 21923, 21925.

In the 'Additions,' cf. ll. 26714-5, 27302-3, 27598-9.

2. F. has the following omissions of lines, when compared with C. G. or G. I first mention the most striking omissions :

l. 316, ll. 3807-8 (cf. the following words 'him' and 'me'), ll. 6195-8 seem to be necessary as concluding lines ; ll. 6383-4 contain a natural explanation of the preceding lines ; ll. 13444-5 contain a comparison which is necessary for the following line : 'þat was neuer fowel sagles (f. sa gleg) of eye ;' ll. 5975-6 are necessary for the corresponding ryme in ll. 15973-4 ; ll. 21841-21 must be compared with the preceding and the following lines ; ll. 22513-4 contain the subsequent sentence to the preceding sentence in ll. 22511-2 ; ll. 24587-92 contain an entire stanza, which is necessary for the contents.

Besides, there are wanting (or incomplete) ll. 135-6, 547-8, 575-6, 781-2, 795-6, 937-42, 1067-8, 1143-4, 1235-6, 1385-6, 1475-6, 1577-8, 1597-8, 1625-6, 1705-6, 1797-8, 1801-2, 1823-4, 1865-6, 1917-20, 1999-2000, 2175-6, 2353-4, 2373-4, 2443-4, 2651-2, 2753-4, 3033-46, 3111-2, 3137-8, 3755-6, 3851-2, 4075-6, 4138 (incomplete), 4190 (incompl.), 4295-6 (incompl.), 5333-4, 5365-6, 5551-2, 5781-2, 6121-2, 6181-2, 6289-90, 6425-30, 6527-8, 6566-7, 6673-6, 6687-92, 6713-4, 6733 ('ox' is wanting), 6837-8, 6977-8, 7091-2, 8105 6, 8377 (incompl.), 8383-4, 9141-2, 9191-4, 9325-11614, 11617-8, 11653-6, 11916 (incompl.), 11917-20, 11924 (incompl.), 11925-6, 11937-54 ('illegible and almost erased'), 11959-62, 12015-28 ('partly erased'), 12031-2, 12575-6, 12579-80, 12675-6 (also in T. L.), 12687-8, 12739-51 (: G.), 13174-5, 13336-7, 13620-3, 13712-3, 13948-9, 14360-1, 14506-7, 14718-21 & 14928-9 (: G.), 15009-10 (some new lines for them : ll. 15015-6), 16199-200, 16227-18512, 18895-19082, 19083-4, 19093-4, 19155-8, 19191-6, 19277-8, 20249-436, 20733-4 (: G.), 20975-6, 20983-4, 21095-6, 21559-60, 21821-2, 21997-8, 22425-6, 22443-8, 22577-8, 23275-8, 23385-6, 23765-6, 23861-2, 23931-2, 24433-6 ('torn'), 24460 (incompl.), 24839-40.

In the 'Additions,' cf. ll. 25451-3 (: C. G.) ; when compared with C. : ll. 26250-1, 26394-7, 27080-1 (additional), 27230-1, 27234-5, 27420-1, 27471-2, 27574-9, 27658-9.

3. F. shows additional lines, when compared with C. G. or with G. or C. I first mention the most striking additions :

ll. 5389-90 are added on account of the preceding mistake ; ll. 6401-2 contain a general conclusion, in which the rhythm is not fluent at all ; ll. 8641-2 contain a general sentence ; ll. 9273-4 contain a repetition of ll. 9271-2 ; ll. 11651-2 and ll. 11761-2 must be compared with their preceding lines ; ll. 11907-10 appear to be quite useless : 'mony selcouth—I haue no tome ham to mouþ'; ll. 12649-52 are useless; ll. 12860-1 betray themselves by theii contents, besides cf. 'þen me,' which is very shocking to the modern reader; ll. 13864-5 betray themselves even by the incorrect rhythm, each line having three accented syllables or stresses; ll. 14160-1 betray themselves by their contents and rhythm; ll. 19617-20 are added for ll. 19619-20 C. G., F. mingling the Bible words with those of the source, so that the thought finds its double wording; ll. 19743-6 are useless; ll. 19817-8 must be examined as to their contents, and the rhythm of l. 19817; ll. 20897-900 betray that the scribe of F. is very well versed in legends; ll. 20923-4 and ll. 22457-8 must be examined with respect to their contents and their rhythm; cf. l. 22457, where the scribe seems to be willing to read : 'wiþ-ín þe spácë óf a mýle.'

Compare besides ll. 521-2, 2277-8, 3409-10, 4663-4, 4682-3, 4897-8, 5981-2, 7137-44, 7273-6, 8609-12, 11993-4, 12438-9, 12485-6, 13110-1, 13185-6 (: G.), 13386-7, 13446-51 (for ll. 13448-9 C. G. are = 13444-5), 13617 (: G.), 13838-9, 13918-9, 14116-7, 14371-2 (: G.), 14382-3, 14468-9, 14520-1, 14524-5, 14724-5, 14924-5, 15015-6 (for ll. 15009-10 C. G. are wanting), 16191-4, 19137-8, 19163-72, 19235-6, 19461-2, 19627-32, 19635-6, 20555-6, 20845-6, 20919-20, 21007-8, 21029-30 (: G.), 21113-6, 21467-8, 21595-6, 21889-90, 22857-8 (: C.), 22939-40, 23033-4, 23169-74, 23739-40 (: G.), 23941-2, 24873-4, 24969-72.

In the 'Additions,' cf. ll. 25349-54 (: C. G.); when compared with C. : l'. 25786-9, 26144-5, 26354-5, 26438-9, 26586-7, 26636-7, 26802-3, 26890-1, 26998-9, 27128-9, 27140-3, 27256-7, 27268-9, 27547-8, 27664-5.

The scribe of F. alters not only because of his dialect, or because his language is later, but he certainly takes a great delight in making many difficult lines more easily understood, or in shortening, or in amplifying with additions taken from somewhere else. In doing so, he often makes mistakes, in which we recognize the source, cf. ll. 3807-8, 5387-8. His way of shortening will be best seen in l. 1867, the beginning of which is taken from l. 1865 (ll. 1865-6 are wanting). The additional lines contain general sentences which usually conclude a thought, or small section. That the scribe intentionally shortens, will be seen in ll. 13120-1, so that ll. 13122-9 are wanting. In still comparing evident mistakes (such as in ll. 2697, 13779, 19153, 25301, etc.) or omissions, such as l. 316, we see from the comparison—the completeness of which is necessary for a correct estimation of F.—that F. is no source of x G., and, judging from its other faithful correspondencies to G. and C. (cf. § 9), that it is no version of a midland or even of a southern original.

§ 7. For the purpose of fin'shing the comparison, I continue stating a conformity of x F., when compared with G. Only slight alterations and some mistakes in G. account for the differences between G. and F.

1. Mistakes and omissions in G. : x F. :

G. :	x F. :
l. 19345 lithed on	lifted on
l. 20111 muntes	nunnes
l. 20813 ' loke' is wanting in G., cf. he mai noght loke tilward hir light.	
l. 21072 spelland (also in T.)	slepand
ll. 22789-90 are wanting in G. (and T.), as well as ll. 23739-40.	
l. 23764 flight	fight.
l. 23950 in x F. is put in G. after l. 23947, and l. 23956 in x F. appears in G. after l. 23953.	
l. 24020 drei dome	dreri dom.
ll. 24050-201 are wanting in G.	

2. Alterations :

ll. 19919-20 Quen he of his comming understode	Quen þai o petre understod
Sone he ras & gain þaim him ȝode (T.)	His cuming son gain him þai yod.
l. 20829 fourti dais in erd he badd (T.)	forti dais & siþen he bad
l. 21901 þe warnes noght (T.)	ne scurnis
l. 22556 bèst / (T.)	nest /
l. 22793 lim & lijf (T.)	ha pith & lijf
l. 23184 samen quiles þai to-gider ware	þai wroght ar þai tuined war.
l. 24034 to bote	of bote.

These passages alone prove that G. is not the Original, nor is the source of F. or x. They withal give me a hint how to go on in my research, that is to say, afterwards to compare G. with T.

§ 8. Some conformity of C. with F., when compared with E. G., is of no consequence at all. Cf. l. 19113 prophetis, C. F., prophecies E. G.; or l. 24658, wit saand of þi succur C. F., wid fand of þi socur. In C. and F. f is mistaken for long s, this slight mistake has often occurred. The meaning of l. 24658 is: "Try thy help;" for 'Jesus has always supported thee (Mary), he will console thee, when thou wilt come to him. Then he will always comply with thee; pray lead us into his communion, only try thy help.'

Nor is a conformity of C. with G., when compared with E. F., of any consequence. Cf. ll. 23809-10, which are inverted in E. F.; both of them could perhaps avoid repeating the words 'sorful time' in the successive lines, 23808 and 23809, for ll. 23808-10 in C. G. have:

> In sorful time þan war we wroght
> A sorful time til vr be-houe,
> Bot godd for-bede þat we it proue.

Nor is a conformity of E. with F., when compared with C. and with G., of any consequence.

Cf. l. 19407 vp þer ras to striue him wiþ   C. : up þar ras to spute him wiþ
                                            G. : up þer ras a strijf him wiþ

nor of E. with G., when compared with C. and F.

Cf. l. 19080, scop E. G., scep C., wanting in F.   It means ' skippe,' as in T., so that the northern ' scop ' is quite correct.   (Cf. l. 3135 and the remark on page 84*.)

    l. 21056, puisund (pussund) G. E., prusund C., poysoned F. ; puisund = poisoned.

    l. 22093, stiglid E. G., titeld C., licande F., stiglid = styled.

    l. 23207, ix paines E. G., viij C., mani harde F.

    l. 24646, in langurs (in lagins) G. E., I languis C., quite different in F.

By these researches, I think, we are enabled to suppose that F. and G. are together derived from the northern version (y), which, with respect to the early age of F. G., may have descended directly from the original (O). From the same source then descends x, which has so much in common with y ; and from x are to be derived E. and C. separately.

§ 9. Among the other manuscripts, I first take into consideration T. as being very near to G. (cf. § 7).   Their conformity with each other (without considering their different dialect) may be proved by a comparison with C., F., and E.

    1. G. T. have alike alterations or mistakes in the expression and the contents, when compared with C., or C. F., or C. and F.

G. T :	C. F. :
ll. 17-18 O tristrem, and ysoude þe suete,	of tristrem & hys leif ysote
Hu þai wid luffe first gan mete	how he for here become a sote
l. 19 Ionet (Ion)	Ionek.
ll. 75-76 treu & lele : to manes lele	lele in like : hony of bike
l. 82 neuer wan (won)	neuer gan
l. 101 ledes (peples) (also L. B.) (sic !)	of leuedis alle
l. 102 meke & mild	mild & mek.
l. 118 hu cristes (us) bote bigan to brewe	how crist brith began to brewe
l. 120 sothli of hir testament	brefly (shortli) o aiþere testament
l. 188 28 ȝere	38 ȝere
ll. 193-4 of lazar þat ded lay under stan	o lazar ded laid under lam
hou iesu him raysed in fless &	how iesus raised his licam
ban	
l. 196 preching þai him thrett	sermon þrali thrett
ll. 221-2 rawe : schawe	raw : daw
l. 246 prechid (sic !)	praised

l. 307 þu understand so	þou underta
l. 316 þat þai noght turne to soru & care	þat þai ne worth to noght als þai war ar (wanting in F.)
l. 332 ouer all oþer he is prines (prince, T.) widuten pere	fra al oþer, sundri & sere
l. 347 to be sett (sic!)	seit (siþen) for to be
l. 449 lightli	hetlik
ll. 519-20 his here of fir	his hete (f. hed = head) of fir
l. 635 naked war þai bath tway	baþ war naked þar licam

ll. 893-8 are in G. T. in this succession : 894, 3, 5, 6, 8, 7.

l. 1031 soun of foulis þere singeth	sune of sautes (santes)

ll. 1067-8 are inverted in G. T., wanting in F.

l. 1240 made	sad
l. 1626 of noe kin	adam kin (ll. 1625-6 are wanting in F.)
ll. 1648-9 of pine is non funden quite	unnes es ani funden quite
l. 2144 o þis same kind	o þis sem (semys) string ('Shem' is to be understood.)

ll. 2219-20 as well as ll. 2249-50 are inverted in G. T.

l. 2264 & went away, sua sais þe boke	quite different in C. and in F.
ll. 2407-8 for þu art fair, quen þai þe se wid niht þai suld þe take fra me	Quen þai þe see for þi fairhede to reue me þe . . þan sal þai wede . . þat God forbede
ll. 2457-8 þen said Abraham wid wordes hend	þen said abraham þat was no sot
"Loth, mi neuow & mi (dere) frend	formast til his neueu loth
ll. 2575-6 are inverted in the endings!	
ll. 3065 lede him ȝender & haue in minde	þou lede him yonder er yon blind (ar to blind) (f. 'lind')
l. 3067 & a tre wid frouit ful gode	on þat tre hinges frut ful gode
l. 3116 foli is gouyn to man to day G. foli is gomen (sic !) now a day T.	to foli giues him man to dai C. fole hede ys giuen al men to pay F.
l. 3135 spille : wille	cole [1] (= to kill) : þole

ll. 3547-8 are inverted, but l. 3548 F. differs from C., and agrees with G. !

ll. 3948-52 are in G. T. in this succession : 3948, 51, 52, 49, 50.

ll. 5051-2 are inverted, in l. 5052 in G. there is mistaken ' blod ' for ' bodi,' so that T. has avoided ' bodi ' altogether.

l. 5056 sexti sith & mar	fourti sithes & mare C. ham (sic !) wiþouten mare F. (cf. l. 5055)
ll. 5119-20 have ' him '	þam
ll. 5143-4 bigod sua dere : ne knightes pere (fere)	eber (foule) pantener : ne er þai noght o þat mister

---

[1] Cole : scop (l. 19080) = quelle(n) : scep = kiil : skip (cf. O. Icel. 'skoppa,' or 'skopa'). Stratmann (cf. Dictionary) should have put ' cole,' which he does not understand, to ' cullen,' which is derived from 'quellen,' and not from 'cole.' Cf. Ten Brink, Chaucer's Sprache, p. 106, § 176 : " skippen (Derivation?) "

l. 5313 his berd was side wid mekil har (wit) hare (= canus)

l. 5321 shows in G. & T. one useless 'him.'

l. 5356 I had of him his (mi) broder benisun — I had his brad beniscun

l. 5376 widuten end / — wit-outen male /

l. 5677 bad alsua — bad als faa

l. 6077 on ilka post, on ilk derner — on aiþer (airer) post þaire (þer) hus to smer

l. 6078 a sine o tau T ('o thayu' in T.) make ȝe þere — a takin o tav on þair derner C. in takenyng of þinges at wald dere F.

l. 6125 wretherale ras — on nightertale ras.

ll. 6289-90 and sua mot he diliuere us ur dere lauerd, suete iesus — sua mot he do þat hei drightin us alsua fra ur wiþerwin C. (wanting in F.)

ll. 6639-40 handis: widstandis — dright: maledight C., fayne: slaine F.

ll. 7023-4 are inverted.

l. 7120 undo him (f. þam) G., so that T. has 'unto him' (sic!) — a redil þam undo he bad

l. 7639 folk of heden lede — folk þat þar fede

l. 8150 þat sekenes on him was þar nan sene — þat he was hale sume ani trote

l. 8197 þan on þe morn quen þai suld lem G. 'þai' is a mistake for 'dai,' so that T. has put 'þei,' with some slight altera- tion: 'on þe morne whenne þei shul so,' and in the next line we read 'go,' while in G. l. 8197 finds its verb in l. 8199. — þan on þe morne quen dai suld leme.

l. 9014 scho bringes him to confusion — he es forcasten als crachon C. he ys umbelaide wiþ tresoun F.

l. 9194 fourti hundrid ȝere & mare — fourten hundret ȝeir & mare C. (wanting in F.)

l. 13506 fisses tua & fiue laues of bred — tua fisches & fiue laues of bere C. ij fisshis & v barly lauis F.

l. 19407 a strijf — to striue E. F., to spute C.,

ll. 21142-3 are inverted.

l. 23206 ix paines — viij paines C., mani F.

2. G. T. have the same omissions and additional lines.

There are wanting in G. T. :

ll. 975—989, in which the Lord declares that he will have only the tenth part of all fruits, though Adam had offered one half, or one third. Does this omission bespeak some shrewdness in the 'clerk' (or scribe) of G. ?

ll. 6123-4 seem to be necessary for the contents.

l. 13617 (cf. in G. l. 13616, farine /, which has no corresponding ryme, so that l. 13616 in T. is also omitted.)

ll. 14371-2 seem to be necessary for the contents.

ll. 21029-30 seem to be original, E. has mistakes, F. differs in l. 21030.

ll. 22857-8 are only in C. :

> þai sal haf noþer o wel ne wa
> Bot in merckenes for euer and a.

These lines seem to be useless, and perhaps caused by the preceding ryme : 'may saued be on nakin wai,' which reminded the scribe of a similar ending, cf. l. 14896, on 'o wel ne wa,' the meaning of which is rather awkward here. F. quite differs in its wording :

> of ham to speke I halde me stille.
> bot ihesu crist mai do his wille.

There are added in G. T. :

- ll. 12744-51 are a mere repetition of ll. 9245-52 ; ll. 12739-43 in G., which represent the genealogical tree in C., are omitted in T., because they are not ryming.
- ll. 14894-5 seem to be a useless insertion, for the rhythm of l. 14895 is not correct, and the connection of the lines with the following is bad.
- ll. 14902-3 and ll. 14910-11 bespeak themselves by their wording to be useless.

From this almost verbal conformity of T. with G. in mistakes, alterations, omissions, and additions, when compared with F. especially, we may easily see a dependency of the one MS. on the other, and that of the younger T. on the elder G. But to finish this comparison, we must also state the differences of T. from G. The obvious relationship between T. and H. L. B. enables me to compare, as far as is made possible by the printed text, T. H. B. L. with G.

§ 10. We must bear in mind that T. and G. dialectically differ from each other, so that the scribe of T. was often compelled to alter expression and ryme, and that he will even correct what he cannot understand, or what seems to him a mistake. Moreover, he will often shorten what seems to him diffuse, and he seldom lengthens the tale. The more modern the text is, the greater will be the desire to make the construction easy, which in T. may be seen in its liking the principal sentence put before the accessory one. Other differences between T. and G. I have not met with.

T. H. L. B., when compared with G., show :

1. The same mistakes or alterations in expressions.

l. 6 mony mon T. L. B., the first 153 lines are wanting in H. [many thosand] G., cf. ' hir' lijf in G. with 'his' lif in T. L. B.

l. 10 was noon in his tyme him liche	G. : was non in his time funden suiche
l. 32 wol flite	wil smite
l. 36 he haþ	he takes
l. 46 men may him knowe	men may þaim knowe
l. 53 þat foles lif	þat foli lune
l. 60 þou shalt from hit or hit ..	þu sal fra hir or scho ..
l. 68 for dew dett	for duel dett
l. 70 þat in our nede	þat in mi [nede ..]
l. 85 shulde ȝe matere take	suld we mater take
ll. 93-94 in dede : rede	brade : made
l. 104 & reiseþ euer þe synful mon	& rayses þe sinful quen þai fall
ll. 105-6 are inverted in T. L. B.	
ll. 107-8 knowe : lowe	ken : men
ll. 111-2 I : lastyngly	biginne : minne
l. 115 sum maner þing is good to knawe	sumkin jeste nu forto knau
ll. 125-6 may : ay	stand : lastand
ll. 139-40 newe : Esaue	ȝou : ysau
l. 150 how he was crafti iustise	hou craftili he did iustise
l. 177 mony & ryf T. H. L. B.	sua rif.
l. 185 o þe spousebriche of o wommon	. . . . , þat womman
ll. 197-8 are inverted.	
l. 207 touchynge þe apostlis of her feest	of þe tuelue apostlis sumkins ieste
l. 214 dredeful dayes	dreri dais
ll. 219-20 spelle : telle	roune ; concepcion
l. 235 for commune folk of engelonde	Englis lede of meri ingeland
l. 236 shulde þe bettur hit understode	for þe comen to unþerstand
l. 247 ȝyue we uche lond his langage	gif we þaim ilkan þair language
l. 252 in pride & boost /	in mekil wast /
l. 268 for almast hit reherseþ alle	for all-mast it ouer-rines all

Besides compare the headings before l. 271 :

Hereþ now of þe trinite dere	Here begines o þe trinite & of þe
And of þe making of his world here	making of all þe worlde.

ll. 593-4, 909-10, 959-60, 2349-50, 5483-4 are inverted in T.

l. 1254 þe steppes of þi moder & me	þi moder & myn oþer broþer (sic !) sloth (G. has mistaken the word 'ouer baþer,' so that T thought it best to omit them at all.)
ll. 3145-6 abide : tyde	bade : made
ll. 3294 to þinke /	in suink /
ll. 5789-90 pay : delay	visite : delite
l. 9846 al is þe wille of god myȝti	Bot monstrus miht men call þaim lik
ll. 9845-6 ferly : myȝti	ferlik : lik.
l. 9894 wiþ feire wardes ..	wid wallis thrinne ..
l. 10052 al hir heuyness	al ille heuynes
ll. 10155-6 dryuen : ryuen	dun : crachun

ll. 10785-6 are wrought into four lines, and ll. 10799-800 into six lines in T. L.

ll. 10835-906 are independent of G., but by 12 lines less than in G. The scribe of T. has made use of a source hitherto unknown.

ll. 13416-7 avow : now	suike : kingrike.
ll. 13174-5 gon : anoon	iaiole : cole
ll. 13220-1 is : blis	iohn : thron
ll. 14878-9 dede : blede	stod : rod
l. 14912 unbynde in dede /	unbidden bede /
ll. 14914-5 gryn : him	passiun : ransum
l. 15060 ioye & game	welcum hame
l. 15806 bet /	forgett /
l. 16022 warnynge /	dring /

ll. 16235-6 and ll. 16237-8 are inverted.

l. 16256 I con no furre þe lede /	men haldes þe for quede
ll. 18015-6 I haue oure iewes made in stryue	I haue him fandit to driue to dede
wiþ bittur peyn him bringe of lyue	mine eldrin folk o iuen lede
ll. 18415-6 bi syde : ful of pride	ihesu : did me tru
l. 18617 þe þridde day in certeyn tide	þe seuend day in paske tide
ll. 20087-8 to : she	to : scho (cf. x F.)

ll. 20817-8 correspond to ll. 20815-8, l. 20833 T. = l. 20834 G., l. 20834 T. is not = l. 20833 G.

l. 20848 in tyme of nede my helpe þou be	sais all amen, þar (f. ' par') charite.
l. 20931 blynde he fel, seynge he ras	seand he fell, bot blind he ras
l. 21315 þe furstes gle o men was	þe fristes greff of irin was
l. 22444 or enten-uale bituir hem bide T. or euyr vale bittir hem bide L.	or enter-uale bituix þaim bide
l. 23738 here is good to make us frende	bot if we here haue mad na freind

ll. 23779-80 are inverted.

ll. 23893-8 contain the conclusion differing from G.

2. The same omissions :

T. H. L. B :

ll. 237-42, 255-6, 259-64.

ll. 1577-8 and ll. 1583-4, for which there are others in T., so that the succession of lines has become quite different : ll. 1569-72 are not in G., ll. 1573-5 T. = ll. 1569-71 G., l. 1576 not in G., ll. 1577-80 T. = ll. 1573-6 G., ll. 1581-4 T. = ll. 1579-82 G., l. 1585 T. = G.

T. L. :

ll. 2011-2, 3461-2, 3483-4, 3583-4, 3919-20, 4293-4, 4319-20, 4323-4, 5197-8, 5219, 5222, 6562-7, 6933-4, 7613-4, 7907-8, 8081-2 (T.), 8165-6, 8790-1 (T.), 9461-72, 9721-2 (cf. B.), 9885-6, 10169-70, 10187-8, 10589-90, 10913-6, 10985-6, 11035-6, 11121-2, 11279-82, 11555-6, 11787-8, 11935-6 (T.), 12675-6, 12908-9, 13046-7, 13507, 13509, 13617, 13840-1 (T.), 13940-1, 14290-1, 14373-4 (T.), 14452-5, 14874-7 (T.), 14916-23 (T.), 14926-33, 15487-90, 15951 (half long line) (T.), 16029-30, 16551-2 (ll. 16549-52 in G. are drawn together into two half long lines in T. L., ll. 1655$^1/_2$ in G. being assimilated to the two preceding rymes), ll. 16787-94, 16815-6, 16859-68 (ll. 1685$^7/_8$ have no corresponding ryme), ll. 16947-8, 16957-8, 16967-17008 containing a copious conclusion on the thought 'none can think how good he was!', ll. 17083-98 (concluding lines), ll. 17099-110 containing the self-praise of him ' þat þis bok gart dight, John of Lindbergh,' ll. 17111-270 ' A Discourse between Christ and Man,' which, as being a useless insertion, may rightly be put aside, ll. 17271-88 containing the introduction to ' Of Joseph of Arimathea,' instead of which T only has :

> O Joseph of Aramathi
> To speke now spede wol I (cf. L.).

ll. 17883-4 (also H.), 18115-6, 18247-50, 18347-8, 18361-2, 18597-600, 18629-30, 18945 (T. H.), 19083-4, 19193-4 (T. H.), 19985-8, 20061-4, 20237-8 (T.), 20293-4, 20539-40, 20767-70, 20783-4, 20797-8, 20809-16 (T.), 20837-42, 20855-6, 20869-70, 20973-6, 21039-40 ; 21347-846, containing a legend, seem to have been rejected by the scribe of T., because they very much interrupt the progress of the narration, ll. 22163-4, 22397-8, 22425-6, 22455-8, 22481-2, 22553-4, 22557-8, 22621-2, 22647-8, 22673-4, 22843-4, 23101-2, 23195-6, 23329-30.

3. The same additional lines :

T. L. :

  ll. 3727-8 being quite different from those of C. F., may serve to connect the successive thoughts.

  ll. 4105-6 are useless, because in ll. 4107-8 we find the same with different rymes; they are, of course, wanting in C. F.

  ll. 6729-30 serve to repeat the subject for sake of perspicuity.

  ll. 9493-4 bespeak themselves by the expression ' in þe lordis þat him owe.'

  ll. 11321-2 are quite useless, and are also wanting in C. F.

  ll. 11651-2 contain the repetition of a just-preceding thought, partly even in the wording, and are quite different from F. ; they are wanting in C. The additional lines are perhaps produced by the conclusion of the preceding line ' and lamb and fox,' which, as being the subject of the preceding verb, seemed to the scribe to want a complement.

ll. 12816-7, so that ll. 12814-5 C. F. G. are wrought into four lines, in order to avoid the ryming words 'hatt: gatt.' l. 12814 in T. ends in 'desert,' to which it was not easy to find a suitable ryming word, so that the next line ends in the general conclusion 'al apert'; l. 12816 T. now contains the thought of l. 12815 in C. F. G., to which a patch-line (l. 12817) is added.

ll. 12876-7 contain an addition taken from Holy Writ; they are also wanting in C. F.

l. 13185, wanting in G., (so that l. 13184 in G. has no corresponding ryme,) is a patch-line, which has not the slightest resemblance to that one in C. F.

ll. 16839-40. The scribe of T. would avoid the ryming words 'one': 'rane' in G. He therefore alters ll. 16837-8, and draws out the l. 16837 into three lines, so that we have three successive ryming words 'one': 'anone': 'mone.'

ll. 16873-4 are in the ryming word assimilated to the preceding 'doun': 'boun,' the omitted word 'smerel' (in T.'s dialect 'oyncment') in l. 16871 in G. is made up for in the diffuse wording of ll. 16873-4.

ll. 17355-6 contain a repetition of ll. 17351-2.

ll. 18417-8 are added, because the scribe seems to have missed some connection between l. 18416 and l. 18419 (there is a gap in F.). He therefore altered l. 18416, and added these new lines, which amplify the thought in l. 18416, and are substantially similar to those in C.

ll. 18711-2 are quite superfluous, and are also wanting in C. F.

ll. 19301-2 (also H.) rather break in upon the contents; they are also wanting in C. F.

It will easily have been seen that any omission in G. is made up for quite differently from C., and only once supplied from the Bible, is somewhat similar to the lines of C., and that any additional lines which are also wanting in C. F. are useless withal.

I therefore state that G., which does not partake in the mistakes, alterations, omissions, and additions of T. H. L. B., must have been the source of T. H. L. B., with the exception of ll. 10835-906. I am now going to state[1] the relationship between the MSS. T., H., L., B.

---

[1] This statement will be of little consequence for a critical edition of the northern version of Cursor Mundi; but I hope that whoever makes researches into the southern dialect, or into that of G., will have an interest in it.

§ 11. I. T. (H. B.) do not partake in the mistakes, alterations, or omissions in L.

1. Mistakes and alterations in L., when compared with T. (H. B.):

l. 16 cawght f. saght.
l. 85 þe f. ʒe.
ll. 91-2 world: rold (T. 'werd': 'herd').
l. 152 born f. bare
l. 253 tyrandise f. trewandise.
l. 9625 they f. þi.
l. 9645 'wiþ' omitted.
l. 9747 suster f. suffer.
l. 9996 suyþe f. swete.
l. 10027 man f. name
l. 10673 must f. nust (= wist not)
l. 11315 & vii hight f. symeon hiʒt
l. 11316 many a shoure (mony a bone T.)
l. 11370 outwerd f. ouerthwert.
ll. 14159-9 ynde: fynde (inde: cuntre T., C. F. G.).
l. 16461 how fondly f. foulely.
l. 16482 to priue f. so priue.
l. 17693 fudary f. sudary.
l. 17895 wreche f. whiche.
l. 17903 noyns f. vois
l. 17937 thou come f. þan come
l. 17982 to reysen f. to receyue.
l. 18018 to symte f. smyte.

l. 18045 fals (T. has the incorrect word 'fas')
l. 18053 a word (T. has by mistake 'awerd')
l. 18065 ys stalworthe (T. has by mistake 'if')
l. 18096 our f. ʒour
l. 18107 ryse & said (T. has 'rise I saide')
l. 18188 distrowbelyst f. distowrbyst.
l. 18199 breuely f. bremely
ll. 18229-30 duke: belsabub (T. 'duk': 'belsabuk')
ll. 18265-6 werrid: ouyr-taruid werrayd: bitrayed T.
l. 18286 thyne (T. has by mistake 'pine')
l. 18438 has the inf. 'sey' inserted after 'herd'
l. 18465 he hath (T. has by mistake 'ʒe haue')
ll. 19005-6 wiþouten let: hight (T. 'let': 'het')
l. 20281 breth (: myrth); T. birþe (: mirþe).

2. Omissions in L., when compared with T. (B.), as far as the printed text enables me to do so.

ll. 81-82, 97-8, 1624-5, 10693, 10927, 11130, 18328.

II. T. (L. B.) do not partake in the mistakes, or omissions in H.

1. Mistakes in H.

l. 18020 furst f. þurst; l. 18023 at þis tyme f. ar.

2. Omissions in H.

The first 152 lines are wanting.

Besides, to judge from the printed specimens, H. agrees with T. word for word, nay, letter for letter. Only compare l. 206, sende T. H., sent L. B.; l. 208, endede meest and leest / T. H., endyd (endid) most and leste (leeste) L. B.; l. 218, henge T. H., hyng (hang) L. B.; l. 254, myʒt amenden in mony wise T. H., might amend in many (manes) wise L. B.

III. T. (H. L.) do not partake in the mistakes, alterations, or omissions in B.

1. Mistakes, or alterations:

l. 10 toun f. tome = tyme.
l. 11 hill f. his
l. 48 regneþ f. rage

l. 49 spenden mane her ʒounge age: spende mony her ʒouþe & age T.
l. 51 stours f. showris.

l. 71 sauit f. saviþ

ll. 72-3 and l. 77 are a little altered.

ll. 91-2 show an alteration in the endings, because the scribe will not
adopt 'werd' (=werld): 'herd';
he changes into 'here' : 'here.'

ll. 97-8 trowhede: spede; trowhede:
spede T.

l. 109 told f. bold.

l. 123 & telle of þe principale :
& telle sum gest principale T. L.

l. 130 beute f. bounte

l. 153 a-ȝene to by f. for to by.

ll. 155-6 are inverted.

l. 159 sowfte f. sowght.

l. 186 stond / f. stone.

l. 188 eght & þrity ȝer (also C. F.).
28 ȝere T. H. L. (also G.). B.
found it very easy to alter
according to St. John v. 5.
The scribe likewise corrected
'preched' in G. T. H. L. into
'praysed' (cf. C. F.).

l. 9541 'in pees' is wanting.

l. 9542 be f. ne.

l. 9553 lokys f. lokyd.

l. 9560 enny f. enemy.

l. 9571 lesse f. leffe = leue.

l. 9588 ȝe f. I.

l. 9594 unto; bitwix and T. (L. has a
different wording).

l. 9610 myght ; wolde T. L.

l. 9638 ȝeff f. ȝeffen = ȝyuen T., yeuyn
L. cf. 9710.

l. 9642 by; bifore T. L.

l. 9654 assayle f. assayleþ (L. assaieþ)

l. 9662 now f. no.

l. 9667 may f. made

l. 9675 no mo liues; mo on liues T. L.

l. 9685 hem & þe; hem þre T. L.

l. 9720 sesiþ; fyneþ T., faineþ L.

l. 9738 here f. praiere

l. 9739 make f. made

l. 9742 sche oght to be herd; she owe be
herde T. L.

2. Omissions :

B. ends with l. 22004, T. H. L. end with l. 23898.

As T. does not partake in the mistakes, or omissions in H. L. B., nor H.
B. in those in L., nor L. B. in those in H., nor H. L. in those in B., it is
evident that T., considering its exact conformity with H. L. B., when compared
with G. (C. F.), must have been the direct source of H. L. B., for L. cannot be
the source of H. B., nor H. the source of L. B., nor B. the source of H. L.

However scanty the materials to be compared were, they were quite
sufficient for this result.

§ 12. The interesting fragment A., containing the Assumption of Our Lady,
is still left. For its exact determination I thought it necessary also to compare
it with Gg, edited by J. R. Lumby.

I. We can first see a conformity of A. with x y [1], when compared with Gg.

1. In expressions and contents :

A. x y :

l. 20068 fleschli kynnes man (G. differs)

l. 20121 naked & hungry sche cloþed &
fedde

l. 20126 she it served, and þat was ryȝt

l. 20140 that faire lade, heuene quen A.
þe leuedi þat es heuene quene x y

Gg :

his oȝe quenes man

poure & hungrie wel faire he fedde

for heo servede hem wel riȝto

Ten wyntere hem amonge.

---

[1] Differences produced by the dialect are not taken into consideration on account
of Gg.

l. 20216 a bone (F. has 'a bede,' in E.   *aboue* (in T. also 'aboue')
    'leaves lost here')
l. 20234 miȝt & space   wille & space
l. 20243 hure sibbe & hure kynnes men   boþe sibbe & *fremde* men.
l. 20252 þat mi saul haf no vnplyȝt   þat mi saule ne beo idriȝt
    (na plight C. y)
ll. 20253-4 the good þat ȝe haue doun me þat god ȝe habbeþ me ydon
    my sone, þat was doun on þe tre mi sone þat was in rode ydon.
l. 20303 wiþ reuful steuene   wiþ milde steuene.

The gaps in F. and E. are of no consequence here.

    2. In additional lines :

        ll. 20105-8 are wanting in Gg, though necessary for the context.

        ll. 20171-2 contain concluding lines of the angel, which may be done without.

        ll. 20263-4 may be disregarded as containing a repetition of a thought which is expressed before and afterwards.

        ll. 20293-6 contain an amplification of the preceding thought :

> Þan I þee se suche sembiant make
> For shal I neuer suche a ladi take
> Hastou ouȝt herde þat I ne can
> Off me or of any oþer man ?

Gg has some other lines (ll. 231-2) ; besides, on account of their simplicity, the lines 229-32 in Gg may be preferred to ll. 233-8 (= ll. 20291-6 in C. G.) in A. Gg has in l. 229 'ised' f. 'he sed.'

    II. We can find a conformity of A. with Gg, when compared with x y.

    1. In expressions and ryming words :

  A. Gg :   x y :
ll. 20081-2 wepe : fete   grete : fete.

It would be quite rash to infer from the ryming words 'grete' : 'fete' that A. Gg should be dependent upon the source of x y. 'Wepe' : 'fete' only bespeak the early age of the manuscripts, and are nothing but assonances.

l. 20088 'alas ! my sone' þo saide sche A. 'Alas ! Alas, alas !' said sco
    'alas, my sone' seide heo Gg.
l. 20098 I shal þee take a trewe fere A. I sal biteche þe a fere
    Ihc schal þe teche a trewe ifere
    Gg.
ll. 20119-20 gode : fote   bote : fote.
ll. 20131-2 to glade hure hymself he cam he self com quilum þat scho bare
    that of hure bodi flesche nam   for to confort his moder care
    (Christ þat fless of hire nam)
ll. 20137-8 while sche was in þat stede   al þat scho badd gladli he did
    al þat sche wolde he hure dede   To quils þai lenged in þat sted
ll. 20141-2 than wolde hure sone sche   hir langed sare hir sun cum to
    com him to
    when he wolde hit was do   & quen scho gernd son was scho

l. 20144 with myrry steuene	wit a mild steuen
ll. 20145-6 Ther sche was & bad hure bede	In the temple wit her he met
Ly3th (li3te) an angel in þat stede	Anurd hir & tar hir grette

ll. 20191-4 (= ll. 139-40 A. & ll. 131-2 Gg):

to þat aungel seide our ladi	þan said Maria, ur lauedi
'what is þi name þat standeþ me bi?' A.	To the angel þar stod hir bi
þanne ansuarde ure lefdy:	'Quat es þi name, þou suet ami?
'What is þi name, belamy?' Gg.	Gladli þar-of wijt wald i.'

It is clear that A. has altered its source here; let us suppose it ran thus:

> to þat aungel standeþ bi our ladi
> saide 'What is þi name, belamy?'

Similar lines are likewise changed by Gg, and could not at all be made use of by the source of x y, which is younger than that of A., and which rejected the concise wording of the supposed lines.

ll. 20205-6 When he had iseide, to heuene he steie	Quen þe angell had his erand made
And Marie þer bi-left he (Marie abod & wel sle3)	He went, ur leuedi efter bade.

In l. 20206 A. as well as C. y have perhaps rejected 'sle3,' because they took it in the bad sense, though it is used here in the good meaning: 'wise, prudent.'

ll. 20241-2 when she hadde praied so hure frendes sche callid hure to	Quen scho had praid tus als scho wald Hir freind-men til hir scho cald.

The scribe of the northern version could not avail himself of these rymes, and therefore altered.

l. 20262 how schulle we louen withoute þee	hou we liue quen þou wil fle.

Gg has the correct reading: 'liue.'

ll. 219-20 (after l. 20276) in A. and ll. 215-16 in Gg:

mi bodi mai no peyne þolen	Mi bodi ne schal no pine þole
for he was þer-of y-boren A.	For he was þer-of ibore Gg

are similar, but inverted, to ll. 20279-80 in C. G.:

> for my licam his bodi bare
> He wel i suffer o na care
> (He wil it suffere of na sare)

l. 20280 being a repetition of l. 20278:

> For my son wil þat it be sua.

ll. 20285-6 as she so spak to þe mon   Quile scho spac þus, þat such woman
      off al þat wist nought seynt   þar-of it wist noght saint iohan.
      Ion A.
      þe while he spac þus to þis
      men
      of al þat þing nuste noȝt Ion
      Gg

l. 20288 ferli him þought þat sche was sory   ferli him thoght þai war sari.
      (& him þuȝte heo was sori)   The scribe must have mistaken ' heo ' or
           ' he ' for ' þai.'

ll. 20291-2 seie me, ladi, what is þee ? he   leuedi qui mas tu sli chere
      sede
      For me were leuer þat I were   ded war me leuer þat i wer
      dede A.
      lefdi what is þe ised (f. he sed)
      Me were leffre to beo ded Gg
      (ll. 229-30)

l. 20293 in C. G. has similar contents as l. 231 in Gg, which line is to be joined to

      ' me were,' etc.: ' þane i seo þe make such chere '

to which will correspond—

      ' what is þe ? ' my lefdi dere ?

2. In additional lines.

ll. 221-2 (after l. 20280 in x y) in A. and ll. 217-8 in Gg :

He þoled deþ himself for me   He þolede pine himself for me.
He honged nailed on þe tre A.   þo he deide upon þe tre Gg.

Gg's reading seems to have the preference for being more closely connected with the preceding ' pine þole.'

III. We can find a conformity of x y with Gg, when compared with A.

1. A differs from x y, Gg in expressions :

A. :   x y, Gg:
l. 20072 & man take hure to moder in   for mans luue thol i þis pine x y
      good wone   þat on þe rode is ispild Gg.
ll. 20077-8 (27-8)
      But þei haue wille to louen me   mine aun þat aght me to louen
      For wham I hange on þis tre   for quam i com dun fra o-bouen
ll. 20085-6 when he þat of hure flesche   for he þat nam of hir fless
      nam
      for his holi swete nam   als his suet wil al wess x y
                              whenne he þat of hire nam blod & fless
                              also his suete wille was Gg.
l. 20091 neuer ere wist I of sorwe nouȝt   ne cuth ic ar o soru noght
                              (ne cuþ ihc neure of soreȝe (sorewe)
                            noȝt.)
ll. 20111-2 are inverted in A.
l. 20117 pore f. þore.
l. 20148 blessed be þou in eche place   wel be þe euer in ilk place
                              (wel be þe in eche place)

ll. 20161-2 thou take þis palme þat I tak þis palme her in þi hand
    bringe þee
  þi dere sone haþ sent it þee it es þi dir sun saand C. y,
             nym þis palm wiþ þi riȝt honde
             hit is þi dere sones sonde.

l. 20183 I f. me.

ll. 20211-2 sche dide of hure clothes alle of scho did tan al hir hater
  & wasche hure wit water o & wesch hir suet bodi in water C. y.
  wille   He dude of al hire batere (f. hatere)
           And wessch hire body with clene watere
           Gg.

l. 20224 to reyne þee (sic !) to deri me (Mary prays Jesus to keep
           her from the devil.)

l. 20232 for man-kynne I praie þee for sinful man bisek i þe
           (For senful manne bid ihc þe)

l. 20251 I it wole amende with my myȝt I wil it mend, & þat is right.

2. A. has additional lines, when compared with x y Gg :

   ll. 21-2 ' & þenketh on my sorwe nowe
     How I hange here abowe '

are added after l. 20072 C. as an amplification of the words 'þi sone,' which
are by mistake referred to John instead of to Christ.

3. A. has these omissions of lines, when compared with x y Gg.

   ll. 20207-8 'þat palme scho nam þat was hir broght
     O þat bode forget sco noght '

are necessary for the following words :

    ' until hure chambre sone sche nam ' A.

   ll. 20239-40 Sun þou kep þam for (fra) þi fa
    For quam þou thold al þis wa C. x

which are inverted in Gg in this way :

    for hem þu þoledest pine & wo
    wite hem wel fram here fo

seem to be necessary for concluding the preceding thought :

    Sun, thinc hou þou has tam wroght
    And hou þou þam has dere boght C.

ll. 20277-8 To me ne sal it negh na wa ne schal no soreȝ come me to
  for my son wil þat it be sua for my sone hit wule so Gg
  C. G.

seem to be in close connection with the preceding lines :

    ' Has na dred, bot wijts it wele
    O pine ne sal i thol na dele ; '

moreover, I would suppose that they are necessary for the rhythm which in
Gg seems to ring in my ears like four-lined stanzas.

IV. A., Gg, x y differ among each other :

ll. 20165-6 he shal sende after þee 　He wile senden after þe
　　　　of heuene ferde moche plente 　from heuene adun of his meigne Gg
　　　　A.
　　　　　　　He sal send efter ful son
　　　　　　　Ne sal þu nawight lang her hon.

l. 20168 that euer was & now is A. 　　þat eure schal leste wiþute misse Gg.
　　　　　　　þar þou sal euer ha mirth i-wisse C. y.

ll. 20181-2 with my frendes & my kynnes 　and nyme lyue of mine kenesmen
　　　　men
　　　　& with hem þat I in erþe haue 　& myne frend þat wiþ me beon Gg.
　　　　ben A.
　　　　　　　I wald wijt gladli tuix & quene
　　　　　　　To tak leue at mi kinesmen C. y.

l. 20183 & hem þat I (sic!) haue fedde 　& of him þat haþ me cloþed & fed Gg.
　　　　& clad A.
　　　　　　o freindes þat me fedd & clad (C. has 'ladd' (sic!)) C. y.

　　　　ll. 20187-8 come: abone A. 　　　come: aboue Gg. doun: bun C y.

l. 20271 lateþ be ȝour greding (f. greting) hit helpeþ noȝt A.
　　　　leteþ ben, ower wepinge ne helpeþ noþt Gg.
　　　　lat be weping, it helpes noght C. G.

ll. 20281-2 mi sone þat is king of heuene 　He þat is almiȝtful kyng
　　　　schal me sende worde wel 　Schal me sende of his geng Gg.
　　　　euene A.
　　　　　　　He þat i bar, þat bligh (f. bliþe) brid (f. bird)
　　　　　　　Sal me sende of heuen wird C. G.

ll. 20289-90 Seie me ladi, what is þee 　and sede lefdy, what is þe
　　　　what is þis folk þat I here 　for mi service tel hit me Gg.
　　　　se A.
　　Fur o grace, leuedi, quat es te 　leuedi, fild ful of grace, quat es ye
　　and tis oþer leuedis þat i se C. 　and þir leuedis þat i here se ? G.

l. 20302 for þi sones loue seie þou me 　For my loue tel hit me (l. 228) Gg
　　　　　　　　　　　　　　(cf. l. 228 with C. G.)
　　　　for mi servis þou sai (þu tel) it me C. G.

These differences are, no doubt, too slight to allow any inferences to be made from them; they generally show a closer connection between A. and x y than between Gg and x y. But to make the comparison complete, I still add such a one between A. and x y, where Gg, which has only 240 lines, can no longer be compared.

V. A. differs from x y :

1. In expressions, rymes, and the succession of lines.

A:

ll. 20311-2 are inverted.

ll. 20327-30 But herestou now my frende Ion

    When þou sest þat I am gon

    Kepe my bodi þat I ne be binomen

    When þe fellon Iewes comen.

ll. 20335-6 mi sone þei hongen on a tre

    wel I wote so wolde þei me

x y:

Queu time es þat he has me

Suet iohn, bi-sek i þe

þou lat na juus negh me to

Despit ful fain wald tai me do.

þai hat na-þing mar þan me

mi sun þai hang o rode tre.

l. 276 A. 'wel i wote,' etc. = l. 20335 C. G., and l. 275 A. 'mi sone,' etc. = l. 20336, in consequence of which the numbering of lines is wrong in the 'Edition,' when compared as far as l. 20395 in C. G.

ll. 20351-2 fare : haue   fare : euermare

Morris would supply 'euermare' after 'haue,' which I cannot agree with ; nor can I do so with J. R. Lumby, who, in his pref. vii., says : 'and bears traces of a more northern origin.' Cf. also ll. 20359-60 !

ll. 20383-4 lone f. loue : i come   understand : hand.

l. 20387 Tho seide Petyr a ferli þinge   Here me now iohn, a ferli þing.

ll. 20395-6 So seide alle þat weren þere

    'Suche wondre sawe I neuer ere'

We se wel þat we all er *her*

Si ferli sagh we neuer *her*

(We se wele þat we all her *here*

Suilk farli sau we neuer *are*)

ll. 20397-8 show indirect discourse 'of hem,' 'þei,' but a direct one 'of us,' 'we' in C. G.

l. 20407 ȝou   us

l. 20410 bi-fore hure knele ȝe alle bi-dene   be-fore hir fair þan kneel yee

ll. 20437-8 are inverted.

ll. 20447-8 To kep þee & be þee by

    Ther-fore we comen to þe lady

To kepe al þe als our leuedi

als lang sai þou ert her us bi.

ll. 20449-50 Ful bliþe sche was of here come

    Blessed,' sche seide, 'be my *sone*.'

Sa fain scho was þat þai þer *wern*

'Blisced' scho said, 'ai be þat *bern* (barn).' C. G.

ho was so faine at þai ware þere

ho blessed þe childe atte ho bere F.

ll. 20457-8 Kepeþ faire my body

    That none do me no vilany

wakes fair now mi licam

wel i wat & traist i am

ll. 20461-2 are inverted.

l. 20250 & siþen I hange on þe rode   þan es it right i do hir gode

ll. 20527-8 That Adam toke & ete it inne   He ete again mi forbidding

    To helle he went & al his kynne

He was tint & all his ospring

ll. 20539-40 Thei token me & bette me sore

    And atte þe last þei dide wel more

þai tok me þan & beft wel sare

& atte last þai did me care

But for other evidences, and l. 20061, one would suppose that these rymes were a proof for a dependency of A. upon the source of x y.   I think, however, no one will doubt that 'more' is no alteration of 'care,' which does not suit at all, for 'þai did me care' is no climax to 'þai beft wel sare.'   On the contrary, I make bold to suppose that 'care' is a corruption or mistake for 'scar' = raillery, *i. e.* they railed on him when he was crucified.   Well, now it is clear that a scribe of the 14th century could not avail himself of those rymes of the early 13th, or even late 12th century.   He was therefore obliged to alter if he found 'sare': 'scare' into 'sore,' and when at a loss for a corresponding ryme, once more to make use of 'sore': 'more,' which had already been used in ll. 20529-30 (*i. e.* ll. 431-2).

ll. 20541-2 swongen : bounden	wrang : hang.
l. 20552 hure f. him.	
ll. 20553-4 & seide, 'Ion, for my lone, kep wel þis wyf, I am hure sone.'	I said til him ' mi leif cosen Kep þis womman, es moder min.'
ll. 20581-2 In to þe chambre þer sche was Inne With ful many of hure kynne	Until hir bure wit miri sang þam thoght til hir wel suith lang.
ll. 20597-8 myȝt : bryȝt	rike : like
ll. 20605-8 'Sone' sche saide, 'I beseke þee' O þing þat þou graunt me that I nought þe deuel se ne none þat euer with him be	'Sun,' scho said, ' bath lauerd & king I þe biseke now of a thing Ouer i sal o þe feind haf sight Or of his þat er maledight. (F. differs in l. 20608.)
ll. 20609-10 fone : none	fa : þaa.
ll. 20613-4 ne wille I neuer þole *more* that any of hem come þee *bi-fore.*	wil i noght thol þe þam to *sei* Sal he noght cum bifore þin *ei* (F. ends in ' be-for þe.')

ll. 20619-26 have these endings:

ȝyue : lyue : þee : þee : þee : pite : praiere : were	þe : fre : giue : liue : dere : praiere : war· bare.

ll. 20619-20 and ll. 20621-2 are, as to the substance, inverted in C. y.

l. 20623 = l. 520 is wanting in C. y, and l. 20626 is wanting in A. Could those readings in C. y be alterations, so that such repetitions as ' þee : þee : þee' would be avoided?

ll. 20627-8 worshipe : treuliche	leuedi : fulli

ll. 20631-2 are inverted.

ll. 20659-60 That no þing with-seie þe Off þat þou wolt biseke me	It was vnright i suld witstand þe of oght o þin erand C. G. hit ware un-riȝt to wiþ-stande þo ani þing þou askis of me F.

ll. 20665-6 'So I auȝt, moder, & so I   'Sua aght i moder, wit-outen wand.'
         wille';
        He left up his houd & blessed   He blisced her wit his right hand.
        hure stille
ll. 20667-8 His blessing sche þouȝt good   Til hir sun þat scho luued mast,
        And he hure soule understode   þan scho yald hir blisced gast

ll. 20715-40 and ll. 20741-64 are, as to the substance, inverted in A.,
which succession does not suit the connection. The number of lines is
quite different. In A. there are in the place of ll. 20741-64 C. G. (containing
the story about a Jewish priest), ll. 611—688 == 78 lines, among which some
insertions must be supposed, f. i. ll. 623—639.[1] The succession of lines in
A. must be: 610, 689—710, 611—688, 753. ll. 711—752 do not correspond
to C. G. ll. 753-4 in A. are similar to ll. 20771-2 in C. y.

ll. 20732 or cast we it in a foul sere   for scho þat ilk traitur bare C. y, to
        sere f. rere, cf. Mark v. 13   which in G. are added ll. 30733-4 :
        (Kent).

                                   þat we quilum hang on rode
                                   For us thoght he was noght gode.
ll. 20735-6 thei comen lepand þiderwarde   þai wend to fill þair fol forward
        & þat hem fel swiþe harde   and son þai lep þider-ward.

ll. 20773-848 in C. y quite differ from ll. 755—904 in A.

ll. 893-4 in A. are given in ll. 2005-8 in C. y ; C. has there the mistake
'tuenti.'

l. 20775 'son þar efter, sum bok sais,' x y, makes us suppose that the
compiler then availed himself of another source.

2. In omissions.

        ll. 20333-4 mi bodi þou kepe fra þaim, i sai
               þou we be sib, bath ic & tai

in C. G. seem to me to be mere additional lines on account of l. 20340 in C.
G. and l. 280 in A.

ll. 20393-4 (between ll. 332 and 333 in A.) :

        als help me lauerd suet ihesus
        I ne wat how i com in þis hous C. G.,

compared with l. 20401 :

        'cums wit me into yon hous' C. G.,

and l. 339 A. :

        '& comeþ wiþ me into þis hous'

which line Morris is wrong to compare with l. 20394, seem to be additional.

---

[1] Cf. Gierth, *Englische Studien*, vii. p. 18.

l. 20409 'cums now all her in wit me,' C. G., seems to be a patch-line for the following line, to which are added, as an amplification, ll. 20411-28 and l. 20430.   In the substance as well as in expressions they remind us of former lines, so that the northern scribe seems to have given his own 'business' here.   l. 20430, 'Blisced mot þou ever bene' (cf. ll. 20153-4), corresponding to 'Suet leuedi of heuen quene,' seems to be a patch-line.   The rhythm seems to bespeak different principles:

Cf. l. 20414 For-þé we er cúmmen to þé leuedí
     l. 20429 Suét leuedí of héuen quéne (A. has : & seieþ 'ladi heuene quene) with
     l. 20424 Ríght bi-fór our léuedi sélue
     l. 20415 Bót a thíng said saínt Iohán
     l. 20416 to pétre ánd to apóstlis ilkán
     l. 20419 þát náman of áll our fér
     l. 20420 bifóre hír mak látli chére C., bifor hir mak na laith chere G.

Notwithstanding the omission in A., we do not want there any link in the connection.

     ll. 20451-2 'I am his moder, wel he me kid
                    I am ful fain yu ar me mid'

are useless for the context, and want an exact collation with the MS., that the question may be decided whether there be any mistake of the editor or the scribe in the ryming words.   'Mid' is southern; and northern 'miþ' is put aside by 'wiþ' as early as the 13th century.

     ll. 20491-508, containing the song of Paradise, the mention of an earth-quake, and how Mary said to those sleeping apostles : 'Wake, sleep not,' seem to be descended from another source, according to l. 20500 (als sais þe bok).

     Besides, there are wanting ll. 20547-8, 20557-8, 20617-8, 20626, 20673-4, 20717-8, 20765-70.

     3. In additional lines.

     We find after l. 20438 two lines in A. (ll. 357-8) which are necessary for the context, but must be done away with in C. y, differing from A. in the preceding lines.   In C. y, John has told Peter and the other apostles how they shall behave to Mary (cf. ll. 20415-22).   This advice is not mentioned in A. The apostles then go and salute Mary with words that we find in A., though they are not spoken by the apostles, but by John, who advises the apostles to use them (cf. l. 348 'and seieþ,' etc.).   So we find after those words of John :—

           Than comen þe apostles alle
           And bi hure bigan to falle.

After l. 20490 there are in A. ll. 409-10:

> ' She badde Ion & þe apostles alle
> To kepen hure what so bi-falle '

which may be done without; C. has in their place ll. 20491-508.

After l. 20598 we find two lines (ll. 495-6) which are a useless repetition of a former thought (cf. l. 492 = l. 20596 C. y). The assonance ' come ': ' bone,' however, would betray their old age.

After l. 20688 we find two lines (ll. 583-4) which are a repetition of ll. 567-8. The printed text gives a strange punctuation,[1] so that one can misunderstand the lines. The punctuation must be: 'Petre, I commaunde þee, mi moder bodi kepe þou me: Iohan and all þine fere; nis no þinge me so dere.'

After l. 20720 there are ll. 711-52 in A., which do not correspond to any lines in C. y, and do not suit the context, so that the scribe of A. may be supposed to have borrowed them from another source. This double source perhaps accounts, too, for the confusion concerning ll. 20715-40 and ll. 20741-64.[2]

This section seems to me clearly to prove that—

1. Gg is no fragment of the original; but it is next to its southern original, which may be marked by Ω.

2. A. is next to the northern source of x y, marked by O., when compared with Gg.

3. A. and Gg point to the source Ω.

4. Gg and O. are independent of A.

5. Ω is not the direct source, either of A. or O.

6. A. and O. are derived from a common source, which may be marked by ω, in ll. 1—610 in A., and in ll. 20057-8, 20065-714 in O. ll. 611—892 in A. are to be derived from another source, which may be marked by ξ, whereas ll. 20715-74 in O. seem still to refer to ω, so that only ll. 20775-848 must be referred to a different source, which may be marked by ε.

In marking the other sources, from which O. is to be derived by α, β, γ, δ, and the source of T. in ll. 10835-906 by η, I may illustrate the filiation of the manuscripts by the following pedigree:

---

[1] Cf. also the wrong punctuation in l. 243: ' Iohan,' seide ladi, ' what is þee,' instead of: Iohan seide: 'Ladi, what is þee, . . .'

[2] Cf. Gierth, *Engl. Stud.*, p. 17 ff.

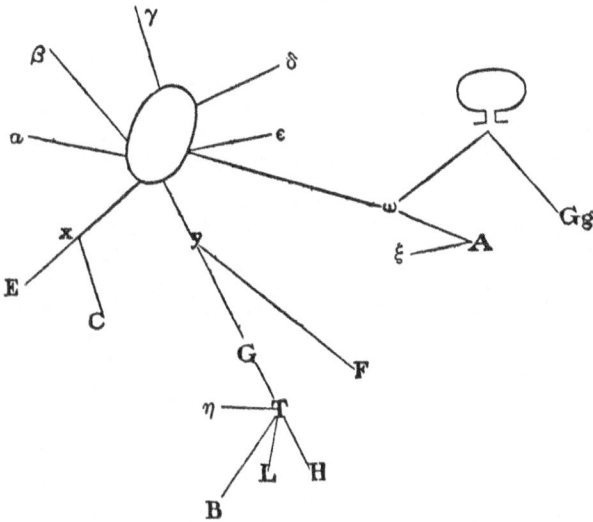

Results which will be available for a critical edition of the northern version of *Cursor Mundi :*

1. C., written in the dialect of the neighbourhood of Durham (but for one exception), must first of all be made use of, and has, where E. is wanting, two votes against F. G.

2. The fragment E., in a Northumbrian dialect, is next to C., but shows too many mistakes and omissions to be used otherwise than comparatively with F. G.

3. G. will be of great advantage (though written in a dialect south of that of C.), where C. shows omissions, or the Midland hand.

4. F., written in a North-Western dialect, without such orthographical absurdities as in the Lancashire dialect of 'Sir Amadace' (cf. Robson, *Metrical Romances*), must be used most cautiously.

5. A. and Gg, both written in a Southern dialect, but of different ages, will sometimes avail, as far as the wording is concerned.

6. T. H., written in a South-Western dialect near the Midland confines, and L. B., in the extremest south of the East-Midland dialect, are quite useless. At the best, T. may perhaps avail once or twice, when the wording in G. is concerned.

I shall now add a careful examination into the sounds and inflections as well as the rhythm of *Cursor Mundi*.

H. Hupe.

CURSOR STUDIES,

AND

CRITICISM ON THE DIALECTS OF ITS MSS.

BY

DR. H. HUPE.

CURSOR STUDIES,

AND

CRITICISM ON THE DIALECTS OF ITS MSS.

BY

DR. H. HUPE.

PART VII.

TABLE OF CONTENTS.

PREFACE.

Motto : Es irrt der Mensch, so lang' er strebt.

It is three years since I wrote for the Early English Text Society an Essay (printed in Part VI) on the "Filiation and the Text of the MSS. of the *Cursor Mundi*." Its German translation, which I wanted for the Göttingen Faculty of Philosophy, underwent some slight changes, but, long after it was originally written, it was published with all its faults of which I then knew. Two years' more work upon the same subject have made me see that a good many things which I took from authorities had better have been left unsaid.

A close inspection of the MSS.—three of which I collated with the text—and a comparative study of other MSS. at the British Museum and the Bodleian Library in the years '86 and '87, have enabled me to take a different view of many points now. But whatever mistakes are in my former essay, printed two years ago, I hope it will not be quite a nuisance to the reader. To me it is a gratification not to cleave to old mistakes : they are useful in some other way. Middle-English philology is still a wretched, barren field, in which a good many workers will rather scramble and err with the multitude, than find a new track where they will encounter difficulties hitherto undreamt of.

To those who best understand how little has yet been done, I need hardly say that I do not imagine I have always arrived at conclusive results. I have not had the opportunity and time to read at liberty in a large library. I am not so happy as to own a set of the most valuable publications of the Early English Text Society. I have also had some difficulty in getting books lent to me again and again when I wanted them, as new views arose.

As to the Pedigree of the MSS., I refer to M. Kaluza's critique of my former essay in the *Englische Studien*, xi. 2, and my reply to it in the *Anglia*, xi. 2.

Grateful acknowledgments are due to the Director of the Society, Dr. F. J. Furnivall, who was kind enough to lend me for a long time the proof-sheets of Robt. Manning's *Chronicle* and the *Pricke of Conscience*. For facilities afforded I am also indebted to the officers of the British Museum and Bodleian Library, and I have been and am under constant obligation to the indulgent officers of the Göttingen University Library.

H. HUPE.

Lübeck, Whitsuntide-week, 1888.

CHAPTER I.—THE PEDIGREE OF THE MSS.

1. In availing myself of the letters of the Pedigree formerly given,— A B C E F G Gg H L T; α β γ δ ε η ξ ω **x y**—I first state that **x** and **y** do not point to the original itself, but to a defective copy (**z**). Both of them have the following mistakes in common :

ll. 21895-6 And he gain vs sa meke and mind (the source had ā = an = on)
   Sua mikel luvis naþing als vr kind C E, similarly in F G.
l. 22402 In papilon that mikel fell (for *Babylon*).
l. 22552 þat al þe erþe it sal to quak C E F T (G has corrected *to* to *do*).
l. 22798 þat mannis fles to mold ᴛo fall E **y**, se C (meant for *do*).
l. 22920 sal com bifor þe demester **x y**. (Compare T : He shuld com, etc.—**x** and
   y have no subject. Qu. : bifor = *he for* (for = before).

2. E seems to point to the common source **x**, for besides the two arguments (l. 20058 and l. 23373) formerly mentioned, there are still other reasons for believing so. Compare :

l. 22450 þat nan it sal in erþ knau **x**, man **y**. Compare l. 22448 þat nan. Qu.
  man for *nan*.
   Compare : þe jugement a litel are
    .   .   .   .   .   .
    Sal vr lauerd his mightes scau
    þat *man* it sal in erþ knau.
l. 20124 þat tai ne had of hir mister[1] þat þai ne had of hir gret mistere
l. 23087 Qwen i in sekenes was sare Quen i was stad in sekenes sare

In both places **y** had no reason to alter **x**'s reading, which is tolerably correct ; but **y**'s reading seems to be original, for it suits both rhythm and sense. I should also be inclined to regard the following readings of G's as original ones :

v. 24642 and þof it was mi (þi E) bale And thoght it was mi bale all bott[1]
  al bett
v. 24646 I languis (in laguis) all for þe In langurs all for þe[1]

      [1] See Addenda.

I should think that if **z** had had *þou*, G would have made the same blunder as C E, for *thoght* is only the repetition of the preceding *thoght me*. F has altered.

v. 22915-6
And o (of E) þat man þat was in were   & to þat man . . .
Þe soth he sceud him al clere

Supposing that **z** had *āto* it is astonishing that both E and C read *and o* and not *vnto* or *& to*, both of which might as well have been taken.

The arguments are not beyond doubt. It is a pity that E is only a fragment.

3. A and Gg must be put in another relation to the original than that which I formerly gave them. There is evidence that A points to a more northern source. Compare the following lines :

A :	x y :
ll. 20081-2 did wepe : at hure fete	His moder stod and sare scho gret : fete

I think there is no reason to fight for an assonance in a late 14th or early 15th century MS. The southern scribes of that time seem rather to avoid the verb *grete*(n).

ll. 20352-3 How schal I lyve, how schal I fare	Hou sal i live, how sal I fare
How schal I blis or ioie have	How sal i ioi haf evermare

A's reading appears to me now to be an unlucky alteration on account of *mare*. Cf. L, which reads : *how shalle I covyr of my care.*

ll. 20403-4 Sche ordeyneþ hure to fare vs fro	And graithes hir to far vs fra
For hure sone hit wolle so	For hir sun will þat it be sua.

Both A and T L have avoided *graithe*, but not the ryme *fra : sua*, though *fro* (for *from*) does not suit the southern dialect.

ll. 20397-8 þorw wham : cam	for quam : þei . . . cam

I do not now think that A has retained a southern original reading; for observe that *cam* is a plural.

ll. 20565-6 Adam & Eue & many mo	Adam *and* Eua and oþer manian
I dide hem oute of helle go	I did þaim vte o þine be tan

A avoided the past participle *tan* for which *take*(n) occurs in the south, but not *I dide hem go* with its causative meaning : to this use of *do* the southern dialect is quite a stranger.

l. 20699 Doþ þe belles alle to ryngen	Dos þe belles all at (to y) ring

1 20736 Thei comen lepand þiderwarde   And som þei lep þiderward (E om.)

The present participle in *and* is unknown in the south.

The arguments are sufficient to prove the above statement.   I shall have an opportunity afterwards to speak of A at full length.

4. There is good reason to believe that E and A point to the same source. It is a pity that only 88 lines can be compared.

1. 20118 Sco serued in baþe les and mare E   þai seruid hir all (bath F G) lesse and
      Sche wolde serue, las & mare A   mare C F G

It appears from the preceding lines that *þai* is the correct reading.

1. 20116
Ful wel þai miȝt in hir forberne E   In all hir will þai hir forbar C F G
Ful wel þei ne miȝt hure forberen A

There is no reason to believe that C F G's source altered the original reading.   On the contrary, as I shall afterwards prove that E A's source is written in the West Midland dialect, I have good reason to suppose that this scribe rejected *forbar*, which does not suit his dialect.   The alteration may be accounted for by a faulty *well* (for *will*).   The relation between E and A is obvious.

1. 20099 þat treulic sal kepen þee E   þat treuli sal ta kep to þe
      That trewly schal kepen þee A

If *kepen* were the original reading, C F G's source could have easily altered it into *kep of*.   But the rhythm in E (þát treulíc) is much stiffer than in C F G, where we read : þat treúli sál ta kép to þé.

1. 20113 þare scho bileui[d] al hir liue E   þar scho bileft for al hir lijf
      Ther sche bileft al hure lyfe A

It excites wonder that both E and A have omitted *for*, which is necessary for the metre.

5. T is not dependent upon G, for it appears from a good many places that T G point to the same source (δ).

1. 2187 G : þat was cechim.   T : oon cechim = oon techim = C's antechim.

It is well known that *c* and *t* are frequently confounded.   G probably omitted *an* (for *and*) on account of its obscurity, and altered it into *þat was*, from which T could never have adopted *oon* if it had not seen *an*.   The correct reading is *and* (= namely) *Techim*.

ll. 15877-80 in T appear in the same succession as in C F, whereas there is no reason why T should have altered G's sequence of lines.

1. 22552 þat all the erd it sal do schake   þat al þe erþe shal to shake

T's reading shows the same mistake *to* as C E F, though G's *do* appears to be a correction.

l. 23764   Certes þai ar feld in fliȝt   Certes þei be felde in fiȝt

G's *fliȝt* is not nonsense, so that T might have had a reason for correcting it.

Moreover, in G there are two omissions: ll. 3727-8 and ll. 18417-8 which agree with C F, so far as T's dialect would allow. The rymes had to be avoided; so we may rightly suppose that C's wording could not be entirely kept.

6. It has been supposed that T is the source of H L B. There is no doubt that it is the oldest, completest, and correctest copy amongst them. T is, of course, not without mistakes. Since the text affords us only scanty materials for comparison, there is no possibility of seeing whether either of the MSS. shows readings which could not be the result of correction. There are some slight corrections in H L B, as I have stated, but there is no evidence to prove that all the differences are due to this cause. I therefore stick to the supposed filiation of T H L B; but I am fully aware that it is not beyond doubt.

7. Considering the age and dialect of the MSS., which are the chief subjects of my further researches, I suppose that neither z nor C is directly drawn from its source. So I beg the reader to accept the following modification of my former statement.

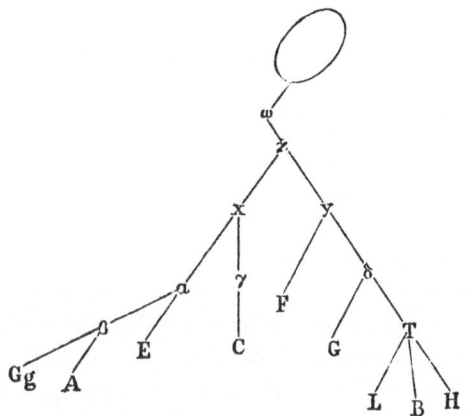

CHAPTER II.—THE COLLATION OF THE MSS.

8. A TEXT copied and printed with diplomatic accuracy is necessary, no doubt. Dr. Morris's edition is splendid in every way; but no human work is without inadvertencies. The collation of his texts with their originals was therefore not superfluous; and it must be inserted here for the sake of my further inquiries. I had an opportunity of collating C, G, A.

9. I begin with C. Curved brackets ( ) denote that the letters or words within them are defaced or rubbed out.

l. 14 For] (F)or
l. 15 How] (H)ow
l. 16 Wit] (Wit)
l. 18 How] (H)ow
l. 42 Both gode and] (Both gode and)
l. 43 Vr dedis] (Vr d)edis
l. 66 *stands in the margin.*
l. 103 neghest] g *is overlined.*
l. 105 oure] oure
l. 168 in] *overlined.*
l. 172 hefdid] he(f)did
l. 209 our] oure
l. 313 his] (his)
l. 337 þou] (þou)
l. 520 hete] *originally not* t, *but perhaps* d.
l. 807 wit hin] within
l. 930 worth *is the old reading,* torne *was put by the transcriber.*
l. 1037 gyon] *only* yon *is in a different hand and ink, and stands on an erasure.*
l. 1038 eufrates *and* fison *stand on an erasure.* C *had no doubt originally the same reading as* F G. *At foot there is a circle divided into four segments in which are written the words — read round from right to left—*'tigre, gison, eufrates, fison.' *The outline is in red.*
l. 1060 was] s *overlined.*
l. 1138 wete] w *not original, altered in a different ink.*
l. 1208 lelli] lelle, *though not quite distinct, but* e *cannot be read for* i.
l. 1237 pastd] pascd *must be read.*
l. 1281 Nou] u *overlined in a different ink.*
l. 1284 ilk way] *between these words something is rubbed out.*
l. 1287 (he)] he *stands in the margin.*
l. 1305 lote] lotti
l. 1407-8 sad : glad] *originally* said : glaid

l. 1461 yer to] þer to. y *and* þ *are not distinguished (only* y *is used).*
l. 1597 Drightun] drightim *for* drightin
l. 1711 ȝow with] vobiscum *in the margin.*
l. 1928 Ti] Til
l. 1951 therst] *I think* theift, *only* i *is mistaken for* r, ft *is often very like* st
l. 2008 *At foot a figure representing the ark, with the words* urcha *on one side, and* Noe *on the other.*
l. 2123 knyth] knytht
l. 2148 (wit)] wit *in the margin.*
l. 2190 At bottom : Divisio terræ

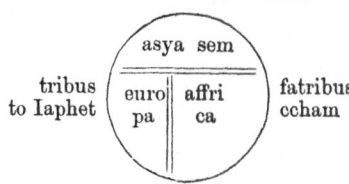

tribus to Iaphet | asya sem | euro pa | affri ca | fatribus ccham

l. 2314 *At bottom, in the space of the pedigree,* Omer *is written in a different ink.*
l. 2315 *At bottom :* turris (*with a figure representing a tower*) babilonie
l. 2348 be] bee
l. 2370 ertd] *originally* th, *but altered in the same hand to agree with* ferd
l. 2419 wit] *originally* wid, *but then altered into* wit
l. 2426 wij] wijf
l. 2427 brokar] *stands on a rubbed place. I suppose it was* brok her, *but the scribe, with his broad pronunciation, preferred* brokar
l. 2452 hild þair store] (hild þair st)ore
l. 2500 to] til
l. 2520 temase] temace
l. 2578 on on] *dele the second* on

E

l. 2610 als] *read* alle, e *is overlined in a different ink.*

l. 2657 sal] sol

l. 2695 scare] *stands on an erasure. It cannot be for* scare, *read* scere

l. 2929 loth] *overlined.*

l. 3220 were] ware

l. 3615 Tac] Gac

l. 3881 *At bottom:* Quomodo laban seduxit iacob cum lya pro rachell.

l. 3910 *There follows the heading:* Quomodo luctatur angelus cum iacob

l. 3975 *Heading:* De reconciliacione iacob et esau

l. 4023 *Heading:* De iacob et ejus filiis et de exsompnia iacob. Cf. *next page of the text.*

l. 4265 *Heading:* Quomodo uxor putifar percunt(atur) Joseph.

l. 4456 *Heading:* Quomodo incarcerabatur ioseph pro eadem uxore. Quomodo ereptus est ioseph a carcere *is the heading of the 2nd column.*

l. 4553 *Heading:* De exsompnia pharaonis regis egypti et de fame eiusdem pat(ri)e

l. 4647 *Henceforth the Latin headings are for the most part cut off by the bookbinder.*

l. 4809 i] þai

l. 5116 þe þen] heþen

l. 5263 for-hond] for-houd

l. 5301-4 *Many words are almost defaced by ink.*

l. 5413 for þair] (for) þai(r)

l. 5529 *At bottom:* De fine joseph filii iacob

l. 5585 demmepster] demmep

l. 5647 him sagh] *repeated by mistake.*

l. 5918 prima vindicta *in the margin.*

l. 5927 secunda vindicta *in the margin.*

l. 5952 Tercia vind. *in the margin.*

l. 5959 iiij vind. *in the margin.*

l. 5993 moru] morn

l. 5999 Quinta *in the margin.*

l. 6009 vj *in the margin.*

l. 6017 vii *in the margin.*

l. 6039 viii *in the margin.*

l. 6051 ix *in the margin.*

l. 6058 x *in the margin.*

l. 6077 ☉ *in the margin.*

l. 6101 had *MS. repeats* had] *is a mistake.*

l. 6389, roche *in* l. 6390, *and it in* l. 6391 *stand on an erasure.*

l. 6428 📖 *stands in the margin.*

l. 6491 oper] oþer

l. 6643 þe MS. ke] *is a mistake.*

l. 6706 him] *overlined.*

l. 6739 þe last] (þe last)

l. 6780 God wil] *is not in a later hand.*

l. 6784 Him to sla] *in a later hand, originally* of slaing. to *is overlined,* of *altered into* hī, *and* ing *rubbed out.*

l. 6916 desert. MS. *inserts* was here] *is a mistake. After* desert *we find* be es *altered into* hees, *which alteration looks bad, so that it is crossed through, and a proper* he es *is added.*

l. 6934 and effrahin] *Between these words something also is overlined in a later hand.*

l. 6964 to] *overlined.*

l. 7083 him] *stands on an erasure, and is in a different ink.*

l. 7094 wal(d) ha] wald haf, d *and* f *being added in the later hand.*

l. 7256 ald] d *overlined.*

l. 7269 left] lelft

l. 7277 hornpan] *first* n *overlined.*

l. 7303 (ar ȝe)] *overlined.*

l. 7304 nise] *on an erasure.*

l. 7409 *Note:* MS. *corrected to* wit gleu wald] *add: in the later hand.*

l. 7507 ren(d)] rend, *originally* t, *corrected to* d.

l. 7649 (wha)] who *overlined in the later hand.*

l. 7659, 60, 61 (þi)s, (And), (þer)] *spoilt by ink.*

l. 8195 sett] seit; cf. l. 8291.

l. 9447 apel] appel

l. 10103 my] mi

l. 10236-10244 *much defaced.*

l. 10932-4 *partly defaced.*

l. 10977-10982 *much defaced.*

l. 11167 (be)] *om.* MS.

l. 11482 sagh] *on an erasure, not distinct, perhaps* sogh

l. 11509 (chere)] *in a later hand.*

l. 11749 At] *crossed through.*

l. 12726 bigun neu] bigunnen

l. 13017 resiun] resum *for* resun

l. 13335 stan] (sta)n

l. 13399 architricline] archidicline

l. 14005 vñtement] vntement

l. 14061 blin] blind

l. 14063 vnttement] *not distinct, perhaps* vintement *or* vnctement

l. 14444 architricline] archidicline

l. 15068 Qua] Q *defaced.*

l. 15141 a] *on an erasure.*
l. 15142 sal] *originally* hal
l. 15154 stable] & stable
l. 15176 (to)] *originally* to, *but rubbed out now.*
l. 15257 þat] *overlined in a later hand.*
l. 15259 wit] *on an erasure.* þat] *overlined.*
l. 15279 sai wirdes] i wirdes *on an erasure.*
l. 15291 boghed] d *overlined, the word is in a different hand, and seems to be a correction of* bued.
l. 15295 (na)] *rubbed out.*

l. 15303 tite] titte
l. 15305 doo] *second* o *seems to be added.*
l. 15330 yuu] y *rubbed out.*
l. 15387 morsel] *correction of a later hand.*
l. 15469, 15479, 15491 *the mark* ⚿ *is not seen on account of the binding.*
l. 15525 ic] c *rubbed out.*
l. 15641 so, *altered from* sa] *there is no alteration.*
l. 15668 be MS. he] *only at first sight;* be *is distinct.*
l. 15720 he] h *nearly rubbed out.*
l. 16099 þai] *overlined.*
l. 16603 caluarie] *on an erasure.*

10. l. 16749.   Here begins a different hand.]   But a much younger man's hand, with the common flourishes and abbreviations of the 15th century.   For a better knowledge of the MS. hands I give a sample of these tags and curls, so far as Messrs. Clay have them.[1]

l. 16754 þere] þer'
l. 16757 son] son)
l. 16760 mone] mon)
l. 16766(4) wore] wor'
l. 8 comforthe] comforth
l. 13 vinegre] vinegr' ; *observe* gall
l. 15 with] w' ; tonge] tong'
l. 36 erthe] erth
l. 40 other] othr, cf. l. 124
l. 48 bone] bon
l. 52 noght] noght'
l. 58 mynd] mynd
l. 68 whether] whethr

l. 73 hand] hand
l. 75 fell] fell
l. 78 drynk] drynk'
l. 121 air] aire
l. 16805 fell] fell
l. 16809 send] send
l. 9 askynge] askyng'
l. 37 iesu] ihu
l. 111 clethinge] clething'
l. 127 soft] soft'
l. 172 kirk] kirk'
l. 17316 wrang] wrang'.   *Here ends the collation of the 2nd hand.*

11. l. 17362 þat] þai

l. 18559 þei] þai   l. 18757 you] yow
l. 18997 sertles] sercles

l. 19243 a] *crossed through.*
ll. 19396-402] *much defaced.*

12. The third hand begins in l. 20065.

ll. 20103-4 might, vnright] might', vn-
l. 20111 a] o   [right'
ll. 20113-4 lijf, strijf] lijf', strijf'
l. 20145 her] hir
l. 20159 thing] thing'
l. 20182 tak] tak'
l. 20232 bisek] bisek'

l. 20334 ic] ic'
l. 20335 hat, na-thing] hat', na-thing'
l. 20368 oþair] ai *is an alteration.*
l. 20576 it] *overlined.*
l. 20790 cark] *on an erasure.*
l. 20822 þe] *overlined.*
ll. 21167-8 tent, brent] tent', brent'.

---

[1] I had noted some 372 instances, but the Director objects to the expense of printing them all, as they have no linguistic value.

Here end the few samples of the collation of the 3rd hand. The full collation shows that the flourishes and strokes occur continually, and not only occasionally, as shown in the edition.

13. l. 22366 strength] strengh

l. 22824 wemed] we*m*med
l. 23340 setlid, MS. seclid] *read* sercled, cf. l. 18997.
l. 23778 chrahun crachun] crachun *is the correction of the badly written word* chrahun.

ll. 24305-10 MS. torn here] *Part of it is torn off, but patched up by the bookbinder.*
l. 24854 drerili] drereli
l. 24928 þisw ord] þis word

14. THE COLLATION OF A (cf. § 12 of the former essay).

l. 67 pore] thore
l. 190 pur] par
l. 438 pore] thore

l. 521 þi] þine
l. 704 sere] rere

15. THE COLLATION OF G. The old paging had 349 pages, but on leaf 145 there is a mistake; from p. 289 a jump was made to 300. The first page containing the table of contents is not numbered. The new paging has 169 folio-leaves. Only the first leaf is a little injured.

l. 48 to] *crossed through and rubbed out.*
l. 53 vanyte] van(yte)
l. 55 to] *defaced.*
l. 86 craftti] craftli
l. 89 set] *defaced.*
l. 91 fantom] o *defaced.*
l. 92 i-now] i *defaced.*
l. 103 nedefull] nedeful
l. 119 entent] ente(nt)
l. 149 syðe, cf. sydē in l. 216. *Both of them mean* sythen; *in* syðe, *standing before a vowel the contraction mark for* n *appears to be left out, and in* sydē *the contraction mark for* th *is disregarded. In this way I explain* wid *and* wit, *occasioned by the abbreviation* w*ᵗ, but in pronunciation likewise meaning* with. The interchange of *d* and *t*, however, stands on a different ground.
l. 150 iustifie] -fie, *badly written for* -sce, cf. manasce 3765, *and* sc = ss *passim. Here. of course, a mistake for original* justise.
l. 258 findes] d *defaced.*
l. 265 and after l. 270 prolouge] p(ro)louge
l. 454 anttour] auctour. *The copier's note goes beyond the mark.*
l. 469 mychal] mychael, e *overlined.*
l. 483 coueryng] couerymg

l. 1312 frott] froit
l. 1440 at] þat
l. 1520 sonne] soune
l. 1522 music] musik
l. 1542 micht] mitht
Heading after 1552 how] hou
l. 1669 festind] festnid
l. 1701 mekil] mikil
l. 1724 hend (*or* heud)] heud
l. 2194 regina] regina
l. 2332 of] *overlined.*
l. 2506 graunted] granted
l. 2508 getun] getûn, *mistake for* getin; cf. ll. 2951, 3421, 3901, etc.
l. 2530 miht] mitht
l. 2569 sal] Sal
l. 2725 efsoins] efsonis = eftsonis, cf. l. 4241.
l. 3386 multeplied] multiplied
l. 3693 leue] *crossed through.*
l. 3915 an] au, *the contraction mark left out,* = aû = aun
l. 4127 saide] *om.*
l. 4482 l(i)uerid] liuerd, cf. ll. 5289, 6176.
l. 4508 eyen = eye n' = eye ne
l. 5114 sal *wanting*] *not om.*
l. 5355 my broder, MS. his] his broð. *Here Wattenbach's observation, that in the* 15*th century* ð *occurs for* de, *may be applied, for* broð *is* = brode (cf. l.

5334 *and* l. 5355 F). *Otherwise, the
contraction mark taken for* ꝺ = th
would be a mistake; cf. T's my broþer.

l. 5329 Fitou] Fiton

l. 5741 nerere] ner'e. *The contraction
mark is wrong, it must be* nēre =
nerre

l. 6098 now] nou

l. 6156 or (ox)] ox

l. 6220 couipil] coiupel

l. 6697 Nedis] N *really looks somewhat
like* M; *therefore, perhaps,* M *in* T.

l. 6965 þai] þaii

l. 7173 oþ(*er*)] oþ(er)

l. 7201 wakind] waknid

l. 7278 wengaunce] wenga(*u*)nce

l. 7281 oft] ofte

l. 7489 wrecched] *doubtful on account of*
cc.

l. 7620 saul] saul(*e*)

l. 7737 saule] saul(e)

l. 7751 sarazins] saraȝines

l. 7792 gunen] guuen

l. 7917 men] *mistake for* inne

l. 8103 us] *overlined.*

l. 8143 unhele] un *overlined.*

l. 8202 processioune] proscessioune; cf.
l. 150.

l. 8407 payre] y *overlined.*

l. 8417 i] *overlined.*

l. 8565 þe] e

l. 8569 be] (b)e

l. 8861 made] *the 3rd stroke of* m *is overlined.*

l. 9214 withest] withtest, t *overlined.*

l. 9233 heard] herd

l. 9250 propantera] .p.pantera = par-
pantera

l. 9280 sua] *repeated from the preceding
line.*

l. 9459 wrecchedly] wrechedly

l. 9485 quihy] h *altered into* li, *but* y *left
standing.*

l. 9506 synays] syttays

l. 10023 so] s *overlined.*

l. 10139 unwon] sone (*from the following
line*).

l. 10242 To make] Go make

l. 10385 þe] þa

l. 10599 frendes] freindes

l. 10610 ilkand] ilkane

l. 10887 wrecchedness] *the second* c *is
again very like* t. (According to the old
paging, p. 146 is = leaf 74*a*, but the
two columns of lf. 74*b* bear the num-

bers 147 and 148, and lf. 75*a* 149 and
150. At foot there is, in a later hand,
an illegible remark beginning: 'this
leaf . . . .')

l. 10980 tale] ta(le)

l. 11021 not] noght

l. 11050 þe] *overlined.*

l. 11055 ȝing] zing

l. 11160 madd] medd

l. 11202 *after* him] mari *overlined.*

l. 11203 gan] gane

l. 11291 on] of *overlined.*

l. 11303 sua] su(a)

l. 11335 skete. MS. *looks like* strete]
skete *quite distinct.*

l. 11358 lauedi] leuedi

l. 11366 þe] *overlined.*

l. 11395 occeane] *the second* c *looks very
much like* t; cf. ll. 7489, 10887.

l. 11407 dozeine] doreine

l. 11416 till] till(e)

l. 11443 tune] time, *mistake for* tune.

l. 11526 als] ales. Qu. alse?

l. 11541 by] bi

l. 11555 Quan herde] Qua herde. *The
contraction stroke belongs to* h; cf. l.
12130.

l. 11946 tinsel] There was originally
another first syllable between *t* and
the supposed *i*, which is not distinct,
and was originally *e*. Some other hand
has overlined a letter which I cannot
read. The word which was wanted
seems originally to have been *ter-
lincel;* cf. *Handlyng Synne,* ed. Furnivall, l. 4266. Look for it in the
Glossary.

l. 12032 rase] rese

l. 12093 leuer] *originally* lauer, *but* a
dotted out, and e *overlined.*

l. 12102 iuen] men, *of course* = iuen.
Leaf 82*a has at foot several names
which are illegible.*

l. 12148 kene] keue, *mistake for* kneue;
cf. l. 11036.

l. 12201 i au] i *defaced, stands on an
erasure, so that the letters may originally have been* tau.

l. 12213 was] (wa)s

l. 12402 oft] ofte

l. 12472 ȝing] ȝung

l. 12527 sprent] *read* c, *which often looks
like* t.

l. 12531 blonand] blouand. The wrong
capitals in the middle of the line are

disregarded in the text; f. i. Helde 12569, etc. If I remember rightly, they are disregarded from l. 10962.

l. 12595 ȝede] *originally* ȝode, *but* o *crossed out, and* e *overlined.*

l. 12648 thritt(i)] thritt(ene), ene *rubbed out;* cf. l. 12829.

l. 12716 spede] sprede

l. 12719 Saint] saint

l. 12828 ner] neȝ *on an erasure, and originally* nere.

l. 13176 commandement] commandenēt

l. 13177 hefedd] hefdd

l. 13260 lou(li)] loi, *the rest defaced.*

l. 13261 war seke] r se *almost erased.*

l. 13321 schipe] schepe, *but* e *not distinct.*

l. 13837 syden] syde, cf. l. 149.

l. 13990 symond] symoᵭ = symo(n)de

l. 14217 i efter] i e *defaced.*

l. 14439 rightwis] rightwais, a *dotted out.*

l. 14465 maidene] maide; cf. l. 149. *There is, no doubt, some confusion in the usage of* ᵭ. Cf. E's archidenis *and* C F G's athes, l. 19395.

l. 14539 Iuus] juus

l. 14670 mistrijf] in strijf

l. 14712 (w)id] wid, w *added.*

l. 14762 Quen] (Q)uen

l. 14783 to man es hete] to manes hete

l. 15137 (A)ll þis world] (A)lle þis werld

l. 15279 walawa] walava. (On leaf 103a there are several biblical remarks in a later hand, which appears to have overlined all the letters and words above mentioned.)

l. 15416 chiþing] chiping, *I think.* (On leaf 106b there is a remark in some other hand quite illegible.)

l. 16182 qwake] (q)wake, q *overlined in the later hand.*

l. 16321 goddes (sun)] goddes sun

l. 16391 barabaras] baraban

l. 16492 he] ha

l. 16660 time] e *overlined.* (All the initials marked in brackets are, for the most part, roughly outlined in black.)

l. 16848 ane] nane, n *overlined.*

l. 16912 þai] þaa

l. 16948 na] ne

l. 17363 look] lock

l. 18369 (A) bacut] bacuc

l. 18371 pepule] ppl'e

l. 18530 keneli] *first* e *overlined.*

l. 18658 all i(n)] all in, *the stroke of* l *going over* i, *and thus joining the contraction mark.*

l. 18693-4 originally in the sequence given by the text, but altered by the scribe, so that = C.

l. 18790 of] *overlined.*

l. 18791 hi(m)] hī, *the contraction mark almost rubbed out.*

l. 19185 (T)ald] *an indistinct* C *is drawn in black for the rubricator.*

l. 19270 þe wich] þe wick

l. 19429 first] firste

l. 20715 were] þar

l. 20847 þar] par

l. 21249 gern] *originally* geen, *but the second* e *dotted out and* r *overlined.*

l. 21822 mon] mou

l. 22029 brim] brime

l. 22530 dome MS. domo] dome

l. 22879 leaf] leif

l. 23002 carked, *it looks like* carijed *in* MS.] carijd

l. 23225 þine] pine

l. 23338 aues] anes

l. 23473 terme] term

l. 23598 mistime MS. mistriue] mistime; *quite distinct.*

l. 24039 blublid] bublid, *read* dublid. Leaf 159 is torn in two; after it one leaf was lost, before (?) the MS. was bound, for the next leaf is marked 160. Cf. p. 26. Lines 24050—24201 are wanting.

l. 24237 s.] o, *but crossed out.*

l. 24461 apone] apon

l. 24485 (w)id] uid

l. 24623 þai] þaa

l. 24921 þroper] proper.

16. l. 25766, *þan of a hundreth lele of dede* are the catchwords for lf. 169b. It is evident that the MS. originally contained more than 170 leaves. Supposing that one quire was lost, the MS. may have run as far as l. 28067 C, and contained 'The Seven Deadly Sins,' as F originally did. From leaf 99 ff. there are no more coloured capitals. They are marked by small black letters, but appear to have afterwards been disregarded by the scribe, who apparently did duty for the rubricator. In the Edition, therefore, these capitals are put in brackets.

17. I will add some remarks on C. On leaf 56 at foot there are two lines turned upside down : 'William Cosyn (repeated) owse þis boke, whoso-euer find . .'

I have taken much pains to make out who this William Cosyn could have been, and my researches will, I hope, be interesting to the reader.

The name occurs a good many times in the old records. Compare *Rotuli Hundred, Temp. Henr. III. et Edw. I.*, etc., vol. i. 1812, under Lincolnshire. ' Extract*us* Inquisic*i*onum factar*um* p*er* precept*um* d*omi*ni Regis in comitati*bus* Lincol*n*iae etc. anno regni Regis E(dwardi) fil*ii* Regis H(enrici) quarto. Wapentak*e* De Asewardbirne (in Kesteven). Membr. 8, p. 387, col. 1. D*i*c*unt* quod Wille*lmus* Cosyn tenuit in Querington (now Quarrington, about three miles, I think, from Sleaford, in Lincolnshire) duas bove*s* terre et dimi*diam* que consueve*r*unt esse geldabile*s* et dare aux*i*lia vica*r*ia et murdr*um* et alia tallagia et modo subtrahunt*ur* per Templar*ios* qui ip*s*a sibi appropriave*r*int.' Page 391, col. 2, 'Membr. 9 d. Wapentake de Langhou (now Langoe, in parts of Kesteven) It*em* qui h*a*bu*er*unt felones inprisonatos, etc. D*i*c*unt* quod Walter*ius* Schelfhanger vic' Linc' & Ra*d*'s de Morwod ceperu*n*t de Will' Cosyn de Marton (in Lincolnshire) XX sol*i*dos ut dimitte*r*ent ip*s*um p*er* pleviñam cum fuit replegiabilis anno regni Regis nu*n*c secu*n*do.'

Hustings Rolls in the Guildhall Library, XX. Edw. I. 'Dictis die et anno venerunt Robertus de Bolesle, Robert de Basing executores testamenti Petri Cosyn civis Londoniensis et fecerunt probare testamentum dicti Petri per Rob. etc. Item lego Ioceo filio meo totam illam domum cum pe:tinenciis quam habeo apud Sanctum Bothulphum (Boston in Linc.) in perpetuum ' (abbr. expanded).

Cal. Inquis. post Mort. et ad quod damn., vol. i. 1806, Anno 32 Edw. I., No. 192. 'Will' Cosyn de London et Emma uxor eius [et Will*us* filius eorundem] Sutton Magna manerium in hundredo de Rocheford cum advo-catione ecclesiæ etc. in Essex.' It runs thus : ' Edwardus . . Vic' Essex Salutem Precepimus tibi quod per sacramentum proborum et legalium homi-num in comitatu tuo, per quos veritas melius sciri potuerit, diligenter inquiras si sit dampnum vel prejudicium nostrum aut aliorum si concedamus Willelmo Cosyn de London et Emme uxori eius et Willelmo filio eorundem Willelmi et Emme quod ipsi manerium de Magna Suttone in hundredo de Rocheford,' etc.

Hustings Rolls, 19 *Edw. III.* (17 Decbr., 1340), No. 72, m. 8 d. 'Dictis die et anno venerunt Petrus Cosyn et Thomas Cosyn filii Willelmi Cosyn de Sutton et probare fecerunt testamentum ipsius Willelmi,' etc.

These inquiries were guided by several conjectures. Nobody could take more interest in a work like the *Cursor Mundi* than a family which belonged to the same county as the author of that poem, whose great authorities of the day had been Robert Grosseteste of Lincoln, and Edmund Rich of Canterbury. Now the dialect of the MS. is not uniform. The dialect of the author seemed to me from the first to point to Lincolnshire. So I could not but rejoice at finding the possessor of the MS. to have been a man whose family—widespread as it is, no doubt—had its origin in Lincolnshire, where the Cosyns are mentioned as early as the last quarter of the 13th century, in well-to-do circumstances.

These suppositions found some support in the Göttingen MS., in which the name of John of Lindberg is mentioned. This name appears to point to Lincolnshire as well, and the reader will afterwards hear what I think of him.

Accordingly, I took down the following pedigree of the Cosyns, whom I believed to be nearly connected. William, mentioned in 1276; his brother Peter, who turned a rich wool-merchant (cf. *Hundred Rolls, Civitas Lond.*, p. 420) in London, died in 1292. Peter's son William, mentioned in 1304 as the husband of a rich heiress, Emma of Sutton, died in 1340. His sons Peter and Thomas lived probably between 1320 and 1370. Peter's son, I suppose, is again called after his grandfather William. It is he who, in my opinion, may have been the possessor of the MS. How his time agrees with the age of the MS. will be seen hereafter.

CHAPTER III.—THE SCRIBES AND THE AGES OF THE MSS.

18. The Cotton MS. is in three handwritings. The second begins on lf. 92, and runs to lf. 93 b, col. 1, l. 8. It begins again on lf. 95 b, col. 2, l. 19, after the rest of the column had been erased. The next three leaves, which contain the insertion, are stitched separately, for they do not belong to the other quires. But on lf. 98 b, col. 2, l. 18, the narrative is continued in the same second hand, and what had been erased on lf. 95 b seems to have been repeated here. The third hand begins on a new quire of 12 leaves, lf. 113, and ends on 119 a, col. 1.

19. It is evident that the three hands belong to the same time. But their handwritings are quite different in style : the first hand belongs to the 14th century, the two others to the 15th century. This difference may easily be accounted for, if we admit that the first hand was written by an old man, who was very careful in transcribing an older copy to the letter, and only sometimes betrayed his old age, and the dialect which he then spoke.

20. The dialect of the scribes, therefore, is much later than that of the MS. from which they copied. But there is some difference as to those parts which do not agree with the *Cursor*, and are taken from other sources. These insertions show a language which is nearer to the age of the scribes. As there is good reason to believe that the common source z was copied in a Northern dialect of the first half of the 14th century, I will give those forms which appear either to be later than the period last named, or not to belong to the Northern dialect.

21. Peculiarities of the first hand :

NORTHERN *A* (SHORT OR LONG) = o, *as*, on (= and) 2802, sol (2 *sg. prs.* = sal) 2657, os (= as) 7526, con (= gan) 1742, non 10, ilkon 25, fro 36, on 187, or 121, gost 308, cloth, both 3695-6, coth 4932, 8951 (cuth 6315), holi 4013, old, told 10587-8, ouen (= awen) 389, maiden, sten (= stan) 3835-6.

NORTHERN *E* BEFORE *R* = *A*, *as*, smart 58, warld 91, hard 551, warryd 1227, answard 1304, gart 1334, sargant 3312, barn 11476, parel 24852, warmstore[1] 4688. *But observe even* durken 24414, feurth (4°) 21590, þorth (= þe erþ), fra no (= nu) forth 3757-8.

NORTHERN *I*, *E*, *Y* (SHORT OR LONG) CONFOUNDED, *as*, hinges 3067, hint (*prt.*) 5055, kiest 5442, kyest 8119, visete 5789, scenshep 18172, frenshep 23637, wirscep 7022, felaghscep 7682, heid (= hid) 11498, merkind (= merknid, 3 *sg. prt.*) 1764, merck (*adj.*) 15726, mercknes 15680, to brin (*trs.*) 1098, hild (*prt.*) 2295, weird (= wird) 3475, friend 14119, priste (*sb.*) 6947, dipe 11603, to wide (= to wede) 13975, isked (= esked, = asked) 11848, wynsþou (= wenestou) 22550, puple (= peple) 7323, puchersum (= wuc her sum, wuc = wicc (= wick, = wicked), p *being mistaken for* þ) 2182, bittur, wittur 697-8, bibul 1900.

O.E. *ēōw* = NORTHERN *ū* = *AU Vōw*, *as*, i trau 3727, traus þou 13671. M.E. *E₃* = EE, *as*, deed 14234, ee cf. mens en 525, etc.

PERSONAL PRONOUNS, *as*, 3 *sg. fem. acc.* brokar = broke har (har Vhere (hiere) = hire) 2427, hur 1898 ; 3 *pl.* him 16449, hem 1703, 6197, ham 4519,

---

[1] Cf. *wermestore* 1698 ; *warnistore* in the text = *warmstore*, and was mistaken by the scribe for O.F. *warnesture*. The Fairfax MS. has the correct *warnestoure*.

4939, of hem 308, mettam 752, settam 4175 (= met tam, set tam, *rather than* meten ham, setten ham).

REFLEXIVE PRONOUNS, *as*, hamself 801.

CONJUNCTIONS, *as*, þof (*used throughout*).

VERBS, *as*, waass (= *to wash*) 1594, was (3 *sg. prt.*) 8149, wassed (*pp.*) 13551.—fan (*prt. for* fined, cf. 14165) = blan 3309.—did turne (= *turned*) 1864, did tan (= tok) 20211.

22. Some peculiarities of the second hand.   (I. II. III. denote its different sections, where the words referred to will be found.

NORTHERN *A* (SHORT OR LONG) = 1) o, *as*, os I. 2, II. 61, oos III. 110, con (= gan) III. 330, non), apon) II. 62-4, or II. 20, quod III. 373, quod III. 345, wore I. 26, byfore, lore II. 22-4, þore II. 60; 2) E : þere, ere II. 69-72.

NORTHERN *E* BEFORE *R* = *A*, *as*, gart II. 33, III. 12, narre III. 387, farrer III. 396, hard I. 140, *beside* herd I. 120.   *Observe* constroyned III. 391, merke (= mirk) I. 23, 26.

O.E. *êôw* = NORTHERN *û* = *AU*, *as*, we knaw, to traw III. 372-4, trawed III. 198.

PERSONAL PRONOUNS, *as*, 3 *sg. fem. nom.* ho III. 178; 3 *pl. acc.* hom I. 37, II. 20; 3 *pl. dat.* hom III. 286.

POSSESSIVE PRONOUNS, *as*, is (= his) I. 111, II. 31.

CONJUNCTIONS, *as*, auther III. 232, nauther III. 449; þaf I. 32, þof I. 4.

VERBS, *as*, clerkez witen I. 109, han. (*pl.*) III. 376, calden (*pl. prt.*) II. 23, seghen (*pl. prt.*) I. 41, risen (*pl. prt.*) I. 84, broken (*pl. prt.*) II. 19; *besides* brake þai II. 21, schold (*pl.*) III. 53, sold (= suld *pl.*) III. 166, dorst (3 *sg.*) III. 189, geue (*pp.*) I. 118, þai bihild III. 128.   *Moreover, I may mention:* dee (= to die) I. 119, deed (*prt.*) I. 121; eghen, geen (*pp.* giuen) I. 75-77, geen (*pp.*) II. 14, egen II. 31, deed (*prt.*) III. 25; byfore, thore III. 157-9, were, ȝere III. 27-8.

23. Some peculiarities of the third hand :

NORTHERN *E + R* = *A + R*, *as*, oþair[1] 20368; *I + R* = *E + R*, *as*, ferst 20383.—na = nu = *now* 20880.—suffurd 20973.—þou = *though* 21026, 20082.—noþer 21044.—*Observe* num (*pp.*), cum (*inf.*) 20685-6.

24. When we consider that a good many of the dialectal specimens above-

---

[1] Cf. the Cambridge Manuscript of 'The Bruce,' *stoutar, blithar*, and *warraying* V. 140, *warray* V. 269, and 'The Townely Mysteries,' p. 52, *marke, warke, dark, clark*, etc.   These are phonetic features of the 15th century.

mentioned occur in every Northern writer of the late 14th and the 15th centuries (cf. *The Bruce*, *The Townely Mysteries*, *Thomas of Erceldoune*), and recollect those forms which are usually taken for Midland ones, we have to look for a county in which the dialect of those portions which do not belong to the *Cursor* can be found in close conformity with that of the scribe. There is no county that suits our purpose better than North Lancashire. Considering the verb *dee*, *deed*, and the ryme *eghen*, *geen*, we may fairly believe that those forms of a more Northern pronunciation were established there in the 15th century.

25. A comparison with the MSS. of *Sir Gawayne and the Green Knight*, *Early English Alliterative Poems*, and *De Erkenwalde* (cf. also *Knigge, Die Sprache des Dichters von Sir Gawayn*, etc., Marburg 1885, and F. Schwahn, *Die Conjugation in Sir Gawayn*, etc., Strassburg ¹/E. 1884), furnishes us with rich materials for our purpose.

NORTHERN *A* = o, *as*, con A 826, A 381, quoth, quod Gaw. 343, etc. ; coþe Gaw. 776, gon, ston, non, upon, Ion A 818 ff., lore, þore G 667, schore, wore A 232, *besides* þare, ware ; owen G 408, *besides* auen G 293, etc.   Dr. Knigge gives average numbers as to the occurrence of *a* and *o*.

NORTHERN *E* BEFORE *R* = *A*, *as*, wary B 51, 1716, smartly G 407, marre G 2262, charre G 1143, gart (*prt.*) A 1150, etc.

NORTHERN *I*, *E*, *Y* CONFOUNDED, *as*, burn, bourne A 711, rurd G 1149, brurd B 1474, urþe A 442 (erþe G, D), gurdel G 2395, gorde G 2035 (girdel G 1829), dunt 452, B 1196, spure B 1606, burde G 2278, murthe D 335, mury G 2295, merke B 1607, worm C 467, busy G 1066, munte G 2262, buried D 94.   *Observe* peple G 123, pepul D 109.

O.E. *êow* = NORTHERN *ú* = *ǎu*, *as*, trawe G 70, 1396, etc. ; trauþe B 1490, *besides* trow G 373, etc.   D (Hm) does not know *ǎu*.

PERSONAL PRONOUNS, *as*, ho (*fem. sg.*) ; her, hor ; hem, ham.   *Mind* vus¹ = vs (so often met with, besides *vure* in the *Cursor*) vs *only* G 2246.

CONJUNCTIONS, *as*, nauþer C 392, þof G 624, D 320.   The common form is þaȝ ; þoȝ only G 69, A 344 ; bot (as the rule in the *Cursor*) A 18, etc. ; bout (*prp.*) G 361, 1285, C 523.

VERBS, *as*, durst G 1493, etc ; dorste A 143, 182 ; ded (*prt.* = dide) C 443 ; withhylde (*prt.*) G 2168.   There is no doubt that these poems have a good many features in common with C.   But the fact is, that some phenomena

---

¹ The MS. has, I suppose, '*vus*,' as in the *Cursor* (cf. p. 985 ff.), so that '*vs*' should be read.

which appear here as the rule, are rather an exception in C, as Northern $\check{u}$ = $\check{u}u$, and *vice versâ*, as þof; others are wanting in the poems, as *dee, eghen*, etc. Especially note the common form þaȝ, which is more Southern, as opposed to þof, or Northern þogh. As most of the instances show the common type of a Western dialect, I may make bold to say, that while C shows a more Northern type—since it may have been spoken near the Northern boundaries of modern Lancashire—the Alliterative Poems are written by scribes of the 15th century living in the Southern part, *i. e.* in the South-West of the ancient archdiocese of York. The consequence is, that the originals were written this side the Dee.

26. The comparison makes it probable that the Cotton MS. was in the hands of scribes who lived in the same district. The dialect of the second and third hands is much later than that of the first, and shows, when compared with the E. E. A. Poems, such forms (*dee, deed, eghen, geen*) as are found in a more Northern source. The first hand, though not destitute of forms like *dee, ee*, copies to the letter, and retains the phonology which is older than that of the source of the second and third hands. For the source from which C copied, must have had such forms as *puc her sum* 2182, or *parn* 24591, both of which C mistook for *puc* and þarn. A comparison with E G gives us some evidence of the same confusion of *i, e, y, u*. So we may believe that some of those peculiarities which are commonly thought to belong more to the South-Western dialects were already in the common source **z**, which derived them from a MS. copied by a Northern West-Midland scribe.

27. THE MS. E. As I have had no opportunity of seeing the MS., I can only take evidence from the text. The late Mr. John Small, in his well-known edition, *English Metrical Homilies*, from MSS. of the 14th century, Edinb. 1862, stated that our *Cursor* MS. was written in the first quarter of the 14th century. There is good reason to believe that this statement, made a quarter of a century ago, is altogether wrong. Moreover, I doubt whether the copy was done on the same rules respecting the extension of the abbreviations as that of C or G; only compare the þate and *ande* so frequently met with.

28. I will give some observations on the third and first hands of MS. E:

þate 19077 *passim*, ande 19205 *passim*, undorn 19830, cod þai 19906, stroid 20246, destroi 22348, sale 22354 *passim*; yong, vprising 22817-8, hondis 22862, royd (cf. roid G) 23911, cod þu 23527, isse 21648, apon 21679, forte (*mistake for* fotte) 21768, op 22548, torn 22538, bot 22770, froit 22880.

29. Differences as to their spellings :

The third hand prefers *sale*, the first always has *sal*. The third has ȝt, *cht*, ȝ, *ch*, the first *ht*, *h ;* the third *gi* (for the voiced friction consonant), the first *y*, very seldom *gi* (f. i. *giern* 2172), *g* in *gern* 22535 *passim*. It is remarkable that the first hand makes the mistake in *you* 22971 (= give).

30. Peculiarities which do *not properly* belong to the Northumbrian or Scotch dialect of the 14th century :

NORTHERN *A* : O—cod 19906 ; A : E—þere / 21104 ; ern : orn—vndorne 19830, I : E *and* E : I—medelerd 22703, lesten 22601, fordreuin, reuin 22635-6, leuin 23940, wet (*vb.*) 22556 ; fild (= *field*) 23852, þrist, brist 22683-4, hint (*prt.*) 19247 ; E : A—arly 19041, *perhaps* marbir 21018, quarner 19155, 21663 (cf. quert, O.F. quart) ; êȝ, êh (EE) : êȝ, EI and îȝ—heier 22287, dryen (*inf.* for *pp.*) 23497 (cf. dreied C, drem G, drowen F) ; UI : OI—destroi 22348, stroid 22247 ; I : U—dunt (cf. dump C, dompit F, bete G) 22643 ; OU : AU—faurtend 22689. D : T—forbot 19328, tendant 19034, liuelate 19835 ; QU : O —cod 19906, 23527 (*but* cf. chone = quone 19782) ; þ : T—tai 19372, 22649, ta 23254, taine 19386, taim 22659, tu 19883 etc., strenket (*sb.*) 23374 ; NG : N —scendin 21005, strenþe 19002 ; T : D—forgied 23177. Remarkable is the mistake *muþis* (= mupis, 3 *sg. prs.*, cf. mous G) 24559. CH, K : UW—lauwe 19998 (cf. lach 21985, lake 19948). Observe some other peculiarities also to be met with in Scotch : W : V—verd 22742, verk 22541 ; GN : GI, NGN—sigine 19282, singnis 19286.

PLURALS IN *N* : erin 19452, eien 19437.

ADVERBS : nauþer-quar 22445 ; on ferrum 18998 (C G), nawiþ 19386.

CONJUNCTIONS : thurȝ 22296, þoȝ 20031, þou 22921, nauþir 23134, auþir 23187, ne 23152.

PRONOUNS : 3 *plur.* hem 22498 ; is (= his) 22732.

VERBS : nis (= ne + is) 24137, 19675, 23635, bes (3 *sg.*) 20056 *passim ;* beþe (3 *sg.*) 23590, bes (*imp. pl.*) 19108 ; arne (*plur.*) 22414, wern 20115, 20138 ; havis 19008 *passim*. tai sul her 22819, þai miȝtin (?) 20116 ; nil we, wil we 23728 (cf. C F G), cun (*sg.* = can, con) 23814 (cf. C G).

INFINITIVES : to letin 19026, turnin 19490, luuen 20077, liuen 20089, 24576, *and* leuen 23940, bitechen 20098, kepin 20099, seruin 20112, 24240, 24965, lastin 21004, deluin 21062, clepin 21994, chesin 22092, hidin 22196, scawin 22272, schawen 24261 (cf. 19194), raisin 22283, scortin 22305, strenþin 22366, fostrin 22102, bene 20914, 22886, don 21004, lesten 22601, mistrun 22796, newin 22924, dredin 23027, rinen 23729, lerin 23864, rewen 24054, þinkin 24055, deien 24139, lengin 24241, techen 24306, wirkin 24724, paien 22776, risin 22931, mensken 23581, witen 23635.

PRESENT 3RD P. PLUR.—flotin 24833, wetin 23685, seruin (?) 21905.

PRETERITES PLURAL IN *EN*: herdin 19539, saldin 19038, wroȝtin 23184. *Besides mind* teld (*prt.*) 24956 (cf. teld C G 7554, teld (*pp.*) C G 7062 (telled F); þei bere 22004 ; scawid (*sg.*) 19145, (*pl.*) 1977. *There are a good many preterites in* it, f. i. wonderit 19082, mengit 19710, gaderit 19136 etc., *besides such in* id : *as*—spellid 19214, finid 19423, foluwid 19483, clepid 19512, forhowid 22772, gernid 23543, graiþid 26584 etc., *and in* ed *passim*.

PAST PARTICIPLES OF WEAK VERBS IN it, id, ed ; STRONG IN in, en, n. *Observe* brote 22263.

IMPERATIVE *laid stress upon by* do : do fles 23159 (cf. dos fles C, do fleis F G).

31. I will add some forms properly Northumbrian : Ic es 20018 *and* ine es 20019, *not in* C F G ; I . . . leies 23807, *also in* F G, *not in* C ; I biguþe 24579. These forms, as well as the Scotch spelling of gutturals, prove that the Edinburgh MS. is a Northumbrian (or Scotch) copy.

32. On the other hand, there is no doubt that E copied from a Midland MS., which is not identical with the immediate source of C. The Midland copy appears to have been written in the West as well as C. First, it is not necessary to claim the preterites and participles in *it*, which so often occur in F, and also in C, for Northumberland or Scotland alone. Secondly, the hissing of voiced restriction consonants, the preference sometimes given to lip-teeth or lip-open consonants before lip-back consonants, or to back- before front-consonants, instances of which are found especially in C, are not phonetic features confined to Scotland, but are common in all mountainous districts, and occur especially in the border counties of the Gaelic tongue. They must consequently appear in the West also. But thirdly, *cod, on ferrum, nauþer nawiþ* (cf. G, th = ght), *dunt* (for *dint*) evidently point to the West. All the other peculiarities above-mentioned suit the East-Midland dialect as well.

33. As to the age of MS. E, the handwriting (cf. þate, ande, etc.) shows that it was written late in the 14th century, or early in the 15th. But there are other reasons. In l. 20061 the original is altered into ' *in opir inglis was it drawn.*' I think that this wording is owing to the Scotch scribe, who betrays in it his natural pride of independence. There is, of course, a vast field for supposition as to when this feeling first showed itself concerning language. The first step to her political independence Scotland took in 1314 (at Bannockburn), but the English supremacy was not given up even in 1329, when Edward III. sought to make peace; and down to 1370 England had her hand in Scottish affairs.   It was not till Robert the Second's accession to the throne, when the Scottish Estates declared against that agreement of succession which Edward III. had made with King David in 1357, that Scotland's relations to England were loosened.   After 1370, therefore, I think that MS. E may have been written.

34. THE GÖTTINGEN MS.   As to its style, I first note that the runic letters p and þ never occur either in G or in C.   The former is rendered by *w*, the latter by *y*, and often by *th*.   Now some Manuscript experts rightly believe that the runic letters were abandoned sooner in the North than in the Midlands and the South, but G shows the same phonetic peculiarities as C, and these point to a much later time, unless we suppose that G was not written at all in the North.

35. *The dialect of G, as opposed to the Northumbrian dialect of the 14th century.*

NORTHERN *A* : *o*—so 9, non 10, ilkon 25, quore 1125, also, slo 1967-8, mohw 2807, grone, one 3731-2, wone, allone 4353-4, done, alon 5285-6, sore, þore 5655-6, to (= *two*) 10345, fro, so 11153-4, strong 5, wold 1105, hold 1198, sond, lond 5855-6 ; : E—quer, her 7209-10, sle 7682.

NORTHERN *E* : *A*—unquart, hart 5721-2, parsonis 6341, barn 11476, garn, larn 19027-8, gart 17100, harke, farli 20387 ; E : o—obber 13041, world 1411 ; E : AY—wraystes 3461 ; I : E—berde, werde 9967-8, wreche (f. wrethe) 3462 ; I : U—durken 24414, bur 24816 ; A : U Vō—us 325 ; U : o—bot 33, hosband 4385, þos 499 ; ô : o—bock 627 ; û : AU—mistrau 3651 ; : oI—roid 23911 ; AW : ow—knou 5857 ; êȝ : I—flie 5959, flijs 5990, dyed 6004, hij 10596. D : þ—wonþer 441, vnþer 1348 ; D : T—formelt, delt (cf. C) 12331-2 ; þ : D— wid 512, erde 1129, diþer 746, dus 886, doqueþer 911, dat 5079, dider 5181, neyder 5857 ; þ : T—trau 22431 ; GH : GHW—doghuti 2112, brohut 2212, dohutyrs 2323, mohw 2807 ; nohut 3538, enohw 4467, enohut 4799 ; vn-lauthir[1] 3283, thout 1344, 1347 ; ȝ (GH) : ȝ, Y—sith, nith[1] 2711-2, nehy (*vb.*) 2422 ; GH : PH—thurgh r. w. skurf (*written* skurth, cf. skurf, thurgh C) 11824 ; KHW : PHKH[2]—fede (f. quede, cf. C 7935 etc.) 12948, fone (f. quone, cf. 15822, 17285 C) 15822, 22740 etc. ; D—GH : T—PH—tifted (*prt.* f. dighte, cf. C *ibid.*, *and* dighted 24828) 19425, tift (*pp.*, cf. tift : gift C *ibid.*, and gift, right G 25647-8) 24807 ; V : W—wessel 6145, wengans 5927.

---

[1] This spelling reminds me of the scribe of *Havelok the Dane*.   [2] Cf. þowf in C 698.

SUBSTANTIVES.   *Plurals:* erin 19452.

ADVERBS : oftin 3520, ʒeis 1249, ʒis 4341, 5859, ʒes 5208.

NUMERALS.   G *avoids* tvinne 3643, *and alters into the bad ryme* : tua, da.

CONJUNCTIONS : þou *used throughout.*

VERBS: wenest þu 7557, cumþs þu 7563, sekist þu 7740, hath 1166 ; sul we 2252, did ken (*compd. pret.*) 2694, made Adam to do 842, þai did him to call 3492, teld (*prt.*) 1296-7, broiden (*pp.*, O.E. brǽdan = *dilatare*, cf. C T) 1008, sy (*prt.*) 5053, sy (*inf.*) 10595 ; G *avoids* blan *as well as* maydan *in* blinne, maydene 3319-10 ; ges (3 *sg. prs.*, ges F 541, ges C 16476, gis C 541) 539.

36. These peculiarities give such a confused mass of details that it is reasonable to take first some examples which G has in common with the scribe of C, cf. a : o, e + r : a + r, i(y) : u, u : o, û : au, *fede, fone, tift, ʒeis, ʒis, ges, did ken, teld, broiden.* These characteristics appear to point to a common source, but the question is, to which of the sources. There is reason to believe that, since these forms do not always occur in the same place, as in C, some of them belong to the direct source of G and F, which must also be sought for towards the West. There are other points which appear to prove that the scribe did not live in the North ; cf. *done, alon, aw : ow, êʒ : î(ʒ), sy* (inf.) *dider, dat, wonþer, brohut, mohw, vnlauthir, sith, wenest þu, haþ, sy* (prt.). Nobody can require me to give certain results here, though I may venture on a supposition. From the fact that G wants several peculiarities which C has, and shows only a few instances properly West-Midland, which C has not, I conclude that the common source of F G (**ɣ**) must have been written a little more towards the East than C. I think it was written in the East of the ancient diocese of Lichfield and Coventry, and that G's direct source (δ), from which T also originated, was copied in the South of that diocese, near the bishopric of Worcester. I may go on to suggest that G itself was transcribed early in the 15th century, in the North-West of the ancient diocese of Lincolnshire.

37. THE FAIRFAX MS.   The peculiarities of the dialect are :

NORTHERN *A* : *o*—con (= can) 86, con (= gan) 5711, go, to 6758-9, so, to 8329-30, : E—þen 4952 ; E : o—ofter (= after) 2004, holpes (*imp.*) 72, vndorun 985, þou chose (*imp.*) 2460 ; E : A—barne, warne 11957-8 ; I(E) : E— worshepe 111, 2439, 3236, 4628, 5980 etc., lordeshepe 24267 ; ei(ê) + LD : I + LD—ʒilde 110 ; U : I—mirþer (*vb.*) 4130 ; ŏw : ăw—I traw 371, tawarde 2474, mistraw 3651, trauþ 3401, flagh (*prt. pl.*) 7592 ; D : T—pynet (*pp.*)

198, endet (*prt. pl.*) 208, blesset (*adj.*) 210; в : p—pot 12294, wardedrope 1686; к : сн—myche (= mikel) 1198; sw : squ—squeven 4455; -rgh : -row —arþorow 9, þorow 57.

SUBSTANTIVES : werkus (*pl.*) 21982.

ADVERBS : ȝus 5859.

CONJUNCTIONS : nauþer 1660.

PRONOUNS : ho (*fem. sg.*) 85, ham (*pl.*) 54 ; suche 66, siche 3219, eueriche 301, iche 35.

VERBS : quoth þai 9321 ; þai þinkyn 727, þai knawen 12373, þai louin 23517, did turne (*compd. pret.*) 1864, dide . . wedde 7249, golias did . . . behalde 7553, made the sunne stille to stande 6955, he did to calle 2995, he seey 3180; nart (= ne art) 656, þou art 21526; telled (*teld* is avoided, wherever it occurs in the other MSS., cf. 7553 etc.) 7062 ; if he sle 6717.

38. There are differences enough from C and G to make us believe that F did not belong to the same district as C or G. F generally avoids $a + r = $ O.E. $eo + r,$ $u = $ O.E. *y, e, i* except in *such, ȝus,* imported from the South, *cod, teld,* þof (C), etc., but it shows some evidence that its scribe copied from a late 14th century MS. written more towards the South, where I supposed the common source of F G was. In other respects the MS. affords a comparison of the 14th century language of the 'northrin lede' with that of the 15th century (cf. *con, go, to; mon, mony;* pp. and prts. in t, *suche, ȝus* (or *siche, ȝis*), *miche* (or *muche*), *euerich,* the compound pret. with the aid of *did,* the preference given to *to make* followed by the prepositional infinitive above *to do* followed by the pure infinitive, all of which peculiarities were imported from the South). The characteristics of Lancashire (cf. *ho, ham, au,* so frequently used for *ow, us* pl. ending for *ys,* the pres. pl. in *en,* the preference always given to final t before d in verbs, adjectives, substantives, &c.) cannot be denied.

Therefore I believe that the Fairfax MS. was copied in the first half of the 15th century in the Western part of the ancient archdiocese of York.

39. THE ADDITIONAL MS. 10,036.

There is no doubt that it depends on a Midland copy. The argument is : (1) participles present in *and : lepand* 613, *liand* 768, *sittand* 868 ; (2) Preterites plur. = sing. : *þei slow* 378, *bigan* 358, *cam* (r. w. *wham*) 336, *þei wist* 305 ; (3) Such rymes as, *beforn, forlorn* 265-6, *fro, so* 341-2, *cam, gan* (inf.) 775-6, *fare, mare* (om.) 291-2; (4) *I did hem* . . *go* 462. Of which 2 and 3 are conclusive for the North-Midland. There is one argument for a dependency

on a Western copy; cf. *he steie, he* 151-2. I know one similar ryme in
Havelok, cf. *hey, fre* (MS. *fri*, more Southern), but the reading is not correct,
and the MS. copy does not belong to Lincolnshire at all. Gg's reading (*Marie
abod & wel sle3*) appears now to be an alteration of A's source.

40. It is interesting to see how, with respect to the relation of **a** and **o**, A
differs from the Northern version. No doubt the Northern scribe had to
overcome the greatest difficulties in this part of the *Cursor*, which was adapted
from a Southern source. Compare *also, to* (*tua, ma*) 17-18, *gone, done* (*gan,
an*) 85-6, *so, to* (*wald, cald*) 183-4, *fone, none* (*faa, þaa,* cf. the wording) 507-8,
more, bifore (to *sei, ei,* cf. the wording of C F: G) 511-12, *fone, anone* (*ennemi,
hi*) 691-2, *done, euerychone* (*done, quone*) 415-16, *wo, ago* (pp.) (*wa, fra*)
209-10; cf. also *fore, more* (N. V. and A) 551-2. Then observe other differences: *throwe, yknowe* (pp.) (*time, hime*) 533-4, *to, do* (pp.) (*to, sco*) 91-2.

41. The scribe of A lived towards the West. He perhaps belonged to the
ancient diocese of Worcester. The argument is:

NORTHERN I : U—gurdel 797, mury 418, furst 323, cust (but *kist* 360)
309, hure (*pers.* and *poss.*) 435, 436.

Other Midland forms are : PHONOLOGY : E : A—wasche (*prt.*) 156, massa-
gere 100; I : E—euelte 439, I : Y, O—mychel 786, mochel 900, moche 412,
AW : OW—throwe, yknowe 523-4. PRONOUNS : sche 680, the (*pl.*) 379, eche
252, euerychone 416, suche 334. VERBS : sitteþ (*pl. imp.*) 2, 11, þenkeþ
(*imp.*) 21, hast 162, hauest 42, haþ 112, beþ (*sg.*) 720, saist þou 44, dide
wepe (*prt.*) 31, wept 241. There is no evidence of a present plural in *th.*

The Additional MS. appears to date from the beginning of the 15th century.
Its source made use of some other MS., which contained the two hundred lines
or so not to be found in the *Cursor*.

42. THE TRINITY MS.

PHONOLOGY : I : U—duden 12, muche 114, furst 131, hud (*prt.*) 863, gult
877, murþe 1004, nust (= ne wist) 1808, buryinge 1190, stude (= O.E. y, e)
477, fuyr (= O.E. ỹ) 520, appul (= i, e) 873 ; I : E—euel 939, merked 1764,
shenshepe 17467, worshepe 2439, felawshepe 1159 ; A : E—meest, leest 908,
cleef, ref 7809-10, in greue (= *in right earnest*) 6547, A : O—eronde 3274,
E3 : I—hy, 17300.

K : CH—mychel 649, iliche 1012 ; D : þ—tenþe 1986.

ADVERBS : 3us 4341, nouþer (neyder G, nauþer F, noiþer C) 7545.

PRONOUNS : sche 2413, hir 191, hem (*pl.*) 251, her (*poss.*) 201, vche 247,
eueryche 510, euervche 1680, sich 1167, suche 3407.

VERBS : þou seest 2936, endeþ (*sg.*) 58, ben (*pl.*) 3577, desiren (*pl.*) 3590, duden (*prt. pl.*) 12.

43. It is not necessary to seek for evidence of T's immediate dependency upon a Northern MS. The pedigree of the MSS., and the observations on G, have proved that T as well as G depends upon a more Northern source, which is not likely to have been purely Northumbrian. Our scribe (T) belongs to the South-Midland, and more towards the West, as is seen from the above phonology. I suppose that T was copied in the south of the ancient diocese of Hereford.[1] As to its age, the difference of style between North-Midland and South-Midland scribes cannot but make me persist in my supposition that T was copied in the first quarter of the 15th century.

CHAPTER IV.—CRITICISM OF THE MSS.

44. The phonology of E offers great difficulties. There is no doubt that the treatment of E in the *Cursor* is not uniform. There are two ways for explaining this singular fact. The reader will afterwards see, and may easily conclude from modern English, or Low German versification in general, that the English verse never was quite pure. A comparison of the *o*- and *u*- rymes in the *Cursor* confirms this statement. So it might be the same with the *e*-rymes. But there are other undeniable evidences that the old vowel-length often began to be rather shortened, so that the vowel was still more opening. The difficulty, however, increases when we take into consideration the frequent interchange between *ēo* and *ēa* in the Northumbrian dialect, our want of safe information about its bordering dialects, and our loss about the quantity of the O.E. vowels or diphthongs in some words. Any comparison with northern manuscripts on this head will, I am sure, give at once some advantage for the statement of the age of the *Cursor*, but an attempt to take slight differences in the treatment of E for dialectical ones would hardly be crowned with trust-worthy results. It seemed to me that a reference to Southern manuscripts would give little interest. The reader will easily see that Ten Brink's Grammar on Chaucer was considered to be the starting-point of my researches.

In order to find a clue to the bewildering rymes in the *Cursor*, I took one of our oldest extant specimens of the East Midland dialect, *Havelok*, for a basis, and compared it with later MSS.

It is worth while to compare the following instances : so god me rede (*prs. subj.*), r. w. bede (to offer) 2085, r. w. dede (deed) 688, r. w. mede

---

[1] But the agreement in words shows that F and T are closely connected.—R. Morris.

(reward) 2901 [cf. spede (*vb.*), mede (*sb.*) 1635].—what shal me to rede (counsel), r. w. mede (reward) 119.—rede (to guess), r. w. þede (*sb.*) 105.— rede (*dat.*, speech), r. w. dede (3 *sg. prt.*) 185.—bedes (*prs.*), r. w. dedes (2 *sg. prt.*) 2393.—red (counsel, *not the verb*), r. w. ded (death) 148.—red (counsel), r. w. ded (*dat.*, death) 2871, r. w. ded (*adj.*) 1194, 1204, 1406, 1975.—red (*dat.*, counsel), r. w. ded (*adj.*) 2211.—It is well known from Skeat's edition that the final *e* was really spoken in *Havelok*, but we see, too, from *red* 2211, *ded* 2870, that it could be dropt. It was a rule to elide it before a vowel or *h*, but some other instances show that it could be dropt in the ryme, f. i. in þe bed, r. w. adred 1258, cf. wedde (*inf.*), r. w. in bedde 2927, þerfram, r. w. sham 56. Now I would conclude from the above instances that O.E. *ǽ*, W. Teut. *â* was generally pronounced with a close *e* in an open syllable, and with an open *e* in a close (shut) syllable.[1] So I would also read with a close *e* : drede (*sb.*), r. w. fede (*vb.*) 828, r. w. bede (to offer) 1665, r. w. lede (*vb.*) 90.—grede (to cry loud, O.E. *grǽdan*, not *grǽtan*, to weep), r. w. stede (horse) 2703.—The same rule holds good in words in which *e* refers to O.E. *ǽ* = Teut. *ai*, as, lede (*inf.*), r. w. drede (*sb.*) 90, r. w. mede (*sb.*) 686, r. w. dede (deed) 550, r. w. wede (garment) 2825, r. w. yede (*prt.*) 1685.—lere (*vb.*), r. w. dere (*adj.*) 2592, r. w. dere (dearth) 824.—sprede (*vb.*), r. w. grede (to exclaim) 96.—mene (*vb.*), r. w. kene (*adj.*) 2114.—hele (*vb.*), r. w. mele (*vb.*) 2059.—clene, r. w. grene (*adj.*) 995.—gnede (*adj.*), r. w. brede[2] (O.E. *brǽdu*) 98.—But read with an open *e* : del (*sb.*), r. w. wel *passim.*—stel (*sb.*), r. w. del (*sb.*) 2503.

This tendency will be seen even in words which have O.E. *ê* ; cf. fet (*dat. pl.*), r. w. gret (wept) 616, 2159 ; fet (*acc.*), r. w. let (*prt.*) 2447 ; fet (*dat.*), r. w. yet 1320, 2041, 1304 (?).—sket (*adv.*), r. w. fet (*pl.*) 1961, (*dat.*) 2303, (*dat.*) 2737. Since *gret* (wept) wants an open *e* (O.E. *ȝrêǽt*, but cf. O.N. *grêt*), I see no other explanation, and would fairly say that *e* in *yet* (O.E. *ȝiet*), and *let* (O.E. *lêt*, prt.) was already pronounced with a tendency to an open *e*, while *yete* 2334, 1288 had a close *e*.

---

[1] This change also occurs in Low German. I was taken by surprise, when I first heard people pronounce even *breeder* or *breider*, pl. of *brœd* (= board). Is 'd' elided, it is *brǽr* again, which is *brǽ'* in *Mecklenburg.* (r, of course, lengthens the preceding vowel.)

[2] There are three ryme-words, *gnede*, *brede*, *shrede*. Is there a mistake? l. 98: *Havede he non so god brede*, makes me suppose so. Is it possible that the West-Saxon should have read *gnede* = O.E. *gnéaȝ*, not *gnéȝ*, and have mistaken *brede* for *bred*, O.E. *brêǽd* (*n.*), so that he altered the second line, which might originally have run thus : *ne hauede he so god shrede in brede ?*

O.E. *êá* appears with an open *e* : glem, r. w. bem (ray) 2123 ; stem (*sb.*), r. w. bem 592.—gret (*adj.*), r. w. net (O.E. néat) 1891, 1026.—grete (*adj. pl.*), r. w. bete (to beat) 1899, etc.—It seems to me very doubtful that *leue* (permission) should be an exception, though it rymes with *reue* (ȝeréfa) 1627, r. w. greue (O.F. vb.) 2593. *leue* is monosyllabic, and will easily find its ryme with *reue.* Of course, one cannot pronounce either pure Æ in *leue*, or pure EE in *reue.* The best orthography for the sound would be *ei* indeed, which is so frequently met with in later times, and the most expedient sign in Low German. The sound would remind of *ei* in modern *day*, with its different shades, without turning into *ai*.

nede (O.E. fem., *ê*, W.S. *êá*) and *yede* (O.E. *éode*, besides *éáde*) appear to have a close *e* : nede (*dat.*), r. w. dede (deed) 2902, r. w. fede (*vb.*) 645, r. w. stede (horse) *passim.*—yede, r. w. wede (garment) 862, r. w. lede (*vb.*) 1685, r. w. dede (deed) 1356. As to the other phonology compare frende (*sb.*), r. w. wende (*prt.*, thought) 375.—fend (*sb.*), r. w. hend (*pl. sb.*) 506, 1412, 2069.— held (*prt.*), r. w. feld (*sb.*) 2911.—helde (O.E. -ê-, e, *sb.*), r. w. welde (*sb.*) 129, 175, 1436, r. w. yelde (*vb.*) 2713. The sound will have been lengthened, but I see no reason for assuming a close *e*.

45. This point of view, I believe, gives us the right clue to an understanding of the phonology of later writers. The tendency of sometimes widening the vowel by rather shortening it, cannot be denied. First we see it in the reduplicative preterites, then often in substantives, adjectives, and verbs which have lost their final *e*, and the stem-vowel of which is either O.E. *ǽ*, or *é*, or *íe*.

1. *Robert de Brunne's Chronicle*, edited by F. J. Furnivall, Roll's Series, 1887. Compare : let (*prt.*), r. w. sett (pp.) 14896, r. w. fet (*pl. sb.*) 12406, 14580, r. w. wet (*adj.*) 15576.—het (*prt.*), r. w. fet (*pp.*) 11996, r. w. set (pp.) 12030, r. w. flet (*sb.*) 14536, r. w. *fet* (inf.) 9776, 11902.—slep (*pl. prt.*), r. w. gan *lep* 9202, r. w. schep (*pl. sb.*) 11492.—dredde (*prt.*), r. w. ledde (sg. prt.) 6310, 7276, r. w. spedde (sg. prt.) 13286. Cf. also ondrédde.—fel (*prt.*), r. w. *Samuel* 2112, r. w. *catel* 5770, r. w. *castel* 7518, r. w. *chapel* 12162. Further compare stel (sb.), r. w. *wel* 1118, 4864.—flet (*sb.*), r. w. met (prt.) 2944, r. w. het (*prt.*) 14536, r. w. get (vb.) 15818.—byleue (to believe), r. w. greue (*vb.*) 9484.—leue (permission), r. w. to greue 5916, 7836.—Further ȝede (*prt.*), r. w. brede (breadth) 3100, r. w. dede (deed) 12576, r. w. drede (*sb.*) 1586, r. w. lede (*vb.*) 1438, 10728, r. w. nede (*sb.*) 1664, r. w. sprede (vb.) 12146, 12784 (pp. ?), r. w. stede (horse) 12680.—Moreover compare sket

(*adv.*), r. w. *gret* (adj.) 9556.—Of French words compare power (*sb.*), r. w. per (*sb.*) 554, r. w. mester (*sb.*) 586, r. w. *wer* (sb.) 4558.—Maumet, r. w. *recet* 1346.—Further: drede (*sb.*), r. w. bede (to offer) 6590, r. w. forbede (1 *sg. prs.*) 1540, r. w. blede (*vb.*) 4378, r. w. *led* (pp.) 1098, r. w. lede (*vb.*) 934, r. w. *rede* (to counsel, Pet. MS. to spede) 4828, r. w. *stede* (place, Pet. MS. thede) 10570, r. w. ʒede (*prt.*) 1586.—drede (*vb.*), r. w. lede (*vb.*) 2942, r. w. lede (*sb.*) 14300, r. w. nede 11878, r. w. rede (to read) 7788.—lete (*vb.*), r. w. *gret* (adj.) 5844, 13292, r. w. *þrete* (prs.) 12658 (prs.), r. w. bete (to amend) 9078, r. w. grete (*prs. sg.,* to weep) 15584, r. w. mete (to meet) 7850.   Cf. *Handlyng Synne:* lete (*vb.*), r. w. *grete* (adj.) 694, r. w. grete (to weep) 716.—ʒer (*sb.*), r. w. *wer* (sb.) 828, 2126, r. w. daunger 2426.—slepe (*vb.*), r. w. *lepe* (vb.) 11530.—schep (*pl. sb.*), r. w. *lep* (vb.) 13898.—bere (*pl. prt.*), r. w. *were* (inf.) 10458.—rede (to counsel), r. w. dede (death) 1262; red (*dat.,* counsel), r. w. ded (*adj.*) 864.   Otherwise I would read with a close *e*: redes (*prs.* 3 *sg.,* to read), r. w. dedes (*pl. sb.*) 66; dedes (*pl. sb.*), r. w. yedes (2 *sg.*) 3232. Finally consider lede (*vb.*), r. w. *brede* (breadth) 6956, 11734, r. w. stede (horse) 12186, r. w. ʒede (*prt. pl.*) 1438, (*prt. sg.*) 10728.—byleue (to remain), r. w. reue (*vb.*) 14522, 15616.—reue (*vb.*), r. w. leue (to leave) 5170.

2. *Hampole's Pricke of Conscience.* Compare: fete (*pl. sb.*), r. w. *hete* (heat) 3215.—here (*adv.*), r. w. *spere* (sb.) 4868, r. w. *were* (doubt) 2511, r. w. *caysere* 883.—stele (*sb.*), r. w. *wele* 6474, r. w. *fele* (adj.) 9460.—dere (*adj.*), r. w. *were* (war) 1469, r. w. here (*adv.*) 4300, 5797.—fende (*sb.*), r. w. *wende* (vb.) 4196.—frende (*sb.*), r. w. wende (*vb.*) 6343.—fendes (*pl. sb.*), r. w. *endes* (prs.) 2219, 3735, 8524, r. w. *wendes* (prs.) 2369, 7240, r. w. frendes 3567, 3623.—felle (*prt.*), r. w. *helle* (sb.) 2065, 2339, r. w. *telle* (vb.) 4848.—Further observe French words: daungere, r. w. *bere* (vb.) 8522, r. w. *er* (adv.) 7982.— apere (*vb.*), r. w. *were* (doubt) 2297, r. w. here (*adv.*) 2885.—prayers, r. w. *ders* (prs., to injure) 2849, 3605.—maneres, r. w. *lers* (prs.) 1525, 4876, r. w. heres (*prs.*) 1591.—clere (*adj.*), r. w. *spere* (sb.) 4868.—Oliuett, r. w. *sett* (vb.) 4098, r. w. *sett* (prt.) 4602, r. w. *sett* (pp.) 5184, 5218, r. w. *lett* (to hinder) 5131.—prophete, r. w. *hete* (heat) 6598, r. w. shepe (*pl.*) 5891, r. w. mete (to meet) 1553, 5152, 6742.—mayntene (*vb.*), r. w. sene (*pp.*) 1109, r. w. wene (*prs.*) 3081 (close *e*).—Observe also sere (*adj.*), r. w. *bere* (vb.) 8736.—More-over consider sete (*sb.*), r. w. *grete* (adj.) 9318, r. w. *mete* (meat) 3059.—drede (*vb.*), r. w. lede (*vb.*) 1607, r. w. hede (*sb.,* heed) 1831, r. w. rede (to read) 1663, 9600.—drede (*sb.*), r. w. dede (deed) 2439, 5743, r. w. mede (*sb.*) 7508, r. w. hede (heed) 276, 9486, r. w. -hed 1177, 2213, 5264, 5391, 8252, r. w.

nede 5935, 8564, r. w. rede (to tell) 2967.—rede (to read, to tell), r. w. drede (*sb.*) 308, 2967, 3969, r. w. drede (*vb.*) 1663, 6287, 6403, 7503, 9600, r. w. -hede 8448, r. w. spede (*vb.*) 2709, r. w. dede (deed) 2485, 3401, 7451, r. w. fede (*vb.*) 6714.—rede (to counsel), r. w. *ded* (death) 1677.—rede (*sb.*, advice), r. w. *dede* (death) 2015, 4304, 4412, 4544.—Finally observe lede (*vb.*), r. w. drede (*sb.*) 158, 2533, r. w. drede (*vb.*) 1607, 6415.—hete (heat), r. w. *grete* (adj.) 6630, 6674, r. w. prophete 6598, r. w. fete (*pl. sb.*) 3215.

46. The following specimens will show that the tendency of widening long vowels before certain final consonants took full effect as early as the second half of the 14th century.

1. *Early English Alliterative Poems.*[1]   Compare : to reget, ȝet (still), reset (*sb.*) A 1064 ff.—sprede (*inf.*), rede (réad), fede (*pp.*), dede (*adj.*) A 25 ff.— grete (*adj.*), forfete (*inf.*), mete (meat), hete (heat) A 636 ff.—hete (heat), counterfete (*inf.*), ȝete (still), grete (*adj.*), þrete (to threaten), plete (O.F.) A 553 ff.—swatte (= swette), prophete, mete (*adj.*), sete (*pl. prt.*) A 828.—lede (*inf.*), schede (depart), godhede, to brede A 409 ff.—cleuen (cléofan), meuen (movoir), sweven (swefn) 105 ff.—swete (*adj.*), strete, ȝete A 1056.—reuerez (O.F.), ferez (ferjan), berez (beran) A 105 ff.—greue (*vb.*), acheve (*vb.*), leue (lȳfan), heue (hebban) A 471 ff.—preued (O.F.), heued (head) 974 ff.—Moreover, compare *Gawayne :* stedde (place), bledde (*prt.*), redde (*pp.*) 439 ff., and fette (*pl. sb.*) B 618, with which we meet also in the Cotton MS. of the *Cursor.*

2. *Sir Tristrem.*   Compare : ete (*inf.*), r. w. mete (meat), gete (*inf.*), grete (*adj.*), sete (prt. pl.) 543 ff.—ete (*prt.*), r. w. *mett* (pp.), *grete* (adj.), swete (*adj.*), ȝete (still) 2505 ff.—*dede* (sb., MS. deth), r. w. lede (*inf.*), bede (prt.) drede (*sb.*) 2597.—mete (to meet), r. w. grete (O.E. grétan), wete (*adj.*), sket (*adj.*) 728 ff.—wede (*vb.*), r. w. stede (steed), drede, blede (*vb.*), nede 1049 ff., etc.

3. *Sir Fyrumbras.*[2]   Compare : dede (death), r. w. spede 998.—ȝed (*prt.*), r. w. forhed (*sb.*) 3925.—wede (wǽde), r. w. hede (héafod) 2419.—deþ (*sb.*), seeþ (*pl. prs.*) 3792.—fet (*pl. sb.*), r. w. gret (*adj.*) 1875 *passim.*—eem (*sb.*),

---

[1] Cf. Knigge, *Die Sprache des Dichters von Gawayn*, etc.   Marburg, 1885.
[2] Cf. *Zur Dialectbestimmung des mittelenglischen Sir Firumbras. Eine Lautunter-suchung* von Dr. phil. Broder Carstens.   I am sorry to say that the material which the author has given is not always trustworthy in the renderings of the rymes, cf. f. i. page 21 deþ (deáþ), teþ (téð) 3189, 2849, and page 24 deþ, ae. déð 3 *sg.* von dôn im reime mit téþ (téð) 3189, or page 25 trowe (treówjan), abowe (âbúfan), 2805 and page 26 abowe (búgan), trowe (treówjan) 2805. The author's argument leaves the question still open. Dr. Furnivall's suggestion is by no means made invalid.

r. w. leem (*sb.*) 1861.—grete (*adj.*), r. w. schete (*vb.*) 3266.—grete (*adj.*), r. w. swete (*vb.*) 2654.—grete (*adj.*), r. w. mete (to meet) 3228. Besides, cf. lede (*vb.*), r. w spede (*vb.*) 908, r. w. stede (steed) 476.

Observ. Of great importance and interest do the following rymes appear: cure (O.E. cyre), r. w. þere 1548.—dur (O.E. dŷre, deõre), r. w. sure (O.F. süur) 2393.—cure, r. w. dure 1063.—fulle (*prt. pl.* of feallan), r. w. reculle (O.F. 971). It seems from these rymes that the Western sound of the so-called French *u* is exactly what I stated in § **53**: short = ĕ or ĕ (f. i. recuver), half-long ĕ͞ᵘ (f. i. sure), long eu͞ (f. i. due). It must be understood from these signs that even the long sound never runs through the full length of the vowel. Whoever knows the phonetic value of the respective sounds as spoken in the West, will easily see that these M.E. sounds came very near to the modern ones; take f. i. *sure* in its rapid Western pronunciation, which sounds to me very differently from the Eastern. The standard pronunciation of *sure*, in my opinion, never weakens *u*.—Compare also O.E. *fŷr*, Western *fur*, *fuir*, *fere*.

4. *Henrysone's Fables*, written in the 15th century (cf. *Anglia*, ix. 337). Compare: to meit (to meet), r. w. greit (*adj.*) 268-70 (in the body of lines *grit* is frequently met with, f. i. 676, 858, etc.).—heit (heat), r. w. meit (*adj.*) 759-60.—greit (*adj.*), r. w. sweit (*adj.*) 780-1.—meill (meal), r. w. to deill, geill 282, 284-5.—greit (*adj.*), r. w. quhite (wheat), to eit 359, 361-2.—beit (to beat), r. w. sweit (*sb.*, sweat), meit (meat) 489, 491-2.—heit (heat), r. w. sweit (*adj.*) 1342-4.—remeid (*sb.*), **r. w.** deid (dead) 511-2.—feid (enmity), r. w. leid (to lead), deid (death) 538, 540-1.—deid (dead), r. w. steid (stead), leid (to lead) 818, 820-21.—heid (head), r. w. remeid (*sb.*) 1522-3.

47. These instances are, no doubt, evidences of the development of a tendency which could be retraced even in Brunne and Hampole. How far this rule already took effect, can scarcely be stated to any certainty. Now we shall find that the *Cursor* rymes are not much different from those of Brunne, though the language is not quite the same. For in *Cursor* several inflectional *e*'s are left, as will be seen in the definite form of the adjective, sometimes its plural when before the substantive, the 3rd person of the present, and the plural of the substantive often not contracted, and some remains of genitives. Therefore we shall find a good many words which are able to retain their close vowels in their full length, but as to the adjective we shall see the difference only in the body of lines. We cannot conclude much from the orthography in C, because it seems to belong to a scribe who lived in a time when the above change had been carried out. Though we shall find that in a good many places the orthography agrees to the pronunciation which I assume the poet must have had, I do not venture to say that the phonology of E in the *Cursor* was quite uniform. Consider that the final *e* in the following instances is silent.

1. O.E. *ê*, M.E. *ee :* BETE (to emend), r. w. grete (*prt.*, wept) 4766, r. w. let (*prt.*) 748, 18691, r. w. prophet 9790, 13219 (bett), 22416, r. w. suete 105.— BREDE (*vb.*), r. w. brede (breadth) 2129, r. w. dred (*vb.*) 16410, r. w. lede (*sb.*) 16414, r. w. lede (*vb.*) 11471, r. w. nede 2945, 23400, r. w. rede (to count) 2569, r. w. sede (*sb.*) 637, 2344, 6870, 9788, 16412, 19022, 22878, r. w. sprede (*vb.*) 227.—DEME (*vb.*), r. w. beme (trumpet) 22712, r. w. barnteme 3432.—fele (*sb.*, feeling), r. w. wele (*sb.*, welle C) 547.—FELE (*vb.*), r. w. wele (*adv.* or *sb.*) 2902 (feil), 18268, 19372.—(VN) FERE (*adj.*), r. w. bere (*vb.*, þe bere F) 12516, r. w. demestere 22920, r. w. dere (*adj.*) 14169, r. w. dinere (*sb.*) 3507, r. w. were (*prt. pl.*) 12078, 14155, r. w. were (doubt) 3829, r. w. vinere (*sb.*) 13765, r. w. yere (yeir) 1237, 1267, 9145, 11409, 13778. The substantive FERE rymes with lere (*vb.*) 12482, pere (*sb.*) 449, 13314 (*pl.*), tresurer 24672.—FET (*pl. sb.*), r. w. grete (wept) 20082, r. w. grette (*sb.*, weeping) 190, 4929, r. w. gret (grett, *sb.*, grit) 15584, r. w. hete (*sb.*, promise, hait C) 11898, r. w. let (*prt.*) 14052, 14091, r. w. lete (*vb.*) 21778, r. w. prophete 14023, 18376 (*acc.*), r. w. sete (*vb.*, Qu. sette) 14735, r. w. wete (*adj. pl.*) 18308, 18688.—HERE (*adv.*), r. w. ber (*vb.*) 904, 3704, 6882, 14367, r. w. clere 9754, r. w. ȝere (yeir) 8514, r. w. nere 3844, 4234, r. w. porter 18258, r. w. sere (*adj.*) 8518, 14453, r. w. stere (*vb.*) 4960, 8230, r. w. torfere 8662, r. w. were (doubt) 3800.—HET (hett, *prt.*), r. w. prophet 10720, 14425, 18106. —LET (*prt.*), r. w. bete (to emend) 748, 18692, r. w. ete (*prt.*) 13295, r. w. fete (*pl. sb.*) 14053, 14091, 15288, r. w. gret (*adj.*) 12496, r. w. mete (*adj.*) 15286, 16566, r. w. mete (*vb.*, to meet) 7674, r. w. sette (*sb.*, seat) 15282, r. w. strete 16568, r. w. swete (*adj.*) 16562.—MEDE (reward), r. w. bede (*prs.*) 15488, r. w. forbede (*inf.*) 17222, r. w. ded (death) 20256, r. w. drede (*vb.*) 272, r. w. dede (deed) 4906, 6778, 7932, 11524, 15264, 15484, r. w. fede (*vb.*) 5638, 15260, 23880, r. w. -hede 4424, r. w. lede (*vb.*) 8354, 12761, 15258, r. w. lede (*sb.*) 15480, r. w. nede 3738, r. w. rede (to guess) 7122, 2326 (to read), 15482 (to read), r. w. spede (*vb.*) 2256, r. w. stede (place F, emedd C) 1004, r. w. vnspede (*sb.*) 15420, r. w. thede (*sb.*) 15490.—METE (to meet), r. w. forlete (*vb.*) 4006, r. w. sett (*inf.*), strete (*sb.*), grett (*prt.*, wept), gett (*prt.*), umsette (*pp.*), grett (greeted), bet (*pp.*, emended) 15001-16, r. w. yete (*adv.*)

1198. REDE (to read, to speak, to say), r. w. bede (to offer) 10636 (*prs.*),
r. w. bred (*vb.*) 2570, 22006, r. w. -hede 10628, 20998, r. w. lede (*vb.*) 6464
(*prs.*), 8544 (*prs.*), r. w. lede (*sb.*) 234, 2654, 4040 (*prs.*), r. w. mede (*sb.*)
2326, r. w. misdede (*sb.*) 4446, r. w. sede (*sb.*) 4026 (*prs.*), 4690, 5488 (*prs.*),
8526 (*prs.*), r. w. spede (*vb.*) 4554, 14927, r. w. sprede (*vb.*) 2322, 12654,
r. w. sted (stede : place) 238 (*prs.*), r. w. thede 4178 (*prs.*), r. w. yede 20882,
r. w. ded (death) 4114.—SLEP (slepp, *prt.*), r. w. kepe (*sb.*) 20128, 20498.—
SUET (*adj.*) r. w. seit (þan can he seit C, þar he sete F, he made a sete G, Qu.:
þan gan him sett) 8292, r. w. ete (*inf.*) 22719.

Besides observe O.E. ê = *i-umlaut of eâ* = Teut. *au* = W.S. *eâ, îe, ŷ*:
EKE (*vb.*), r. w. seke (*vb.*) 17560.—HERE (*vb.*), r. w. bere (*vb.*) 10726, 12228
(*v. r.* lere), r. w. boteler 13407, r. w. chere (*sb.*) 4964, r. w. clere 15600, r. w.
dere (*adj.*) 14641, 15594, r. w. emperere 16036, r. w. gospellere 13523, r. w.
lere (*vb.*) 13657, 13697, 15598, r. w. langer (*comp.*) 14535, r. w. manere 11990,
r. w. nere 7412, r. w. sere 12214, 14579, r. w. stere (*vb.*) 8230, r. w. were
(doubt) 12839, r. w. were (*prt. pl.*) 4393, 5330.—NEDE, r. w. bede (*vb.*)
14581, 14913, 15317 (*prs.*), 15426 (*prs.*), r. w. forbede (*subj. prs.*) 4826,
15314, r. w. dede (deed) 15320, r. w. dred (*vb.*) 2554, 3996, 4442, 7502,
12442, r. w. fede (*vb.*) 13321, r. w. gnede (*adj.*) 15424, r. w. -hede 1142,
1440, r. w. lede (*vb.*) 8560, 9018, r. w. mede (*sb.*) 3738, 15442, r. w. red (*sb.*,
counsel) 8398, r. w. rede (*subj. prs.*, to counsel) 8398, r. w. sede (*sb.*) 2156,
5408, 7694, r. w. spede (*vb.*) 9496, r. w. spred (*vb.*) 3792, vnspede (*sb.*) 15420,
r. w. ʒedd 10300, yede 10620.—GNEDE (*adj. and vb.*), r. w. brede (breadth)
9934, r. w. nede, unspede (*sb.*), mede (*sb.*), bede (*prs. pl.*), lede (*vb.*), spede
(*vb.*), rede (to counsel, *only in* C) 15418-32, r. w. sprede (*vb.*) 2448 (*vb.*),
r. w. nede 13385, 17218.—LEUE (to believe; liue C) r. w. leue (permission)
6033.—eke (*adv.*, O.E. eâc, êc), r. w. meke (O.N.) 23900, r. w. seke (*vb.*) 6332,
23760, r. w. chek (*sb.*) 24534, r. w. speke (*sb.*) 18056, 18438, r. w. speke (*vb.*)
18982, eth (*adj.*), r. w. meth (*sb.*), 10012.—Compare also STELE (O.E. stêle,
stŷle), r. w. wele (*adv.*) 18088, 24708.—Moreover consider O.E. eâ in NERE
(neir), r. w. dere (*sb.*) 3602, r. w. here (*adv.*) 3844, 4234, r. w. here (*vb.*) 7412,
14123, r. w. yeir (yere) 12648, 12829, r. w. messager, 3328, 5240, r. w. mister
11840, r. w. schere (scissors) 7240, r. w. were (*prt.*) 4672.

2. OE. êô, M.E. EE. Let us first consider such spellings as remind us of
those in the Psalter and the Rushworth Manuscripts. The spelling *ei* seems,
upon the whole, to indicate the lengthened sound and a wide articulation.
Compare TRES (*pl.*), r. w. sees (3 *sg. prs.*) 862 (treis, seis G).—KNES, r. w. seis

(2 *sg. prs.*) 14292.—BES (3 *sg. prs.*), r. w. seis (3 *sg. prs.* of to see) 4508, beis
(3 *sg. prs.*), r. w. sais (for *seis*, 2 *sg. prs.*) 2138 (C).—chese (*vb.*), r. w. lese (*vb.*)
7614, chesse (*vb.*), r. w. heess (C F, he *om.* C) 8410.—Besides compare PREIST,
r. w. neist 7264, 11498, 20640, r. w. breist (*sb.*) 12897, 17722.—BREST (*sb.*),
which is known to *Havelok* and *Chaucer*, occurs also in the *Cursor*, cf. brest
(*sb.*), r. w. best (*sup.*) 894.—Consider also the adjective *prest*, likewise spelt
preist, of course, ryming with *best* (sup.) 26, 3450, r. w. *fest* (prt.) 21256.

Further compare LEIF (*adj.*) 15509 ; LEUE (*adj.*), r. w. leue (permission)
8340.—THEIF (*sb.*), r. w. greif (*vb.*) 7234, THEFE (*sb.*), r. w. leue (permission)
14745 [cf. leue (permission), r. w. greue (*vb.*) 2920, 5950, 24734, r. w. breue
(*sb.*) 19606, r. w. leue (to belieue) 6034].

Quite different appear to me the following instances : DERE (*adj.*), r. w.
chere (*sb.*) 4220, 11510, 10434, 12626, r. w. here (*vb.*) 14641, r. w. yeir (yere)
6918, 10212, 11102, 13183, r. w. jailere 4434, r. w. pere (*sb.*) 4356, r. w.
prayer (*sb.*) 3442, 3978, r. w. sere (O.N.) 9962, 10056, r. w. were (*sb.*) 8746,
r. w. were (*prt.*) 5300.—LEM (*sb.*), r. w. barntem (*sb.*) 18194.—*leme* (*vb.*), r. w.
ierusalem, 8197.—SMEKE (*sb.*), r. w. speke (*vb.*) 2928.—Compare also KNELE
(*vb.*, O.E. ?), r. w. wel (*adj.*) 17696.

Further compare FREIND, r. w. hende (heinde, *adj.*) 4258, r. w. leind (lend,
vb.) 9652, r. w. sceind (*vb.*) 4398, 24022, r. w. teind (10°) 14119, 24436,
r. w. wend (weind, *prs.*) 3808, 6832, 14191, 18790, 24297 (*inf.*).   No doubt,
an open sound.   It will be the same with *feind*, 23740.

Moreover, consider LEPP (*prt.*), r. w. step 5194, 19078, r. w. iosep[h]
17318.—BETE (*bet*, prt., beat) without a ryme, seems to show the same tendency.
—wepe (wep, *prt.*) I have not found in a ryme, nor are the spellings *weped*
and *wepped·* or *sleped* proved by a ryme.   But cf. *Brunne's Chronicle*, *slept*
(prt.), r. w. kept (*prt.*) 290, and *slep* (prt.), r. w. schep (*pl.*) 11492, while I
know only *slep* (slepp), r. w. kepe (*sb.*) in the *Cursor.*—HEILD (*prt.*), r. w. eild
(*sb.*) 5166, r. w. feild (**y**) 3832, r. w. queld (*prt.*) 19468, r. w. teld (*pp.*) 17490,
18551, r. w. weld (*prt.*) 8446.—YEDE (yeide, ȝeide, ȝedd, cf. O.E. ẽode, ẽade),
r. w. dede (deed) 1086, 7404, r. w. -hede 6544, 11232, r. w. lede (*vb.*) 12030,
11632, r. w. lede (*sb.*) 10946, 11348, 12596, 20904, r. w. nede 10300, 10620,
r. w. rede (to read) 13879, r. w. sede (*sb.*) 12324, r. w. thede (*sb.*) 11104, r. w.
ded (adj.) 14235, r. w. *brede* (breadth) 16602.—FELL (*prt.*), r. w. hell (*sb.*) 478,
r. w. tell (*vb.*) 134, 3322, 4536.

OBSERV.   *feild, scheild* (O.E. ë) seem to have an open *e*.   Compare *feild*,
r. w. cild (*sb.*) 4714, r. w. yeild (*inf.*) 6762, dounheild (*sb.*) 3822, 6432, r. w.

schcild 7672, and *scheild*, r. w. weild (*sb.*) 20818.   Compare for the ryme-
words heild (inclinare), r. w. yeild (*inf.*) 24408 ; weild (*sb.*), r. w. yeild (*vb.*)
3818, 6742, r. w. eild 5650, 10328 ; eild, r. w. feild (*sb.*) 4714, r. w. biheild
(*prt.*) 5166, r. w. donheild (*sb.*) 5468, r. w. beild (*sb.*) 10516, r. w. weild
(weld, *vb.*) 5650, 10328.

3. The same observations will be made on words of French origin, and will
serve to illustrate and explain the above-mentioned rymes.

O.F. e = Lat. *a:* CLERE (*adj.*), r. w. baner (*sb.*) 22764, r. w. cher (*sb.*)
19418, r. w. here (*adv.*) 9754, r. w. messager 7988, r. w. stere (*vb.*) 6056.—
PERE (*sb.*), r. w. bachelere 8542, r. w. fere (*sb.*) 450, r. w. messagere 12720,
r. w. were (*prt.*) 776, r. w. yeir (yere) 1468, 1702.

O.F. IE, monophthongized in Norman French : GREUE (greif, *vb.*), r. w. leue
(permission) 2920, 5950, 24734, r. w. theif (*sb.*) 7234.—MAINTEIN, r. w. barntem 7374.—CHER (*sb.*), r. w. bere (*sb.*) 10448, r. w. dere (*adj.*) 4220, 11510,
10434, 12626, r. w. here (*vb.*) 4964, r. w. manere 12052, 12350, r. w. messager
8548, 10314, r. w. sere (O.N.) 4232, r. w. were (*prt.*) 4458, 10942, 14302.—
MISTER, r. w. ber (*vb.*) 3248, r. w. nere (*adv.*) 11840, r. w. squier 4670, r. w.
stere (*vb.*) 5560, r. w. webster 1526.—PRAYER (*sb.*), r. w. dempster (demester)
9738, r. w. ere (*sb.*, ear, cf. O.E. éare, éore) 10514, r. w. dere (*adj.*) 3442, 3978,
20624, 20654, r. w. maner 10488, r. w. unfer (*adj.*) 20964, r. w. yere 9152.—
MANERE, r. w. ber (*vb.*) 10672, r. w. cher (*sb.*) 12350, r. w. here (*vb.*) 11990,
r. w. lere (*vb.*) 12422, r. w. nere (*adv.*) 5240, r. w. praier (*sb.*) 10488, r. w.
were (*sb.*) 10846, r. w. were (*prt.*) 4068, 12790.—MESSAGER, r. w. answer (*sb.*)
1890, r. w. ber (*vb.*) 3334, r. w. clere 7988, r. w. chere (*sb.*) 8548, 10314, r. w.
er (*sb.*, ear) 5140, r. w. dere (*adj.*) 17934, r. w. foriner (*sb.*) 13209, r. w. here
(*adv.*) 20150, 20178, 20306, r. w. nere (*adv.*) 5240, 3328, r. w. peer 12720.—
IAIOLER, r. w. stere (*vb.*) 4450.—MORTER, r. w. ber (*vb.*) 5524.

5. O.F. e = Lat. *e* resp. Greek *η* : PROPHETE (PROPHET), r. w. bete (to
amend) 9790, 13219, 22416, r. w. fete (*pl.*) 14023, 18376, r. w. het (hett, *prt.*)
10720, 14425, 18106, r. w. hette (*pp.*) 6872, 14783, r. w. let (*sb.*) 9150, r. w.
lete (*vb.*) 22296, r. w. lete (*prt.*) 14609, r. w. sete (*prt. pl.*) 17872, r. w. skete
(O.N.) 2988, 7396, r. w. strete 17904, r. w. mete (*vb.*) 22964, r. w. oliuete
22982.—OLIUETE, r. w. sitte (C G, Qu. : sett, *pp.*) 17743, r. w. gret (*sb.* grit)
15582, r. w. suete (*adj.*) 17484.—MAUMET, r. w. sete (sett G, *pp.*) 11754.

6. O.N. Ê, IÛ, ÊÓ : SEIR (sere), r. w. conceiler 9314, r. w. chere (*sb.*) 4232,
r. w. dere (*adj.*) 9962, 10056, r. w. here (*adv.*) 8518, 14453, r. w. here (*vb.*)
12214, 14579, r. w. riuere 3506, r. w. were (doubt) 9276, r. w. were (*prt.*)

3340, 10784, r. w. yeir 1434, 6840, 11378.—MEKE, r. w. eke (adv.) 23900.—
SKETE (adv.), r. w. prophete 2988, 7396, r. w. fete (sb. pl.) 4172, r. w. ete (sg.
prt.) 5706.—Observe here KEPE (sb.), and KEPE (vb.), the etymology of which
is not quite settled : kepe (vb.), r. w. depe (adj.) 21360, r. w. scepe (pl. sb.)
5730, 6764, 14657, r. w. slepe (vb.) 626, 8210, r. w. on- slepe 7986, r. w. yepe
(adj.) 4924.—kepe (sb.), r. w. scepe (sb. pl.) 10368, r. w. on- slepe 7428, r. w.
slep (slepp, prt.) 20128, 20498.

48. O.E. *æ̂* and *ê* = W. Teut. *â*. Compare SPEKE (sb.), r. w. eke (vb.)
12198, r. w. seke (adj.) 13261, 13349, 24321, r. w. eke (adv.) 18056.—CHEKE
(sb.), r. w. eke (adv.) 24534.—SLEPE (sb.), r. w. kepe (vb.) 7986, r. w. kepe
(sb.) 7428.—SLEPE (vb.), r. w. kepe (vb.) 626, 8210.—DEDE (deed), r. w. drede
(vb.) 8570, 11788, r. w. forbede (vb.) 1106, 3204, r. w.—hede 1160, 3402,
9978, r. w. lede (vb.) 6866, r. w. lede (sb.) 1746, 9062, r. w. mede (sb.) 752,
4906, 6778, 7932, 11534, r. w. rede (to read) 11582, (to say) 4446, r. w.
spede (vb.) 224, 8228, r. w. thede (sb.) 4484, r. w. weede (1 sg. prs.) 3750.—
DREDE (vb.), r. w. dede (deed) 8570, 11788, r. w. lede (vb.) 5768, r. w. lede
(sb.) 2406 (prs.), 3122, 5220, 8226, 12068, r. w. mede (sb.) 272, r. w. nede
2554, 3996, 4442, 7502, 12442, r. w. rede (to guess) 16624, r. w. rede
(sb., reed) 16622, r. w. sede (sb.) 5230, r. w. wede (vb.) 13035, r. w. wede
(garment) 16620.—DRED (sb.), r. w. lede (vb.) 5767, r. w. ded (adj.) 20236.—
SEDE (sb.), r. w. brede (vb.) 638, 2344. 5574, 6870, 9788, 22876, r. w. gnede
(adj.) 5392, r. w. -hede 2324, 2330, 5582, r. w. lede (sb.) 10284, r. w. lede
(vb.) 4936, 5230, r. w. nede 2156, 5408, 7694, r. w. rede (to speak, to read,
inf. and prs.) 4026 (prs.), 4690, 5488, 8526 (prs.), 598 (to expound), r. w.
wede (garment) 1140, 5136, r. w. yede 12324.—WEDE (vb.), r. w. dede (deed)
3750 (prs.), 16010, r. w. ded (adj.) 12040, r. w. drede (vb.) 13035, r. w.
-hede 2454, r. w. lede (vb.) 16006, r. w. nede 10014, 16014, r. w. rede (prs. pl.,
to read) 16016, r. w. yede (prt.) 16012.—BIDENE (adv.), r. w. wene (vb.) 1457,
1814, r. w. clene (adj.) 1959, r. w. mene (vb.) 5395.—YEPE (O.E. ӡêap = yǽp,
cf. Ormin), r. w. iosep[h] 5370, r. w. kepe (vb.) 4923.—YERE (YEIR), r. w. bere
(sg. prt.) 2170, 11800, 20824 (cf. also ber·(sg. prt.), r. w. eliezer 6440), r. w.
dere (adj.) 6918, 10212, 13183, r. w. dempster (demister) 7006, r. w. fere
(adj.) 1238, 1268, 9146, 11410, 13779, r. w. here (adv.) 8514, r. w. lere (vb.)
1546, r. w. neir (ner) 12648, 12829, r. w. pere (equal) 1468, 1702, r. w.
praiyer 9152, r. w. seir (sere, O.N.) 6840, 11378, r. w. unfere 238, 1268, r. w.
were (doubt) 7070, 12136.—ETE (prt. sg. and pl.), r. w. stret (sb.) 4176 (pl.),
r. w. skete (adv.) 5706, r. w. forlete (prt. sg.) 9448, 13295, r. w. mete (meat)

22898.—SETE (*prt. pl.*), r. w. prophet 17872.—SETE (*sb.*), r. w. grot (*adj.*) 13371, r. w. lete (*prt.*), mete (*adj.*), fete (*pl.*) 15282.—STRETE (*sb.*), r. w. let (*prt.*) 16568, r. w. prophet 17904, r. w. mete (*vb.*) 3354, 6182, 11542, 13526, r. w. ete (*prt. pl.*) 4176, r. w. sett (*vb.*) grette (*prt.*, wept), to mete (to meet), grett (*prt.*), umsette (*pp.*) grett (greeted), bet (*pp.*, amended) 15001-16.—WET (*adj.*), r. w. fete (*pl.*) 18308, 18688, r. w. grett (*prt.*, wept), suett (*prt.*), sett (*pp.*) 15626-30.—LETE (*vb.*), r. w. flete (*vb.*) 2288, r. w. fete (*pl. sb.*) 21778, r. w. mete (to meet), 4006, r. w. suete (*adj.*) 17254, 24093, 24282, r. w. yeit (*adv.*) 2288, r. w. prophete 22295.—THERE (*adv.*), r. w. spere (*sb.*) 21104, 20546, r. w. dere (*adj.*) 21088.—BERN (*pl. prt.*), r. w. wern (*pl. prt.*) 20716. —WERN (*pl. prt.*), r. w. ern (*pl. sb.*) 8080, r. w. stern (*sb.*) 11490, r. w. bern (*pl. prt.*) 20716.—WERE (*prt.*, *sg.*, *pl.*, *subj.*), r. w. bere (*vb.*) 9072, r. w. chere (*sb.*) 4458, 10942, r. w. dere (*adj.*) 5200, r. w. here (*vb.*) 4394, 5330, r. w. lere (*vb.*) 10608, r. w. manere 12790, 10846, r. w. nere 4672, r. w. pere (*sb.*) 776, r. w. sere (*adj.*) 3340, 10784, r. w. scere (*prt.*) 2696, r. w. stere (*vb.*) 4296, 12230, r. w. were (doubt) 2426.—BERE (*prt. pl.*), r. w. sere (O.N.) 386.—WELE (weel, whirlpool), r. w. sele (*sb.*) 2903, r. w. quele (*sb.*) 23720 (cf. 21273).—METH (*sb.*), r. w. eth (*adj.*) 10011.—DEDE (*prt.* of *to do*), r. w. drede (*prt.*) 3414 (MS. *didd*), r. w. stede (place) 8892, r. w. fede (*quede* = fiend) 19358, r. w. -hede 21706.—MELE (*vb.*), r. w. hele (*sb.*) 8014, 13785, 22302, r. w. fele (*adj.*) 9166, r. w. israel 5476, 5848.—REDE (to counsel, to expound), r. w. ded (*adj.*) 906, 3452, r. w. ded (death) 4317 (*prs.*), 22972, r. w. mede 7122, r. w. sede 598.—REDE (*sb.*, counsel), r. w. dede (death) 3994, r. w. ded (*adj.*) 4032, 6938, 20358, r. w. red (*adj.*) 4678, r. w. ned (*sb.*) 4636.— QUEDE (evil, fiend), r. w. dede (death) 16256, 22822, r. w. bred (bread) 17216, etc.—SELE (good fortune), r. w. dele (*sb.*) 23796, r. w. bitele (*vb.*) 6890, r. w. wele (*adv.*) 1166, 2904, 4432, 5564, 6982, 8320, 23094, r. w. wele (weel, whirlpool) 2904.

Amongst these words open e only seems to be known in : *dede* (prt.), mele (vb.), *rede* (to counsel, to expound ; advice), *sele* (sb.). Open e seems to prevail in : *ete* (prt.), *sete* (prt.), *strete* (sb.), *wet* (adj.), *lete* (vb.), *there*, *wern* (pl. prt.), *bern* (pl. prt.), *were* (prt.), *yeir*, *drede* (sb.). Unsettled seems to be the e-sound in : *yepe*, *drede* (vb.), *rede* (to read, to say), *wele* (whirlpool), *sede* (sb.), *wede* (vb.), but I strongly believe there is a tendency to open e. Close e seems to prevail in *dede* (deed), but its articulation is wide. Doubtful appears e in : *meth* (sb.), *speke* (sb.), *slepe* (sb. and vb.), *cheke* (sb.), but its articulation is wide.

Where open E only is known, E seems to be much broader than the E of those words in which open E seems to prevail, so that we have perhaps to distinguish three E's : Very long, broad E (wide articulation), Long open E (narrow articulation), Long close E (wide articulation).

I do not mention the dissyllabic rymes, as in plurals of substantives, the 3rd person singular present, the 2nd person singular present and preterite, which end in *es*, because the *ē* = O.E. *œ̄*, *ē* in an open syllable seems to keep close, f. i. *dedis* (deeds), r. w. *redis* (3 sg. prs.) 42. When the form is contracted, so that *e* in the termination *es* is silent, the preceding *e* appears in a shut syllable again. This rule seems also to hold good in French words, as, *porters*, r. w. *ders* (3 sg. prs.) 10014 (cf. 12061), which ryme can be read only with an open E.

49. Nor is the phonology uniform in words in which E refers to O.E. *œ̄*, *ā* = Teut. *ai* or *ai -i*. Compare : TECHE (*vb.*), r. w. leche (*vb.*) 21203, r. w. reche (O.E. rǣcean) 3650, 5307, r. w. preche (*vb.*) 13251.—BREDE (*sb.*, breadth), r. w. brede (*vb.*) 2130, r. w. -hede 1642, r. w. lede (*sb.*), nede (*sb.*), spede (*vb.*), yede (*prt.*) 16594-602, r. w. vngnede (*adj.*) 9934, r. w. lede (*sb.*) 22386, r. w. sprede (*vb.*) 21974.—SPREDE (*vb.*), r. w. brede (breadth) 21974, r. w. brede (*vb.*) 228, r. w. forbede (*subj. prs.*) 17436, r. w. gnede (*vb.*, MS. knede) 2248, r. w. -hede 600, r. w. lede (*sb.*) 10684, 20944, 22336, r. w. lede (*vb.*) 5222, r. w. nede 1222, 3792, r. w. rede (to read) 2322, 12656.—LEDE (*vb.*), r. w. bede (to offer) 12732, 16282, r. w. brede (*vb.*) 11872, r. w. dede (dead) 6866, r. w. dred (*sb.*) 5768, r. w. fede (*vb.*) 2402, 18474, r. w. -hede 7422, 8422, 8470, r. w. lede (*sb.*) 13831, 14407, 16274, r. w. mede (*sb.*, reward) 8354, 12761, r. w. nede 8560, 9018, r. w. rede (to read) 6484, 8544, r. w. sede (*sb.*) 4936, 5230, r. w. wede (*vb.*) 16276, r. w. spede (*vb.*) 9608, 18278, r. w. sprede (*vb.*) 5222, r. w. yede (*prt.*) 6970, 11632, 12030, 19322.—LERE (*vb.*), r. w. baner 12722, r. w. fere (*sb.*) 12482, r. w. here (*adv.*) 6882, r. w. here (*vb.*)· 13657, 13697, 22870, r. w. manere 12422, r. w. messageres (: leres, 3 *sg. prs.*) 12782, r. w. yere 1546.—The suffix -hede[1] (once -*hade*, in maidenhade, r. w. made (*pp.*) 10360) rymes with : bede (to offer, *prs. pl.*) 5404, r. w. brede (breadth) 1642, r. w. dede (deed) 1160, 3402, 9978, r. w. dede (*prt.*, MS. did) 21706, r. w. lede (*sb.*, people) 1190, 2454, 2954, 5648, 9488, 10166, 13235, r. w. lede (*vb.*) 7422, 8422, 8470, r. w. mede (*sb.*, reward) 4424, 10350, r. w.

---

[1] Compare from the *Additions: manhed*, r. w. ded (death) 25611, *goddhed*, r. w. rede (*adj.*) 25650, *drunkenhede*, r. w. we sprede 27877, etc., and *preisthade*, r. w. to bere þair lade 27501.

nede 1142, 1440, 4838, 9820, 12929, r. w. rede (to read, to speak) 98, 11928,
10628, 20998, r. w. sede (*sb.*) 5582, 2324, 2330, r. w. sprede (*vb.*) 600, 2064,
r. w. wede (garment) 9868, r. w. wede (*vb.*) 2408, 2454, 13975, r. w. yede
(*prt.*) 6544.—HELE (*sb.*), r. w. castel 13985, r. w. del (*vb.*) 8144, r. w. fele
(*adj.*) 8992, 19516, r. w. israel 11318, r. w. lele (*adj.*) 10364, r. w. mele (*vb.*)
13785, 22302, r. w. mesel (*adj.*) 8138, 14447.—DEL (*vb.*), r. w. lele (*adj.*) 1626,
r. w. mele (*sb.*, flour) 4680, r. w. Samuel 7302, r. w. [un]hel (*sb.*) 1984, 8144.
—dele (*sb.*), r. w. wele (*adv.*) 2428, 9533, 10022, 13493, r. w. sele (*sb.*, bliss)
23796, r. w. wele (*sb.*) 24190.—BILEUE (to remain), r. w. weve (O.F. *sb.*)
22928, r. w. reue (*vb.*) 14501.—HETE (HEITE; *sb.*, heat), r. w. swete (*vb.*)
11872, r. w. geite (to watch) 998, r. w. gret (*adj.*) 1173, r. w. grete (*vb.*) 4700.—
RES (*sb.*), r. w. moyses 6550, r. w. les (*sb.*) 7166, r. w. blese 8878.—QUETE (wheat),
r. w. grete (*adj.*) 4578. —SWETE (vb.), r. w. hete (*sb.*) 11872.—MENE (*vb.*), r. w.
ben (*pp.*) 8900 (*prs.*), r. w. bedene (*adv.*) 5396, r. w. clene (*adj.*) 3108, 9330
(*prs.*), 23580 (*prs.*), r. w. kene (*adj.*), r. w. sene (*pp.*) 4456, 5252, 8496.—
[VN]CLENE (*adj.*), r. w. bene (*pp.*) 2984, 10890, 10912, 21034, r. w. bedeine
1960, r. w. mene (*vb.*) 3108, 9330 (*prs.*), r. w. scene (*adj.*) 9986, 18204, r. w.
sene (*pp.*) 4918, 10598, 10630, 12891, r. w. wene (*prs.*) 9794.—SEE (*sb.*), r. w.
be 382, r. w. se (*vb.*) 708, r. w. liuere 2121.

Among these words only close e seems to be known in: *mene* (vb.), *clene*
(adj.), *see* (sb.), and only broad e in: *hele* (sb.), *hete* (heat), *dele* (vb.), *dele*
(sb.), *bileue* (to remain), *quete* (wheat) and *res*. Open e seems to prevail in
lere (vb.). The e-sound seems to be unsettled or doubtful in: *teche, brede*
(breadth), *lede* (vb.), *sprede* (vb.), *-hede*. The latter, I believe, show a close
e, when they appear in an open syllable; *lere*, I think, shows contracted forms
only.

50. O.E. ĕ in an open syllable, which was lengthened in M.E., has
remained open and long in the *Cursor*, but, as final e is silent, it seems to be
rather shortening before d, t, though its articulation is wide.

Compare: ber (vb.), r. w. ansuer, 11320, r. w. demester 23060, r. w. ger
(*vb.*) 2598, 7534, r. w. gospeler 12582, r. w. her (*vb.*) 10726, 12228, r. w. her
(*adv.*) 904, 3704, r. w. kaiser 9410, r. w. langer (*comp.*) 12991, r. w. maner
10672, r. w. messager 3334, r. w. mister 3248, r. w. morter 5524, r. w. suere
(*vb.*) 3226, r. w. sauuer (*sb.*) 10542, r. w. sper (*vb.*) 13329, r. w. were (*prt.*)
9072.—bere (sb.), r. w. dere (*vb.*) 692.—*were* (to defend), r. w. heer (army)
23766.—*were* (*weir*, doubt), r. w. dere (*adj.*) 8746, r. w. fere (*adj.*) 3830, r. w.
here (*adv.*) 3799, r. w. here (*vb.*) 12839, 20043, r. w. samplere 10891, r. w. seir

(*adj.*) 9276, r. w. yeire 7069, 12135.—*speke* (vb.), r. w. amalec 6404, r. w. freke 5198, r. w. iosep 12290, r. w. smeke (*sb.*) 2928, r. w. wreke (*vb.*) 2928.—*ete* (vb.), r. w. sett (*pp.*) 12558, 13501, r. w. grett (*adj.*) 19834.—*fett* (vb.), r. w. mett (*prt.*) 19940, r. w. grete (wept) 9046.—*met* (sb.), r. w. sett (*pp.*) 13993, r. w. bete (*prt.*, amended) 14415, r. w. sett (*prt.*) 4472, r. w. umsett (*prt.*) 9212.—*to gett* (cf. on account of *g* O.N. geta), r. w. sett (*pp.*) 7902, r. w. lett (*pp.*) 10326, r. w. dett (*sb.*) 21428, r. w. recett 5300.—*geten* (pp.), r. w. forgeten (*pp.*) 13043, 14799, 24904; *forgeten*, r. w. etin (giant) 21708.—*forgett* (pp.), r. w. lett, umset (*pp.*), sett (*pp.*) 15806 ff.—*wele* (sb.), r. w. sele (good fortune) 6982, r. w. israel 5714, r. w. feil (*vb.*) 2902.—*fele* (adj.), r. w. unlele 13173, r. w. morsel 13485.—Compare also *e* = O.E. *y* in an open syllable : *stere* (O.E. styrian), r. w. clere (*adj.*) 6056, r. w. here (*adv.*) 4960, 8230, r. w. iailer 4450, r. w. mistere 5560, r. w. were (*prt.*) 4296.—Besides, consider *e* = W.S. *ea*, *ie*, after a palatal, and before *r* + *w* (cf. on *g* also O.N.) : *geyre* (gere, *sb.*), r. w. bere (*vb.*) 7534, r. w. sper (*sb.*) 7728, r. w. were (*vb.*) 3300.—*gere*[1] (vb.), r. w. ber (*vb.*) 2598, 11214, r. w. wisliker 11786 ; gers (3 *sg. prs.*), r. w. afers (*pl.*) 11962, r. w. forberes (3 *sg. prs.*) 13835. The MSS. have also *gar* (*gart* prt.) which never occurs in a ryme.

Of the words of the above kind I especially take into consideration *stede*, *sted* (place), r. w. rede (redd, 1 sg. prs. of *to read*) 238, r. w. bedd (*prt.*, offered) 8820, r. w. bede (*sb.*) 17672, 19210, r. w. bedde (*sb.*) 902, r. w. ledd (*pp.*) 4968, r. w. ledd (*prt.*) 6666, 8874, 11984, 16098, r. w. brede (board), redd (*pp.*), ledd (*pp.*) 16577-84, r. w. forbedd (*prt.*), ledd (*pp.*), bedd (*sb.*), bled (*prt.*) 16913-22, r. w. fledd (*pp.*) 17459, r. w. redd (*pp.*) 21182, 24926.— Besides, cf. *stedd*, r. w. *emedd* 1004, where we are likely to read *o mede*, so that C confounded *o* and *a mede* with *amid*, *emid*, cf. F's reading : Paradys ys a preuey stede—þer many mirthes ar *and* mede, and G's alteration : *Paradys es a priue place—Ful of mirth and of solace.* The Latin text leaves us in the lurch. Or should the scribe only have wanted to make the vowels agree? For compare did, *takenhid* C, takin hede F G 21706, where the correct reading must be *dede* (prt. of *to do*) which C avoids, but which is proved by ll. 3414, 8892, 19358. Now why did he not correct into *stid*, *emid* 1004, though he wrote did, *stid* 380, or make the vowels agree in *stedde*, *did* (prt.) 20012, 20138, in which the *Add.* MS. has *stede*, *dede* (prt.)? I therefore believe that the

---

[1] I'll mention that *gere* also occurs in *The Meditations on the Supper of our Lord :* þey were : gere 658 ; he gert : smert 140 ; þey gerte : herte 654. Cf. *Helmers*, p. 54 ff.

Northumbrian by-form *styd* (cf. St. Mark, ch. i. 10, *oustyde* R, 35 *stouo* t *styd* L, *stowe* t *steyde* R) must be rejected. Moreover, compare the remarkable difference between the ryme-words in the *Cursor* and *Brunne*, and in *Hampole*, *The Towneley Mysteries*, *Barbour's Bruce*, and the *Insertion in Cursor* (*Of the Resurrection*, p. 985). In the latter piece we find such rymes as, *sted*, r. w. *ded* (adj.) 115, r. w. *hede* (head) 219, r. w. *brede* (bread) 414, 430, in the *Pricke of Conscience: sted*, r. w. *ded* (death) 1865, 3025, 3317, 3811, 4614; 1745, 1819, 1931, 2091, 2145, 2610, 2667, 2969, 3287, 6710, 7272, 7814, 9062; r. w. *ded* (adj.) 1705, 2193, 3879, 5216, 6510, 8548; 859, 2807, 3649, (*pl.*) 3981, 4608; r. w. *hed* (head) 3043, 5002, 5659, 9146; 8874; in the *Towneley Mysteries: stede*, r. w. *red* (counsel), *lede* (lead), *hede* (head) p. 227, r. w. *ded* (adj.) p. 262, r. w. *red* (adj.), ded, med (O.E. medu) p. 283, r. w. *bred* (bread) p. 234; in *Barbour's Bruce: steid*, r. w. *dede* (adj.) I. 609, IV. 421, VI. 312, IX. 46, XVI. 438, 664, XIX. 721, XX. 254. I'll add *deid* (adj.), r. w. *steid* 818, 820, from Henrysone's *Fables* (cf. Anglia, IX. 337) c. anno 1460, and *stede*, r. w. *ded* (adj.) 218, r. w. *red* (adj.) from *Lancelot of the Laik*, ab. 1490—1500. These rymes do not occur in the *Cursor* and *Robert de Brunne's Chronicle*, nor do they, so far as I know, with any Midland writer. As to the other ryme-words with *stede*, I do not see any difference between the *Cursor* and the properly Northern or Northumbrian writers.

Observ. 1. Remarkable are the two rymes : *pott* (sb.), r. w. *fott* (inf.) C y 12310, and in the *Additions*, which are likely to belong to the same dialect as the *Cursor*, *þou sotte, to fett* C 27025 (F v. r.). In the body of lines the reading *fott* occurs in several places, cf. *fot* C, *focche* F, *fet* G 5625, *fotte* C, *focche* F, *fete* G 5091, 14965, 19704 (also E), *fott* C, *fot* F, *fett* G 7394, 7395, *fote* C', F om., *fett* G 16570, *fottes* (imp. 2 pl.) C, *ga focche* F, *fettis* 5021, *fott* (prt. 3 pl.) C F, *fett* G 5705, *fott* (pp.) C F, *fette* G 7292, and in the *Additions: fott* (imp.) C, *focche* F, *fott* G 25462. The form *fott* is unknown to *Robert de Brunne* and *Hampole*, but I was happy enough to meet with O.E. *ȝefotia* Mr. 15, 44 (cf. Zur altnorthumbr. Laut- und Flexionslehre, von H. Hilmer, Goslar 1880, page 10). This northern form (besides *to fett*) deserves our particular attention.

Observ. 2. The abbreviated participles past are the same in *Brunne's Chronicle*, f. i. *get* (pp.), r. w. sujet (*adj.*) 15322, r. w. set (*pp.*) 648.—*steke*[1]

---

[1] As to the pp. *ysteke* (see Kölbing, *S. Tristrem*, page lxxvi), cf. *Seven Sages* 1360, from *steken* (st. vb.) trs. : to transfix, fix, fasten, shut up, close, cf. *E. E. A. P.*, B. 157, 352, etc., *intrs.*: to stick in, *pret.*: stek = stuck (was fastened) *Gaw.* 152 (see and correct

(*pp.*), r. w. *breke* (inf.) 13048.—Compare also the weak participle past *fet* (pp.), r. w. het (*prt.*) 11996, r. w. set (*pp.*) 8784.

Observ. 3. The same E (long and open) appears in French *were, werr* (war), r. w. forbere (*vb.*) 3453, 7355, r. w. ferre (*adv.*) 7071, r. w. nerre 7579.

51. O.E. *ea* before *ld* = M.E. *a* + *ld* and *e* + *ld*. The *Cursor* has both forms. Compare FALD (*adj.*), r. w. bald (*adj.*) 110, r. w. fortald (*prt.*) 9857.— FALD (*vb.*), r. w. tald (*prt.*) 8965; falden (*pp.*) 24348; fald (*pp.*), r. w. cald (*adj.*) 24491.—to HALD, r. w. wald (*prt.*) 6903; to behald, r. w. fald (*adj.*) 23451-2; heild (*prt.*), r. w. weld (*prt.*) 8446; halden (*pp.*) 51, 2664, 3981, 6560 etc., bihalden (*pp.*) 8103; helden (*pp.*) 9504 (C G), 9508 (C).—YEILD (*prs.*), r. w. heild (1 *pl. prs.* = *to incline*) 260, r. w. weild (*sb.*) 461; yald (prt.), r. w. tald (*pp.*) 209; he yeld C 21260, [y]eild (*prt.*), r. w. in weild 9484 (cf. T, F *om.*, biheld G); yolden (*pp.*) 9581.—to TELL : tald (prt.), r. w. ald (*adj.*) 2993, r. w. thicfald 11257; teld (prt.), r. w. held (*prt.*) 24956; tald (pp.), r. w. sald (*pp.*) 141 (teld, seld G), r. w. cald (*pp.*) 320, r. w. to behald 1331, r. w. fald (*sb.*) 23876; teld (pp.), r. w. feld (*pp.*) 7062, r. w. feld (*prt.*) 7174, r. w. biheild (*prt.*) 7398, 7554, 17490, r. w. geld (*adj.*) 10346, 10493, unteld (*pp.*), r. w. heild (*prt.*) 18549.—to QUELL 17268, queld (*prt.*) 17268; queld (*prt.*), r. w. held (*prt.*) 19467.—DWELD (*pp.*), r. w. teld (*pp.*) 17708, r. w. held (*prt.*) 19526.

Compare also *Tristrem*, which, besides *a, o*, has forms in *e*. Kölbing, in his edition, p. lxi, mentions l. 1073 ʒeld (= O.E. ʒeald), l. 1075 queld, r. w. scheld, feld, biheld (= biheŏld); l. 2311 held, l. 2315 teld, r. w. unselde, ʒeld (= ʒeldan); l. 3248 ʒeld, l. 3250 biheld, l. 3252 teld, r. w. feld. Mind that the forms *held, biheld* (infin.) are wanting in the *Cursor*.

Besides, compare *Sir Perceval*, from which Kölbing cites p. lxx, l. 1224 beholde (f. bihelde), r. w. schelde, felde, ʒelde.—In *Horstmann's Legenden*, 1881, we find, according to Wende,[1] p. 23, I. l. 141 bihelde, felde, VII. l. 534 dwelt (*prt.*), held.—*Sir Gawayn* has welde (*sb.*), forʒelde (*inf.*), felde (fealdan) 837-41, besides forʒelde 1279, double felde 890. Otherwise *a, o*. The *E. E.*

Morris's Glossary of *E. E. A. P.*). Further, compare 'Lancelot of the Laik' : *Quhill tyme cum eft that we schal of hym spek This processe mot closine ben and stek* (pp. = shut up, concluded) 315-16. The *Lancelot* also teems with the form *tone*, r. w. *gone* 2145, besides cf. 1054, 1071, 2299, 2713, 2921, 2939, 3344, 3399. The ryme in *Tristrem* (*ton*, r. w. *don* 1484) seems to me to prove that *o* in *ton* is rather shortening. Moreover, cf. *Gaw.* 2155 ff.: *one, grone* (vb.), *tone.*

[1] *Ueberlieferung und Sprache der me. Version des Psalters*, etc., von E. Wende. Breslau, 1884.

A. Poems have welwed (wealwian) C 475. Otherwise *a, o*. Mind that the *Cursor* only knows *fald* (adj. and vb.).

Robert de Brunne's Chronicle has *a + ld* and *e + ld*, besides *o + ld*. Cf. Helmers, *Ueber die Sprache Rob. Mannyng's of Brunne*, etc. Göttingen 1885, p. 20 : l. 16198 y halde, calde; l. 16502 hald, cald (*pp.*), l. 16124 Osewald, cald ; l. 3714 halde (*prs.[1] pl.*), calde (*prt. pl.*). There are, however, a good many instances in *e + ld*, about which Helmers is altogether silent. Cf. teld, eld (*adj.*) 854, elde (*adj.*), to bihelde 1802, telde, of elde 7284, which are not strictly conclusive. Compare, however, teld (*prt.*), r. w. held (*prt.*) 10798, 11910 etc.; teld (*pp.*), r. w. held (*prt.*) 11258, 12816, 14054 ; besides ʒelde (*vb.*), r. w. wolde (*prt.*) 6268. Consider also : ʒold (*pp.*), r. w. wolde (*prt. pl.*) 10808 ; calde (*prt.*), r. w. halde[2] (*pp.*, Qu. ʒif = is) 282, cf. l. 5520.

Hampole knows only forms in *a + ld*. The *Bruce* has also *a + ld*, as, tald, to hald IV. 68, hald (*inf.*), yald (*prt.*) IV. 172, tald (*prt.*), sald (*prt.*) V. 610, ʒald, vald VII. 118 etc.

I beg the reader still to compare *delf* (prt.) C, *dalue* F 21146, *delf* (prt.) C G, *dalue* F 21530. The weak form *delued* C G 18562, 16877 seems to be a younger form. Besides, *threll* r. w. *tell* 10914 etc., *thrall* r. w. *all* 5506, 9480, r. w. call 5718 etc. ; *barn* r. w. *forfarn* (pp.) 1232, 20050, *barn* r. w. *warn* 12453, 17732 etc., *bern* r. w. *wern* (pl. prt.) 20450 etc. ; *ern* (eagle) 21314, 21333, *arn* 13444. As regards *er* (pl. sb.) 2541, *ern* (2 pl.) 4878, *are* 221, we have probably to think of O.N. influence and O.E. *aron*. But cf. *earon*, which seldom occurs in the *Psalter*.

52. The *Cursor* reads *yet* and *yit* (O.E. ʒêt, ʒîͤt[*a*]).

The East-Midland dialect of *Havelok* knows *yete* and *yet*. *yete* occurs in the body of lines, and *yet* is proved in its ryming with *fet* (pl. sb.) 1320, 2041.

Robert de Brunne's Chronicle has, so far as I know, only one ryme of *yit*, r. w. Berit 5760. In the body of lines, ʒit and ʒut occur. There is no trace of *yet* in the Lambeth MS. I have no references to *Handlyng Synne* at present.

The West-Midland dialect of the *E. E. Allit. Poems* knows *yet* only.

---

[1] Helmers has by mistake *prt. plur.*

[2] As to *halde* (pp.), the two passages cited by Kölbing, *Tristrem*, p. lxxv from the *E. E. Psalter* (xviii l. 11, and cxviii l. 72) do not hold good, for in both places the adjective *hold* (cf. the common ryme *gold, hold* in other Northern writers, f. i. *Cursor* 13264, 21318, 23861, 27602 ; *Brunne's Chronicle* 16230) is meant. Compare *O. E. Texts*, and the various readings of the passages.

Compare strete, r. w. ȝete A 1058-60; hete, counterfete, r. w. ȝete A 533 ff.; to reȝet, reset (O.F.), r. w. ȝet A 1063 ff. Besides cf. swete, strete, mete (adj.), r. w. ȝete A 1056 ff.

The Northern dialect of *Hampole* has only ȝyt, cf. *The Pricke of Conscience*, as, ȝyt, r. w. it 1048, 8220, r. w. writ 4292, r. w. wit (sb.) 7806, r. w. pyt (sb.) 8770; writ, r. w. yhit 4068, 4148; visit, r. w. ȝyt 1981; wit (sb.), r. w. ȝyt 22, 6468, 7433; witte (vb.), r. w. yhit 8198, 4735.

The *Cursor* has mete (vb.), r. w. yete 1198; ȝeit, r. w. forleit (vb.) 2288. The other readings are worth mentioning at full length.

> ll. 795-6 For of that ilk appul bitt
> Þair suns tethe ar eggeid yitt (ȝeitt G, F om.).

The reference is found in ll. 28700-1:

> And al bot for an appul bitt
> Þat godd forbedd and þai it ete (ett it C G).

C G's reading *ett it* seems to deserve the preference.

> ll. 1875-6 How sal we o þis waters weit (wete F, witt G T)
> Quedir þai be fulli (aught G) fallen yeit (ȝete F, ȝeitt G, ȝitt T).
> ll. 13082-3 Iohn bigan at þam to wijt (asse F, witt G T)
> Quer iesus crist, his lauerd, yeitt (wasse F, ȝeitt G, ȝitt T).

I have not been able to find any line that would confirm *weit*, O.E. weotan. The forms *wite, witt, wit* are just as common in the *Cursor* as in *Hampole*, and in *Brunne's Chronicle*, where also *witen* is proved by *wyten* (vb.), r. w. *wryten* (pp.) 1618.

> ll. 20053-4 And mare þar-of i sai þe yett (ȝou ȝet F, ȝu ȝeit G)
> Qua hertili hers or redis it.

I have no reason for altering the ending. *yett*, therefore, must be changed into *yit*.

53. The *Cursor* reads *proue, couer*.

The North and North-East-Midland shows the same phonology.

O.F. *ue* (= Lat. ŏ (ŭ) *sine positione*), which seems to me the *i*-umlaut of *o* = Mod. Fr. *eu*, when in the same position (cf. *heureux*), turned into *e* in Anglo-Norman, as spoken in the South and West of England, while it returned to *o* in the mouth of an Anglian man.

ov as well as *ev* is capable of being vocalized, so that we meet with the diphthong *eú* final in the West Saxon dialect, while the Anglian monophthongizes *ou* into *ū* (still written *ou*). I see a remarkable difference between *eú* final, and *eu* followed by consonants.

In M.E. $\breve{y}$, $\breve{\imath}$, $\breve{e}$ are sometimes confounded, as on the Continent. So Western u stands in place of these sounds, all of which are very like an open i sound ($= y$ in Scotch). The sound is far from being the Modern French u, or the proper German $\ddot{u}$. I rather compare it with a High German $\ddot{u}$ in the mouth of a Low German; and this must be what the Normans (of Low German descent) adopted from the Franks. Therefore, I do not think that in *bicuver*, E. E. A. P.-B 1327, there is any sound like French $\ddot{u}$ or $\ddot{o}$; but I see in it only the Southern representative of $\breve{e}$, to which it is nearest in sound.

A spelling like *controeved*, B 266, shows us a scribe who only assimilates the original orthography to his pronunciation. The same is found in *doel* G 558, B 158 etc., or in *dulful* T 1517; cf. *delful* G 560, B 400.

Quite a different thing is French $\bar{u}$. Cf. 'Sir Gawayne,' *hewe*, *salue*, *remwe* 1471 ff., the E. E. A. P. *trwe*, *blwe* (adj.), *grewe* (prt.), *remwe* A 421 ff., *knewe*, *swe*, *due*, *hwe*, *vntrwe*, *remwe* A 889 ff. Here we see that, in *remeve*, *ev* is vocalized into *eú*, so that it is the diphthong *ew* with which *salue*, *due* (cf. O.F. *dëu*) ryme. It must be understood that the articulation is loose and open, which is quite contrary to French and High-German habits. Therefore I may adopt for *salue*, *due* the phonetic value of $\dot{u}$, without thinking of a modern French $\ddot{u}$-sound; but, as the figure implies, my articulation begins with a short e and ends in an open, rather half-long u-sound, which is liable to be confounded with both Scotch y and English $\breve{o}$ ($\ddot{u}$). In this way I explain the *Bruce's* ryme: *verty*, *douchtely* XVIII. 439, and Hampole's *accuse*, *dos* 5485, *duse* ($=$ *dos*), *use* 6381, 7634, *stature*, *pore* ($=$ *poure*). Besides, it regularly rymes with the diphthong *ew*, and with u in the *Towneley Mysteries*, as *trew*, *verteu* p. 65, *vertue*, *new* p. 75, *trew*, *new*, *Iesu* p. 157, *Iesus*, *us*, *vertus*, *us* p. 173, *Iesu*, *rew* p. 231. Observe, too, *Iues*, *rues* ($=$ rewest) p. 228, *rew*, *trew*, *Iew*, *new* p. 271. In *Hampole* we meet with such rymes as *Ihesu*, *dru* (prt.) 9616, besides *vertue*, r. w. *Ihesu* 6255, r. w. *value* 9199; in 'The Bruce' *reskew* (inf.), *now* XI. 275,[1] *aventure*, *sture* (adj.) XII. 92. The *Cursor* has rymes with $\bar{u}$, as, *tru* (vb.), *vertu* 11792, *scou*, *iesu* 12033-4, *iesu*, *nu* ($=$ now) 11360, 22474. Besides observe *destru*, *iesu* 22133, *now*, *juu* 3943-4. The *ew*-rymes are strictly observed in the *Cursor* with two exceptions. The one exception is *juu*, which is easily explained, inasmuch as the initial j absorbed the following glide-vowel, which is very like y. The other is *throu*, *drou* 24317-8, where the spelling of the scribes is striking, so that I have no doubt that the glide-vowel in *throu* was dropped.

---

[1] In 'Bruce' *trow* (inf.), *now* IV. 238, and *trew* (vb.), *rew* (vb.) II. 327.

Now I can bring forward the following rymes from the *Early-English Alliterative Poems*. I remark here that *e·* in an open syllable can turn into *e.* in a close syllable, f. i. *preved*, where the final *e* does not prevent the first *e* to stand 'in positione' (= *vẹd*); but it is not necessary to declare *e* in *vẹd* to be altogether silent. A 'slurring-over' takes place, as Prof. Skeat justly calls it; and it is by this way of pronouncing that Ten Brink's 'schwebende betonung' is produced. Compare *heved* (sb.), *veved* (leafed), *dreved*, *keved*, *preved* A 973 ff., *sweven*, *meven*, *cleven*, *dyscreven*, *leven*, *weven* A 62 ff. *gef* (prt.), *pref* (sb.), *þef* (O.E. *þẹof*) A 270 ff. Besides compare *kever* C 223, 485, G 750 etc., *kerchefs* (MS. *kerchofes*) G 954, *bicever* (MS. *bicuuer*) B 1327; *recever* (MS. *recover*) C 279, *contreued* (MS. *controeved*) B 266; moreover, *peple* G 123, C 371, *pepul* D 109, *del* A 250; *preve* G 262, *kevered* G 1755.

The same phonology is found in *Chaucer*, whose dialect has undergone the influence of the South (the Court language). Cf. *Ten Brink*, § 67 δ, *beef*, *preef*, *repreef*, *preue*, *repreue*, *remeue*, *keuere*, *peeple*.

Quite different is the phonology in the East-Midland and North-Eastern dialects. Compare *R. de Brunne's Chronicle;* as *loued*, *proued* 2312, *proue*, *loue* 2494, *proued*, *loued* 14406, *pouere* (= poor), *recouere* (sb., *recouerere* Pet. MS.) 16216; also *proue*, *byhoue* 2422, *byhoue*, *proue* 2704, 6516. As to the vocalization of *ov* into (*ou*) *ū*, cf. *vertu*, *prou* 7766, *Dertmue* (Pet. MS.), *rescue* 9982. Note the argument: *vertu*, *remue* 9945-6, *remue* (MS. *remewe*), *rescue* (MS. *rescuwe*) 9176, *Minumue* (f. *Minnmue?*), *remue* 164. Besides, compare *neuow* (*neuow*, Lamb. MS.), *prow* 4432, *rescue* (MS. *rescuwe*), *neuow* (MS. *neuew*) 5256.

Hampole's *Pricke of Conscience* has the following rymes: *loue*, *byhoue* 70, r. w. *proue* 1087, 6221, 8380, *proue*, *loue* 3531, 9492, *loued*, *byhoued* 945, r. w. *proued* 9040, *loues*, *proues* 1081, 1113, 1845, r. w. *byhoues* 1365, r. w. *moues* 4708, 8398, *proues*, *droues* 1319, r. w. *controues* 1561. Besides observe *stature*, *pore* (= poure) 8258.

The *Towneley Mysteries* have: *proue*, *louf* (*sb.*) p. 36, *foode*, *behoued* p. 46. From the *Bruce* I have only taken down *couir*, *discouir* IV. 124. The *Cursor* has the following rymes, *loue*, *proue* 9038, *pouer*, *couer* 1798, besides take *dole*, *fole* 13040, 10456 (G); *behoue*, *proue* 3656, *proue*, *behoue* 4384. Moreover, note *neuow*, *enow* 2443 (G). In the body of lines, C as well as G, of course, has *neueu*, cf. 2443 C, 3885 G.

54. The *Cursor* reads *wiꝥ*, but *mid*, too. The various readings of the MSS. are *wid*, *wit*, *with*, and *emid*. There are a good many passages in which

the scribes use *emid*, when *with* would be expected, and there is no doubt that
it is used in the same way as *a mel*, *emel*. Its proper meaning is found in
ll. 14620, 17482, but instead of *emid* or *amid* we can read *o* (= *on*) *midde* (cf.
O.E. *on middum, middan*). *emid* appears to be a weakened form from *amid*,
and *a* in *amid* is nothing but Western *an* = *on*. Ormin, who reads *a mang*,
a weȝȝ, cannot be considered on this account as a model of a purely Anglian
dialect. He must have lived near the West-Saxon area. The *Cursor*, therefore, would have to read *omidde*.

Now observe ll. 4251-2, *in all þe dedis þat he did, He sagh driȝtin was him
emid*. F as well as G has various readings. There is no doubt that *emid* is
wrong. I would, therefore, alter C's reading into *mid*, which could still have
been used by a Midland writer of the 13th century. The same correction
will be found necessary in ll. 4626, 10051, 14015, 23490 (where *has* must be
altered into *is*, cf. F's alteration). *mid* is retained in l. 20452, in that part
which treats of the Assumption, and is declared to be of Southern origin. It
is also found in the *Finding of the Cross*, l. 21590. There is some reason to
believe that the author was rather a stranger to *mid*, and that its use in his
dialect was somewhat obsolete at the time he wrote the *Cursor*. However,
we must remember that by his stay at Cambridge,—where he must have
studied at a time when the memory of Edmund Rich of Canterbury and
Robert Grosseteste of Lincoln was still living,—and by his study of more
Southern sources, he may have been led to use a word which his own country-
men had almost forgotten.

55. The *Cursor* reads *to schaw, schawed, schawn*.

The M.E. development of O.E. -êaw- is not alike in all words or dialects.
We see at the end of the 13th and 14th centuries, *þeu* (O.E. *þêaw*), *deu*
(O.E. dêaw), *hew* (O.E. hêawan) in all dialects. It is in the South and West
that the latest examples of -eaw- can be given, cf. þeau, eau, *Hom.* ii. 47,
þeawes, *A. R.* 240, þeauwes, þewes, þæwes, þeuwes, *Laȝ.* 2147 etc. (cf. *Stratm.*[3]
585), forheawed, ystrawed, *Sir Ferumb.* 2689. But see in *Hampole* thewes
5548, the *Towneley Mysteries* to hew p. 48, *The Cursor* theu 13275, deu
22464, *Havelok* þewes 282, *Rob. de Brunne's Chronicle* þewes 9767, *Chaucer*
hewen (*Ten Brink*, § 43, γ), *E. E. A. P.* þewes C 30, *Sir Tristrem* hewe
190, *Sir Ferumbras* hewe 986, tohewe 676 etc.

But as *to schaw*, we see in *Hampole*, Berthelmewe, shewe 967, 1163,
shewe, Mathewe 4354, 5121, 6131, besides cf. shewes, thewes 1883, shewed,
lewed 2608, 4414, 5302, thewes, shewes 5549, lewed, shewed 1118, 2445,

6267 ; in *E. Metric. Homilies* schau, knau p. 3, in *Havelok* shauwe, knawe 2206, 2784, 1401 (where *sheue, knewe* must be altered), mawe (O.E. mâwan[1]), shawe 1853 (MS. mowe, shewe), shawn (*pp.*), knawn (MS. shewed, knawed) 2056, shawe, lawe (MS. shewe, lowe) 1698, in *Rob. de Brunne's Chronicle* þewes, schewes (Pet. MS. om.) 9768, shewed (*pp.*), lewed (*adj.*) 16151, in *Tristrem* shewe (*inf.*), hewe, newe, trewe 1565, shawe (*imp.*), drawe, rawe, knawe, plawe 3097, in *E. E. A. Poems* (but without ryme) shewed B 122 etc., shawe B 1599, 1626, in *Sir Gawayne* shawe G 27, in *Sir Ferumbras* shaue, haue 1542, in *Bruce* shawis (*prs.*), blawis (*prs.*) IV. 122, shaw (*inf.*), saw (*prt.*) IV. 621, aw (*sb.*), shaw (*inf.*) V. 132.

The *Cursor* has : to scau, he sau 1351, drau (*inf.*), scau 2366 etc., knaun, scaun (MS. knaud, scaud) 1162, scaun, draun 19890. Besides cf. *laud* (O.E. lǽwed) in the *Cursor*, and *E. Metr. Hom.* (p. 5), while other dialects have *lewed*. The total absence of *schew* in the rymes, and the very rare occurrence of *schaw* in the body of lines, make me believe that *schew* belongs to the Northumbrian scribe.

To find our way thro' this comparison, it is necessary not only to view the change from a question of dialect, but also from that of a difference of time. In the North—where the inflection of the infinitive was dropped at the earliest time, and sooner in the East than in the West—it is evident that final *aw* was easily changed into *ew*. But on account of the different ways of accentuating the diphthong, it was also retained much longer in the West than the East. This difference may be seen to this very day in such words as *house*, which is vulgarly pronounced as far as the West of Yorkshire like *háus* (as Germans generally do in speaking English), while the standard pronunciation requires *hæûs*.[2] It is known that *shawen* is to be derived from *schǽwen*, so that *æ* was broadened by way of lowering. Now, when in the East the inflection of the infinitive was weakened more and more, the stress was felt at the end ; and by way of raising the first element of the final diphthong into *æ* or *e.*, the result was *ew*. This change is very likely to have taken place in the 14th century, as may be inferred from *Robert de Brunne's Chronicle*, while towards the end of the 13th century (cf. *Havelok*) *aw* was still used. In the

---

[1] Cf. L. Hohmann, *Ueber Sprache und Stil des ac. Lai Havelok þe Dane*, Marburg, 1886. He, besides some other mistakes, makes another when he puts *mowe = movoir*.

[2] It is interesting to compare in this respect the Cockney pronunciation of *house*, which is very like *û*. But mind, it is a shut syllable which is shortened, while in *how* the tendency must be towards *heû*. Thus O.E. *êaw* appears to me pronounced like modern *æû* in *house*.

North (Yorkshire), of course, this change may have taken place some time earlier. *Hampole* gives no sufficient evidence of its earlier occurrence in the North. But we see that in the Scotch dialect (*Bruce*) broad *a* has still been kept. However, let us consider that from this reason (and others still to be mentioned) the *E. Metrical Homilies* do not belong to *Hampole*, as J. Small supposed. In *Tristrem*, where *shewe* and *schawe* appear, the infinitive *schewe* points to Southern influence.[1]

In the South, the development took its origin from *êaw*, which changed into *ew* directly; for no intermediate link like *aw* have I ever met with. Our modern pronunciation seems to want an explanation either from the analogy of other verbs, as *sow*, *mow*, *strow*, or from Scotch influence.

56. The *Cursor* reads *giue, liue*.

In O.E. occur *ȝeofan, ȝiefan (ȝyfan, ȝifan)*; *leofian (liofian), lyfian (libban)*. In M.E. there are *geuen, gyuen, giuen; leuien, leuen, liuien, liuen*. The East Anglian dialect appears to know only *ȝiuen, liuen*, cf. *Ormin, Havelok, Brunne*, and also *Chaucer*. In the North and the North-West, *geue, leue* are the usual forms; cf. *Hampole* (14th cent.), Cotton Insertion (14th cent.), *The Bruce* (14th cent.), *Henrysone* (15th cent.). In West-Midland and the bordering Northern districts, in the South and South-West, both forms are usual, cf. *E. E. A. Poems, Sir Gawayne, Langland, Ayenbite, Shoreham*, etc.

Wherever the forms *ȝeue, leue* only occur, it is easy to find conclusive rymes, but it is very difficult to account for the other rymes. We must recollect that short *i* and short *e* are frequently bound in rymes in every dialect, while long *i* and long *e* but seldom ryme with one another. Therefore, the argument *e contrario* must be admitted in a large work which afforded ample opportunity of using the well-known ryme-words in the same way.

I. HAMPOLE'S PRICKE OF CONSCIENCE: leue (to liue), greue (O.F.) 749, mischeues, leues 699, forȝeue, greue (*adj.*) 8344, ȝeue, greue (*vb.*) 4260, leued, greued 4596, 7088, Eue, leue 492, greues, leues 2889, 3007, 3355, 3521, 3609, 7437, forȝeue, greue 3861, greue (*vb.*), leue (*vb.*) 4352, 4646, 7670, 8012, 8154, byleue (*dat.*), ȝeue 4336. It is the long close *e*. The past participle has a rather short vowel, so that the ryme *schriuen, forȝeuen* 3197, 3301 is not con-

---

[1] This Southern influence may account also for the occurrence of *ew* in all other districts where *aw* had been pronounced before. So Hampole and Robert de Brunne may have adopted it during their stay in the South.

clusive. The scribe,[1] whose pronunciation is *giue, giuen, liue, liued*, writes : *lyues* 699, *lyfe, griefe* 748-9, *forgyue, gryfe* 8343-4, *gryefe, lyefe* 4645-6.

II. COTTON INSERTION (2nd hand), page 958, l. 77 geen (*pp.*), eghen.— HENRYSONE : geif (*inf.*), leif (*inf.*) 507-8. THE BRUCE : leif, geue (*prt.* MS. E, gaf C) VI. 158 ; the ryme *giffin, driven* IV. 136 is not conclusive, but cf. *dreuen* in *Cursor* MS. E. As to *geue* cf. E. E. A. P. : *gef*, pref (sb.) A 270 ff.

III. E. E. A. POEMS : gef C 226, geuen B 259, 1627, geuen, þriuen, striuen A 1190.—'Gawayne,' *as*, ȝef 1964, geuen 920, gif 288. These instances are not conclusive for the author. But cf. A 68 dyscreuen, cleuen, leuen and *Hampole's* leued, descreued 1923.

IV. SIR FYRUMBRAS : leue (*inf.*), greue 4560. Otherwise compare *Carstens, Zur Dialectbestimmung*, etc., p. 12, where the material given is only conclusive for the scribe.

V. HAVELOK : shriuen, gyuen 364-5 (cf. striue, on liue (*sb.*) 362-3), liueden, clyueden 1299-300, liue, ȝyue (*sb.*) 357-8. The scribe writes f. i. ȝeue, liue, cf. Glossarial Index, p. 156.

VI. ROBERT OF BRUNNE'S CHRONICLE : gyue (*sb.*), lyue (*vb.*) 13481-2, vn-gyuen, þryuen 6545-6, giue, liue *et vice versâ* frequent. The argument may be taken from an alteration adopted by the Lambeth scribe, cf. ll. 5425-8 :

> He saw wel—weel he mought hit leue
> þat oþer truage wold he no geue
> Ne þe Romayns schuld it neuere wynne
> Whyle Wyder rengned kyng þer-ynne.

Now the Petyt MS. has *till he mot lyue*, and omits ll. 5427-8. There is reason enough to believe that Robert meant to say : 'He saw well that as long as Wyder should live he would give no other tribute.' The source of the Lambeth MS.—for this MS. is a second-hand one—preferred *geue*, and perhaps rejected *till that*, used like the Latin 'donec' ; or, which is more likely, *weel he mought hit leue*, is an alteration of the Lambeth scribe, who knew *geue*, but (as is seen from the MS.) preferred *liue*. He then added ll. 5427-8 to make

---

[1] I have worked out a critical ryme-index which I shall publish with the text to be edited. In the same way I have been working on *Tristrem, The Early English Psalter, The Seuen Sages, Robert of Brunne's Chronicle, Havelok the Dane.* I had an opportunity of collating *Havelok* with Laud MS., and shall have some emendations to give. In the summer of 1887 I copied, by the advice of Dr. Morris, *The Seuen Sages* from Cotton Galba E IX. without knowing that Prof. Kölbing had done so previously. Besides, I collated *The Early English Psalter.* As my criticism stands on a different ground, I hope I shall not interfere with Prof. Kölbing. Dr. Furnivall has printed in his edition a Ryme-index to *Robert's Chronicle* from the Lambeth MS.

up the preceding patch words. So that I have good reason to believe that the
original ran very like this :

> He saw weel til he mought liue
> That he ne wold other truage giue.

In the North the negation *ne* was generally abandoned as early as the 14th
century.

VII. THE CURSOR, as, fordriuen, giuen 23655-6 (cf. fordriue (*inf.*), liue
(*sb.*) 23753-4), driuen (*pp.*), for to liuen 24575-6, thriuen, giuen 14806-7, liue,
give very frequent. The scribes often prefer *e* instead of *i*; f. i. *fordreuen*,
reuen E 22635-6, etc., but that cannot surprise us after what I have stated
about the dialect of the MSS. It is important for me that I never found in
such a large work as the *Cursor* any such ryme as occurs in *Hampole*, the
Cotton Insertion, or *Sir Fyrumbras.*

Of a like interest is O.E. -*scipe*, seldom -*sciepe;* cf. Sievers, § 98, Rem.
I have observed in Hampole's *Pricke of Conscience* that the common suffix is
-*shepe* proved by rymes, as, kepes, worshepes 1139, worshepes, kepes 56,
felawshepe, kepe 5032, r. w. slepe 8076, shenshepe, kepe 381, r. w. depe
7136, worshepe, kepe 597, 5785, 8528, 9022, depe, schenshepe 7932. It is
worth while to mention the various readings of the MSS. which, as was to be
expected, use *schipe* and *schepe*, as *shenshepe* T 17467, *shenshepe* F 19448,
scenscep C T 18172, *wirscep* C, *worshepe* F, *worshepe* 7022, *worshepe* F 4628,
5980, F T 2439, 3236, also *to worshepe* F T 1937, besides *felawshepe* F T
1159, *felaghscep* C 7882, 15929, *felawshepe* F 13267, *frenscep* C F T 23637.
In all these passages *worshipe* occurs in G. I have found -*scipe*, as, *egypte*,
r. w. *wirscipe* (worship) 5980, 4628, r. w. witslip 12901, r. w. scipp 24830; so
so that I would read *worschip* or *wirschip, frendschip,*[1] *felawschip, schendschip*[1]
for the *Cursor.* Compare Ormin's and Chaucer's -*shipe.* Noteworthy is
felawscap, r. w. *spak* C F (G T have *spak, evyl pack*) 2212.

57. I. The CURSOR reads the diphthong *eʒ* or *ey* :

(1) = O.E. -*œh* (W.S. -*eah*), as, sey (*sg.* and *pl. prt.*) 3779, 18961, etc.
(*besides,* sau).

(2) = O.E. *éʒ-, -éh* (W.S. *œʒ-, éaʒ-, -éah*), as, eye 3780, wreye (to accuse)
16466, ney 732, hey 1041, stey 22724, vpstey 203. As to *stey*, cf.
O.Northumb. *sté*[*h*], O.N. *steig*, and after *g* having been dropped, *sté* (= *stei*),
so that O.E. *stiʒan* (Class I. according to Sievers) must be referred to the
second class of strong verbs.

---

[1] Cf. *frendschip* E 23637, *scendscip* E 19448.

(3) = O.E. êȝ-, ǽȝ- (W.S. ēoȝ-), as, ley (inf.) 659, fley (sb.) 5959, fley (vb.) 1782, drey (to suffer).

(4) = O.E. êȝ-, ŷȝ- = i-umlaut of auȝ, as, leyne 2738 G, 1549, 5281.

(5) = O.E. iȝ-, *eh-, as, wey (O.E. wìȝa) 8419, stey (inf.) 17758, 18668, sey (inf.) 4077, 6706, etc.

Apparent exceptions are hiȝt (height) 1339, 22994, sliȝt (sleiȝt) 5562, 6662, and wiȝt (weight), though, in the body of lines, occurs once weȝht 21429.

Further observe : dey (O.N.) 660, etc., sley (O.N.) 4312, drey (O.N.) 731, 5511.

These words are never found in rymes with ē close or open, nor with ī.

II. HAVELOK.   hey, sley 1083-4, eye, fleye 1812-13, 1826-7, leye, hey 2010-11, heye, eie 2544-5, heye, fleye 2750-1.   hey, fri 1071-2 is to be altered into hey, sley, cf. 1084.

III. HAMPOLE.   deghe, heghe 2177, r. w. eghe 8160, dreghe (vb.), deghe 2045, etc., r. w. eghe 6524, etc., eghe, dreghe 2235, r. w. fleghe 6884, deghed, fleghed 2173, heghe, deghe 2205, etc., r. w. sleghe 7570, fleghe, heghe 9550, r. w. eghe 7738, etc., [vn]sleghe, deghe 1939, 2663, sleght, weght 1790, r. w. heght 7698.

IV. ROBERT OF BRUNNE'S CHRONICLE.   In Robert's as well as Chaucer's dialect (cf. Ten Brink, §§ 40 and 41), O.E. êȝ-, êh, ëȝ- have become ē·y, ē·i, ɛī, ī, i. e. East-Midland, in general, vocalized the final consonant earlier than the Northern dialect did.   While we still have in Hampole's dialect ē·ȝ, it has often turned into ɛī, through ē·i, in Brunne's Chronicle.

A. ē·i, as, seye (1 sg. prs.), deye (inf.) 1084, to wreye (MS. wrye), weye (way) 1105 (cf. weye, valeye 1115, seys, weys (pl.) 1372, seye (1 sg. prs.), weye 1732, etc.), deye, weye 1259, on hey, þey fley 1413, þey fley (MS. fleyghe), to deye 1468, seye (inf.), deye 2216, fleye (inf.), sleye 2257-8, seye (inf.), eye (sg.) 2894, heye (pred. pl.), eye (dat.) 3447-8, in a tour hey, fley (sg. prt.) 5291, ley (1 prs. sg., tell lies), fley (pl. prt.) 8189, stey (prt.), fley (prt.) 8341, deye, leye (to lay) 9023, fley (prt. sg.), ney (adv.) 9792, hey, fleye (inf.) 10891-2, stey (pl. prt.), pley (sb.) 11375, drey (adj. far), ney 12205-6, ney, a drey 1041-2, deye (inf.), aweye 12285, weye, fleye (inf.) 13872.

B. ɛī, as, dreye (to suffer), Italye 745, worthy, hey 2698, affye, heye 2452, felonye, deye 2790, heye, abye 3481, hey, ky 4731, curteysly, hey 6884, hardy, sley 12092, ney, maistri 12517, eyne (pl.), pyne 6939, Quyntalyn, eyn (pl.) 12672, body, hey 16404, dreye (vb.), bye (to purchase) 16421, flyes (sb.), styes (sb.) 2625, lye (to lie), flye (inf.) 12104, hye (to hasten), eye (sg.)

15868, cry, ney 1654, sleye, vndermye (*inf.*) 3431, glorie, flye (*inf.*) 7078, lye (*pl. prs.* tell lies), dye (*inf.*) 14305-6.

I have good reason to believe that the monophthongization of ē·i began to take place at the end of words, *i. e.* in adjectives when not in an oblique case, or in a plural attributive, in adverbs when the final *e* could be given up, in infinitives when the final *en* could be dropped, and in substantives not in the dative. The final *es*, where they appear in the MSS., must be considered from a different point of view than that generally taken. In the 15th century, when the tendency of shortening long vowels before final consonants was evident, such as had been kept long were marked by an additional final *e*, which had no phonetic value whatever. Therefore I read *eyn*, r. w. *pȳn* 6939.

Chaucer, whose South-Midland dialect shows the vocalization of ȝ in ēȝ by at least one generation earlier than the North-Midland, has gone one step further. In his dialect we meet only with *flyen*, *flye*, *dryen*, *lyen*, *ye*, *sly*, *hy*. In double forms, like *se·igh*, *sy*, *deyen*, *dyen*, *sleight*, *slight*, *ne·igh*, *ny*, the latter seems to me the development of the former. As to *abeyen*, *abyen*, *seigh*, *say*, I refer to Ten Brink, *Chaucer*, § 41, Anm.

V. TRISTREM, as, beiȝe, heiȝe, neiȝe, sleiȝe 265 ff., neiȝe, sleiȝe, beiȝe, heiȝe, seiȝe 3016 ff., sleiȝe, neiȝe, seiȝe, heye, dreiȝe 3027 ff., deiȝe (MS. *dye*), heye, leiȝe (O.E. lêȝ, lŷȝ, flame,[1] MS. *lye*), seyȝe 3125 ff., deiȝe (MS. *dye*), wreiȝe (MS. wrie), heiȝe, leiȝe (1 *sg. prs.*, tell lies) 2148 ff. Besides, there is *hiȝt*, as in the *Cursor* and *Chaucer*.

VI. E. E. ALLITERATIVE POEMS AND SIR GAWAYNE. In order to understand the phonology of these poems, with which several scribes have meddled, it is necessary first to advert to such rymes as A 800 : felonye, query (lat. quære), debonerte, he (*pron.*); A 231 : Grece, nece, pryse, spyce; A 68 : dyscreuen, cleuen, leuen, or such spellings as folé G 1545, sorquidre G 2457, contraré B 4266.

The phonology of the *E. E. A. P.* and *Gawayne* is almost the same as is found in the Northern dialect as early as the second half of the 14th century. In late 14th and 15th centuries the purely Northern writers teem with instances in which the (front) palatal is given up, and even rymes between *e* and derivative *y* (for which slight *e* is put) are allowed. Compare *Barbour*,

---

[1] Kölbing's translation of *Ysonde biheld þat lye vnder leues liȝt = Ysonde sah die an welche unter leichten blättern liegen* (?) is wrong, as the editor has admitted by the point of interrogation. The text runs on thus : *Tristrem hye þer seyȝe.* Ysonde's fancy is inflamed with love. The poetical description of her vision is not unusual. (þat can never be ' those who.')

as, de, he; de, fle (= to flee); e (eye), he (*pron.*); *Morte Arth.*, as, sey, me; leye (MS. sye, lye), he (*pron.*); he (high), be (*inf.*); *Thom. of Erceldoune*, as, wree (MS. wrye), me; hee (MS. hye), tre; lee (to tell lies, MS. lye), me; dee (MS. dye), be; and *Town. Myst.*, as, de, he; thirte, be, the; companye, se;[1] *Henrysone*, as, de, fle (to flee) 1126, ee (eye), he (*pron.*) 11643, ee (eye), diuinitie, slie (*adj.*) 664, 666-7, hie (*adj.*), tre 871-2, pietie, crueltie, degree 1595, 1597-8, hie (haste), be (*inf.*) 307-8, sensualitie, fle, propertie 783, 785-6.

The *E. E. A. P.* and *Gawayne* represent the transition period (ab. 1350). The palatal is vocalized and forms a glide, as in modern *day* (= dēᵉ). In the Anglian dialect the chief vowel is close, in the Saxon it is rather open.[2] I'll first give the MS. readings, and add my own spelling: discrye (*inf.*), syʒe (*pret.*) G 81, yʒe, studie G 228, in hyʒe, cortaysye, wyʒe (man) G 245, hyʒe, by (*prep.*) G 2087; yʒe, lyʒe (*sb.*), dyʒe, syʒe, sorquydryʒe, tryʒe (*vb.*) A 302, hyʒe (*adj.*), cortaysie A 453, byʒe (*sb.*), cortaysie A 466, byye (to buy), cortayse A 477, hit, Iustyfiet, tryed, asspyed, dyed A 697, Galalye, Ysaye, professye, dryʒe (O.N.) A 816, sye (*prt.*), asspye (O.F.), plye (O.F.) A 1032.

Whatever may be the spelling of the scribe, it is hardly possible to represent exactly the sounds as spoken in the West. In adopting final *ie*, I connect with it the idea that *i* is open, and rapidly slides into half-long *e*, so that I do not hear any remarkable difference between the endings in *heie* and *cortaisie*. It must be understood that a word like *by* is pronounced differently in the West and East. Therefore I would write *eie, studie; hie* (sb.), *cortaisie, wie; heie* (adj.), *by*, etc. It is even worth while to think of a modern spelling, like *eye*, etc.

VII. SIR FYRUMBRAS. The West-Midland (Southern division) dialect of the late 14th century is nearly the same as Chaucer's on this ground. Cf. fleʒ (*prt.*), neʒ 2183, steʒe (*pp.*), heʒe 5163 (corr.), steʒ (*sg. prt.*), heʒ 5731, slegh, hegh 3116.—nubbye, ounwrye 1849, ny, socoury 3168, hye, Normandye 1859, heʒ, þer-bey 623, dye, company 2507, crye, flye (*sb.*) 4930, vylonye, eye 2255, folye, ye 3433, Normaundy, wey (*sb.*) 3999 (cf. pray, way 1703, praye, away 1477, etc.).

I have no reason to believe that the rymes show a pure *i* sound; but as the South vocalized the guttural at a very early time, the diphthongal pronunciation produced the tendency to quicken at the end. The first element

[1] Cf. A. Brandl, *Thom. of Erceldoune*, Bln. 1880, where the question has been already broached.

[2] Now-a-days, too, there is a remarkable difference between Anglian 'day' and Southern 'day,' and between Northern and Southern 'day.'

lost its full sound on account of its being less open than in the other diphthongs of French origin, or in such as are derived from a short (open) vowel
and a guttural. There is no doubt that the West-Saxon dialect with its
broader pronunciation of diphthongs, never attained to a pure monophthongization, such as is seen in the purely Anglian dialects.

Compare also *Castle of Loue*, which is by about thirty years older than *Sir
Fyrumbras:* fey (faith), ney₃ 467-8 (Vernon MS. and Add. MS., while the
later Halliwell[1] MS. avoids the ryme), mastri, hye H, alast, fast V A 991.

58. O.E. ēōw, ēōw-, o₃-, u₃-, ó₃-, óh, ú₃-, úh have become *û* in the *Cursor.*

I. ēōw˙, which appears to consist of short vocal elements, turns into ow˙,
the glide vowel being dropped. M.E. *o* in *ow* remained short, as may be
proved by Ormin's spelling (cf. *trowwen*). But its further dialectic development appears different. While it is rather open in the West-Saxon dialect
when kept in the body of the word, it is rather close in the Anglian dialects
and such Northern districts as may have undergone the influence of Anglian
emigrants. Here *ow* turns into open *ū*[2], when it stands at the end of words;
there it turns into *aw*. The spelling of *ou* must have been retained for a long
time, though the ryme was in *ū*, or in *o.u.* But in the South, where the
inflection was kept, *ow* of the Anglian dialect remained in the body of the
word, and inclined towards *aw* only when it was spoken near the boundary
line of the West-Saxon dialect. The broad open *ow* is very well rendered by
aw in North West-Midland and in Lancashire; but the occurrence of *ow* in
the South of the Western dialect does not imply that *ow* is here close; nor are
the rymes which are found in this dialect always conclusive. It seems to me
quite wrong to take for granted that M.E. rymes must be correct. Old poets
were never better than modern ones. Therefore I believe that in the Midland
and Southern dialects of the 14th century, when *ow* from O.E. ēōw, ú₃, ó₃, etc.
is seen to ryme with *ow* from *âw*, the former must be considered to be
fluctuating between close *o* and open *o*. I need not refer to the different
shades of modern pronunciation which open *o* is liable to assume; my readers
will also know J. Wallis's chapter on the diphthongs.[3] The other sounds above-

---

[1] Now in the possession of the Bodleian Library.

[2] þó˙u = 'though,' is an apparent exception to this rule, for, though it may have been
borrowed from the Low German dialects, it might be expected that, when the guttural
was lost, the diphthong would also turn into *u*. But as it does not bear the stress in a
sentence, there is reason to believe that it retained its more backward sounding on that
account, and the spelling would not mistake much by keeping ₃ (þou₃).

[3] I. Wallisii Grammatica Linguae Anglicanae. Lond. 1765. Cap. I, Sect. iii.

mentioned change in nearly the same way when the gutturals become labialized, and the vowels are shortening.

Now we have in the *Cursor* tru (a remnant of historical spelling is *trow*, from *trowen*), r. w. nu 375, ȝow, i tru 5146, i tru, now 5249, tru (*inf.*), pru 5829, ȝow, tru (*inf.*) 5826, nou, to trou (tru C) 7222, we tru, r. w. vertu, hu (*adv.*), iesu, avou 17002, gru (to grow), r. w. tru 24495.

In *yu* (historical spelling *yow* = O.E. *ēow*) 4395, r. w. *hu*, I see[1] the general development of O.E. *ēow* final into *ew*, *w* being vocalized = *ĕú* (diphthong). Such a diphthong beginning a word has scarcely any other effect than *iū*, which gave *yū*.

II. O.E. *forhoȝian*, A.R. *forhowien*, Orm. *forhoȝhen*, later *forhowen* gives, when the inflection is lost, *forhu* 19949, r. w. *tru* (vb.).—O.E. *muȝan*, Orm. *muȝhen*, later *mowen* likewise turns into *mou* = *mu*, r. w. *þou* (pron.) 23559. A final *l* (as well as *m*, *n*, *r* in my opinion) does not retain the preceding diphthong, cf. O.E. *foȝel*, *fuȝel*, which changes into *ful*, r. w. *bul* (O.F.) 21269.— Very remarkable is the ryme *flou* (sg.), r. w. *wyndou* 1881-2. O.E. pl. prt. *fluȝon* gave *fluȝen*, *floȝen* (by analogy of the pp.) = *fluwen*, *flowen*, then *flow* = *flou* (*flu*). So *flou* (sg.) is originally a plural form. O.N. *windouga* underwent a monophthongization of its diphthong,[2] perhaps even before it was introduced into English, cf. windoge in *St. Genesis* and *Exod.* 602, then windowe, windou = windû. In the *Promptorium*, the historical spelling windowe[3] 529 is retained. Besides, compare a similar development in Dan. *vindue*.

III. O.E. *ȝenōh*, *ȝenōȝ* turned into *ynowȝ*, *ynow*, *ynou* (*inou*) = *ynū*, r. w. *drou*, 2190. Most remarkable is the ryme *throu* (prt.), *drou* 24317-8, which seems inaccurate, though the general pronunciation of Northern *ew* after *thr* must have soon become rather like *u*, in opposition to Southern usage.—O.E. *bōȝ*, *bōh*—*bouȝ*, r. w. *drouȝ*, *wouȝ*, *louȝ* 15024.—O.E. *slōh*, *slōȝ*—*slou* (historical spelling *slough* 152, or *slogh* 5662, partly owing to the more Northern scribe), r. w. *drou* 5662, r. w. *wou* (MS. wogh) = O.E. *wōh*, *wō*, Orm. *wōh* 1213-4.— O.E. *bāȝan*—*bu*, r. w. *nu*, *iesu*, to *tru* 15094; *bu*, *iesu* 17533, *buud*, *troud* 19379-80.

---

[1] Ten Brink prefers for *y* in *yu* the analogy of the O.E. nominative ȝe = M.E. *ye;* but Chaucer's *yow* ends likewise in a *u* sound.

[2] It is very likely that even in O.N. such forms as *windo·uga*, *windo·ga* were admitted, and that one of them was introduced into Old England; cf. A. Noreen, *Altisl. and Altn. Grm.*, Halle, 1884, 92 Anm., § 93 Anm. etc.

[3] From this spelling nothing whatever can be inferred for the pronunciation of the 15th century man. Final *e* had no phonetic value in his time.

For an illustration of the *Cursor*, compare *Havelok: plow* (sb.), *inow* 1017-8, *utdrow* (sg.), *slow* (sg.) 2632-3, *slowe* (pl.), *flowe* (pl. prt. of *flêân*) 2432-3, *trou* (MS. *trǫ*, printed text *tro*), r. w. *do* (inf.) 2862, *troud* (printed text *croud*, but MS. quite distinctly *troud*, as Stratmann had already conjectured), r. w. *God* 2338. From these few instances, which cannot be made stronger by other examples still found in *Havelok*, it may be justly inferred that final *ow* alone was = *ŭ*, but that the pl. prt. distinguished by *en* or *e* had the old pronunciation, the diphthongal character of which cannot be denied. Such forms as *trou* (inf.), *troud* (pp.), however, must be compared with the full forms *trowë* 1656, *trowedë* (*prt.*) 382, so that we have in *trou'*, *trou'd w* vocalized, and we see a tendency to open *u*. Rymes even between open *u* and *o* are not uncommon in Middle English, nor even now-a-days.

Robert of Brunne's Chronicle appears to confirm our supposition, cf. *God*, þey *trowd* (Pet. *trod*) 7358, 8112, *y trowe*, *bowe* (O.E. *boʒa*) 1523-4. Further compare *bowe* (inf.), *ynowe* (pl.) 899-900, *ynowe* (pl.), *bowe* (inf.) 3523-4, *ynow* (sg.), *bow* (inf.) 4009-10, *bowe* (inf.), *slowe* (pl.) 16221-2, *slow* (pl.), *ynow* (sg.) 9773-4, *ynow* (sg.), *drow* (pl.) 2465-6, *ynowe* (pl.), *drowe* (pl. prt.) 871-2, *now*, *slow* (pl.) 13676, *slow* (sg.), *now* 2601, *how*, *slow* (sg.) 2662, *ynow* (sg.), *now* 4609, *ʒow*, *ynow* (sg.) 8907, *how*, *slow* (pl.) 6638, *ynow* (sg.), *prow* (sb.) 2303, *drow* (sg.), *prow* (sb.) 1882, *loughes* (lakes), *trowes* (pl. of O.E. *troʒ*) 10217-8, *flowes* (sg. prs.), *growes* (sg. prs.) 10331-2, *ynowe* (pl.), þey *ne mowe* (Pet. *mouh ; mowe* = O.E. *muʒon*) 7335-6; but *ynowe* (pl.), *to* þrowe 1039. This is all I could find in the *Chronicle*. More conclusive material would be wanted for the first part. Then it seems to me a quite vain attempt to make a difference between the singular and plural of *ynow*, or the strong preterites. The singular does office for the plural, as is proved. Nor have the auxiliary verbs any inflection, sing. and pl. are alike ; cf. *gaf* (pl.), *have* (pl.) 13754. Only some remnants of *to be* and *to have* in the prt. occur, cf. þey *hadden*, þey *ladden* (they led, Pet. MS. : *laden*) 13257-8. It remains, therefore, to remove the ryme *ynowe* (vb.), *to* þrowe 1039, which would be otherwise conclusive. On looking at the Petyt. MS., which has þat þei *without agayn* þam *throwe* (prt.), I have no doubt that, in preferring this reading, we have a similar ryme to *throu* (prt.), *drou* 24317, or *blu* (prt.), *nu* 6503 in the *Cursor*. As to the above spelling, I'll mention that the Lambeth scribe belongs to the West-Midland (cf. þaw = *thóu* 7159, *whuche* (= *qwilke*) 7116, þulke (þe *ilke* = *swilke*) 7341, *furst* (= *fyrst*) 7419, *hure* (= *hire*) 7566, *ʒut* (= *ʒyt* or *ʒeit*) 4688, *beye* (which seems to stand for *tweye*) 544, *swiche* (= *swilke*) 3238, *deþ* (= *ded*, sb.) 217 etc. etc., but depends on a Lancashire or West-Riding transcript.

As to Hampole, I see the same use in the *Pricke of Conscience* as in the *Cursor;* cf. trow (*vb.*), now 12, 4005 etc., trowe (*cj. pl.*), bowe (*vb.*) 333, bowes (boughs), growes (3 *sg. prs.*) 659, Iesu, dru (*prt.*) 9616. But it must be borne in mind that the transcript belongs to the 15th century.

On the Northern border of the West-Midland there is a different development. Compare *Syr Gawayne*, snawe, lawe (MS. lowe, O.N. *lâgr*), trawe (MS. trowe) 2234 ff.; ȝe mowe (O.E. maȝon, muȝon, moȝon), lowe (O.N. lâgr), innowe 1397 ff.; to blowe (O.E. blôwan), innoȝe 512 ff. Further, compare readings without ryme, like trawe G 70 etc., trawþe G 626 etc.; rawþe *E. E. A. P.* B 233 etc., faure B 958 etc., faurty B 741 etc., flawen (O.E. flŏȝen) C 214; baw (O.E. boȝa) G 435, bawemen[1] G 1564.—Otherwise compare: doun (*adv.*), soun (O.F.), boun (O.N.), ȝe moun, broun (*adj.*) A 536.

Moreover, compare *Cotton Insertion*, p. 990, l. 372-4, we knaw, to traw, and in F 1883: flaghe = flau (flew) etc.

Sir Tristrem furnishes a remarkable instance: now, trowe (1 *sg. prs.*), Petricu, ynouȝ, hou (*adv.*) 3104 ff. I have no reason to pronounce a diphthong here. Cf. *The Aunturs of Arthur*, xvi: trowe (*vb.*), thou (*pron.*); Horstmann's *Altengl. Leg. N. F.* 1881: trow (*vb.*), how 39, 409, trow (*vb.*), bow (O.E. *bûȝan*) 40, 449 (See *Knigge*, p. 37).—*Syr Tristrem* has only *may*.

In *Syr Fyrumbras* belonging to the South-West Midland (late 14th cent.), we find the rymes: abowe (bûȝan), trowe 2806, rowe (rûh), Ynowe (ȝenôh) 1955, draȝe, mawe 3581, adrawe, mawe 1691; but mowñ, [a]doun (dûn) 855, 4998, idon (dôn), mown 2923, rowe (rûh), þrowe (*pp.*) 4618, socoure, foure 1192.

59. As to consonants, there is a striking difference between the Anglian and Saxon dialects.

I. DENTALS. There is a remarkable instance, which seems to prove a difference between the dialect of the author and that of the scribe. There occur two verbs *to dight* and *to tight*, which appear to be sometimes confounded by the scribe. We must distinguish *to dight* = O.E. dihtan = to prepare, to dress, to adorn, from *to tight* = O.E. tyhtan, tihtan = to lead, instruct, design, set, set about, purpose. Stratmann is wrong to compare *tight* with Germ.

---

[1] Such forms as *warlaȝe* B 1560, *warlawe* C 258, which require *werlau* (*wærlŏga*) are not remarkable, because unaccented *o* remained short in all dialects, so that we get *werlou* = *werlau* everywhere.

dichten, tichten, which is O.E. dihtan. The instances he gives only suit to O.E. *tyhtan;* cf. þe sones of Israel . . tiȝten shiltron, *Wicl. Judges* 20, 33 (put themselves in array). The *Cursor* has *tight* (prt.) 12032, 3157, 15888, 24488, (*pp.*) 5432, 18323, 24344, 1301, 25243. In these passages *tight* is kept according to its meaning; F has *diȝt* in l. 15888, and T *diȝt* in l. 1301. But there is another form *tift,* which is used in the same sense as *diȝt.* The true meaning of *dight* may be seen in ll. 3364, 3630, 3645, 6661, 17100 (G), (*prt.*) 3673, 11179, dighted (dight) 19835, 24828, (*pp.*) 3649. The confusion is seen in l. 24807, where C G have *tift,* and E has *diht,* r. w. *gift,* though the meaning of the line : *Wit trisor (tresorie) son* (E *om.*) *his scipp was tift (diht* E) only suits to *diȝt* = (prepared, fitted out). Compare now *tifted* (prt., made ready F) 19425, *tift* (pp.), r. w. *drift,* cf. þe castel þat sua es tift 9931, *tift* (pp., wroȝt F, done G T) 1761, and *redi tift,* r. w. *gift, resp. lift* 5089, 12864. On the ryme see hereafter.

Halliwell's Dictionary gives to *tift* the meaning of *to adjust,* ' North. dialect,' but I believe that it rather belongs to the North-Western dialect, as an interchange between *d* and *t* seems to be characteristic of that dialect. Compare *late* (adv.), *abate* (prt. of *abidan*), *gate,* ' E. E. A. P.,' A 614, *malte, walte, halte, swalte, litalt, bycalt* (pp.) A 1162, *yot* (= *yode*), *spot* A 10, *dyt* (= dyde) A 680 etc. (cf. also Knigge, etc., p. 56).

A striking difference may be observed between the *Cursor,* and *Hampole* and *Rob. de Brunne,* as to the weak preterites and past participles in *nd.* There are a good many remnants in the *Cursor,* as can be ascertained by the rymes. Compare *blend* (pp.), r. w. hend (*pl. sb.*) 17334, r. w. mend (*inf.*) 18842, r. w. wend (*prs.*) 24806; *brind* (pp.), r. w. find (*prs.*) 9206, r. w. send (*pp.*) 13239, (*prt.*) r. w. hint (*prt.*) 13237 ; *kend* (pp.), r. w. lend (*prs.*) 1152, r. w. wend (*prt.*) 10610, 1584, r. w. send (*pp.*) 3424, r. w. hend (*pl. sb.*) 6418, r. w. end 8478, 10358, r. w. spend (*pp.*) 8840, r. w. descend (*vb.*) 22640; *bekend* (*prt.*), r. w. hend (*pl. sb.*) 7242 ; *lend* (prt.), r. w. send (*pp.*) 10776 ; *lend* (pp.), r. w. end (*sb.*) 23648, r. w. wend (*vb.*) 4214 ; *send* (prt.), r. w. end (*sb.*) 5916, 10944, 13943, r. w. hend (*adj.*) 2256, r. w. spend (*vb.*) 17508, r. w. wend (*vb.*) 6180, r. w. wend (*prt.* of *to wene*) 736, 4892, 7680 ; *send* (pp.), r. w. brend (*prt.*) 13239, r. w. hend (*pl. sb.*) 19686, r. w. kend (*pp.*) 3424, 14338, r. w. lend (*prt.*) 10776, r. w. mend (*vb.*) 10316, 14699, r. w. onend (*adv.*) 1296, r. w. wend (*vb.*) 14217, r. w. wend (*prt.*) 12688, 20408; spend (*pp.*), r. w. entend (*prs.*) 23896 ; stund (*pp.*), r. w. grund, 12962 ; *wend* (prt. of *to wend*), r. w. end (*sb.*) 6160, r. w. kend (*pp.*) 10610, not particularly to mention *wend* (prt. of *to wene*), r. w. send (*prt.*) 736, 4892, 7680, r. w. kend (*pp.*) 1584, r. w. lend (*vb.*) 1868, r. w. send (*pp.*) 12688, which is also found in Brunne's *Chronicle*, cf. ll. 4605, 4619, etc.　From these facts also it appears that the *Cursor* dates earlier than the *Pricke of Conscience* and the *Chronicle*.

60. II. GUTTURALS. I am concerned about *thof, thowf* in C, *quon, fon* C F G, *quede, fede* C F G, *thoru, thurgh* C G.

As to *thof*, J. A. H. Murray (*Dial. S. C. Scotland*) gives the following statement, p. 119 : ' In " Cursor M." *thof* is an exceptional word, for in the Northern counties of England the rejection of the guttural has taken place within living memory.' The explanatory addition is quite true.　But *thof* is not Northern, *i. e.* Northumbrian or Scotch, or belonging to the mountain districts in the North-West, but is especially the Saxon (North-West) pronunciation of the 15th century ; cf. *Sir Gawayne, Syr Amadas,*[1] *Syr Gowther,*[1] *Sevyn Sages,*[2] and even *Hampole.*[2]　As I believe that *thof* is of M. L. G. origin (*thoh*, cf. ' Ten Brink ') there is no reason to identify it with the O.E. þeah,[3] which shows quite a different development.　The form þawf, which I have met with in the *Cursor Insertion*, gives us the right clue to the several steps of W.S. þeah: þah, þaȝ, þawh, þawȝ, þawf.　Now there may be some difficulty about the quantity of the vowel.　Orm's þohh and þoffe in *Syr Amadas* decidedly show the shortness that was to be expected, for I take M. L. G. *thoh* to be likewise short.　Otherwise the shortness could have been inferred from the Western treatment of similar words.　The stages through which *h* must have passed, before it advanced into *f*, are: 1. labialized guttural thŏkhw (acc. to Sweet), 2. gutturalized labial (thŏwh or thŏphkh [lip-back-open]), 3. labial thŏph (lip-open) and thŏf (lip-teeth-open).　The same result took place, but later, in words in final *h* preceded by long *o* or *u* ;[4] cf. ȝenôh, rûh.　In the East, the treatment of *thoh* was different.　Here the pure guttural at the end never had the same effect as in the North-West.　Final *h* became *g* or *ȝ*, so that we have *thowȝ* (cf. ꝺog in *Gen.* and *Ex.*) ; and as the guttural was soon lost, we get *thow*, which, by lowering the tongue, has the diphthong ; cf. þou in *Havelok*, and in the Göttingen MS. of the *Cursor*.　Such spelling in *ou* will be found in similar words of the neighbouring dialect, so that *gh* is a merely historical

---

[1] MS. 19. 3. 1. Advoc. Lib. Edinbg. ; cf. Breul, *Sir Gowther.*　Oppeln, 1886.

[2] Cotton Galba E IX.　　　　[3] Cf. Ten Brink, *Chaucer Gramm.*, § 46, Anm.

[4] It seems to me a mistake that Chaucer's language should be taken as the starting-point from which to construe the stages of phonetic development of every word to the present day.　We should never forget how much political changes bore on the Southern dialect of the capital, and do bear even now.

remnant. My spelling *þóu* for the *Cursor* appears to be confirmed by the mistake of C in once confusing it with *þou* (pron.).

No attention has ever been paid to the fact that *quone* and *fone* are the same words in M.E. Both of them are to be derived from the O.E. pron. *hwon* [1] (*hwan*), originally the instrumental of the interrogative pronoun *hwá*, then used as an indefinite pronoun of the neuter gender (adverbially and substantively) ; cf. Lat. *quod* in *aliquod*. Its short quantity can be seen from the interchange between *hwon* and *hwan* (cf. *Mark* i. 19, *Matth.* xxvi. 39). On this account, Grein's reasoning (cf. *Glossary* ii. 123) is not sound ; compare, therefore, *Grimm Gr.* iii. 182, and *Dietrich*, H. Z. xi. 407. This *hwon* is met with in M.E. as *whon* and *quon*. The latter is Northern, as it is afterwards (15th cent.) rendered by *whune*, according to Halliwell, *Dict.* 930 ; but in a purely Northumbrian (Scotch) dialect we should expect *qwhune*, or *chone*, *chune*, and we meet indeed with *chone* in the Edinburgh MS. of the *Cursor*. Now there is no doubt that *qu* (= labialized guttural) passed through the gutturalized labial *wh*, and advanced into the labial *ph*, *f*. We meet with *fon* especially in C F ; besides, cf. *Cotton Galba* E ix. (*Pricke of Conscience*, *Minot's Poems*, *Sevyn Sages*, etc.), the *Psalter* (*Cotton Vesp.* D vii.). As to *fone*, *fune*, in *Pricke of Conscience*, Morris has justly observed that it is unknown to *Barbour*. I am of opinion, indeed, that those transcripts in which *fone* occurs were taken down in the North-West. The boundary line of its area may be looked for in Lancashire and the West Riding of Yorkshire.

After this discussion I only take notice of *quē.d*, *fē.d*, both belonging to O.E. *cwéâd* = *cwǽd* (cf. *cwed* in the *Blickling Homilies*). Its meaning is ' evil,' ' the evil,' and personified, ' the fiend ' ; cf. *quede* C G 16256, *qued* E **y** 22822, *qued* C G 17216, *qued* C **y** 19575. The same interchange that is found between *quone* and *fone*, cf. *quone* **x**, *fone* **y** 23922, quon C, fone G, chone E 22740 (cf. also l. 25121), may be seen between *quede* and *fede*, cf. *fed* C, *qued* G 7935, *fed* C, *qued* E **y** 22822, *þi fede* (enemies) C G, *quede* (evil) T L 16254.

As to *thorw*, *thurgh*, I have to remark that *ðurh* occurs in W. Saxon and Kentish, and *ðorh* in the O.E. *Psalter* (Merc.). The interchange between *ŏ̆*

---

[1] It is interesting to see how the modern ' the little ones, some one, any one ' (from which *one* alone came to be used), are to be traced to O.E. *hwon*; cf. O.E. *lyt-hwon* n. It has nothing to do with the numeral, which, in its pronunciation, was confused with the indef. pron. Compare Mr. A. J. Ellis' statement in the Proceedings of the Philol. Society XXXVIII (*Transactions of Phil. Soc.*, 1885-87).

and *ü* is old, and is a characteristic of all Low-German dialects. We meet
with þurh, þorh in 'Laʒamon,' þorʒ in 'Shoreham,' 'Ayenbite,' etc. ; and þurh
in 'Orm.,' ꝺurg in 'St. Genesis and Exodus,' thurgh in 'Chaucer.' The
Pricke of Conscience has *thurgh*, Havelok *thoru*. Now I have met with two
rymes of *thurgh* in the *Cursor*: *skurf*, *thurgh* 11824, *burgh*, *thurgh* 11070,
while, in the main of lines, we find throughout *thoru* (*thorw*) x G þorou F,
þourʒe T. But cf. also þurʒ E III and *thurg* E I 23412, when þoru is used
elsewhere. It is remarkable that even *thrugh* (grave) occurs as *thorw* 17390.
I was not surprised to find similar forms in *Brunne's Chronicle: Lambeth MS.*:
þorow, þorough, and *Petyt MS.*: þorgh, þorhout. These forms could hardly
be convenient in the rymes, and the attempts to meet the ryme look rather
strange. *Arthur*, which is the regular form, and occurs thus in the body of
lines, and is convenient for the ryme, as *iogelour*, *Arþour* 9842, *honour*, *Arthour*
10556, 10606 etc., is drawn into such forms as *Arthurghe*, *Arthoru*, *Arthorow*,
only to meet rymes like *burghe*. The ryme, of course, shows that *r* has the
Northumbrian burr (back-trilled-voice), but I do not think it necessary to spell
Arthurghe, to meet the ryme-word *burghe*, which seems to be *burwʒ* (back-lip-
open-voice). Now let us compare *Conyngesburgh*, r. w. þer-þorough 8492 ;
þorow, r. w. *Arthorow* 13854 (*Pet. MS.* þorgh, *Arthorgh*) ; þorow, r. w. *Scarde-
burghe* 14816, and *Arthurgh* (*Pet. MS.* Arthoru), r. w. *burghe* 9904 ; *burghe*,
r. w. *Arthurghe* 10810, and I hope the reader will be convinced that *Robert de
Brunne's* genuine form was *thurgh* = *thurwʒ*, as in the *Cursor*. The ryme
skurf, *thurgh*, in the *Cursor*, reminds me of such rymes as *noght*, r. w. *loft*
2086, *diht* (E), r. w. *gift* 24808, *gift*, r. w. *right* (G) 25647, and in *Havelok*:
bouth, r. w. *oft* 883, and, to a certain extent, of such as *slawen*, r. w. *raven* in
Havelok 2676, and *haven* (harbour), r. w. *drawen* (*pp.*) in *Brunne's Chronicle*
7722.—I'll still notice the changes from *thorgh* or *thurgh* into þorwʒ, þurf, cf.
Legends of the Holy Rood, by R. Morris ; *Treatises on Science*, by Th. Wright ;
and *E. E. Poems*, and *Lives of Saints*, etc. (*Life of St. Catherine*), by F. J.
Furnivall. þurwʒ, þurw, derived from þurh, can, in my opinion, give only
þoru, so that this form may be derived from *thorgh* as well as *thurgh*, cf.
Havelok's þoru, boru.

61. The numerals also afford some samples which are characteristic of the
Author's dialect.

1. Cardinal numbers.

Notice *baþer* (gen. pl.) 1254, 23958, *tuai*, r. w. *sai* 12700, 21756, *tuain* C
4032 ; besides *tua* 723, etc., and *tuin* (O.N.) 523, etc. Now we know for

certain that *tuai* (O.E. twǣȝen) is a Midland form, and so far as we know, never occurs in Northumbrian writers; cf. Brunne's *Chronicle, twaye*, r. w. *Maye* 296, *tweye*, r. w. *weye* 3682, *tweye*, r. w. *deye* 5136.

Further consider *thre* / 3474; *þrin* / (O.N.) 353; *four* 356, 592, *fourteen* 4577, *fourti* 510. It has already been stated that the *Cursor* is quite a stranger to *au* = O.E. -ēow; therefore all such forms as *faur, faurten*, etc., which point to the West, and occur even in E (cf. l. 23372) must be disregarded.

Moreover compare *aght* C 188, *nine* (9) / 11178 (cf. Hampole *neghen* 729), and *hundreth* / 9228.

2. Ordinal numbers.

Consider *thridd (thrid)*, r. w. *bid* 974, r. w. *unhid* (pp.) 21308, r. w. *mid* 21590, r. w. *kidd* 22494. The scribes of the *Cursor* MSS. occasionally use *thred* (cf. C 18567, and E 24258, 24549). This form seems to be Northumbrian, as is proved by Hampole's *Pricke of Conscience* þredde, r. w. *bredde* (pp.) 4210. Brunne's *Chronicle* has *þrydde*, r. w. bytydde (*pt.*) 15162.

Further consider *sevend*, r. w. neuend (*pp.*) 22546; *agten*[d] C 10573, besides *aghtand*, f. i. 2669; *thritteind*, r. w. heind (*adj.*) C 11374.

Moreover we meet with *niinde*, r. w. *finde* 23257. Since we have *nine*, r. w. fine 11178, and þe *nine* (9°), r. w. mine 970, I think such Northumbrian forms as *neynd* E, *neinend* C 22579, must be rejected. Compare also *nend* 26685, *neent* C, *nighend* C G 29314, *neuent* C, *nighend* C G 29470, and *neghent* C second hand, p. 958, l. 59. Noteworthy are such forms as neind G, nyend F 22579. Hampole has the well-known form *neghent* 3988, 4790, 6571.

Finally consider *elleuend* (11°) 2003, and *elleven*, r. w. *be leuen* G 22628, while **x** F have *elleft*, r. w. *be left*. The passage runs thus:

> þe signe of the day elleuen (elleft **x** F)
> It es (nes E) na skil þat it be leuen (left **x** F)

Now it is remarkable that E has þe *signes*, and l. 22629 runs : *Sair þai sal do for to grise* though the following line has *winde on ilka side sal rise* E **y**, whereas C has *windes*. I have no doubt that l. 22629 (*þai*) can only refer to þe *signes* mentioned in E, so that in l. 22628 *it* should be altered into þai, and we have a plural present in *en*, not uncommon in the *Cursor, be* and *leuen* being contracted. The loss of *d* in *elleuen* is illustrated by þe *nine* (9°), r. w. *nine* 970 and other well-known instances.

Take also notice of *fourtend* 22689, E's *faurtend* belongs to the Western source. As to other forms I'll mention *ferthe* (4°), r. w. *erthe* 358, 13441 (cf. *Chronicle, ferthe* (MS. forthe), r. w. *erþe* 12366); *twelfed* 29326, *thrittend* 29920, *fiftend* C 29328, etc.

62. PRONOUNS.—A. Personal.

Sg. 1st Pers.: I (*i*) and *ic* occur in C E, *i* only in G F. *ic* seems to have the preference before vowels, etc., f. i. *ic understand* C E 21746, *ic of men* C E 24917, *ic hope* C E 23930, *ic ask* C E 23921, *ic haue* C 208, *ic hight* C 1975, but *ik bisek* E 23930. *i* has the preference in C.

2nd Pers.: þu 15414, 16107, etc. The scribes' spelling generally is þou. Mind the assimilated and contracted forms : *ertu* C 18326, C 20596, C E 24193, þat tu E 24182, *wist tu* 24707 ; in the objective case : *latte* C 16330, *waste* E 24665.

3rd Pers.: objective case, feminine gender : *hir.* The scribe's spelling is *hur* C 1898.

Pl. 2nd Pers.: ye (*ȝe*) and *yee* (*ȝee*) / 18457. Objective case : yuu 15869, youu C 13047, 13481, 15445, 15447, etc., besides *you.* The spelling *yee* seems to be preferred to avoid a confusion with *ye = þe*, and *yuu* to avoid such a one with *yu = þu.*

3rd Pers.: þai / 2046. Besides þei C 1039, G 21632, þaij G 23555. Objective case : þaim / 8703, 12381, 12811, 18533, 23154. There also occur in x G þam passim, þem C 13725. In F occurs the Western form *ham*, which we occasionally meet also with in C, as, ll. 4519, 4939, 6350, 7088, 8568, 16439, 17389, *hamself* C 801. In E occurs the mistake þaim for þain' 23762 etc.—But we also find *he* (= þai) C E 23025 ; cf. also þai C, which seems to be mistaken for *he* G (3 *sg.*) 5527, 21516. The objective case is, by mistake, *him* for *hem* C 7030, G 6430, C 16449 ; hem C 308, 1703, 6197. Cf. also *cun þai* C þai con F, *gan he* G 2009.

B. Possessive.

Sg. 1st Pers.: mi (my), and before vowels and h, *min (myn)* 119, 365, 1971.

2nd Pers.: þi, and before vowels and h, þin. Besides mind *was tin* E 24675, *was ti* E 24671, and the mistake in C þat þin for þat tint E G 24268. Observe þin behoue x 23916.

Pl. 2nd Pers.: yur C 13936, 15409, 15545, 15577, C G 15411. The scribes' spelling is *your, youur.*

3rd Pers.: þair passim. Besides we meet with þeir C 1716, 2045, 2221, 4457, 6984, þaier C 4057, þere C 50, þer C 6, 201, 4148, 5535, 17300, *hir*

G 6.   It is not unlikely that the original spelling was þeir, which would suit better to the less broad articulation of our author's dialect than þai, and it would perhaps be worth while to compare, on this account, the spellings of the several manuscripts of Robert de Brunne's *Chronicle*.

C. Demonstrative.

þis (sg. and pl.) 39, 221, þijs (pl.) C 4985.   Besides we find þes (pl.) in F 221, 5127 etc., þese passim in T, and the mistake in C þis for pes 5333.

þir (pl.) 294.   Besides, there occurs þer passim in F, and þeir C 5831, þier C 5938.

þat (sg.) 18572 etc.   þaa (pl.) 861, 8204 etc., and used substantively, like þai: þaa þat (= those who) 251, 6118, o þaa (= of them) 1958, 20610.   þaas oþer 491, 7134, 10000, 11258 etc., besides þaas wandas C 8187, to þaas iuel . . þat C (to þaim . . . þat G) 90209, þais unbestes C (þa G) 19859, þe ilk blescedhedes C (þas y) 23475.   þaas seems, though rarely, to be used only before vowels, h or a semi-vowel.   þe ilke (sg. and pl.), followed by a substantive, passim; likewise þis ilke 39, etc., þat ilke 22731, etc., þas ilke 23475 (MS. *ilk*).   all þa ilk (*subst.*) F 20585 (þai ilk C, ilk *om.* G).

swilk / 10379, etc., slik / 9775, 23153, etc.; sli C 66, 259, 13405, etc., scli C 114.   Compare suilkins C 18064, slikins C 12010.

D. Relative.

þat passim, and in the objective case, the verb is followed by the preposition.—qua 3880, seems to be used more frequently in a generalizing sense, cf. 81, etc.   Genitive case: quas 1490, 5732, etc.   Objective case: quam 10, 1509, etc.   þe quilk, with reference to things, 146, 529, 1367, 2176, 6252, etc., þe quilk þat 3922, used adjectively 421.   Quilk used adjectively, the substantive being followed by þat C 1205.

Generalizing are qua passim; qua þat 52, 509, etc.; qua sa (swa) 96 etc.; qua sum 1953, etc.; quat contre sum 1149.

Determinative: he þat 61; þai þat 1809; þaa þat 251, 6118, etc.

E. Interrogative.

qua passim, quas, quam; quat.—quilk (subst. and adj.).—queþer of þir tua C 14045.

F. Indefinite.

all þat (sg.) 7133, (pl.) 1955, etc.—ilk passim; ilka, ilke, ilkan passim; ilkane (subst.) passim.

quon / 24686, C 24305, C 10047; C 22740 (chone E, fone G), x 23922. quoner (comp.) 19495.

aiþer C **y** 723, 800, 12378, etc. *neiþer* (MS. *neþer* C, *neyder* G) 1660. *ouþer* (*oþer*), *nouþer* (*noþer*). The MSS. show these spellings : *oþer* C *ouþer* G T 6198, *ooþer* C *ouþer* G E 21949, besides *oiþer* C ; *noiþer* C 2092, etc., *noþer* C *nouþer* G T 6197, *nouther* G E 19306. *auþer* and *nauþer*, which occasionally occur in C and E, and have the preference in F, belong to the scribes, as has been above proved by phonological reasons.—Genitive case of *oþer* : *oþers*, cf. *of oþers wrake* C 21927.

Compare also the contractions : *sumkins* C 115, *sumkines* G 207, *anekines* G 276, *alkines* G 578, 695, 825, *nakins* C 9486, C 17128, *nankines* C 9486, C 17344, G 574, 1990, C G 5575, etc., *serekines* G 5448. The MSS. generally show the loss of *s*, as could be expected, cf. Hampole and others.

63. ADVERBS.

The final E of the adverb is silent as a rule. Besides those forms in *-like* which E seems to prefer as the older form, there occur such in *-ly*, *-li*, f. i. *openlik* 175, *wonderlik* 2322, *straitlike* 6105, *witerli* / 6419, *tenderli* / 5057. Some remnants of an old *e* in monosyllabic adverbs seem to be kept in *dere* 20238 (Ç), *bliþe* Add. MS. 20482, cf. 20604 (þan *add.* **x** G, ai *add.* **y**), *ilike* **y** 1012, 1989, C **y** 1421, *ful harde* **y** 496, 16014, cf. also 24364. The rymes cannot be conclusive, for a final E is always silent in the ryme, nor can be so the spelling of C, which so often drops final *e* when **y** and also E still keep it, and the metre seems to want it. From this point of view the reader may consider such rymes like *ilike* / 75, *lik* / 9776, *euer ilike* / 18446, *her* / 8699, and *hard* / 4919, 24766. Moreover, I beg to observe that a final E can also be dropt before a semi-vowel, f. i. *swa hard wiþin* 3447, *ful hard was* 3470. Therefore the final *e* is never sounded in *softe, ofte, lange, lude* (16353), etc., and the MSS. are right to drop it, as they generally do.

ogain C 20956 and in sixteen other places, such in E included, and where it is a preposition. Besides *again, egain.—o wai* C 6008, 8067, 20792, 20953, *on-wai* C F 8067 (cf. also the spelling *wei* C 11738, *wey* C 11665). Besides *awai.—*As to *obouen* C 3366, 20078, *obute* (otherwise MSS. *abouen, abute,* etc.), consider the peculiar mistake in C *a-boute* for *of bote* / 8458.

The spelling in *o*, which I prefer, may be ascertained to be the original one by the fact that *o, on* is in a good many places confounded with Western *a, an ;* cf. *a = of* C 1367, *a = of* C F 555, *A = of* C 12888, *o = a* (article) C 19951, *a = o* C 21105, *and = on* **x** G 21895, *and = on* C **y** 23677.

sumdel (= somedeal, in some measure ; somewhat ; rather) 1280, 19942 (*sundir* E) ; 18836 ; 785, 2492, etc.

PREPOSITIONS.

hu of (O.E. *hû* c. gen.), cf. *If þou wil wijt hu o þair eildis* C 22814, *of faire statur hu sal it be* G 22842.

64. PREPOSITIONS.

omang C 967 and in seventeen other places, *omanges* C 2833. Besides occur *amang, emang.*

opon C 198, 497, E 21139, G 1824 and in five other places in C, *vpon* G 1099, 7199, 21687, (C *up apon*). There needs no great discussion whether *upon* or *opon* should be preferred; for in my opinion, there is scarcely much difference of pronunciation when the last syllable has the stress. But I mean to reject *apon.* Cf. also the mistake *at apon* C = *to opin* 25066, and even *op* E 22548, 22569.

onend C 1295, cf. Seth then sette him spell onend. *onend,* of course a contraction of *on* and *end,* means *over-against, opposite to, against, compared to, considering,* so that the sense of this passage is: Seth replied to him (*lit.*: Seth set a tale (cf. T) against him). I do not understand how M. Kaluza, in his Glossary, gets at the meaning 'anon, immediately.' Cf. Hampole's *onente* (*onence* is a misreading) 1355, 3678, etc. Now compare *anent, enent* in the MSS., cf. 10858, 14878, etc., and the reader, I hope, will be convinced that they are nothing but Hampole's *onente.* There are some other interesting instances, as, *anentes* C, *anyendis* F (cf. ʒende, Brunne's *Handl. Sinne,* 2347) 26957, *anentes* C 27234, *anentis* C, *onente* (*onence* is a misreading) CG 27653; further *enentes* (*enent þis* G; perhaps *enentis* = *enent þis*) 6880, *enentis þe Iuus* (perhaps = *enentis Iuus* = onent þis Iuues) 14459, cf. 23722, *enents* C, *anyent* F, *enent* G 25312.

unto and *vntil* seem to deserve the preference before *into, intil,* cf. *until* **x y** 19825, E F (intil C G) 20106, E F (*intil* C, *vnto* G) 22959, C (*intil* E **y**) 23286, C F (*intill* G) 20209; *vnto* **x** F 19846, **x** (*into* **y**) 20051, **x y** 20837, **x y** 20014, **x y** 23055, **x** F 23350, **x** (*into* **y**) 22978, E (*into* C **y**) 23049, **x** F (*into* G) 23350, F (*vntil* G, *into* C, *intil* E) 22834, C G (*vntil* E F) 22962.

at, followed by a infinitive; besides *to;* cf. *at write* C (*to* G) 18514, *at ga* C G 14595, *at here* C (*to* G) 18542, *at mend* C 18442, *at come* C G 19534, *at light* C G 19588, *at ete* **x** F 19833, C **y** 15512, *at end* **x** G 21855, *at turn* C (*to* C **y**) 22351, at ask **x y** 22524, *at understand* **x y** 23295, 23409, 24894, etc. In the two latter instances a slurring-over is wanted by want of a kind of aphæresis. There seems to be a mistake in l. 21420, where G has *make he cuth,* but C *at mak.* There is a mistake in E 20032 *ai be* for *at be* and in G *ay to be*, which seems to be an alteration from *ai be;* *at* is likewise read for *ai* in C 20968.

ogains C 1617, 16947, E 21981, *ogain* 2633, etc.; elsewhere *again, agains*

65. CONJUNCTIONS AND NEGATIONS.

Bot passim, but we meet with *but* C 13182, E 21858, besides there are two remarkable instances: *beit* C (*bot* G *but* T) 17621, *bit* E 22740. If we consider that short open *u* is generally written with *o*, though the rymes want *u*, and there are spellings like *vnto couer* C = wont to couer G 10119, and *luue*, etc. changes with *loue*, I think we may be right to adopt for our 13th century writer *but*, which is still in use in the 14th century with the Midland writers. But its spelling matters little.

sin = since 5172, etc., apparently a contraction of *siþen*, is used in **x** F, while G uses *siþen* as a rule.

As regards the negations employed, the final *e* in *ne* (= nor) can never be dropt, f. i. nē wen*e* wat 23736, nē was he ferde 21832, nē ouertan 575.

The weak negation *ne* if joined to a pronoun ending in a vowel, is always enclitical, though it does not always appear in writing, and never counts as a syllable. There is an elision before a vowel and the verbal forms beginning with *h* or *w*. It is of great importance and interest to observe that *ne* is often omitted in C **y**, when it is still kept in E. The contraction with the following word is sometimes marked in writing.

First observe the common mistake þ*am* C = þain' 14667, E 19432, 23762, (ne *om.* C **y**) 23289, 23923.

Then notice:

ine E F 22909, (*printed* me) E 21823, 21824.

þ*oune* 20157.

hene 19651, E: 19945, 20813, 20917, 21071, 21091, 21854, 21908, 21922, 22042, 22181, 22183, 22454, 22769, **x y**: 22171, 22436, 23417, C G: 22567, **y** (he *om.* C, ne *om.* E) 22516.

wene E: 20820, 20858, 21885, 22558, 23718.

yene E: 23718.

þ*aine* 19182, 20214, 20808 (faire *om.* C), E: 22853, *taine* 19386, 19547, **x** (þai ne **y**) 20124, **x y**: 23145, þ*ain* E: 19453, 23362.

nes E 20857, E 22628, *nis* E: 23100, 19671, *ne es* (nees) C **y** 329, C 929 (ne art G), **y** (þat is E, it es C) 23413, E **y** (na E, it es C) 22169, *neys* C 55.

ne bes **x** G (best C) 23201.

nart F 656.

ne war C E 21681.

ne *has* C (na hauis E) 21708.

ne hauid E 23164.

nil we **x y** 23728.

ne mai **x y** 23244, **x** G 23206, E F (it mai C G) 23468, E: 23213, 23220.

ne moʒt E 23415.

ne sal (it sal G) **x** F 23489, **x y** 22480, 23498, **x** 22500.

ne sulde E 23212.

ne wald C E 23285 (*and walde* **y**).

ne sagh (na E) 22464.

ne appears separated from the personal person : *he . . . ne fand* E 22902, *þai . . . ne mis* E 23288.

Compare now *Es nan* **x y** 20479, *Es na* **x y** 22340, *Es tar na* **x y** 23812, 23813 ; *sal nan haue* **x y** 22342, *þai sal na* E G (þat C F) 23480 ; *þai wald noht* **x y** 23287, *we fin noht* **x y** 23784, *þai mai haf na* **x y** 23264, and *criste sal noʒt come* **x y** 22411, *þat es na* **x y** 22419, 22433, *þat wald na* **x y** 23301.

66. NOUNS AND ADJECTIVES.

NUMBER.—The plural terminates in : *s, ës, es.* Observe the following in : *-en (-in), -n* ; as, *eien* passim, *erin (ern)* / 8090, 21333, but *eres* C **y** 18836, and such in: *er*, as, *childer, breþer* passim. Consider *breþer* G (*brothers* C, *brethers* F) 2054. Moreover, take into consideration *freind* (plur.) 13389, 23738, besides *frendes.*

CASE.—The genitive ends in : *ës, es, s.*

The following phrases contain remnants of genitives of old feminine nouns ; as *handëwerc*, 132 1155, *hellë pit* 506, *hellë pine* F 23187, E F 19578, E F 23199 (cf. 10072, 19578, 20524), *rodë tre* 15344, 16358, 16604, 24062.

No inflection appears in : *heuen blis* 20465, *heuen king* (heuenes G) 20438, *heuen court* 20619, *heuen wird* 20282.

Contrary to the general old Northumbrian usage appears no inflection in : *his fader schame* 2026, *his fader hiʒte* C **y** (fadires E) 19006, *mi fader name* C **y** (fadiri E) 22311, *in moder wambis* C **y** (moderis E) 22465, *his modir gin* C **y** 3716, *mani moder son* C **y** 7061, *þi moder . . slogh* (moders C F) 1254, *þi broþer blode* 1135, *þi breþer* (pl.) *stat* 4092.

This well-known O.E. usage must not be confounded with another to which the original does not seem to have been quite a stranger, but which seems to have been a common feature of the Northumbrian dialect of the 14th century, and to have been imitated from O. French, that is to drop the genitive inflection of nouns denoting persons, when the genitive is followed by the governing substantive, f. i. þi sun messager C G, sonis F Add. MS. 20150, cf. 20177, it es þi dir (dere) sun (sone F, sunes G) saand 20162, suns child C 3700, his kinges (king C) wande 22267, crist laghes C, cristis E y 23132, of cristes heuen x y 22170, cristes kne x y 22664, vr lauerd wiþerwines x y 23320, Antecrist come 213, but antecristes come E F (antecrist C G) 22217, and a great many instances where the MSS. have various readings. The dropping seems really to be allowed in proper nouns, f. i. David kin 15055, David fot 7795, þat anticrist of Danis sede (dane F) 21975.

One remnant of an old dative is : on rode C F (rode-tre G) 20560.

OLD COMPOUNDS. Notice his endë-dai E F 21062, paskë-day 18606, 22953, paskë-tide 18617, euë-sang 6286. Besides, consider þe pask dai messe quen þat he sang (þat om. y) 21253. Observe here also hindëwin (hindwin x y) 22395.

As regards the final e elsewhere, it is always silent.

The adjectives employed have two forms—Definite and Indefinite.

The definite form preceded by the definite article, or demonstrative adjective, or a possessive pronoun and followed by a substantive terminates in -ë in the singular and the plural, as, þe heye curt F 22718, þe harde tre F 22878, þe alde lau y 116, E 21644, þalde time 22284, þe strange soru F 15703, þe laste day E 19109, G 22423, þe lesse folc E F 21724, þe maste king E 22258, mi leue sun 24125, þat fule folk 22333 ; þe laste daies E 22257, þe grete kaisers E y 22127, his suete willes F 20086 ; his right hand 20666, etc. The final e seems always to be silent before a vowel, h and a semi-vowel.

The ordinal numbers are treated like adjectives, as, þe þridde dai E 19959, þe fifte mett G 2410, cf. 22519, þe ferthe pin E 23233, þe sixte dai G 401, 22531, þe tende part F 978, y 22764.

Such adjectives of more than one syllable always drop the final e, as well as such as are not followed by a substantive. Examples abound.

Putting aside the numerous examples in which the scribes dropt the final e, we still meet with a good many exceptions to the above rule ; as, þe wers part (?) 21446, þe god baptist 11113, þald testament 12886, þe first passage 19990, our grete prophete 19523, ur dere driȝtine 22267, mi leif cosen C G 20553, his hey palais G 413, þat hei (?) ture 98005, þat hey (?) curt 472. I think we should read þe werse part, þat heye curt, þat heye ture.

When the adjective forms a compound with the following substantive, the definitive form is never used, even if preceded by the definite article, etc.; as, þe wisman 27, þis godman 16225, þe godmen C 22165, þe dedman 11504, etc.

Such adjectives as terminate in *-e* in O.E., generally keep *ë* in every form, except in the ryme; as, *þat suete tre* 16585, *hir suete sun* 85, *mi suete* 24128, 24140, cf. 24179, *þat suete mighti king* **y** 15161, cf. 16431, 17071, 17083, *his suete muth* **y** 15767 : *þo riche man* (instead of *riche* read *rike* according to ryme) 7925, *his riche croun* 9097, *þis riche man* 14037, *þe riche men* 16611 ; *þis wreche Iudas* 15433 ; *a grene gate* 1252, *in grene tre* 16663, *a riche gift* 24803, *a riche land* 3252, *a wreche man* 18404, *to riche gestning* 3326, *with riche weede* 3341, *in riche pall* 5147, *riche giftes* 11375, *suete smelles* 1014, *suete spices* F 1028, *as trewe fere* Add. MS. 20134, *treu* (*probably* trewe) *men* and *lele* 4909, *a neu* (*probably* newe) *smock* 20214. Exceptions are : *treu luue* 20300, *his new vessel* 22938, *a neu biginning* C G 2008, *a neu liuelade* C **y** 2009, *suet iohn* (*perhaps* iohan ; suete **y**) 20328, *suet iohan* 2037 (suete **y**), *suet ihesus* C (suete **y**) 20393 ; *þat suetę woman* (*on account of w*) 20285, *þis wrechę woman* (*on account of w*) 13717, *suet colures* E 23964, *his suetę gleuing* C 7411, *þat suetę meigne* 15536, *yur suet discord* **x** 24593, *suet spiceri* E 23456, *suet grennes* 9917, *suet sauur* C 20788, *a suetę fernet* 15213, *clenę forgiuenes* 19107. Remarkable is the mistake *a neu sang* for *an euë-sang* C G 6286.

Some remnants of an old vocative case in *-ë* appear in : *leuë sun* E **y** 20092, E **y** 20094, E **y** 20229, C **y** 24509, but *lef sun* 20610 ; the same in : *suetë moder* **y** 20601, 20611, cf. 20617, suete leuedi G 20429, etc.

Putting aside such adjectives as generally keep final *e* everywhere, the plural generally drops *-ë*. Remnants may be found in *gode peres* **y** 37, *alde sakes* **y** 4949, *grete stremes* G 1316, etc., but *all landes* 1001, *ferr landes* 1034, *fair kij* (faire F) 4566 ; *fair iuels* 23458, *gret signes* 22437, 22176, *hard* (harde F) *þrous* 24317, *hard* (herd C) *werkes* 5527, *ryȝt limmes* 22839, *sere maneres* 21900, *wiss clerkes* 1552. As to *fair*, I may say that whoever sticks to the metre (which is not consistent) will easily read it in two syllables.

Adjectives of Romance origin drop *-ë ;* but there are some instances where I should be inclined to restore final *-ë*, as *þat fals file* 715, *þair fals fame* 11183, *þat fals fede* C G 18045, *þe fals Iuus red* 20354 ; while it is evident that final *e* is dropt in examples like *wit his fals felauscip* 15743, *þe fals felun Iudas* 15878, *ur fals seruis* 21894, *þat fals prophet* 22415, *þe fals witnes* (pl.) 19457.

A remnant of an old genitive singular is *goder* (= ȝôdre) in : *Ful goderhail* 23527. Kaluza, in his Glossary, gives the peculiar rendering : *better*

health. An old genitive plural in *er* (= *re*) appears in *aller*, 469 (*alder* G),
etc., *alþermast, alþerheiest,* etc.

Some remnants of an old dative case in -*ë* appear in : *wiþ a milde steuen*
E F 20144, *with heie* (hei C **y**) *note and lude steuen* 22467, *wiþ ful harde
paine* E F 21111, *in forme tide* E F 22193, and also, *in alde lawes* E F 21711.
Besides, observe *on ferrum* 11744, 18998.

67. Verbs.

Though the infinitive generally has no inflection, a good many instances are
still found even in our MSS., f. i. *askin* C 5299, *deri* C 20224 [cf. also won
(ai *add.* C G) 23364, and *Tristrem*], *ben* / 20430, 20603, *bun* C **y** 22666 (*bow*
E), *deluen* / C E 21063, *hiden* C E 22196, *lasten* 13892, *liuen* / 24578, *lenden* C
9806, *louen* / 20077, *knaun* / 18730, *makin* C G 9876, *mistrun* / 15498, *rasen*
(*raisen* E) C 22272, 22283, *witten* (*witin* E) G 23635, *wacken* (*trs.*) 8409, *sen* /
24081. Besides, compare those instances in § 30 taken from E.

The plural present shows either no inflection or northern *s*, seldom the
older Midland inflection in -*en;* as, *gaas* / 6822, *hers* / 12191, *redis* / 23943,
beginnes / 1035 etc.; *wern* / 12106 etc.; *luuen* / 20375, *wetin* E 23685.

The preterite singular of strong verbs usually does duty for the plural, as,
gan / 1050 etc. Some remnants of an old preterite plural appear in *wern* (*weren*),
warn, bern (*beren*) 8079, 20715-6, 22004, *þai stungen* C 20545, *þai runnen* C
(*ran þaim* G) 18730, 18952, *suonken* C G 23051, *begun* C 5942, G 17898,
G 17976, *gun* C G 19452. Besides, there is some confusion in the use of *gun*
(sg.) C G 20940, C G 20966, C G 22906, G 18369, *con* C F (*gan* G) 1869 etc.

Wrong strong preterites of weak verbs frequently met with in the 15th
century should be disregarded, as, *fan*, from *finen*, used by analogy of *blan*,
from *blinnen;* cf. 1835, 8135, 4108.

The preterite of weak verbs has lost its inflection as a rule. There are
some remnants of full weak preterites plural, as, *herdin* E 19539, *miʒten* E
20114, *seldin* E 19038, *wrohten* E 23184.

Wrong weak preterites of strong verbs are : *delued* C G 16877, 18562,
delued G 21146, perhaps *sleped* (*slepe* G) 12572.

The sharpening of final -*de* behind *n* has not come into its full effect,
cf. § **59.**

The past participles in -*n* seldom lose their inflection; but cf. *wite* (=
gone) / 10551, *forget* / 15806, *get* / 17418, *num* / 12730, *do* G 4870 (rymes
with *Pharao*, cf. 4660). Besides, observe *gotten* / 13662 (transition from
the fifth class; according to Sievers, into the fourth class).—Final *t* and *ed*

contracted, of course, give *t*, as, *translāt* / 232; cf. translated 9162. The sharpening of final -*de* behind *n* into -*nt* has not come into its full effect, cf. § **59**.

Moreover, consider *liggen* 10084, and līn[1] / 11297; castin 9947, 10100, 10116, and *cast* 5289, *kest* C G 19614.

The prefix *y-* (*i-*) seems to be unknown; but cf. *i-beft* E 20974. Wrong weak participles past are *schawed, scaud, sceud* 1162, 23194, 4588, *knaud* 1161.

The present participle terminates in -*and*. There are some printed mistakes like *mirkind* = *mirknid* (pp.) 1764, *glopind* = glopnid (*pp.*) 10308, cf. 11611.

The subjunctive seems to have lost its inflection; as *blin* / 121, *begin* / 1495, *forget* / 1686, *grant* 5466 etc.

Besides, compare the following remarkable rymes, *stern* (sg. sb.), r. w. *wern* (pl. prt.) 1490 (cf. *sterne, zerne* (adv.) 23587), *wern* (pl. prt.), r. w. *ern* (pl. sb. = ears) 8080, *lantern*, r. w. *to bern* G 12911, *wern* (pl. prt.), r. w. *bern* (sb.) 20450, *wern* (pl. prt.), r. w. *bern* (*pl. prt.*) 20716, *wern* (inf.), r. w. *bern* (*pl. prt.*) 22004, *warn* (pl. prt. = were), r. w. *forfarn* (pp.) 4760, cf. ware (*pl. prt.*), r. w. forfare (*inf.*) 4966.

68. AUXILIAR AND DEFECTIVE VERBS.

A. Verb substantive.

Sg. 1st pers.—*am* passim, 2nd pers.—*ert, art, es* 18120, 18193, 18189, 18216, 5262, 10888 etc.; 3rd pers.—*is*, passim *es* C 13564, 17686, 20784, 23508 etc. *es* in the 1st person sg. occurs in C 5444, in E 20018, 20019, but I think they should be disregarded as belonging to the scribes.

Pl. *er, ar, ern, es*, 3541, 4824, 4878, 24147, 24256 etc., 4847, 21945 etc.

Sg. 3rd pers.: *bes* / 4507, 2137.

Pl. *ben* C 20479, *we ben* C 9712, *bes* 23672.

B. Auxiliaries.

Inf.: *haf* 430, 9532 (printed *has*), *haue* 124, *a* C 1117, 5284.

Sg. 1st pers.: *haf* 73, 4623 (C F printed *has*), *haue* 70; 2nd pers.: *haues* C 2464, *has* 300 etc.; 3rd sg.: *hauis* E passim, but *has* (printed *haf*) 23367, *as* 23114, *hafs* 23030, *haues* C 13889, *has* 31. G's *hath* 547 must be disregarded; cf. also *had* E 23336.

Pl. *haf, haue, ha* C, *has* 8510, 92, 4912, 2062, 23706; *hauis* E passim.

---

[1] *līn* is not a contraction of *leyen*, from *lezen*, but of *lizen*, cf. *Medit. on the Supp. of our Lord* 771: *lyne, pyne* (cf. *Helmers*, elsewhere, p. 56), *Tristrem* 2909.

Pres. *can.* Pret. *cuþe* (r. w. *muþ* passim).

Pret. *gan* 1490, 838. As regards *can, con, gun,* see § **67.** *biguþe* E (cf. *and I biguþe it withald* E, *and I bigan it to withald* C **y**) 24579, E (*in sinagoge spel biguþe* E, *in synagog bigan to spell*) 19698, which is used here as an auxiliary verb, seems to be Scotch, cf. *The Bruce,* II. 393, V. 9, VIII. 308, and appears as an obvious alteration in l. 24579, while in l. 19698 the reader will see that the context in C **y** ll. 19695-98, of which two lines are wanting in E, gives no objection.

Pres. *þar.* Pret. *þurt* 1993, 6979. Cf. *þis tar = þis þar* E 24743.

Pres. *mun (mon)* 18246, 15980, 21822, 24867. Pret. *mund* C E 23179, (*mond*) C 12359, C 1105.

Pres. *mai* (sg. and pl., cf. besides O.E. *mæʒon*) passim ; *mu* (3 pl., O.E. *muʒon, moʒon*) / 23559. Pret. *might* passim, *moght (mught* F) 23772, 24432, etc.

Prt. *doght (dught* C F) 16204, 23771.

Prs. *mot* (= may, to denote a wish) 3737, 7867, 6289, 23099, 23932, 21471.

Prs. *most* (= must) 916, 1243 (*bus* G), 5984, C 948, C F 333 (*bos* G). Pret. *most* 2400, 2249.

C. Defective Verbs.

Pret. *quaþ* / 22973, *coth* C (*quod* F, *said* G) 20751, C G (*cod* E) 23560, C G (*cod* E, *quoþ* F) 23527, C G 24476 ; cf. O.E. (North.) *cwaᵭ,* and W.S. *cwellan* = quell and O.E. (North.) *cuœllan* = cole 3135, 11862.

Pret. 3 sg. *bird* 10695, 12988 etc.

69. The rymes.

It is a general mistake to believe that all M.E. rymes must be pure as to the quality and quantity of their vowels, or as to the consonance. As to their quality, I dare to say that rymes in *i : e,* or *o : u* would be more frequently found in every dialect, if the scribe's spelling (generally 14th cent.) were not made too much of. The slightest knowledge of modern English rymes and of the Continental Low German dialects must suggest such an idea.[1] In such *i : e* rymes, *e* must be rather close, and generally short, and *i* open, because the assimilation between ĭ.· and ĕ· is easiest. When ŏ and ŭ ryme, *o* is open indeed, and ŭ. would be practically close ŏ, which so often changes with ŭ. in the same word. A difference between ŏ· and u is scarcely felt. There is no

---

[1] Cf. the rough list of *i : e* rymes, which A. Brandl gives in *Ang. f. d. Altertum, N. F.* xix. 1, and *Litteratbl. f. Germ. and Rom. Pe : e* iv. 135 The late Dr. Wissman (in 1876) started the wrong idea that *i : e* rymes could be dialectic criteria.

particular period, when f. i. *abŭ.ve* is *abŏ·ve* alone, but when the tendency to put *o* for *u* is complete, it is ŏ open.

As to the origin of this interchange, there is some reason to believe that surrounding consonants originally influenced the utterance of the vowels, but this phenomenon did not make its first appearance in M.E. A list of consonants from M.E. rymes before which this interchange took place would imply first that such ryme-words were then preferred in verse. Any attempt at a solution of this question in Middle-English would have to begin with Old English materials.

As to their quantity, I would say that rymes in ā· : ă· or ō : ŏ are the common exceptions to strict purity. Where the first class appears, there is reason to believe that *a* has an obscure close sound, and inclines to *o*. Otherwise the distance would be felt much more. So I believe that a ryme like *ras* (prt.) : *was* must be pronounced with an obscure (broad) sound, whereas *place* : *was* would show a clear, open (French) *a* which is not so long as the *a* in *ras*. As to ō : ŏ rymes, ō and ŏ may be either open or close, and *vice versâ*.

As to the consonants, the rymes show the same liberty, so that neighbouring sounds like *d* : *t*, *m* : *n*, etc. are allowed. But the pronunciation of rymes consisting of dentals does not seem to be the same in the Saxon dialect, where it is sharpened.

I'll add a rough list, which contains several corrections of the scribe's spellings and readings.

I. Difference in quality :

A. *Short or lengthened i : e·, or e· : i,*—togedir, hider[1] 6554, to bren, witin C 5750, hent (*prt.*), stynt (*sb.*) (stent C) 3841, 17699, steng (*aculeus*), ȝyng 24029 (cf. stang, amang 693), ryn, bren 7157, leng, thyng 8181, dynt, hent (*prt.*) 3176, 12315, vphent, dynt 12183, wild, feld (*sb.*) 6079, unweild (= impotens), child 10539, dere (*vb.*), scire (*adj.*) 23470, tint, jugement 945ᶜ heuen, dryuen, 22110.

B. *Short or long o : u*—Salamon, ton 14612, Salamon, promissiun (MS. -o- 14432 (cf. Salamon, don (*inf.*) 9075, don (*pp.*), Salamon 9116, but : to hon, Salamon 8791), dome, cume 23056, *sooth, Eliud* 9241, aboven, oven (*sb.*) 2926, coue, lufe (*vb.*) C 11617, behove, love 3646, luve, prove 9038. Open o : close o : Iohn, bone 10966 (Iohan C). As to *abouen* and *luue* we may see in the rymes the state of transition from *u* into *o*.

---

[1] Compare also *hing* (inf.) 4992, 8905, 16020, (subj. prs.), *dring* (sb.) / 15414, 16022, hint (*inf.*) / 21624.

II. Difference in quantity :

A. $\bar{\imath}$: $\check{\imath}$ or *VICE VERSA*,—fine (*vb.*), wiðerwin 7206, pris, his 6732, nine (numeral), driȝtin 2644, this, paradis 20492, him, tim 13773.

B.[1] $\bar{o}$: $\check{o}$,—Iohn, bone (prayer) 10966 (cf. yon, Iohn 14471, apon, Iohn 23202), fordone, quon (fune C, fone G) 18246, Iŏhn, tron 13221.

C.[1] $\bar{a}$: $\check{a}$,—Adam, allan 1112, gan (*pp.*), Abram 5724, nan, Iohan 11078, Iohan (*v. r.* Iohn, Ion), on an 11095, to wale, sale 7952, þan, nan 13780, sale, dale 1252, gate, hatt (*prt.*), 10546, yatt (*prt.*), gate (gatt C) 8806, yate (yatt C) (*sb.*), forgat (*prt.*) 12594, make, Isaac 3016, wrake, spak 890, nightertale, sale 2783, spade, sad 1240.

D.[1] $\bar{e}$: $\check{e}$: forgett (*pp.* for *forgeten*), lett 15808, gett (*pp.* for *geten*), dett 17418, snell (*adj.*), Israel 7754, Samuel, tel (*vb.*) 7360.

E. Diphthong : monophthong : destrui (MS. destru) : iesu 22134, threw (MS. throu), drou 24318.

III. Difference in consonance :

A. m : n—Abraham, man 2756, Adam, allan 1112, name, tan 5646, man, nam y 12737, gan, abram 5724, man, adam 9784, name, nan (nam C) 9830, gan (*pp.*), ham (*sb.*) 13191, tuin, Effraim 5236, grim, Benjamin 7008, Sichim, kin 6964, time, latine 7040, thrin, him 3382, time, Sarȝine 11072, wiðerwin, venim 14871, sun, cum 20326, toun, capharnaum 12488 ; lend, demd (MS. dempt) 23054, luuen, cummen 20376.

B. d : t—vmstund (MS. umstunt), wont 13693, cf. .21073. *Besides*, cf. demẹd, *and* lend, dempt 23054.

C. th (þ) : d or t—quaþ, Iosaphat 22974, forþ, word 11084, sooþ, Eliud 9242, ferd (*adj.*, orig. *pp.*), erth 2370.

D. b : p—Jacob, biscop 19492, 21170.

E. p : k—Iosep, spek 12174, 12290.

F. pt : p—Egipte, wirscippe 4628.

G. ȝt : ft.—diht, gift E 24808, moght, loft 2086, kniȝtes, giftes F G 18570.

H. f : wȝ—skurf, þhurgh 11824.

I. z : s—wisẹ (*sb.*), it hisẹ (hastens) 21278, wisẹ (*sb.*), unwisẹ (*pl. pre.*) 2224, chesse (*inf.*), beess C 8410, in þi servis, in paradise 20844 (cf. wis (*adj.*), of paradise 21026).   Final *s* seems to be sharpening though it is derived from soft *s*.

---

[1] The difference in B C D seems to be slight, as the short vowels allow of being lengthened.

70. *The Author's Time and Dialect.*

Since Dr. J. A. H. Murray wrote in 1868 his unrivalled book on the dialects of the Southern Counties of Scotland, no attempt whatever has been made to inquire into the validity of his suggestions. In his opinion, the *Cursor Mundi* was written near Durham, about 1275-1300 (while Alexander III. reigned in Scotland), and was preserved in an orthography not much later. The abstract he gives is taken from the Cotton MS. Vespasian A iii. After having shown that the MSS. which have come down to us are much later than is generally believed, and that the Cotton MS. was written late 14th or early 15th century, in a dialect far different from what Dr. Murray supposed, I am now certainly entitled to conclude, from the comparative view of the author's language, that he was a *Lincolnshire man*.

A comparison with Robert of Brunne's dialect has proved that the author of the *Cursor* was his elder, so that he belonged to the 13th century. He finished, as we may justly suppose, his education at Cambridge at a time when the 'age of Robert Grosseteste' the 'Linconicus' [1] was still in living memory. He 'understands' (l. 20060) that Edmund Rich of Pontigny, where the famous Archbishop of Canterbury died on the 16th Nov., 1240, composed the poem of *The Assumption of our Lady*. The whole literature, religious and profane, of the first half of the 13th century was an object of his studies. He calls his authority in l. 9516, 'Sant Roberdes book,' and makes us suppose that he wrote his *Cursor* when Robert Grosseteste had been canonized. According to Pegge [2] (p. 250), the Dean and Chapter of St. Paul's in 1307 solicit Pope Clement V. to canonize Robert, but their request is without result. Nor do we know whether Robert was canonized at all. I hardly believe that the *Cursor* was composed after this date, and it is very likely that the author was not particular about the title 'Sant,' which Robert really deserved after his death in 1253, but which was never granted by a Pope whose predecessor Robert had called a heretic and an antichrist. From philological reasons, as we have seen, it is certain that the *Cursor* was written as early as the second half of the 13th century : to give a nearer date would be a mere guess.

Remembering the disgraceful expulsion of the Jews, which was due to the bigotry and rapacity of Edward I. in 1290, and proved such a severe blow to the commerce of the kingdom, I should think that the author, who treated fully of the 'felun Juus,' would have made some allusion to this fact, if he had

---

[1] Cf. *Sammlung der Würtemburgischen Schul-Gesetze III.*, p. 91.
[2] Cf. *The Life of Robt. Grosseteste.* 4° : Lond. 1793.

written after its date.   But I have not been able to find any allusion to it.
The suggestion will therefore be allowed that the *Cursor* was composed between
1254-90.   There is another fact which I will mention, though it is trifling.
In 1279 Edward had issued a new silver coin, of the value of four pence, and
called a gross or groat, that is, a great penny.[1]   Considering the eagerness with
which clerks caught at new expressions, one would expect that the *Cursor*-
writer might use this new term—for instance, in speaking of ' the xxx penis '
which Judas got for his treachery, or somewhere else—but he does not, and so
one may venture to say that the *Cursor* was written between 1255 and 1280 ;
but this is all I can urge in favour of my supposition.

71.   *The Author's Name.*

My argument that the author must have been a Lincolnshire man, and
lived near the borders of Yorkshire—to judge from some Northern particular-
ities of which he was aware (plural in *s*)—is confirmed by another fact.   The
Göttingen MS. has some most remarkable lines (ll. 17087-17110), which have
been supposed to belong to the scribe.   Part of these lines, which are coloured
in red, are found in the Cotton MS., which breaks off at l. 17094, and con-
cludes with three new long lines which show the same end-ryme, but also a
ryme at the middle and end of the first half-line (f. i. *and send space al of his
grace vr wranges here to right*).   It seems to me that these three long lines do
not belong to the Cotton scribe, nor do they betray an ignorant one.   It is
very likely that the *Cursor*—which no doubt was widely known and highly
appreciated by ' clerks '—went through the hands of several monks ; so that
the lines were probably written in the second half of the 14th century.   The
lines in G appear to have a different view.   There are ten rymes in ' ight,' and
after the fifth ryme the half-lines likewise ryme.   Such concluding lines are
not without a system, and appear to have been intentional, so that they do not
look like patch-work.   The Cotton MS. has two equivalent rymes among the
three new ones (right, light, right) which are found among the ten of G, all of
which are different from each other.   Northern spellings are found in *bock,
gart* 17100, and *dune* 17103, while in l. 17110 *boke* appears.   The rhythm
in G is quite correct.   The whole is shut up with two other rymes ; the long
half-lines likewise ryme.

If none of G's lines (which do not exist at the end of the *Cursor*) were
preserved in the Cotton MS., if the three new lines in C did not betray a

Cf. Geo. L. Craik, *History of British Commerce* (vols. i.-iii.   Lond. 1844), vol. i.
p. 156.

clerk who, in his different ending, perhaps used well-known lines (which he remembered when he saw concluding rymes in G), if G's lines did not show a well-considered and well-proportioned change in rymes, and if there were not an undoubted context with the preceding matter (cf. ll. 17096 and 17098), I might think that these lines belonged to the Northern transcript (y), on which the Göttingen MS. depends. However, I should wonder what interest the Göttingen scribe—whose copy is fairly done after his Northern source, but shows a good many inconsistencies with the Northern dialect—had in retaining in these lines a name which was to be considered that of a scribe. He certainly did not think so. The words ' JOHN OF LINDBERGHE, i ʒu sai þat es mi name ful right' appear, therefore, to betray the author's name. But there is still some apparent difficulty. In the preceding line we read : ' þat þis book gart dight.' The expression suits capitally. There is no doubt that the clerk who wrote this book got it ' ornamented.' But the Göttingen MS. shows no ornaments at all, and the few red lines, and red initials (which are left out at the end of the MS., and are then only marked in black) prove that the rubricator and the scribe are the same person : another reason why John of Lindbergh must not be confounded with the Göttingen scribe.[1] So the first possessor, *i. e.* the Author, had an interest in saying :

> And speciali for me ye pray þat þis bok gert dight:
> Iohn of Lindberghe, i yu sai that es mi name ful right,
> If it be tint or done oway, trewli mi trowþ i plight,
> Qua bringes it me wiðuten delay, I sal him yeild þat night;
> And qua it heles and haldis for me, trewli i yu tell
> Curced in kirk þan sal þai be wiþ candil, boke and bell (ll. 17099-110).

I can give some further researches about *Lindbergh*. There are two names between which we have the choice. First there is ' Lindbergh Magna[2] in Northridinge Ebor.', mentioned 1 anno Edw. I., in the *Cal. Inquis. post mortem*, vol. i. 50, 1806. But this cannot be meant. The author's dialect differs from Hampole's, whose birthplace is in the neighbourhood, and who, though younger than the Author of the *Cursor*, used such forms as could never be developed from the forms of our Author. The differences are of course not great, and that is just a comfort for me. For we see that the other Lindbergh, which must be preferred, is in the neighbourhood of Yorkshire.

---

[1] Similar concluding lines, as above mentioned, may have afterwards been used by scribes, but they stand apart from the context.—The above lines are written in the spelling which I think suitable for a critical edition.

[2] Now-a-days Limber Hill, a hamlet in the parish of Egton, North Riding, co. York, 7 miles S.-W. of Whitby.

In the North of Lincolnshire there lie two 'Limbergh's' close by each other, one called 'Magna,' the other 'Parva.' The former is often mentioned without the addition in the Hundred Rolls, and is the seat of a monastery. The latter is a hamlet, and can be found in *Cal. Inquis. post mortem*, vol. i. 195. There appears no doubt that the former, called Limberge Magna, or Limberge, Limbergia, is meant. As to the spelling, we are assured by the name Lindberge registered in *Rotuli Hund. Temp. Henr. III et Edw. I. In Turri Londin. et in Curia Recept. Saccarii Westm. asservati*, vol. i., 1812 (The Lincoln Rolls are in the Tower). Cf. 312, col. 2, ' *Com'. Linc'. Edw. I.—Willata Linc'. de magno anno domini Edwardi Regis tercio.* No. 17a m. 4, *Veniunt omnes subscripti*, etc. etc.; *abbas de Torneton* xx s. . . . *Item abbas de Ramestrey* xviii s., *Item priore de Lindberge* xiii s. iiii d. This Lindberge is now-a-days LIMBER MAGNA, a parish in the Ecclesiastical division of the hundred of Yarborough, parts of Lindsey, co. Lincoln, 5 miles S. of Ulceby, 5 N.-E. of Caistor. I add its general description from Hamilton's *National Gazetteer:* 'The village, which is small, is situated on the Wolds. The church, dedicated to St. Peter, is an ancient structure with a tower containing 3 bells. The church was given in the reign of Henry III. to the Cistercian abbey of Aulnoy, in Normandy, by Rich. de Humet, Constable of Normandy. At the suppression of alien priories it was sold to the Carthusian abbey of St. Anne, near Coventry.'

John of Lindberȝe is a true-born Englishman. He wants his English congregation to read English rymes. For of what use are French romances to those who don't understand French?

> ' þis ilke boke it is translate
> Into Inglis tung to rede
> For þe luve of Inglis lede,
> Inglis lede of Ingeland,
> For the commune at understand.
> Frenkis rimes here i rede
> Communlike in ilka stede;
> Mast es it wroȝt for Frenkis man:
> Quat is for him na Frenkis can?'—ll. 232-240.
> ' Give we ilkan þair langage
> Me þink we do þaim nan vtrage.'—ll. 247-8.

CHAPTER V.—THE PHONOLOGY OF THE RYMES AS A RESULT
OF THE CRITICISM.

72. Vowels.

A. *Short i.* It is generally open in M.E., as is seen from the regular
confusion between *i* and *e*.

1. O.E. *i, y, as*, mid (with) 21590, þridd 21589, bigyn 111, myn 112, blin
121, wiðin 5750, rin 7157, þinges 21, kynges 22, to give, to live 145-6, his
2390, myrth 2319, byrth 2320.

2. O.E. *î, ŷ, as*, kydd 7954, hydd 21308, bliss 442, wiss (to show) 14643,
tynt 1587.

3. O.E. *e,*[1] *as*, dill (O.E. dwellan = to prevent) 202, 13031.

4. O.N. *i, e, as*, flit (O.N. flytja) ?450, [un]skil 201, gin 3644, twin
(O.N. pl. tvenner, tvenne, *e* = former *i*) 1536, þrin (O.N. pl. þrenner) 353.

B. *Half-long i.*

M.E. *i before ght* = ʒt, *as*, myʒt, forsyʒt, wyʒt, lyʒt, nyʒt, plyʒt, bryʒt,
hyʒt (was called), flyʒt, maledyʒt, wyʒt, dyʒt, fyʒt, ryʒt, hyʒte (height).

C. *Long i.*

1. O.E. *î, ŷ, as*, tijm 1359, mijn 564, nijn 2643, pijn 9799, þijn 15686,
tijne (*vb.*) 9457, vijn 180, lijke 10, ilijke 75, rijke, kyngrijke 415-6, wijke
(angalus) 2090, wijke (= village) 7917, swijke 2097, þe wijs (*adj.*) 149,
wijs (*pl. adj.*) 435, wijse (*sb.*) 2223, flijte 7556, nijte, wijte (= poena) 883-4,
smijte 3173, quijte (*adj.*) 8120, wrijte 18518, ij 2219, forþij 309, forqwij
813, bij (*vb.*) 2036, bij (*prep.*) 2207, tijde 447, abijde 466, hijde (*vb.*)
777, sijde 1681, wijde 1682, lijf 6, lijve 1456, rijf 177, wijf 830, fijve 1455,
rijve 1855, strijve 9306, belijve 7508, drijve 9100, ijre, fijre 1981-2, clijve
(*sb.*) 1856.

2. O.E. *i, ŷ, î, y + palatal, as*, bij (to buy) 152, bij (village) 8538, drij 309,
hij 2605, lij 8537 (but cf. *to ligȝe* 8946), lijs 1129, stij 3779; (gastlij, bodilij
427-8, myʒtilij 1614, on account of the ryme).

3. M.E. *i before ld, nd, as*, chijld 156, mijld 155, scijld (*sb.*) 10808, blijnd
184, fijnd 183, brijnd (*sb.*) 9206, strijnd 2144.

4. O.N. *î, ŷ, as*, knijf 7511, skij 3780, bijke 76, tijte 500, sijte 6288, lijte
(origin?) 17633, 17899, 18517, 24589.

5. O.F. *î, as*, partie 370, trecherie 730, mercij, crij, envie, maistrie, cries,
folie, multiplie, etc., fijle 715, vijle, exijle 1153-4, gesijn 11298, nocijn 5372,

---

[1] Qu.? hing (*inf.*), dring (*sb.*), hint (*prt.*), cf. § 69.

5802, fijn 8802, justijs 150, paradijs 606, parties (*pl.*) 344, prijs 436, truandijs 253, scrijt*e* (*sb.*) 18492, coverlijt*e*, tapijt*e* 11239-40, despijt*e* 7555, quijt*e* 7568, visijt*e* 5789, etc.

73. A. *Short e.*

1. O.E. *ë, e, eo, y, as,* spell 95, tell 12, fell (*sb.*) 584; himselue 173, twelue 174, welth 755; merr (*vb.*) 2254, werr (*comp.*) 12952, ferr (*adv.*) 2253; smert 58, hert (*heart*) 57, hert (*hart*) 1787; went (*prt.*) 1090, biwent (*pp.*) 825; west 2120, fest (*pp.*) 558; neuen 303, euen 335, heuen 336, seuen 508; heðen, aneðen 5117-8.

2. O.E. *œ, ǽ, ëö, as,* togedir 582, 10107, þrell 10914, gress 545, wes (= *was*) 8867; neuer, euer 83-4; fell (*prt.*) 11.

3. O.F. *e, a, as,* clerk 1178, quert (O.F. quart, *dwelling, shelter, safety*) 1803, unquert (= *harm*) 1788.

4. O.N. *ë, e, a, as,* es (3 *sg. prs.*) 1021, 1406 etc., emell 1445, kest (*prt.*) 1080, 1087.

B. HALF-LONG, OPEN E in a close syllable.

1. M.E. *e* (O.E. *ë, e, é, ïë, eo, ea, ëö, ǽ*) + *l* + *d*, or *n* + *d*, or *r* + *d* or *th* or *n, as,* beild 22852, sceild 2497, feild 2498, 3821, eild 585, 923, 10544, 22851, 10594, heild (*prt.*) 259, 587, 907, dunheild 3822, weild (*vb.*) 462, 586, 788, 10593, yeild (*vb.*) 260, 461, 908, 924, teld (*prt.* and *pp.*) 24956, 7062, queld (*prt.*) 19467, dweld (*prt.*) 19526; leind (*vb.*) 9652, sceind (*vb.*) 4397, seind (*vb.*), weind (*vb.*) 1271-2, heind (*adj.*) 431, 13888, teind (10°) 432, 968, freind (*sg.* and *pl., besides* freindes) 4398, 961, 1150, 1061, 1207, 14119, 24436, 13389, 23738, feind 23740; erth (erd) 2370, wer(l)d 91, answerd 4143, bern (*prt. pl.*) 20716, bern (*vb.*) 12911, bern (*sb.*) 20450, wern (*pl. prt.*) 8079, wern (*vb.*) 22003, 21334, stern (*sb.*) 23587.

2. O.E. *ë, e, œ* (= *ea* after ȝ), *a in an open syllable, as,* stede (*sb.*) 238, 8820, 17671, 19210 etc., bede (*sb.*) 17672, 19209; speke (*vb.*) 1643, 2927, 12289, wreke (*vb.*) 2928; fele (*many*) 8991, 6823, 10105 etc., stele (*vb.*) 4910, 6477, mele (meal) 4680, wele (*adv.*) 1165, 4431 etc., wele (*sb.*) 672, 8883, overwele (*sb.*) 2901; bere (*vb.*) 904, 3704 etc., forbere (*vb.*) 3454, forbereṣ (*prs.*) 13834, bere (sb., *barley*) 13506, bere (*bear*, sb.) 691, dere (*vb.*) 692, 7731, 23469, here (*host, army*) 7732, 13507, were (*to wear*) 9072, spere (*sb.*) 7728, 20545, pers (*sb. pl.*) 37, swere (*vb.*) 3225, were (*to defend*) 3299, were (weir; *doubt*) 2425, 3299, 3453, 3698, 8746, 9276, 10891 etc., demestere 22920, gere (*vb.*) 2598, 7727, gereṣ (*prs.*) 8221, 13835, gere (geyre; *sb.*) 3300, answere (*sb.*) 11320; stepę (*sb.*) 5194, 4816, 9248, 17704; gete (gett; *vb.*) 1015, 3603,

3629, 4990, 17947, mete (sb., *meat*) 4340 etc., mete (measure) 22897, ete (*vb.*)
passim, forgete (forget) *passim*, fete (*vb.*) 9046 etc.   *Observe, too*, stere (O.E.
styrian) 4295, 4450, 4959, 5559, 6055, *and* O.N. ë *in* gete (*to watch*) 997.

3. O.E. *ê, ǽ, by way of syncope, as*, delt 1068, melt (*pp.* and *prt. of* O.E.
mǽlan, *besides* meild (*prt.*) 27214) 2268, wend (*prt. of* O.E. wênan) 23737,
herd (*prt.* and *pp.*) 92 etc., ferd (*prt.*) 2849, 4144, ferd (*adj.*, orig. *pp.*) 2369,
grett (*pp. of* O.E. ȝrêtan) 4339, 10834, *besides* bedd¹ (*prt.*), forbedd (*prt.*),
bredd, bledd, fedd, fledd, ledd, left, spredd, scedd, spedd, threst (*pp.*) 557 (*sb.*,
3279), uncled (*prt.*) 16666.

4. O.E. *œ, ǽ, eâ, eô, as*, flex (fless) 80, 1857, lest (last) 208, neuerþeless 79,
less 2112, 2168, 18504, lest (*least*) 1659, 2119, 4849, 6004, alðerlest 10423;
wess (wex, wesc, *by analogy of* O.E. wêðx, cf. *Northumbrian* wôx) 1997, 2713,
stepe (*prt.*) 10764; grett (wept) 4765, 5248, 9045, 15006, lep (*prt.*), bet (*prt.*),
wep (*prt.*); nerre (*comp.*) 7580, 12366, 12953, ete (*prt., by the influence of the
plural*) 22898 etc.   *Besides, observe* stele (O.E. stệl, stýle) 18188 etc., yeit
(*adv., besides* yit) 2287, 1198, *and proper nouns like* Ierusalem, Iersalem,
Samuel, Israel, Iosep.

5. O.F. *e* = Lat. *e, a, as*, best 737, 1660, fest 10424, geste 207, tempest
6027, pres 5608, cypres 8007, morsel 13485, catel 3103, 4953, castel 10035,
angel 1391.   Besides, observe O.F. *e* = Teut. *e, as*, were (werr) 7579 etc.

C. *Unsettled, but, in my opinion, generally inclining towards² half-long
open e (narrow).*

1. O.E. *ê, as*, fele (*sb.*), fele (*vb.*), deme (*vb.*); (un)fere (*adj.*), fere (*sb.*),
here (*adv.*), mede (*reward*); het (*prt.*), let (*prt.*), slep (*prt.*); bete (*to emend*),
brede (*vb.*), fet (*pl. sb.*), suete (*adj.*), mete (*vb.*), rede (*to read, to speak, to say*).
Besides, O.E. ê = *i-umlaut of* eâ, *as*, here (*vb.*), nede (*sb.*), gnede (*adj.* and
vb.), *perhaps also* leue (*to believe*); O.E. *eâ, ê, as*, eke (*adv.*), nẹre (neir),
perhaps also neist (*sup.*).

2. O.E. *eô, as*, dere (*adj.*), lem (*sb.*), lem (*vb.*), smeke (*sb.*), lede (*sb.*), yede
(*prt.*); *perhaps also* leif (*adj.*), theif (*sb.*), breist (*sb.*), preist (*sb.*).   *Compare
also* knele (*vb.*).

3. O.E. *ǽ, e* = W. Teut. â, Goth. ê, *as*, dede (*sb.*), drede (*vb.* and *sb.*),

---

¹ Where no references are given, look for them in the critical part.
² I beg the reader once more to consider that, according to dialect, a half-long open *e*
spoken with a narrow articulation slightly differs from a half-long close *e* spoken with a
wide articulation, cf. modern *hare* and *say* in the context of a sentence. This may
perhaps account also for the interchange between *ǽ* and *ê, eô* and *eâ, eo* and *ea* in the
Anglian dialects.

sede (*sb.*), sete (*sb.*), wede (*vb.*), wede (*sb.*), scep (*sb.*), yepe (*adj.*), yere (*sg.* and *pl.*, *besides*, yeirs) ; sete (*prt. pl.*), strete (*sb.*), wet (*adj.*), lete (*vb.*), there, were (*prt.*), bere (*prt.*), scere (*prt.*), *perhaps also, according to the rymes*, speke (*sb.*), slepe (*vb.* and *sb.*), cheke (*sb.*).   *Compare also* bles (*sb.*) 7160, 8877.

4. O.E. *ê, â* = Teut. *ai* or *ai-i*, *as*, brede (*sb.*), sprede (*vb.*), lede (*vb.*), lere (*vb.*), -hede.

5. O.F. *e* = Lat. *a, as,* clere (*adj.*), pere (*sb.*).

6. O.F. *ie, monophthongized in Norman French, as,* cher (*sb.*), mister (*sb.*), prayer (*sb.*), messager (*sb.*), iaioler (*sb.*), morter (*sb.*).   maintein (*vb.*) 7374 seems to have kept its diphthongs.

7. O.F. *e* = Lat. *e resp.* Greek *η, as,* prophete, Oliuet.

8. O.N. *ê, îu, as,* seir (sere), sketc (*adv.*).   *Observe also* kepe (*sb.*), kepe (*vb.*).

D. LONG, OPEN E.

1. O.E. *ê* = W. Teut. *â,* Goth. *ê, as,* dede (*prt.*), rede (*to counsel, to expound ; advice*), quede (*sb.*), mele (*vb.*), bitele (*vb.*), sele (*sb.*) ; *probably also* leche (*vb.*).

2. O.E. *ê, â* = Teut. *ai* or *ai-i, as,* dele (*sb.* and *vb.*), hele (*vb.*), res (*sb.*), hete (*heat*), quete (wheat), swete (*vb.*), biyeit (O.E. beʒêat) 2206, bileue (to remain) ; *probably also* teche (*vb.*), reche (*vb.*).

3. O.E. *êâ, as,* bred (*bread*) 4601, 12949, led (*lead*) 16454, ded (*adj.* and *sb.*) 905, 4113 etc., red (*adj.*) 4678, 5919 ; eme 3789, beme (beam) 11228, *ryming to* leme 9946, drem (*sb.*) 5069, tem (*vb.*) 6170, 12797, 14791 ; ere (*ear*) 5140, ern (*pl. sb.*) 8080, les (*sb.*) 5747, wemles 5748, 7165, faðerles 6787, ches (*prt.*) 144, 5642, 13304, 20914 ; grete (*adj.*) 2205, 4598 etc., grete (*vb.*) 4700, nete (*sb.*) 4597.   *Perhaps also* leue (*permission*).

4. O.F. *ei, ai, monophthongized, as,* peis (pees, *sb., besides* pais 2589) 2793, 5971, males (malees) 6300, es (ess, *sb.*) 8757, 13305, ses (*vb.*) 6032, weue (O.F. [N] weif) 22927.

5. O.F. *ei + ê.* or *e + â contracted, as,* sele (*sb.*) 6889, 17411, 18565, lele (*adj.*) 1625, 4909, 6478, 6824.

E. LONG, CLOSE E (*wide*).

1. O.E. *ê, e* = W. Teut. *â,* Goth. *e, as,* bidene (*adv.*), wene (*vb.*).

2. O.E. *ê, as,* kene (*adj.*) 213 etc., grene (*adj.*) 1012 etc., scene (*adj.*) 2416 etc., fiuetene 214, scuentene 9142, sene (*pp.*) 4918 etc., ben (*pp.*) 2984.

3. O.E. *â* = Teut. *ai* or *ai-i, as,* clene (*adj.*), mene (*vb.*), sec (*sb.*).

4. O.E. *êô, as,* be 289, thre 182, fre 664, gle 54, tre 761, tres (treis) 7159,

knes (kneis) 14292, fre 1059, bene (*inf.*) 20430, lese (*vb.*) 7613, chese (*vb.*) 7614, quele 23719 (*but* cf. wele (*adv.*) *ryming to* quele 21274).

5. O.F. *final e* = Lat. *a, as,* meyne (meigne, *sb.*) 1862, 3208, pite 1861, trinite 561, vanite 53, liuere 2122.

6. O.F. *ie, ei monophthongized in Anglo-Norman, as,* vele (veil; MSS. wele) 23717.   Cf. *also* vayl (*Cotton Insertion,* p. 957, l. 85).   *Probably also* greif (*vb.*) 7233.

74. A. *Short open a.*

1. O.E. *æ, as,* spak 890, 1242, 2811, craft 426, 511, scaft 425, 512, scap 733, was 479, 2845, gras 2846, fast 169, last 229, stedfast 281, formast 433, brast (*prt.*) 1538, 1766, gave 667, stave 7322, þral 2055, stal (*prt.*) 8635, smal 376, 972.

2. O.E. *a, as,* have 769, 668.

3. O.E. *a, ea before l, m, n, as,* al, alle, all 101, 268, 395, 340, 538, 971, 2056, 8635, galle, calle, falle, scal, stalle, halle, als, cam (*prt.*) 1205, 2383, suam, ram (*sb.*) 1785-6, can 240, blan (*prt.*) 744, wan (*prt.*), bigan 1050, lemman, wan (*adj.*) 82, man 513, yoman 7821, woman 185, 629, 886, þan 269, 423.

4. O.F. *a, as,* principal, bale (*vb.*) 13139, 13195, pan 4387, mat (*vb.*) 8479, matt (*adj.*) 10041.

5. O.N. hap (O.N. happ) 734.   *Observe, too,* Ir. Gæl. crag 9885.

B. *Half-long open a.*

1. O.E. *a, æ, as,* sad 1240, glad 1408, 3199, bad (*prt.*) 1291, 1750, 3200, forbad 673, spade 1239, hag (cf. on *g,* O.N. hagi) 9886, make 3016, wrake 890, hake 1241, tale 124, niȝertale 2783, smal 393, licame 635, schame 2026, 2202, name 406, 2769, 4808, 5755, tame 17326, mischapen, schapen 367-8, vndertaken, forsaken 917-18, naked, maked 989, 900, saked 1223 ; lake (O.E. lac, lacu) 2887 ; dale (from O.E. pl. *dalu*) 1251, slade (from O.E. pl. *sladu*) 1259.

2. O.E. *a, æ, ea, ǽ before final r, rn, nd, ng, as,* care 483, 615, hare (= hare) 687, ȝare 915, fare (*sb.*) 1831, spare 5966, bare (*adj.*) 801, 1321, bar (*sg.* and *pl. prt.*) 158, 1069, 4485, 1051, 3211, 493, 1185, 3636 ; swar[1] (*prt.*) 4650, forfare 2829, war (*adj.* warr) 2787, sparr (*vb.*) 2788, mar (hindrance) 8634, answar (*sb.*) (besides answere) 5853, barn (*sb.*) 1231, warn (*pl. prt.*) 4759, warn (*vb.*) 12453, fand (*prt.*) 1293, stand (*inf.*) 1184, land 12979, wand 12970, hand 601, sand (*sb.*) 679, vnderstand 337, aand 541, faand (*vb.*) 542,

---

[1] *swar* by analogy of *bar.*

fourtiand 1465, Ingeland 8, sang, amang 87-8, stang 693, gang, lang 949-50, wrang, sprang 1599-600. *Observe also* O.E. *e* in *errand* 1294, þusand 1466.

3. O.F. *a*, *as*, heritage 609, vtrage 975, grace, manace 1833-4, allas 6128, pas 15392, cas 16348, blame 4027, state (cf. also O.N. staðr) 1551, 1999, 2982, 10042, 10410, 5418. *Observe, too, knaulage* 610, 976, *but cf. the explanation below.*

4. O.E. *a*, *ea before ld*, *as*, wald (*sb.*) 2393, saald (*prt.* and *pp.*) (5407), 4241, talde (*prt.*) 2393, taald (*pp.*) 8765, cald (*prt.*), caald (*adj.*) 15910, hald (*inf.*), behald (*inf.*) 1332, bald 2675, fald 110, yald 209, ald 2994.

5. O.E. *â*, *æ by way of syncope*, *as*, cladd 1046, madd (*adj.*, orig. *pp.*) 2799, badd (*adj.*, orig. *pp.*) 1801, dradd, last, etc. *Take also* stadd (*besides* stedd, *from* stedan, cf. L.G. steden, O.N. steðja) 674, 1045, 1269. *Observe, too, proper nouns, as,* Adam, Iohan (*besides* Iohn), Iordan, Cham, Caiphas, Iudas, *which often find their rymes with long a.*

6. O.N. *a*, *æ*, *as*, take 86, 333, 820, 838, 2881, 2814, lake (O.N. hlak) 138, gate (way) 6262, wale (cf. O.N. val) 5375, raadd (O.N. *pp.* hræddr) 1292.

C. *Long close a.*

1. O.E. *â*, *æ*, *as*, alswa, twa, wa, brade 93, 347, 1667, 2241, bade (baide, *sb.*) 490, 607, 943, 2535, liuelade (liuelaid) 1506, 1962, þrafe (*prt.*) 3911, hale 419, 684, swak (*prt.*) 819, lam 191, ham 994, ane, nane, onan, allan, ilkan, ban, stan, lan (loan) 12835, gran (*sb.*) 3731, gan (*pp.*) 927, 5723, scan (*prt.*) 2022, wan (hope) 980 ; þare, mare, quare, ware, are (*pl.*) 4486, ar (*adv.*) 802, 916, sare (*sb.*) 688, lare (*sb.*) 999, har (hair) 3662, fas 5539, ras 5540, smat (*sg.* and *pl. prt.*) 2495, 6261, wate (*sg.* and *pl.*) 301, 1552, hate (*adj.*) 302, mast 205, 434, gast 170, wrast (*vb.*) 19353, gnast (*vb.*) 19354, biyate (*sb.*) 5417, laþ 29, 1102, wraþ 30, 1091, claþ 3809, lave 7116. *Observe also* stra (O.E. strêâw) 7204.

Remark 1. As regards *knawlage* 610, 976, cf. M.E. -lêche, -leeche, -lêche, -lâche, O.E. lêcke, lâke, O.N. leikr (cf. *lik*, body) = posture of body, play, dispositio, modus, ludus. The ending *-lage* appears to be influenced by the common French one, and belongs, on that account, to the same heading as *heritage*, *vtrage*. It is, therefore, useless to refer to O.N. *leggja* (disponere), *lag* (dispositio, societas, conjunctio) and Lat. *lex*.

Remark 2. As to *waan* 980, which is in O.E. wên, wên, wân, in O.N. wân (hope, doubt), observe the common M.E. phrases *wille of wan* (hopeless), *wille of rede* (helpless). *wille* must, I think, be directly referred to O.N. *villr*.

Halliwell's explanation, cf. *The Thornton Romances*, Lond. 1844, *Sir Isumbras*, l. 391, *for fulle wille I am of wone* r. w. *allone* = 'at a loss of a dwelling,' is beyond the mark.

2. O.E. *a lengthened by the syncope of a consonant, as*, made, mad 94, 348, 489, 608, 944, tan (*pp.*) 299, 928, 14514, overtan 575, mistan 911, taa (*inf.*) 1822, vnderta (to vnderstand[1]) 307. *Observe also* slan (*pp.*), O.E. slaȝen, 5260, 5671, 14515.

3. O.N. *á, as*, fra 1180, wan (abundance) 641, 652, bath 793, 1101, braith (O.N. *braðr* = violent) 1092, 2632, waith (O.N. *váði* = danger) 794, male (O.N. *mâl* = speech) 5376, scale (O.N. *skâli* = house) 8592.

4. O.F. *a + n + consonant, as*, chance, France, penance, meschance, vengeance. The MSS. often have *au* as a right representation of *a* low-back before *n*, when English *a* before *n* had generally turned into *o*.

75. A. *Short open o.*

1. O.E. *o in a close syllable, as*, oft 531, o loft 532, beforn 1413, morn 1414, born 1057, forlorn 1058, corn 2148, forbod (*sb.*) 13032, grot 2378, scort (O.E. sceort), *but confer* scort, hert (O.E. heort) 8347, þole 22490, cole (*sb.*) 22489, cove 11617.

Observe also Lot 2377, 2443, 2458.

2. O.F. *o (a), as*, flote 2444, sot 2457, pott 12309, skorn (cf. O.F. escarn, escharn = derision) 8963, 2723 G.

3. O.N. *a, as*, fon (O.N. fani = fool) 9186.

B. *Half-long open o.*

1. O.E. *o in an open syllable, as*, unbroken, spoken 611-12, loken 8323, vnwroken 13067, cropen, open 22609-10, hoven 8035, oven 2926.

2. O.E. *o before ld, as*, hold, gold 13264-5, 21317-8.

3. O.F. *o. (Lat. ŏ, au), as*, host 6223, note, rote 7407-8, fole (= fool) 12089, trone 8540, 20836; los 1452; pover 1797, warnestore 1698.

4. O.F. *ue* (= *Lat. ŏ), as*, cover 1798, prove 3656, 4383, dole 13040.

5. O.N. *o, as*, stoven (O.N. stofn = stem) 8036. *Moreover, observe* bost (Welsh bôst) 6224.

C. Long close *o*.

1. O.E. *ó, as*, blode, rode, mode, fode, flode, god, brode, boke, toke, vndertoke, skole 12090, son 339, 617, doon 340, 618, 387, mone 388, hone 8413, bote 44, 1376, fote 3730, glove 8116, behove (*sb.*) 3655, 4384, dom 2906, kingdom 2127, wisdom 1540, forsooþ 1253, oðer, broðer 853-4, 1219-20,

---

[1] On its meaning cf. vndertook in l. 2050.

1573-4, do 7417, lo (from looke, *vb.*) 17911.—*Observe that* don *is also ryming with* quon, sune (= son); Sodom, Rome *with* doom; fote *rymes with* goddote (= God wât) 3729. *Note also* droue (Du. origin = *droeven ?*) 11974.

2. O.E. *êô, as,* sco 634, yode 681, 1044, 1806.

3. O.N. *ô, as,* rote 43, bone 8814, crok 700, sloþ (= track) 1254, tom (= leisure) 2128, fro (= good) 23568, ro 7418.

76. A. *Short u and û.*

1. O.E. *u, as,* lust, rust, þus.

2. O.E. *u, as,* lure 3646, oboven 2925, lufe (loue, luue, *sb.* and *vb.*), born (brook) 8964, cume (come) 23056, sune, tunge, sunne (= sun), yung (yong) (*pl.*) 1418; numen, overcumen 805-6, wonder, vnder, drunken, wun (won) (*adj.*), won (*vb.*); *also* þrum (O.E. *þrymm*).

B. *Long open u.*

1. O.E. *û, as,* nu, þu, hu, ku, sku 12033, dun 1847, rune 219, bure 9806, fus 23749, hus 192, obute 8149, lute 1305. *Observe the proper nouns* Jesu, Esaü, Juu (originally Jew).

2. O.E. *u before nd, as,* grund 128.

3. O.E. *-êôw, -ôw monophthongized, as,* yu 139, 3597, tru (*vb.*) 24673, truus 22441, mistru 8433, gru 24494. *Observe* gru 24494 (O.E. greôwan (?) = Germ. *sich grauen*) 23027.

4. O.E. *o, u* + ʒ, *and û* + ʒ *vocalized by way of w, as,* forhu 19949, fule 21269, bu (*inf.*) 17533; flouʒ (*sg. prt.*) 1882.

5. O.E. *-ôʒ, -ôh, as,* slouʒ[1] 162, 1214, 2502, 5662, louʒ 2028, drouʒ 2189, 24318, bouʒ 4467, 8044, inouʒ 1557, 2027, touʒ 24439, wouʒ (injustice, falsehood) 162, 1213, 1558.

6. Anglo-Norm. *u,* O.F. *o·, as,* pru 784, avu 8434, concepciun 220, 24759, naciun, commune, tresun, pardun, felun, sun (*sb.*) 2359, chesun, paramur, socur, commandur, auctur, honur, (h)ure, labure, tur, creature, mesure, fund (*vb.*) 127, curs, vertu 11792, bule (Pic. boule, Lat. bulla = bubble,—deceit) 21270. *Observe also* trute (O.F. truite) r. w. abute 8150, destru r. w. Iesu 22133. *But* destrui *without ryme.*

7. O.N. bun (O.N. *pp.* bûinn[2]) 1651, drun (O.N. drukna[2]) 1652, 1848,

---

[1] I don't suppose that any writer spelt *slû*. The general spelling was *slouʒ*, but ʒ was silent. Our MSS. have spellings like *flou,* flogh, slo, slogh, logh, drou, inou, inogh, etc.

[2] The two etymologies appear to me rather doubtful. I should like to put O.E. ʒebûn, pp. of *bûa,* in its transitive meaning ; and O.E. *druncnian* (trs.), which is used in the same way as modern 'drown, *to be* drowned.'

5592, souȝ (O.N. sog = sentina, hence generally 'pool, slough') 2501, windouȝ (= O.N. windo·uga, orig. windo.uga) 1881.

77. Diphthongs : *ay*, *ey*.

1. O.E. *æȝ*, *as*, day 215, sayd 323, may 509, slayn 1128, fayr 1211, fayn 1387, lay 2045, frayn (O.E. fræȝna, freȝna against W.S. friȝnan, cf. O.N. fregna) 5777.

2. O.E. *á* = O.N. *ei*, *as*, ay 48, nay 1283, wayth 3524, (3522), layte (to ask) 5977.

3. O.E. *eȝ*, *as*, says, layd, flayn (*pp.*) 21112 ; *say* is formed by analogy of the 2nd and 3rd sg. prs. (only one ȝ).

4. O.E. *ëȝ*, **eh*, *as*, wai (wey) 1250, play 2816, rayn 1769, ogayn 1550, always (alweis) 10445, vpbrayd (pp. *contracted from* vpbreyded) 5673, tway (O.E. tweȝen ; the usual form is twa, O.E. twâ) 21756 ; sey (*inf.*) 7446, 4077, 6706, 18500, 16460 (besides, se, sen 23026, 23064, etc.).

5. O.E. *æh* (W.S. *eah*), *as*, sey (*sy. prt.*) 3779, 5960, 204, 1345, 10595, 5053 (*plur. prt.*[1]), 18961, 22724.

6. *æȝ-*, *ëȝ-* (W.S. *êâȝ*), *êh* (W.S. *âh*, *êâh*), *as*, clay 402, eye 3780, 1346, 4078, 4311, 6705, 13547, wrey (to accuse) 16466, ney 732, 767, 1042, 14908, hey 1041, 1684, 10596, 7445, stey[2] (*prt.*) 22724, vpstey (*prt.*) 203 (cf. O.Northumb. stê[h], O.N. steig, and stê [= stei]).

7. O.E. *êȝ-*, *æȝ-*, *êûȝ* = W.S. *êôȝ*, *as*, ley 659, 3613, 5054, fley (*sb.*) 5959, fley (*vb.*) 1782, 23621, drey (to suffer) 951, 1025, 2248, 1300.

8. O.E. *êȝ-*, *ŷȝ-*, *îȝ-*, *as*, layn (= to deny) 1549, 5281, wey (O.E. wîȝa) 8419, stey (*inf.*) 17758, 18668.

9. O.F. *ai*, *as*, delay 2253, claym 8704, reclaym 1577, 8578, playn (*adj.*) 929, (*sb.*) 2466, playnes (*plur.*) 1775, ayr 520, palays, vnpays 413-14, ayse 10446, surfait 22884, glaive 7445. *Mind also* Iordain 2465 (*besides*, Iordan).

10. O.F. *ei*, *as*, parfay 298, pray 833, 1818, fay 2354, lay (= law) 1428, 1474, 3194, renay 8995, fraid (frightened) 5814, purveyd 324, 1612, feyne, atteyne 1113-14, payn 5282, eyr (heir) 4016, payre (to grow worse) 8407, streyt 24745, receyve 7746, conceyve 22076. *Observe* valay 2380; maintein (?) (O.F. *-ie-*) 7374.

11. O.F. *a* or *e before l* or *n mouillée*, *as*, travail (traveil) (*sb.*), avayl 89-90, fayles, travayles 3525-6, fayle (*sb.*) 1827, conseil 1828, montaynes (*pl.*) 1776.

12. O.N. *ei*, *as*, dei (O.N. dyja, deyja) 660, 768, 952 etc., grayd (*contracted*

---

[1] O.E. *séȝon* (W.S. *sǽȝon*) can also give only *sey*.   [2] Cf. also *stei* (pp.) 20908.

from graiᵭed, *pp.*) 550, 1708, 3534, graith (*sb.*) 3523, frayst (O.N. freistni = temptation) 9884, layr (*sb.*) 519, nayte (O.N. neyta = to use) 22883, 24746, vnnaite (= vseless; cf. O.N. *adj.* neytr) 5976, rays (*vb.*) 7949, raym (to sound, O.N. hreima) 23156, trayst (trustworthy; orig. O.N. pp. *treyst*, cf. adj. *traustr*) 9883, þay 1427, þaym 8703, 23155. *Observe also* sley (O.N. slǽgr) 4312, vnsley 1683, on drey (cf. O.N. drjûgr, W.S. *on drey* and *a*¹ *drey* = at a distance) 731, 5511.

78. *oi*.

I have met with this diphthong only in French words, as, crois, vois 11419-20; oile, boile 11885-6. Cf. *Ten Brink*, § 90.

79. *eú*.

1. O.E. *êôw, íw, as*, newe (neu) 117, 1281, 1522, 21450, 4226, 6567, 6783, hew (colour) 4225, 9913, glew (glee) 1521, 4210, trew (*adj.*) 2149, 2663, 9914, vntrewe 6902, 13947, brew² (*inf.*) 118, 4137, rew (*inf.*) 1281, rewes (*3 pers. prs.*) 7968, knew (*prt.*) 4209, 6576, 6901, 13946, blew (*prt.*) 6503, 6575, sew (*prt.*), grew (*prt.*) 12325-6, treuth (13891), 9661, 24054 (*besides probably* truth), reuth 9662.

2. O.E. *êâw, as*, þew 13275, dew 22464, schrewes (*pl.*) 14825. *Besides observe* hew (*inf.*) 16571, *without ryme; its preterite is* hew 2497 (*no ryme*). *Note also* deus (God) 7967, Phariseus (*pl.*) 14824, Andrew 13274.

As regards O.E. *êôw* (orig. eow), it must be borne in mind that the by-form in *êô* has given long *e*; cf. gle, tre, kne. See § 73 E 4. As to O.E. *êôw* in *trêôwan*, we have seen that it is *tru* (cf. § 64) in our dialect, but compare O.E. *trûwian*. O.E. *-êûwan* is *awe* in *schawe* (cf. § 54). There is some reason to believe that the inf. *hew* has undergone the influence of the preterite.

80. *ăw*.

O.E. *âw, âʒ-, as*, knaw 4852, 5107, 7394, knaun (*pp.*) 2701, law (O.E. *hlâw*, hill) 7393, raw 221, 4851, saw (*prt.*) 1352, 4533, saun (*pp.*) 1949, 4698, saun (*pp.* = sown) 4697, þraw (*sb.*) 757, awen, aun (*adj.*) 1950, 3091, maw (O.E. *mâʒe, daughter-in-law*, or *son-in-law*, cf. l. 7650) 2807, waw (wall) 7667. *Besides observe* law, O.N. lâgr, 481, 1774, 2808, 7668.

As regards *maw* in l. 2807 (cf. *maues* = sons-in-law 2811), observe that F G have altered the entire wording 'sun or doghter, mik or mau,' C. It is

---

¹ Cf. Brunne's *Chronicle*, ll. 1042, 6048; *E. E. A. P.*, B 71. I suppose that *a* is = W.S. an = on, and not O.N. *á*. The Lambeth MS. of the *Chronicle* is not conclusive for either explanation.

² *Observe the Northern spellings* bru, ru 4137-8, blu, nu 6503, *and* truth, reuth 9661-2.

evident that *mik* stands in some contradistinction to *mau ; mik* is a Lancashire
form introduced by the scribe, as will be seen from the following comparison :
O.E. mấȝ = M.E. mey, mi, mēgh, mīgh ; Lanc. mik = cognatus, generally
' cousin ' ; O.E. mâȝ = M.E. ·maw, magh = cognatus.   Cf. also O.E. mâȝe,
mấȝe (*fem.*).

2. O.E. *ẽaw, as,* scaw[1] 1351, 2366 etc., scaun (*pp.*) 19889.

3. O.E. *aȝ, o.ȝ, as,* daw (by analogy of the plural) 2931, 5108, draw 222,
758, 791, draun (*pp.*) 2701, 4698, saw (O.E. saȝu) 791, 1569, 2931, law (O.E.
laȝu) 1569, 9053, werlaw (wấrlo.ȝa) 9054.   *Besides observe* O.N. agi = aw
482, 1636, 1773, O.N. fêlagi = felawes (*pl.*) 13442.

4. O.E. *æht*[2] (*aht*) = W.S. *eah, ealht, as,* faȝt (fauȝt) 15, 855, 3447, maȝt
6720, naȝt 3448, 3931, saȝt 16, 856, 1656, 3964, 3540.

5. O.E. *âht, ẫht, as,* taȝt (tauȝt) 3396, bitaȝt 3539, laȝt 3932, aȝt (property)
3963, 3395, 6727, aȝt (*prt.* O.E. âhte) 6719, 6728.

81. ó.u

1. O.E. *oht, ôht* (in which *ó* was shortened), *as,* wroȝt (wrouȝt) 311, 345,
397, 445, 517, 553, boȝt 821, 3553, doȝt 16204, moȝt (*prt.* of muȝan) 7708,
24431, broȝt 63, 160, oȝt 473, noȝt 312, 346, 398, 446, 613, soȝt 159, 7707,
þoȝt 3553, doȝter 2330.

2. O.E. *ów, ẽow, as,* nouẟer, ouẟer (besides *noþer, noiþer, nour, ooþer, oþer,
ouir*) 7227, 13165, 19306, 19422, 21949, 22445, 24155 ; four (O.E. fẽ̃ower ;
no ryme) 356.

82. ó·u

Observe *þow* (þowȝ) (= though ; no ryme).

I break off here.   As to the consonants and the inflections of the noun and
verb, the critical part must be sufficient until I have prepared a critical text of
the whole *Cursor.*   It is only then that the versification of the poet can also
be treated of thoroughly.   From the two following specimens of a critical text
the reader will be able to form an idea of my views.   In the Notes I shall
have an opportunity to enter upon several questions relative to the same
subject.

---

[1] In the body of lines still compare ll. 12979 C, 16266 (cheu G), 18172 C, 18471 C G,
20855 C, 21039 G, 22916 G.

[2] For practical reasons I put here the development of O.E. ẫht, æht, aht, âht, as
well as of O.E. oht, ôht, though I have shown elsewhere that the analysis is = *a* + *wȝ*
and *o.* + *wȝ*, i. e. the labialization is part of the guttural.

CHAPTER VI.—TWO SPECIMENS OF A CRITICAL TEXT
(ll. 1-1044 and ll. 22427-23194).

THE CURSOR O WERLD, PERHAPS BY JOHN OF LINDBER ЗE
(ab. 1260-90).

Man yernes rimes for to here
 And romanz rede on maners sere;
Of Alisander þe Conquerur,
4 Of July Cesar þe Emperur ;   4
Of Grece and Troy þe strange strijf,
þer many þusand les her lijf;
Of Brut þat bern bald of hand
8 First conquerur of Ingeland ;   8
Of Kyng Arþur þat was sa rike;
Quam nan in his tim was like;
O ferlijs þat his knyЗtes fell,
12 Of aunters sere i here of tell,   12
Als Wawayn, Kay and oðer stabel
For to were þe runde tabel;
Hu Charles Kyng and Rouland faЗt,
16 Wiþ SaraЗins ne wald þay na saЗt; 16
O Tristrem and his leif Ysoud,
Hu he for hir becom a sot;
Of Ionek and of Ysambras,
20 Of Ydoyn and of Amadas,   20
Storijs als o serekyns þinges,
O princes, prelaates and of kynges,
Sanges sere of selkuþ rime,
24 Inglis, Frenkis and Latine   24
To rede and here ilkan is prest,
þe þinges þat þaym likes best.
þe wijsman wil of wisdom here,
28 þe fole him drauis to foly nere, 28
þe wrang to here of ryЗt is lath,
And prijd wið buxumnes is wrath ;
O chastite has lecchur leth,
32 On charite ay werreys wreth. 32
Bot bi þe fruit may ilk wijs se
O quat vertu is ilka tree.
Of alkyns fruit þat man schal find,
36 He fettes fra þe rote his kynd. 36
O god pertree cums godu peres,
Wers tre, wers fruit it beres.
þat i speke o þis ilke tre

1 Men **y**, iestes G 2 romans C romance **y**, maner G, *alt*. F 3 Alexand*er* G 5 strang C
grete F strong G 6 lesis C lost F *def*. G, þer C þaire F hir G 7 bern] was F 8 þe first C
def. G 9 sa] so C G *om*. F 10 *alt*. **y** 12 of] þat C *def*. G, aunters sere] mony aunters F
auntris did G 13 als] of F *def*. G 15 charles þe k. F king ch. G, rauland C 16 wiþ] *def*.
C wit F wid G, ne *om*. C F noЗt s. F never be s. G 17, 18 *alt. in* G, hir] here C 21 serekyn]
ferekin C divers G 23 selkuþ] divers G 24 frankys C frenche F frauss G 25 ilkon C G
26 þam C ham F þaim G, liked G 28 draghus C 29 wrong G 30 wit C F wid G 31-2
alt. in **y**, *inv. in* F 33 ilk wijs] scilwis C ilk man G, men F 35 alkyn C ilk a G iche F,
mai **y** 36 fecches F takes G 37 cums] *om*. **y**, god C 38 wers f.] wer f. G vers C

40	Betakens man, bath me and þe:	40
	Þis fruit bitakens all vr dedes,	
	Bath god and ill, qua ryȝtly redes,	
	Vr dedes fra vr hert tas rote	
44	Queðer þey be worþ bale or bote;	44
	For bi þe þing man drawes till,	
	Men schal him knaw for good or ill.	
	A sampel herbi þaym i say	
48	Þat rages into þayr riot ay;	48
	In riot and in rigolage	
	Of al þeyr lijf spend þay þeyr stage.	
	For nu is halden nan in curs	
52	Bot qua þat luve can paramurs,	52
	Þat foly luve, þat vanite,	
	Þaym likes nu nan oðer gle.	
	Hit nys bot fantum for to say	
56	To day it is, to morwe oway	56
	Wiþ chance of ded or chance of hert:	
	Þat soft began has endyng smert.	
	For wen þu traistest wenes at be	
60	Fra hir schaltu, or scho fra þe.	60
	He þat stiþest wenes at stand	
	War him his fal is neist at hand.	
	Ar he sua braþly dun be broȝt	
64	Quiðer to wend ne wat he noȝt,	64
	Bitwixand his luve have him ledd	
	To swilk mede als he him forbedd.	
	For þer sal mede wiðvten lett	
68	Be sett til him for dolful dett.	68
	Forþi blisce i þat paramur,	
	Quan i have nede me dos socur	
	Þat saves me first in erth fra sin	
72	And heven bliss me helps to win;	72
	For þów i quijlum haf ben vntrew,	
	Hir luve is ay ilike new.	
	Hir luve scho haldes lele ilike	
76	Þat swetter es þan hony o bike;	76
	Swilk in erth es funden nan,	
	For scho es moder and maydan,	
	Moder and mayden neuerþeless,	
80	Forþi of hir took Crist his fless.	80
	Qua trewly luves þis lemman,	
	Þis es þe luve bes never wan.	
	For in þis luve scho fayles never,	
84	And in þe toðer scho lastes ever.	84

40 both C   42 Bath god] *def.* C   43 takis F   44 worthi or C turne to G   45 him *add.* F   48 into G, þare C, alway G   49 rekelage G   50 þere C   51 holdẏn G, non C G   54 þam C ham F him G, non G   55 ys **y**   56 morne F   58 smart C   59 quen **y**, wenis traistiest to be G sicurest w. t. b. F   60 fro C, schalt þu C þu sal fra h. G   61 w. stiffest to G stiþest wenes to F   62 nexst his C   66 sli C suche F, as **y**, forbedd] forwit C *alt.* F   67 þer] þair G þan C   67-8 *alt.* C *om.* F   68 dolful] duel G   69 blisce] blesse F   70 *half def.* G   71 first] *om.* **y** erþe F herth C erde G   72·*alt.* F   73 þof C if F, suntyme **y**, have ben] be G   74 euerelike G   75-6 *alt.* G   77 non G   78 maydan] maiden alone G   80 iesu G   81 þat *add.* G, ay *add.* F   82 wan] gan C began F, Scho es . . . þat G   84 þe] þat C, scho *om.* G

Of swilk an suld ye mater take,
Ye crafty þat can rimes make,
Of hir to make bath rim and sang.
88 And luve hir swete sun omang. 88
Quat bote is to sett travayl
On þing þat may noȝt avayl.
þat es bot fantum o þis werld
92 Als ye have sene ynouȝ and herd. 92
Mater find ye large and brade
þów rimes fele of hir be made.
Qua-swa wil of hir fayrnes spell
96 Find he sal ynouȝ to tell: 96
Of hir godness and hir trewþhede
Men may find euermar to rede
O reuth, o luve, and charite
100 Ne was neuer hir make, ne neuer sal be. 100
Lavedij scho es of levedys all
Mild and meke wiðvten gall
To nedy neȝest on to call,
104 And rayses sinful quen þay fall; 104
Til all vr bales for to bete
Vr lauerd has made þat mayden swete;
þarbi man may hir helping kenn,
108 Scho prayes ay for sinful menn. 108
Qua menskes hir, þay may be bald
Scho sal þaym yeld an hundreth fald.
In hir worschip wald i begin
112 A lastand werc opon to myn, 112
For to do man knaw hir kyn
þat us sli worschip gan to win,
Sumkyns gestes for to scaw
116 þat done were in þe alde law 116
Bitwix þe ald' lawe and þe new,
Hu Crist birth began to brew;
I sal yu schaw wiþ mijn entent
120 Breflij of ayðer testament. 120
Al þis werld, ar þis book blin,
Wiþ Cristes help i sal ouerrin,
And tell sum gestes principal,
124 For all may na man have in tale. 124
Bot forþy þat na werc may stand,
Wiðvten grund-wal to be lastand,
þarfor þis werc sal i fund
128 Opon a selkuþ stedfast grund, 128

85 mater *om.* C   86 ye *om.* C   87 ieste G   88 emang G   90 not C, may noȝt *transp.* G
91 warld C   94 þof C, mani G lyte F   95 swa *om.* G   96 may y   97 trouthhedd G   99
reuth] petey F   100 was C y   101 Lady G ledes G   102 meke a. mild G   103 nedeful y,
neghest C next F neist G   104 doun *add.* F   105 Til] *and* F, bale C F, ai *add.* C   106 Iesu
made G, nayden] lady F   107 men G   108 prais C G   109 Q. þat worschipis G, he G
110 him G ham F, ʒilde F, a C, hundre F   111 wirschip C worshepe F   112 warc C, apon
C y   113 *alt.* F men G   114 *alt.* F, scli C swilk G cum to w. C   115 sumkin G þerfore
sum F, nu *add.* G   116 was G, hald C   118 cristes y, brith C bote G   119 schew C y
verrament F   120 sothli G shortly F, hir G   121 or C F   122 ourrine G   123 ieste G
124 no G, mon F   125 forþer   127 i wil G   128 Apon C F on G, selkuth] secure F

           þat es, þe haly trinite
           þat al has wroȝt wið his bunte.
           First at himself i sett my merc,
132   And siðen to tell his handewerc;   132
           O þangeles first þat fell,
           And siðen i wil of Adam tell,
           Of his oxspring and of Noe,
136   And sumquat of his sunnes þree,   136
           Of Abraham and Ysaac
           þat haly war wiðvten make;
           Siðen sal i tell to ȝuu
140   Of Jacob and of Esau.   140
           þar neist sal be siðen tald,
           Hu þat Josep was boȝt and sald;
           O þe Juus and Moïses
144   þat Goddes folk to lede him ches,   144
           Hu God bigan þe law him give
           þe qwilk þe Iewes in suld live.
           Of Sawl þe king and of Davi,
148   Hu þat he faȝt ogayn Golij;   148
           Siðen of Salamon þe wijs,
           Hu craftilike he did iustijs,
           Hu Crist com þurȝ prophecie,
152   Hu he com his folk to bij;   152
           Siðen hit schal be redd ȝu þan
           Of Ioachim and of Saynt Anne,
           Of Mari als hir doȝter mild,
156   Hu sco was born and bar a child;   156
           Hu he was born, and quen and quare,
           Hu sco him to þe temple bar;
           O þe kynges þat him soȝt,
160   þat þre presandes til him broȝt,   160
           Hu þat Herode kyng wið wouȝ
           For Cristes sake þe childer slouȝ,
           Hu þe child to Egipte fledd.
164   And hu þat he was þeðen ledd.   164
           þar sal ȝe find sumkyns dedes
           þat Iesus did in his barnhedes;
           Siðen of Baptist saint Iohan,
168   þat Ihesus hoof in flum Iordan;   168
           Hu Ihesus, quen he lang had fast
           Was fanded wiþ þe wicke gast,
           Siðen of Iones baptising
172   And hu him hefded Herod kyng;   172
           Hu þat Ihesu Crist himselve

130 beute C   131 First at h.] *transp.* C, first *om.* F   132 handwerc C handwarke G   133 angels C F   136 sunns C   135-6 *om.* F   137 of *add.* C y   138 lake y   139 to *om.* C F, yaw F   141 here G, teld G   142 þat *om.* y, bath *add.* G, seld G   143 Of *add.* y   146 Iuus C G, in suld] *inv.* G   150 craftily y, iustisce G   151 cam G, *alt.* F, thoro C thoru G þorow F   152 *alt.* G   153 reddynn C rede C   154 sant C   155 mare C   157 quen] how F ware C   158 ho F, til F   160 presantes G   161 herodes G   162 crist C   163 til y   164 þennis G   165 And *add.* y, suld G, find] here G, sumkyns] sum gode F mani a G, dede G   166 barnhede G childchedis F   167 of þe baptist Iohan C   168 baptist C G, þe *add.* G   169 wan G, longe G   170 fondid C temped G, wik C wicked G   171 Ions C

Ches til him apostels twelve
And openlik began to preche
176 And all þat sek war to leche,   176
And did þe miracles swa rijf,
þat þe Juus him held in strijf;
Siðen hu þat halij driʒtin
180 Turned water into wijn;   180
O fijve þusand men þat he
Fedd wiþ five laves and fisses þre,
Of a man sal ye siðen find
184 þat he gave siʒt, þat born was blind;   184
Of a spusebreke womman
þat þe Iewes demd to staan;
Hu he heled an al vnfere
188 þat sek was þritty and aʒt yeir;   188
Hu þe Maʒdaleyn wiþ grete
Com for to wass vr Lauerdes fete;
Of hir and Marþa þat was fus
192 Obvten þe nedes of þayr hus,   192
Of Lazar ded layd vnder laam
Hu Ihesus raysed his licam,
Hu Iewes Ihesu oft vmsett,
196 And for his sermun þraly þrett;   196
Huu þay schedd his blisced blode,
And pijned him opon þe rode;
Wiþ Cristes will þan sal i telle
200 Hu he siðen harwed helle;   200
Hu Jewes wiþ þeyr grete vnskill
Wend his vprijsing to dill;
Hu he vpraas, hu he vpstey,
204 Many man onstandand sey;   204
Hu he þat of myʒtes mast
Send intil erth his haly gast;
O twelve apostlis sumkyns gest,
208 Bot hu þay ended at þe lest;   208
Hu vur levedy ended and yald
Hir sely sawl, hit sal be tald;
O þ' haly crois, hu it was kidd
212 Lang efterward þat it was hidd;   212
Of Antecrist com þat sal be kene,
And of þe drery days fijftene
þat sal cum forwiþ domesday;
216 Siðen of þe dome yu sal i say;   216

175 openli y   177 þe om. G, meracles C, so F   178 Quarfor G, hild C   179 godd all-mightin G   180 vyn C   184 þat born] and b. C   185 and add. G, a om. C þe y, spouse-breche G, of a F þat G   186 Iuus C G, dempt C demed G walde deme F   187 on C, a man G, al om. y   188 eght and tuenti G   189 Mari add. G, þe om. G, Maudalan F   190 lorde C cristes F   191 þat wild noʒt blinne G alt. F   192 þare C inne G   193 þat add. G, lay G, stan G   194 in fless and ban G   196 preching þai him G   197 blesset F   198 apon y   199 crist C   200 hared C heried F harud G   201 þer C, vnschill C   203 vprais C   204 a add. y, on stad and C it herd and G wit eghe it F   206 erde G   207 sumkin C F   208 Bot om. G and F, mast and G   209 lady F, endet F   210 semeli G, blesset F   212 efter y   215 bifor G

Þan of vr levedys murnand mod*e*,
For hir sun*e* scho saw on rod*e*.
Þe last resun of al þis run*e*
220 Sal be of hir concepciun.   220
Þijs are þe maters redd on raw
Þat i þink in þis bok to draw,
Schortly rimand on þe ded*e*,
224 For many are þay herof to sped*e*.   224
Nedful me þink it war to man
To knaw himself, hu he began,
Hu he began in werld to bred*e*,
228 Hu his oxspring began to spred*e*;   228
Bath of þe first and of þe last,
In quatkins curs þis werld is past.
Efter haly kirkes state
232 Þis ilke book it es translaat,   232
Into Inglis tung to red*e*
For þe luve of Inglis led*e*,
Inglis lede of Ingeland,
236 For þe commun at understand.   236
Frenkis rijmes here i red*e*
Communlijke in ilk a sted*e*;
Mast es it wroȝt for Frenkis man:
240 Quat is for him na Frenkis can?   240
Of Ingeland þe naciun
Es Inglis man þar in commun.
Þe spek*e* þat man may mast wiþ sped*e*,
244 Mast þarwiþ to speke war ned*e*.   244
Selden was for any chance
Praysed Inglis tung in France;
Give we ilkaan þayr langage
248 Me þink we do þaym nan vtrage.   248
To lawed and Inglis men i spell
Þat vnderstandes quat i tell,
And to þa speke i alðermast
252 Þat won in vnwerc er to wast   252
Þayr lijf in trufel and truandijs
To be war wiþ þat self and wijs,
Sumquat unto þat þing to tend
256 Þat al þayr mode myȝt wið amend.   256
Ful il hayl þai þayr spending spend
Þat findes na fruit þarof at end.
Sli word and werc, sum we til heild,

---

217 ladi F leudis G   218 quen he hing G   221 i redde G   222 draw] schawe G   223 renand on G, *alt.* F   224 þai *om.* G, þarfor G   227 he *om.* C   230 quatking C quatkin **y**, world C   231 kyrc C   232 ilk C, is es C, it *om.* **y**   233 vnto G vntil F, engliss G   234 englijs G englis F   235 Ingland C engelande F, meri *add.* G   236 to vnþerstand G, fortil F   237 Frankis C frenche F, redd C   238 comunli G, a *om.* C, iche F   240 *alt.* **y**   241 Ingland C G engelande F   243 speche C **y**, wit *transp.* C   245 seldom G   247 þare C   248 non C, na G   249 leuid G lewet F   250 quat i can G   251 to þoo C til þaim G, mast F   .252 unvarc es C *alt.* G   253 *alt.* **y**   254 *alt.* **y**   255 tent C   256 al] þai G, þar C, mede G, may G   257 wa til þaim G il ha þai C, hir love to G   258 fro C, frute F, þir of no fruit G   259 sumkin G, and] or G, werkis F, sum we til] as we to G as we in F, lyue F

260 Treystlij acountes sal we yeild.   260
      Þarfor to draw yu hiderward
      Þat of þe pardun wil ha part;
      Þa here and hald, sal have pardun
264 O plyȝt, wiþ Cristes beniscun.   264
      Nu of þis proloog wil we blin,
      In Cristes name vr book begin;
      Cursur o werld man auȝt it call,
268 For almast it ouerrennes al.   268
      Take we vr biginning þan
      Of him þat al þis werld began

INCIPIT DE TRINITATE ET CREACIONE MUNDI.

      Of all, men aw þat driȝtin drede
272   þat mirþes mettes man to mede,   272
      Þat ever was and ay sal be
      Wiðvten change in trinite,
      He þat Lauerd, bath God and man,
276 Alkyns good of him began.   276
      Þow he began all oðer þing
      Himself had never biginning,
      Of him com al, in him is al
280 He haldes vp al fra dunfal;   280
      He haldes heven and erth stedfast
      Wiðvten him may na þing last.
      Þis lauerd þat es swa mykel o myȝt,
284 He purvayd al in his forsyȝt   284
      And þat he ordaynd wið his wit
      He multiplijs and governs it.
      Þerfor es he cald Trinitee,
288 For he es anfald God in þre.   288
      And if þu wenis it may noȝt be,
      Behald þe sunne and þu may see.
      In þe sunn þat schijnes clere
292 Es a þing, and þre þinges sere,   292
      A body rund, and hete and lyȝt,
      Þir þree we find all at a syȝt,
      Þijs þinges þree wiþ nankins art
296 Ne may man nan fra oðer part,   296
      For if þu taa þe lyȝt oway,
      Þe erth it has na sunn parfay;
      And if þe hete oway be tan
300 Sunn forsooþ ne has þu nan,   300
      Bot ilk wijsman it wate,
      It es þe kind of sunn be hate.
      Þe sunnes body þat i neven

---

260 Suilk a font G, armites C, suld G   261 yu] þam C   263 To C G, *alt.* F   264 and part G, crist C, *alt.* F   266 crist C   267 þe *add.* G, au G   271 Of *om.* G, laverd G, dride C 272 settes G   274 ende G   275 He þat *om.* F, louerd C   276 Alkyn C anekines G al F, god] thing G   277 þof C if F   279 can G   280 he haldes vp al] *inv.* G   282 no C   283 so C, mikul C mekil G   284 He] *om.* G, forsyȝt] aun sight G   287 þe *add.* G   289 wynus C 293 and *om.* G, hote G   294 þer F   295 wit C F wid G, nankin y   296 Ne *om.* C noght be G   300 þen C, ne *om.* C   301 on ilk a maner ilk man G   303 sun C

304   Betakens þe fader self of heven,   304
     And bi þe lyʒt þat is lastand
     Þe sunn þu aw at vnderstand,
     And bi þe hete þu vndertaa
308   Þe haly gast cums of hem twa.   308
     Fader is he cald forþi
     Þat he is well þat neuer sal dri,
     Or forþy þat he self has wroʒt
312   All þinges quen þat þey war noʒt.   312
     His sune wisdom es þat waat
     All þinges þat he haldes in state,
     And haldes þaym up fra misfare
316   Þat þayn' worþ noʒt als þay war ar.   316
     Þe haly gast es tat godhede
     Þat gives lijf and mas anhede
     Minning es þe fader cald,
320   Þe sune es vnderstanding tald,   320
     Þe haly gast es ay þat will
     Þat fader and sun will bath fulfill.
     Þis driʒtin, als i forwiþ sayd,
324   First in his witte he al purvayd,   324
     His werc, als dos þe sotil wryʒt,
     And siðen he reyses it in syʒt.
     Forþij is God, als says scripture
328   Nan elder þan his creature,   328
     Elder o time ne es noʒt he,
     Bot elles wel mare in dignite.
     Þis wryʒt þat i speke of here
332   Fra all oðer is sundry and sere   332
     For þay most oðer timber take,
     Bot he himself can timber make;
     For of himself he toke his even
336   Þat he of wroʒt bath erth and heven.   336
     Bot þun' sal noʒt understand
     Þat he wroʒt al his werc wið hand,
     Bot sayd wið word, and als son,
340   Al his commandement was don,   340
     Swiftliker þan eye may wink,
     Or any mannes hert may þink.
     Als clerkes seys þat are wijs
344   Hen' wroʒt noʒt first wiþ partios;   344
     Bot he þat mad all þing o noʒt
     Togeder he al þis werld wroʒt,
     Seit for to be on lang and brad.

305 be C   306 it es G, aw at] *om.* G aghe to F   307 *alt.* G   308 gost C, þaim G   310 þat n. is drey **y**   311 And ouyr G, himseluen **y**   312 þat *om.* C F   313 wisdom es] *transp.* G, al thing *add.* G, þat *om.* F, wele *add.* F   314 þat haldes stat C, for all þe werld G   315 He haldis all thinges G, fro C   316 to *add.* C, þai noght turne to soru and care G, *the whole line om.* F   318 onede G   320 vnderstanden G   321 ay *om.* G   322 wil *om.* G   323 lauerd G, bifore G   325 vs G, a G   328 non G   330 wel *om.* G   332 is *om.* C, *alt.* G   333 oþer writhes bos G   334 he] þis G, himself] þisself C   337 ne *om.* C **y**   340 comament C comandmont G   341 smartlier G, squyfter F, þen C, hee C   342 mans C   343 sayne F   344 ne *om.* C **y**   346 all þis werld togider he G, he al þis werld] *transp.* F   347 to be sett G, in lenth and brede G, in F

348   Þe mater first þerof he mad   348
       Þat es þe elementz to say.
       Þat first scapless al samen lay,
       He delt it siðen in sex days
352   In parties als þe scriptur says,   352
       Þe elementz first in dayes þrin
       Þree þinges þaym es wiðin;
       Þijs elementz þat all þing bindes
356   Fowr er þay, als clerkes findes.   356
       Þe neðermast es water and erth,
       Þe þridd es ayr, and fijr þe ferth.
       Or say we þus þat he began
360   Als Awstin says, þe haly man,   360
       Als we in his boke writen find.
       First þan wroȝt he angel kind,
       Þe werld, and time, þir þinges þre
364   Bifore all oðer þing wroȝt he;   364
       Þe werld i call wiþ min ententz
       Þe mater of þe fowr elementz,
       Þat yeit was tan o forme unschapen
368   Quarof was sereness siðen scapen.   368
       Al scapless was it noȝt forþij
       Þat it o scap ne hadd partie,
       Bot þarfor scapless was it, i truu
372   Þat it hadd nan þan swilk als nu.   372
       He wroȝt opon þe toðer day
       Þe firmament, þat es to say,
       Þe lift wiþ sternes grete and smale
376   Wið water sunded als cristal,   376
       Þat es þarouer fra þat þarvnder
       In þijs he sunded al wið wonder.
       Þe þridde day þat driȝtin dede
380   Þe waters draw unto a stede,   380
       And badd a drij sted suld be,
       Þe waters all he cald þe see,
       Þe drij cald erth þat laverd king,
384   And badd it gress and fruit forþ bring: 384
       Alkyns þinges gruand sere
       Þat in þaymself þayr seding bere.
       Þe ferth he badd, and it was don
388   Bath war mad þe sunne and mone   388
       Ayðer wiþ þayr awen lyȝt
       For to twin þe day fra nyȝt:
       In takening o tides to stand
392   Days and yeiris bath dwelland,   392

348 þar y, i rede G   351 ham F þaim G, sin G   353 elementes y, days C y   354 ar ham F, wit in C F wid in G   356 als] as y   357 lauest þan G   357-8 erde : ferde G   359 Ayder G, þus *transp.* G   360 as G, þat G   361 bokis y, writen *om.* y   363 þis G þes F   365 entens C ententes y   367 þan G *om.* F, mischapen (?) C F   368 sereness siðen] *transp.* G   370 þat] for G, ne *om.* G, sum *add.* G   371 a tru C, hou G   372 nogh G, as it has G   373 apon C y 375 light C, sky G sterris G   376 sonded C schinand G clere F   377 *alt.* y   378 wið] to G 379 thrid C y, did C, *alt.* G   380 vntil F, place G   383 he *add.* G   385 waxand þare G 386 bare G   387 feird G, it *om.* G   389 þer C þayr *om.* G, sere G, ouen C   390 to part þe G, þer til tyne F

And þe sternes grete and smale
Þat we may see wiðuten tale
In þ'ouermaast element of all
396   Þer þe fijr in has his stall.   396
Þe fifte day þat fayled noȝt
Of water fuul and fiss he wroȝt;
Þe fiss to water, als we find,
400   Þe fuul betaȝt he to þe wijnd.   400
Al gangand best þe sexte day,
And Adam bath he wroȝt o clay ;
He was last wroȝt als laverding
404   Vt over alkyns oðer þing.   404
In a dale he wroȝt Adam
Þat Ebron hatt, in Hebru name.
Þir sex days he wroȝt his will
408   Þe sevend of werk he heild him still.   408
Himself gave vs ensampel þare
Þat we suld hald it evermare.
His first werc als yee herd me neven,
412   He wroȝt þe angels all of heven,   412
And sett þaym in his hey palays,
Þar neuer may be of pride vnpays ;
For to þis palays at was swa rike
416   Als myȝtij king in his kingrike   416
He fordestined twin creature
To serve him in þat haly ture ;
Þat suld be of a numbre hale,
420   And many þuusand have in tale,   420
Þe qwilk tale nangate suld be mare
And nede behoved it fulfild ware.
Þis numbre þat he ordeynd þan
424   Suld be bath of angel and man,   424
For mensked wiþ twin maner o scaft
Wald he be, þat king o craft,
Þat es wið angel þat es gastlij,
428   And wiþ man þat es bodilij.   428
Of angels wald he served be
Þat suld of ordres have þrijs þre,
He ches til him, þat laverd hend,
432   Þe man suld mak þe ordre tend.   432
Bot þangeles he wroȝt formast
Of all he gave an poustee mast,
For þow þey all war fayr and wijs,
436   And sum of less, and sum mar prijs,   436

393 sterns C   395 heiest G   396 in] he C transp. G   397 faylis y   398 On C, fuxol C
399 watur C   401 bestis y sext C F   402 made y, on C   403 made G, laverþing G lord-
ynge F   404 al oþerkin C, to be maister ouerall G   406 hate G, ebreu G   407 þe C F, sext
(day) F, þat was add. C   408 hild C   409 þan add. C, gaf vs] transp. G, sample C   410
halghe F   412 Godd G, angelis G, all om. G   413 þam C, his om. C, haly C   414 widuten
pride to be in pais G, alt. F   415 to om. G, in F; ryme riche : kingriche G   417 fordestend
C ordaned him G   419 of om. G   420 to add. G   421 nagat G   422 nedeful G, fulfild om.
G transp. F   423 numbrari G, ordend C F (-t)   425 worschipd wid to G alt. F   427 þat es]
bath F, gostli G   429 If G   430 ordres] transp. G   432 men C   433 angel C   434 þaim G
ham F   435 þof C, all om. G, bath add. G   436 of add. G, more G

He gaf an mast of all þat sele,
If þat he cuþ have born it wele,
And sett him heyest in his hall
440 Als prince and sire ouer oðer all;   440
And for þat he was fayr and bryȝt,
Lucifer to name he hyȝt.
Wen he perceyved him be þis
444 Þat he was ouer all oðer in bliss,   444
Allas, caytif! he knew him noȝt
Þat hey driȝtin þat hadd him wroȝt;
For ilhayl saw he þat tide,
448 Ogaynes him he took a pride,   448
Heðelik he lete of ilka fere,
To God himself wald he be pere,
Noȝt pere alan, but mikel mare,
452 For vnder him he wald all ware,   452
And be himself þayr comandur.
Qua herd euer a werr auntur,
Þat he þat noȝt hadd bot of him,
456 Ogayn him suld becum swa grim?   456
'Sett,' he sayd, 'mi sete i sal
Gayn him þat heyest es of all,
In þe norþ side it sal be sett,
460 Of me servijs sal he nan gete.   460
Qui suld i him servijs yeild,
Al sal be at mijn awen weild.'
Bot he was merred of his mynt,
464 Ful sone he fand unstern stynt.   464
For langer þan he þoȝt þis pride
In heven moȝt he na langer abide
For in þat curt þat es sa clene
468 May na filþ dwell wiðvten wene.   468
Saynt Michel for þayr aller ryȝt
Raas ogayn him for to fyȝt,
Ogayn him gave a batayl grim
472 Vt of þat heye curt kest him;   472
Lucifer first dun he broȝt,
And siðen þat til him helded oȝt,
And skuurd þat curt of þaym sa clene
476 Þat siðen þayr stede was never sene.   476
Þis es þe feind þat formast fell
Þurwȝ his ouergert into hell;
Fra þan his nam changed was,

437 He gaf an] *transp.* G, þat *om.* C, to knaue and fele G   438 þat *om.* C, him G   439 best G   440 of G   441 þat *om.* G   443 quen G, parceved C, þus *add.* y, him *om.*G, he C G 446 hee C, *alt.* G   447 soruful G   448 Agains C   449 Hetlik C lightli G heþeli F   450 him *om.* C, selven G   451 mikul C, alon G   452 vnd*ur* C, were G   453 he G   454 of *add.* G, warr C, auctour G   458 ys lord F, es best G   459 it sal] *inv.* G, I sette my sete F   460 o m. serv.] *transp.* G, non C G   463 marrid E   464 sturne F   465 þen G   466 bide F 467 so sclene G   468 in *add.* C   469 micheal C mychal G, þare C, alder G   470 again C egaynes G   471 Again C Gaynes G, he *add.* G, batell C   472 hei C, *om.* y, he *add.* G, cast G   474 all þas G alle þat F, to G, wit F, held y   475 schurd C, þam C ham F   476 þar C 478 ouergart C awgart F, for his pride fra heven to hell, unto F   479 schangid G

480 For nu es he cald Satanas.   480
     Fra ful hey he fell ful law
     Þat of his lauerd wald stand nan aw,
     Wiðvten covering of his care,
484 Þar hen' has mercy nevermare,   484
     For God awȝt noȝt give þaym mercij
     Þat þar-after wil noȝt crij.
     And þus he les his grete honur,
488 Þar hen' baad noȝt fullik an vre,   488
     For alswijth als he was made,
     He fell, was þar na langer bade.
     Þas oðer gastes þat fell him wiþ,
492 Þe qwilk forsoke Goddis griþ,   492
     Efter þe will þay til him bar;
     Þan fell þay depe, or lesse or mare,
     Sum in þe ayr, sum in þe lift,
496 Þar þey drey ful harde schrift,   496
     Þayr pijn þey bere opon þaym ay,
     And swa sal do to domesday.
     Bot þai þat left wiðvten wite,
500 Þay ware confermed þar als tite.   500
     Þat þay may neuermar held til ill
     Namar þan wick may to good will.
     Þe numbre þat vt of heven fell,
504 Þa can na tung in erth tell,   504
     Ne fra þe trone quar he gan sitt
     Hu ferr es into helle pitt.
     Bot Bede says fra erth to heven
508 Es VII. M. yeir and hundreth seven,   508
     Bi jurnes qua þat gang it may,
     Fowrty mile on ilk a day.
     Als i tald ar, þat Kyng o craft
512 Wald mensked be wiþ twinkyns scaft,   512
     Bath of angel and of man.
     Adam þerfor was wroȝt þan
     Þe tende ordre for to fulfil
516 Þat Lucifer did for to spill.   516
     Of erth alan ne was he noȝt,
     But of fowre elementes wroȝt,
     O water his blood, his fless o layr
520 His hete o fijr, his aand of ayr,   520
     His heved wiðin has eyen twin,
524 Þe lift has sunne and mone wiðin,
     Þat als mans eyen er sett to syȝt,

480 Now es he cald fuul G   483 wild G   485 au y, þaym] þam C him G, om. F   487 leses
C tint G   488 he ne] transp. G, badd C G, on our G   489 alswijth] alswa suith G, as G sa F
490 no G   491 þe toþer G, angelis G, wiht C wid G   493 to G, alt. F   494 fell þai to hell
G, or om. G   495 & add. G   496 drift G   497 þar C, þine (?) G, apon y, þam C ham F   498
tille F   499 þos G, þai C, witoten C   501 hald G, to G   502 þe add. C, wikket F   504 þo C,
om. G, noght G, can transp. G   505 can C, of þat bliss G   506 farr C, hell pitt C G, es
transp. G   508 VII. M.] seven thousand C . VII. thousand y hundret C hundredis G,
seven] . VII. G   509 iournays F iornayis G   510 euerilk G   512 twyn y   515 for om. y
517 ne] made F   520 here G, -ond G, two lines ins. F   521 (523) widine G, has] bath G
haþ T   522 (524) skey G, has] bath G haþ T, sōn C   523 (525) þat] Right y, men sen C
men eien G mon e. F, ar F

Swa serves sunne and mone o lyȝt.   524
Vij mayster sterns er sett in heven,
528 And mannes heved has þirles seven,
Þe qwilk if þu wil þe vmþink,
Þu may þaym find wiþ litel swink.   528
Þis aand þat man drawes oft
532 Betakens wijnd þat blaws on loft,
O qwilk es þoner and leuening ledd,
Als aand wiþ hoost in brest is spredd;   532
Into þe see al watres sinkes,
536 And mannes wamb al licur drinkes;
His fete him beres vp fra fal,
Als þe erth vphaldes al.   536
Þe over fijr gives man his syȝt,
540 Þat over ayr of hering myȝt,
Þis vnder wijnd him gives his aand,
Þe erth to tast, to fel and faand;   540
Þe hardnes þat man has in banes,
544 It cums him o þe kijnd of staanes;
O þerth it gruues, trees and gress,
And neyl and here of mannes fless.   544
Wiþ bestes dumb man has his fele,
548 O þing man lijkes, ill or wele.
Of þir þings i have her sayd,
Was Adam cors togedir grayd.   548
For þis resun þat ye have herd,
552 Man is cleped þe lesse werld.
Bot resun yeit al herd yee noȝt
Quarof mannes sawl was wroȝt.   552
O gastly lyȝt, man says, it es
556 Þat God has mad til his licknes
Als preynte of seel in wax es þrest,
Þerin he has his licknes fest.   556
He has it wroȝt als freind and fere,
560 Forþij es naþing him swa dere.
His godhed es in trinite,
An sawl has propre þinges þre: 560
Minning and þat of þinges þrin
564 Þat es, þat was, þat sal be mijn,
It has als vnderstanding clene
O þing it sees, and of vnsene,   564
It has als skilwisnes o will

524 (526) To seruis G So serveþ T þe s. F   525 (527) seven C G   526 (528) mans C, hede G, thirls C   528 (530) þam C ham F, litul C   529 (531) men C G, he F, draus C G, oft C y 530 (532) blauis G, ys F   532 (534) bredd y   533 (535) watir G   534 (536) mans C, womb C F   535 (537) duun add. F, alt. F   536 (538) alsua G   537 (539) gis C ges G gifues F, mon F manes G   539 (541) vnderþ G, gis C ges F, ond G   540 (542) þe t. C, to om. G, fond G   541 (543) bones G   542 (544) is mad G, stonis G   543 (545) on G, groues C y, gris G 544 (546) neis C, of om. G, mans C   545 (547) hath G   546 (548) liks C   547 (549) þir C G þer F   548 (550) layde F   549 (551) hard C   550 (552) es man callid G   551 (553) yett C yet F, al om. y   552 (554) mans C   553 (555) a C F of G T   554 (556) liknes C F   555 (557) prient C prent F T, es om. G   556 (558) licam C   558 (560) him om. G   560 (562) and y, þe add. G   561 (563) pre G, alt. F   562 (564) alt. F, ay sal be G   563 (565) also G om. F, vnderstand C   564 (566) seis C G, alt. F   565 (567) also G, schilwisnes C wisdam G, in G, hit is resonable F

568 Þe good to take and leve þe ill.
    All þe myȝtes þat may be,
    Wonis in þat haly trinite.   568
    All virtûes has sawl ywis
572 Þat vt o sinne vnsaked is,
    And als God þat es an and þre,
    Wiþ nankyns creature may be   572
    vnderfanged ne overtan,
576 And he ouertakes þaym ilkan,
    Alswa þe sawl, wiðvten wene,
    Til alkins þing it es vnsene;   576
    Þow it of all þinges have syȝt,
580 To see þe sawl have ye na myȝt.
    Nu have i scawen yuu til hider
    Hu twa þings man halds togedir,   580
    Þe sawl, of gastly þing to tell,
584 If bodily, his fless and fell.
    Adam was maad o mannes eild
    Als he moȝt wele himselven weild,   584
    Als Austin says, þat leyes noȝt,
588 And vtwiþ paradijs was wroȝt.
    Here nu þe resun of his name.
    Qui þat he was cald Adam.   588
    In þis name er fowr lettres layd
592 Þat o þe fowr yates er sayd
    Swa mikel es Adam for to muþ,
    Als est, and west, and norþ, and suþ.   592
    And þu may ask wiðvten blam
596 Qui God him gave swa mikel a nam.
    Parfay þat es bot eeþ to rede,
    It takens Adam and his sede!   596
    Ouer al þe werld þan suld þai sprede,
600 And þerof bere þe laverdhede.
    Als vr lauerd has heven in hand,
    Swa suld man laverd be of land.   600
    Þerfor he gave him to begin
604 A luvesum land at lenger in,
    A land o lijf, o beild and bliss
    Þe qwilk man clepes paradijs.   604
    Into þat land widvuten bade
608 Was Adam broȝt qwen he was made.
    He gaf it him als in heritage
    To yeild þerfor na mar knawlage,   608
    Bot for to hald it wel vnbroken

569 (571) a *add.* G   570 (572) clensed G, es G   571 (573) in on G   572 (574) nankyn C nankines G, *alt.* F   573 (575) vnderfanding non G, vndirgroped ny T   (575-6) *om.* F   574 (576) þam C   575 (577) witoten C   576 (578) to **y**, ilk a man F   577 (579) þof C, þing G, *om.* F, has (?) C   578 (580) þe] na G, þai G   579 (581) scheud C **y**, hiþer G   580 (582) togiþer G   582 (584) *and add.* F, þe bodi **y**, his *om.* F   583 (585) mans C, *alt.* F   584 (586) might G, *alt.* F, welle C, *om.* G, him self C   585 (587) leis C lies G   586 (588) widuten G, was *om.* C   591 (593) micul C mekil G   593 (595) witoten C   595 (597) es *om.* C, etht G   597 (599) þan *om.* G   598 (600) þarof **y**   601 (603) þarfor **y**   602 (604) to **y**, duell G, lenge F   603 (605) beild] ioy G   604 (606) mon F men G, calis **y**   605 (607) witoten C   607 (609) as G, *om.* F   608 (610) þarfor **y**, mar] *om.* G

612   Þe forbod þat was betwix þaym spoken.
      Bot forþy þat he heild it noȝt
      He did vs alle in bale be broȝt.   612
      In bale he broȝt vs, and in care,
616   Sum i schal tell yu furðer mare.
      Wen Adam wroȝt was als son
      In páradijs þan was he don.   616
      Þe bestes all, bath sco and he
620   War broȝt forwið him to see.
      Fiss on sund, and fuul on flyȝt
      Was broȝt all forth in his syȝt.   620
      All war broȝt to serve Adam,
624   And þat he suld give ilkan name.
      Þan gave þat king his craft to kepe
      Sleyly þen Adam gert he slepe.   624
      Vt of his side, als says þe book,
628   Widvten sare a rib he took,
      And of þat rib he mad womman
      Til Adam þat was first his aan.   628
      Quen sco was broȝt befor Adam,
632   Virago gaf he hir to name;
      Þarfor hiȝt sco virago,
      For maked o þe man was sco.   632
      Bath war naked þayr licam,
636   Bot þarfor þoȝt þaym þen na scham.
      Driȝtin þaym blessed and badd þaym brede,
      And multiplij wiðin þayr sede.   636
      ' Adam,' he sayd, ' hu þinkes þe
640   In þis stede es fayr to be.
      Þis es a stede of welþful wan,
      Þar all godes wantes nan.   640
      Here lastes lijf wiðuten end,
644   Her es naþing for to mend,
      Her es bliss þat lastes ay,
      Never nyȝt, bot ever day.   644
      Nys nan forsooth wiþ hert may þink,
648   Ne writer nan may write wið ink
      Þe mikel joy þat þaym es lent
      Þat dos her wele mi comandment.   648
      O trees, o fruit es her good wan,
652   All sal þay be þijn bot an,
      O þaym all þi will to do,

---

610 (612) forbot C F   614 (616) als G   615 (617) quan F quen G   616 (618) into F, þen *om.* F   617 (619) he and scho G ho and he F   618 (620) befor F, *alt.* G   619 (621) in water G, to G   620 (622) before him F, his *om.* F *alt.* G   622 (624) for *add.* G, þaim G 624 (626) þen *om.* **y** Adam, *transp.* G gart C made F, to *add.* G   625 (627) bock G   626 (628) witoten C, sor G   632 (637) maket *transp.* F, mad *transp.* G   633-4 (635-6) *alt.* G 633 þar C   634 þarof F, þam C ham F, þen *om.* F   635 (637) þam C ham F, blisced G blesset F, þam C ham F   636 (638) wiðin] in C in *transp.* G   637 (639) thinkt C likes F 639 (641) of *om.* C, weltful C welful F, wone G   640 (642) *alt.* **y**   641 (643) witoten C widuten G   642 (644) a thing non G, amende F   645 (647) Es C G   646 (648) *alt.* G. 647 (649) mekil G, þam C ham F   648 (650) will C wele *trsp.* G   649 (651) fruttes C, wone G.   650 (652) oute-take F, one G   651 (653) þam C ham F, þou F

Bot yon tree cum þu nawyȝt to   652
þat standes in midward paradijs;
656   For if þu do, þu nart noȝt wijs.
þís tree haf I don in friþ,
For i wil þat it havę my griþ.   656
If yee it tuch, i sal noȝt ley,
660   O duble ded þan shal ye dey.
Lok forþij, þat ye take tent
þat yee ne brek my comandement.'   660
And herby may we all wel see,
664   Hu he þaym gave þeyr will alfre,
þe good to do, to leve þe ill;
Bath he sett in þayr free will.   664
Witt and wisdam he þaym gave
668   Miȝt and fayrhed for to have;
Of al þis werld made Adam king
Euer to last widvten ending.   668
Omang his many serkyns sele
672   I sal tell sumquat of his welе:
Ar he brak þat God him forbadd,
In mikel blisse þan was he stadd,   672
Of his wijf sa fayr and fre
676   þat mikel mirth was on to se ;
þe bestes buud him all obutе
Als to þayr lauerd vnderlute,   676
Fuul o flyȝt, and fiss on sand,
680   All fell him duun to fote and hand;
At his will þay com and yode,
Als he war fader of þayr fodе.   680
þe bestes self war samentalе,
684   Widvten hurt þayr herd ay halе;
Betwix þe wolves lay þe shepе,
Sauvely moȝt þay samen slepе.   684
þe hund ne harmed noȝt þe harе
688   Nē nan soȝt on oðer sarе.
Bi þe dere þat nu es wild,
Als lamb him lay þe leon mild.   688
þe grijp alswa bi sijdе þe berе,
692   Nan best wald til oðer derе,
þe scorpion forbar his stang
Fra bestes þar he lay omang.   692
Ilkinnes þing, on serkinnes wisе,

652 (654) yonder F, a *add.* G, ȝe G, noȝt **y**   653 (655) a m. F emiddis G   654 (656) ȝe G,
es C er G   655 (657) ys done F   656 (658) have it to G, mi *om.* F   657 (659) i wil ȝou say
G wiþouten leghe F   658 (660) þan *om.* F, sul G   659 (661) Bi war G, þat *om.* **y**   660
(662) ne *om.* **y**, noȝt *add.* **y**, commament C   661 (663) ȝe **y**   662 (664) þam C ham F, þer
C   664 (666) þare C   665 (667) þam C ham F   667 (669) þis werld] erd G   668 (670) euer
om. G.   669 (671) Emang C, meyne G, serekin C F divers G   671 (673) iesu G, him *om.* **y**,
forbedd G   672 (674) mikul C mekil G, he *om.* G, stedd G   673 (675) wis G, sa G so F
674 (676) mekil G   675 (677) cam G   676 (678) þai er *add.* G   677 (679) and *om.* G   679
(681) ȝede and cam G   680 (682) maker of þaim G   681 (683) samert. C in samen t. F so
meke t. G   682 (684) þar C in F þai G, ȝode euer G   683 (685) Tuix G   686 (688) na best
G   690 (692) na **y**, til] do G *om.* F   691 (693) tunge G tang C   692 (694) emong G   693
(695) Ilkin C alkines G iche F, (of) in divers **y** serekin C

696 Yeld til Adam þayr servise;
    Nē þe neddre was noȝt bitter
    Þan þow he was ever witter,   696
    For of alle als schawes þe book,
700 Maast he cuþ of crafte and crook.
    Þe sunne was þat tijme þat i say
    Seven sijþ bryȝter þan þe day;   700
    Þe mone was þat time alswa bryȝt
704 Als es to day þe sunne o lyȝt,
    Hald na man þis for folie,
    Þe prophet sayd it, Isai;   704
    Of all þinges þat we here se,
708 On hey, on law, on land, on see,
    War of gretter strengþ and piþ,
    Ar Adam had fordon þe griþ.   708
    Bot Adam sone was send a saand
712 Þat soȝt him wiþ ful fell a faand.
    Quen Satan saw þat he was chosin
    To win þe bliss he had forlosin,   712
    Sorwful becom þat false file,
716 And þoȝt hu he moȝt man bewile.
    Vmþoȝt o þat þing to stynt
    Þat God til ending good had mynt;   716
    Ogaynes God wex he sa grill
720 Þat all his werk he wend to spill,
    And wend wele wiþ his grete envie
    O God himself to win þe maystrie.   720
    Man is nu sett bitwix twa,
724 On ayðer side he has his faa;
    Betwix þe werlaw and his wijf
    Adam es stadd in strang strijf.   724
    Bath þey werreyd on Adam
728 For to bring him into blame.
    Bath ar nuu on aan partie
    To confund man wiþ trecherie.   728
    Þat wily werlau him heild on drey,
732 And gayned noȝt cum him to ney,
    Namly in his awen schap,
    To sped hen' hoped have na hap.   732
    Forþij a messager he send
736 Wiþ quam best to spede he wend;

694 (696) ȝeilded G, to G, þar C   695 (697) bittur C   696 (698) For he was G, þan þowf C,
wis and G, wittur C   697 (699) bot F, bestes add. F, als om. F, scheus C says F   697-8
(699-700) alt. G   699 (701) as G   700 (702) sith om. F sitht G, bright G, þen C F, to d. G
701 (703) als C F   702 (704) þe d. C, a. is þe s. nu on day l. G   704 (706) it s. C it says y
705 (707) of] þat F, þe add. G   706 (708) on om. G or l. G, or s. G   707 (709) þai add. G
708 (710) or F, bifor þat G, brac G   710 (712) alt. y   711 (713) alt. F   712 (714) þat add.
G at add. F, lorne F lorin G   713 (715) sorful C sori G, he cam G   714 (716) mith G, bi-
gile y   715 (717) he thoght y, o om. y, for add. y   716 (718) to gret goddnes G   717 (719)
A-ganis C agaynes y   719 (721) troud G þoȝt F   720 (722) þe om. F   722 (724) his] a y
723 (725) sathan C   725 (727) werhaid C war G, þinkyn F   726 (728) in G   727 (729) in F
a C G   728 (730) trechuri G   729 (731) feind G deuel F, heij G   730 (732) And] him G,
ganid C, Adam G, to om. G   732 (734) ne om. C y   733 (735) sent G   734 (736) whom G,
for til spede ful wele F

To þis he ches a litel best,
Þe qwilk nes noȝt vnwiliest,   736
Þe neddre þat es of a scaft,
740   Þat mast can bath in crook and craft.
Grayðly taȝt he him þe gin
Hu he suld at þe wijf begin,   740
And þurwȝ þe wijf to win þe man.
744   Þis neddre forþ þat he ne blan,
Bot in his slouȝ was self Satan;
Selcuþ was hit he þider wan.   744
Bot wiþ his suffrance he it lete
748   Þat best wist hu þe bale to bete:
Forþi he mad þaym þat þay moȝt
Sinne or leve, if þaym good þoȝt;   748
Þat þurwȝ skil of þayr awen dede
752   Suld be mettaim al þayr mede,
To bu and live wiðvten end,
Or elles of ded in langur lend.   752
Adam yode walkand in þat welth
756   Þat halden was in mikel selth;
Quen he was fra his wijf a þraw,
Þe neddre nerhand hir gan draw,   756
And sayd: 'Womman, tell me nu quij
760   Þat yee ete noȝt al comunlij
O paradijs of ilk a tree?'
'Certes,' sayd sco, 'swa do wee   760
Of all þe treës but of an
764   Þe midward tre is vs vttan;
Vr lauerd in forbod has it layd.'
'And wat þu quarfor?' 'Nay,' sco sayd.   764
Bot sco sayd, 'if we cum þer ney,
768   Of ded, forsooþ, þan suld we dey.
Þis tree suld himselven have,
And we all oðer þen þat lave.'   768
'And wenes þu þat it be swa,
772   Sum hee has sayd yu?' 'Certes, ya!'
'Nay, goddot,' sayd þat felun,
'Þar es vnder al sere resun.   772
He dos it, for hene wald ye were
776   Perigal til him ne pere;
Þe sooþ fra yu wil i noȝt hide.
He wat wele wat time or tide   776
Þat yee had eten of þis tree,

736 (738) nes] es C **y**   737 (739) of a] of suilk a G, *alt.* F   738 (740) þat maast c. b. in cr. a.] Mast of quantise es in G   739 (741) Graitli C Quaintli G   743 (745) Bot *om.* G, slught C slohu G, selven G   744 (746) Wonþer G, diþer G   745 (747) it] ham F   749 (751) on C, þar C þaire F hir G   750 (752) mettam C markyd þ. G her m. G, þaym *om.* F, sulde þai merke F   752 (754) to *add.* **y**   753 (755) ȝede G, wanderand G   754 (756) þaim *add.* G, micul C mekil G, elth C   755 (757) Adam G, f. eve G, tharu C trawe G   756 (758) gun C 759 (761) in G   760 (762) sayd scho] sir G, so G, nou *add.* G   761 (763) þe *om.* G   763 (765) forbot C, had G   764 (766) qui G   767 (769) a *add.* G   768 (770) we *om.* G, til vs be laue G, *alt.* F   769 (771) trous G   770 (772) as G, has *om.* G, ȝu said G   771 (773) goddot] said he G, forsoth F, wid gret tresun G   772 (774) Bot *add.* G, al sere] anoþer F suilk G 773 (775) It es G, ne *om.* **y**, noght *add.* **y**   774 (776) to G, na G   776 (778) þat *add.* G, wat] quat G, fra þat F   777 (779) þis] þat G

780 Als Goddes suld yee selven be;
 On witing bath good and ill,
 Yee suld be laverds at yur will,   780
 Of it ye ete, swa red i yu,
784 For yee schal find it is yur pru.'
 Þis hyȝt was þan sum del mikel
 Þow it was ful fals and fikel.   784
 Sone quen sco þis fruit beheild,
788 Scho yerned it to have in weild,
 Ne left sco noȝt for drede o blame,
 But took, and ete, and raȝt Adam.   788
 Quat bot es lang my tale to draw,
792 Quat sum first þar was gayn saw?
 Al for noȝt þay ete it bath,
 Þat al þeyr kyn þurwȝ fell in wath,   792
 For of þat ilke appil-bitt
796 Þayr sunes tethe ar eggid yitt,
 And sal be ay to domesday,
 Her ogayn may na man say.   796
 Quen þay loked on þeyr licam
800 Ayðer þoȝt of oðer scham;
 For quen þey saw þaymselven bare
 Þat welth and blisse had cleðed ar;   800
 Þey cledd þaym þar in þat mister
804 Wiþ leves brad bath of figer.
 Quen þe feind þus had hem numen
 Wele he wend have God ouercumen,   804
 And sayd wiðin his sary þoȝt:
808 'Ic have him don to swinck for noȝt;
 His heven he sal have his aan
 O Adam lott ne getes he naan   808
 To bring into that heritage
812 Þat i have tynt with mijn vutrage.'
 He leyed, þat eber file, forqui
 Þat yeit of man had God mercij.   812
 Adam war tynt, God wald it noȝt,
816 For he wið wicked rede was soȝt.
 Þe feind was mar worþi to blam
 Þat wiþ his swijk biswak Adam.   816
 God wist wel þe feind him swaak
820 Forþi yeit wald he wiþ him take;

778 (780) godds C, ȝur G 779 (781) o C, To knau G, þe g. G 780 (782) aun *add.* G 781 (783) so G, nu ȝu G 782 (784) and G, for **y.** p. G 783 (785) heting G, þan s. d.] þat time ful G 784 (786) Bot ȝeit G, ful] bath G 785 (787) quen] als F 786 (788) desirred C 787 (789) Ne *om.* C, ne bl. G 790 (792) Bot som of hoting w. g. s. G, *alt.* F 792 (794) Quar thoru all þ. king wer wrath G 793 (795) aplis G, (795-6) *om.* F 795 (797) A. sua G, ay *om.* G 796 (798) egain C G, mon F 797 (799) *alt.* G 798 (800) Aieþer C, *the whole line alt.* G 799 (801) quen] þen F þan G, hamself C F, al *om.* C F 800 (802) In w. G, had] was G, clad G 801 (803) þan *om.* G, i tell it þe G, for velane F 802 (804) b. b. o. f.] of a fike tre G 803 (805) quen G, þam C him G 804 (806) ha C 805 (807) sori G 807 (809) sal he **y,** allan C, him a. F, by h. a. G 808 (810) part G, now C, non G 810 (812) for G 812 (814) þat] *om.* G, *and* F, Adam G 813 (815) þat *add.* G, were G, wild G, *alt.* F 814 (816) vikced C 815 (817) find C, w. m. F G wele m. G 816 (818) þ. sua falsli bigiled G, þ. wiþ his gawdes begylet F 817 (819) wel *om.* G, find C, had adam blent G 818 (820) ȝeit wild he noght þat he war schent G, *and* þoȝt ofter wiþ him to take F

Bot þow he siðen of him roȝt,
He wald it first full dere war boȝt.   820
Son quen þay had bath don þat sin,
824   Began al baret to begin.
Alkynes bliss was þan biwent,
Fra þaym þat brak þis commandment.   824
Sone bigan vengeance to kiþe,
828   Al blured þat was forwiþ bliþe;
Al bigan to strut and strijve
Ogaynes Adam and his wijf,   828
Bitwix þaym twa to strut alswa,
832   Þe stranger þe weyker for to sla,
Ilkan to make of oðer prey,
Als we may see þaym do to day.   832
Fra þeþen first com ded to man
836   Þat fra þat tide al waa bigan,
Þe wrangwijs wiþ þayr waful wrak
Þar þay biginning gan to tak,   836
Sinne and sake, and schame and strijf
840   Þat nu es ouer al þe werld sa rijf.
Mercy, lauerd, strang wickedhed
Broȝt Adam to swilk a ded.   840
Þat had him tynt and al his kyn,
844   Bot vr lauerd had ranscund him,
On swilk a wijs, als he forþoȝt,
Befor ar he þis werld had wroȝt.   844
Bot that was noȝt al don for nede,
848   Bot þurwȝ his awen doȝtyhede.
Þan if he wald, he moȝt man
Wel better mak þan he was þan ;   848
Wiþ fless forþij he com in place,
852   And fild þis werld al wið his grace.
His grace it was and naþing oðer
Þat he wald bicum vr broðer.   852
Wiþ þe feind þerfor he faȝt
856   And wið his fader he mad vr saȝt.
Leve we nu o swilkyns spell,
Of vr story forth to tell.   856
Wen Adam saw he had misdon,
860   He went to hide him als son ;
He wend to hide him omang þa trees
Fra his syȝt þat al sees.   860
Al for noȝt hidd him Adam,

820 (822) first it f. d. G   821 (823) als fast als G, bath *om.* **y**   823 (825) Alkin C, fra þaim was went G, *alt.* **y**   824 (826) Fra þai had broken . . . G   825 (827) he *add.* G, wenganz C   826 (828) blurded C lourid G, *alt.* F   827 (829) to *om.* G, stour G   828 (830) Agains C **y**   829 (831) twa] selven G selfe F, to strijf G to flite F   830 (832) strang C strenger T 832 (834) nou ilk a day G, *alt.* F   833 (835) Fra þaim G, þen at first F, deþ F   835 (837) þe w. wight wid il w. G   836 (838) þar þai] þair G, con F gan þai at him G   838 (840) es *trsp.* G, þis **y**, sa *om.* G   840 (842) Made A. to do G   841 (843) Himself had tint G, *alt.* F 843 (845) forþoȝt] had þ. G, he] him F   844 (846) had *om.* G   845 (847) all *transp.* G   847 (849) For G, might **y**   849 (851) cam G   850 (852) fulfild G, world G   852 (854) aller *add.* G   853 (855) find C, þarfor **y**   854 (856) he *om.* G   855 (857) swilkins] þis ilk G   856 (858) st. nu G, for G   857 (859) quen G   859 (861) amang C emang G, in F   860 (862) þing *add.* G

864   Vr lauerd cald him bi his nam.
     'Lauerd,' he sayd, quen i þe herd,
     For i saw wel þat i misferd,   864
     I and my wijf yode vs to hide;
868   Fór vs þoȝt scam þe to bide;
     For vr bodys ar nu all bare.'
     'Goddot, Adam! þis sayd i ar,   868
     þe waath i tald þe wel forwiþ
872   Wat it war to brek mi griþ;
     Bot nu it es þis appel eten,
     And swa mi forbod es forgeten.   872
     Forþi þat þu has don þe mis
876   þyself þu wite þi wa, y-wis.'
     'Lauerd,' he sayd, 'o þis gilt here,
     Sco es to wite þat es my fere   876
     þat þu me gaf my wijf to be;
880   Ful þraly first sco bedd it me,
     For sco me bedd, wiðvten blin,
     Sco has me filed wið hir sin.   880
     Al þat i say, may scoo noȝt nite,
884   Forþij aw sco to ber þe wite.'
     God spak til hir, and sayd on-an:
     'Quy did þu þus, þu ful womman?'   884
     'þe worm,' sco sayd, 'me draf þartil,
888   þat i have wroȝt ogayn þy will.'
     Til þat worm þat driȝtin spak
     Wordes bathe o wrath and wrak: 888
     'þu worm, þu sal be malediȝt
892   Mar þan any oðer wiȝt;
     Mar þan any oðer best,
     For þu sal slide opon þi brest.   892
     Fra þis day forþ fareden sal be,
896   Forsoþ, betwix womman and þe,
     Betwix þyn and wommans sede
     Mold sal be þy mete for nede.   896
     þu sal wayt womman for to sting,
900   And sco sal yeit þy heved þring;
     þow þu wald euer haue hat sted,
     In cald sal ever be þy bed.'   900
     'And þu, womman þat standes here
904   In sorw sal þu þy bernes bere,
     þu sal be slaan wiþ duble ded,
     Hard it es þe for to rede;   904
     þu sal be to man vnderheild,

864 (866) misfard C   865 (867) vs ȝode C went vs G   866 (868) For *om.* F, him t. abide G
867 (869) er G aren F, nu *om.* y   869 (871) þu wat it iteld þe formest G, *alt.* F   870 (872)
was G, hest G, *alt.* F   872 (874) so G   874 (876) þiselven es þe wite G, þu] may F   876
(878) sco es] *inv.* G   878 (880) stiffli G, bad G   881 (883) all þis may scho noght gain say
G   882 (884) scho au to b. þe gilt away G, aw sco to] sulde ho F   883 (885) Iesu G, he F,
spak til hir] *inv.* G   884 (886) dus G, ille G, wommon F   886 (888) agayn C y   887 (889)
þan dr.] vr laverd þan G our lorde F   888 (890) wreth G   891-92 (893-4) *inv.* G   893 (895)
forþ *om.* C, foredin G departynge F, sal *trsp.* y   895 (897) *trsp.* G, womman C G wommon
F wommones T   896 (898) *trsp.* G, erd G   897 (899) stang G   898 (900) þin G, hede C
hefde G, thrang G, *alt.* F   899 (901) þof C, wild G, *alt.* F   902 (904) childer G   903 (905)
slain y   905 (907) be *trsp.* F, vnder mannes ȝeilde G

908   To him þy buxumnes to yeild,
    To scaw þy scath be noȝt vnkidd,
    Þu scal haf euer þyn heved hidd.   908
    Þat þu þowqueðer has nu mistan,
912   It sal be bett wið a womman.
    O sinles man þan mad i þe,
    In womman sal my wonning be.   912
    Bot þat bes noȝt kidd sa yare
916   For i most cover þis tinsel ar.'
    ' And þu, man, þat has vndertaken
    Þy wijves red, and mijn forsaken,   916
    Ne sal þu nawiȝt þarwið win,
920   Þe werld es werid wiþ þy sin ;
    Of erth þu sal wiþ swete and swink
    Win þat þu sal ete and drink.   920
    All þe dayes o þyn eild
924   Brembil and þorn it sal te yeild.
    Þarof þu sal ete gresses sere,
    And þu sal bij þy bred ful dere,   924
    Betwix and þu ogayn be gan
928   Vnto þe erth þu was of tan.
    For þu ne es bot a pudre playn,
    To pudre sal þu worth ogayn.'   928
    He turned þan his wijves nam,
932   And Eve fra þan hir cald Adam,
    Eve sco hiȝt euer fra þat day,
    Þat moder of many es for to say.   932
    God mad þaym kirtels þan of hide,
936   And cled þayr fless wiþ for to hide.
    ' Loo,' he sayd of Adam, ' hu
    Lik he's mad tilward vs nu,   936
    Bath þe god and ill knawand ;
940   Nu forþij ar he strek hand
    To þat tree þat lijf es in,
    And siðen he live wiðvten blin.'   940
    He put him vt wiðvten bade
944   Vnto þe werld þar he was made :
    ' Ful dere, Adam, sal it be boȝt,
    Ar it be bett þat þu has wroȝt.'   944
    Tak þy wijf nu in þy hand,
948   For ye most leve þis luvesum land,
    Vnto þe wrecched werld to gang,
    Quar þu sal þink þu liues to lang,   948
    Ful lang penance for to drey
952   And siðen wiþ duble ded to dey.

907 (909) sceu C F   908 (910) hefd G   909 (911) þoqueþe C doqueþer G   911 (913) s. m.] *trsp.* C   912 (914) yet *add.* **y**   913 (915) yeit *add.* G, so C G   914 (916) mast G   916 (918) wijf C F   917 (919) Ne s. þ. n.] Naþing sal þu G   919 (921) on F in G   921 (923) on C 925 (927) Tuix and G, *alt.* F   926 (928) To G, þat *add.* G   927 (929) ne *om,* F, art **y**   928 (930) turn G   931 (933) euer] eue C *om.* G   932 (934) es] it es G   933 (935) m. þ. þan k. G 934 (936) And] þarwid, G cled *om.* G wiþ] þan G   (937-42) *om.* F   936 (938) he's] es C es he G   938 (940) Nu *om.* G, er G, h. st. h.] þai bath strikand G   939 (941) ȝon G   940 (942) ȝe leue G   942 (944) Into G intille F, world G   943 (945) sal it] *transp.* G   944 (946) Till G   946 (948) *alt.* F, sal G   947 (949) Into F Intill G, world G, to] þou F   948 (950) Þare G, þi life **y**, ful G   949 (951) Ful *om.* **y**, pining G   950 (952) wiþ] *òm.* G, dobil G

Ye sal be flemed fra my face
Betwixand i yu send my grace;   952
þe oyle of mercy most yu bide,
956 I hyȝt at send it yu sum tide.'
'Allas!' sayd Adam, 'wa es me,
Lauerd þat i ne had truud þe,   956
Lauerd þat euer i mad þe wrath,
960 Forþij my lijf es me too luth.
I wat hot þe haf i na freind;
Tell me ar i fra þe weind   960
Hugate and wiþ quat kinnes þing
964 I sal cover þi saȝtling.'
He sayd: 'Adam, nu wel seis þu
I sal þe tell, and herken nu,   964
Omang þyn oðer werkes hend
968 O þi winning give me þe tend,
Of alkins fruit have þu þe nijn,
For i wil þat þe tend be mijn.'   968
'Lauerd,' he sayd, 'þu gives al,
972 Quij sal þy part be sa smal?
þe half part gladly or þe þridd,
We wil þe give if þu it bidd.'   972
'Adam, i wil ask nan vtrage
976 Bot þe teind als in knawlage;
For sum o þijn ful mikel wil þink
To give þe teinde part þayr swink,   976
Ye sal do bren it on a stan.'
980 Adam went vt ful wil of wan,
Had noȝt Adam ben in þat bliss
Bot tides þre dwelland ywis,   980
Quen he gan brek þe commandment
984 þat al his oxspring did be schent.
For he was wroȝt at undern tide,
At midday Eve drawn of his side.   984
þay brak þe forbod als sone
988 þat þay war bath don vt at none.
Adam was vt don neyss and naked
Into þe land quar he was maked.   988
þar he ledd a lang lijf,
992 And gat his childer wið his wijf.
Vt es put swa wrecched Adam
Of paradijs, þat rike haam.   992
A fijren wal þar es abute

953 (955) bos you G, abide G   954 (956) hete G, to G, yu om. C, alt. F   955 (957) ful w. G
956 (958) in add. G, trawet F   958 (960) to] ful G   959 (961) bot þe] bot i of þe G, haf i]
have G   961 (963) quatkin C F quat G   962 (964) Mai c. nu G   963 (965) sais þou C F, nu
transp. G   965 (967) amonge F emang G   967 (969) alkin C F, hald G, neien G, alt. F
968 (970) þat om. G, þan add. G   969 (971) gafs C   970 (972) suld G, so F   971-984 (973-
986) om. G   973 (975) haks C om. F   974 (976) part om. F   975 (977) sal C   976 (978)
þare C F   979 (981) Adam dwelled noȝt F   980 (982) tides þre] þre owres F   981 (983) can
C con F, comament C   983 (985) vndorun F   985 (987) forbot C, als sun C   987 (989) nars
C nerehand G   990 (992) bi G   991 (993) he add. y, swa om. y, put] now F   992 (994) rich
C riche y   993 (995) firir C, Meruail F

996 May nan winn in þat es wiðvte.
      An angel has þe yate to geite
      Wiþ swerd in hand of mikel heite.   996
      ' Tell me, man, yeit wiþ þi lare
1000 Quat land es paradijs and ware,
      Sin i sal her þe þerof spell ? '
      Blithli, sir, i sal þe tell.   1000
      Paradys is a prive stede
1004 Þar many myrþes er o mede
      Þe luveliest of all landes
      In erth toward þe est it standes,   1004
      Land o lijf, o ro, and rest,
1008 Wiþ bliss and beild broyden best;
      Þar never neȝes ned ne nyȝt
      Bot euer umlayd wiþ leme and lyȝt;   1008
      O selines es it wel seene,
1012 Þe gress es ever ilike grene,
      Wiþ alkyns bliss þat þar es elles,
      Fluurs þar es wiþ swete smelles.   1012
      Trees o fruit þan es þar sett
1016 Þat serkyns vertu has at ete,
      Þat if man ete in tyme of an,
      Hunger suld he neuer have nan,   1016
      And if he ete of anoðer tre,
1020 Ne suld he never þristy be.
      Þe þridd, qua ete o þat þar es,
      He suld have never werines;   1020
      Of an qua siðen ete at þe last,
1024 He suld in eild be ay stedfast,
      Seknes suld he never drey
      Ne never mare his body dey.   1024
      It es a yard cald o delices
1028 Wið al manere o swete spices.
      Qua lenges þar, þar þaim noȝt lang,
      Þar suun es soft and swete sang.   1028
      Suun of saintes þat þar singes,
1032 Midward þat land a well springes
      Þat rennes vt wiþ fowr strandes
      Flummes farand in ferr landes.   1032
      Þijs flummes fowr þat þar biginnes
1036 Þurwȝ vt all oðer cuntres rynnes,

994 (996) cum G, wid-in G, þar v. G   996 (998) suord G   997 (999) yeit] om. G   998 (1000)
quare y   999 (1001) sal om. G, þareof G, alt. F   1000 (1002) Blethli C Gladli G   1001
(1003) place G   1002 (1004) emedd C and mede F, Ful of mirth and of solace G   1003
(1005) leueleist C, place add. F   1006 (1008) beild] bote G, ioy and blis F   1007 (1009) þar
euer es day widuten night y   1008 (1010) Bot e.] And G, and euer F   1009 (1011) it es G
1010 (1012) griss G, elike G   1011 (1013) all G, blisses G   1012 (1014) þat er G alt. F, of y
1014 (1016) diuers y   1016 (1018) sal G   1018 (1020) Ne om. C, sal G, thresti C   1019
(1021) þe th. q. it etes of þ. þere riss G, alt. F   1020 (1022) sal he G, h. n.] transp. y   1021
(1023) Of ane quaso it etes at þ. last G of þe firthe qua ete a. þ. l. F   1022 (1024) sal G,
ay be F, euer G   1023 (1025) sal G, non add. G   1024 (1026) mare] sal G   1025 (1027)
orichard G, delites C delijss G   1026 (1028) suet C, alt. G   1027 (1029) þam C, him y
1628 (1030) suet C, alt. F   1029 (1031) sautes (print.) C, foulis G   1030 (1032) In middes
G   1032 (1034) Stremes G   1033 (1035) þat] at F   1034 (1036) rennes G

þe first es Tiger and siðen Gyon,
Siðen Eufrates and Fison.   1036
þay bring o paradijs þe stan,
1040 Swa precius es funden nan.
þis paradijs es sett swa hey
þat moght neuer flod any þar ney;   1040
Forþij was it of Noë flode
1044 Free, þat al þe werld oueryode.

OF þE XV SIGNIS BEFOR THE DOOME.

Bot ijn' may nangate bot i meene   1044
22428 þaa cruel dayes and þaa kene,
For doomesday þay sal be sene
Wiþ sorwful signes yaa fiftene.
If ye of þaym wil listen a þraw   1048
22432 I sal yu tell of þaym sooþsaw,
þat es na man in erth swa fell
þat herken hertly wil þis spell
Of þis wrecched werldes end   1052
22436 þat hen' his lijf aw for to mend.
Gret signes sal vr laverd make
For to schaw þe wick his wrake,
Als it es tald of Jeremie,   1056
22440 Zorobabel and Ysay,
Als Jeronim þat man wel truus,
Tells, he fand in þe book of Juus.
Queðer þey sal all on raw betide   1060
22444 Owðer interval bitwix þaym bide,
þat vndos he nowðerquar
þow he was mikel clerc of lare.
þe jugement a litel ar,   1064
22448 þat nan sal of þe feluns spare,
Sal vr laverd his myȝtes scaw,
þat man it sal in erth knaw.
Hider nu i bidd þeym draw   1068
22452 Al þai þat of him standes aw,
And herken swa þat i sal say
þat hen' wend noȝt hafles oway.
Swa sorwful syȝt was never aa   1072
22456 þat þai sal bijd sal tell of waa.

1035 (1037) þe first hatte tigre þe toþer ganges F, *of* gyon C *only the first letter kept,
but illegible,* þe f. es tyger and g. G   1036 (1038) Siþen eufrates and fison *(on erasure)* C
Siþen nil. and euf. G þe þrid nilus. þe firþ eufrates F   1037 (1039) stanis fra p. G, mony a
stane F   1038 (1040) naquar funden es G   1039 (1041) þ. might (muȝt F) n. fl. cum þar
ney **y**   1041 (1043) fre *add.* G   1042 (1044) fre *om.* G, warld C, yodd C it ȝ. G   1044
(22427) Nu mai G, na gat C G   1046 (22429) Forn G, þat C   1047 (22430) sorful E C G,
þaa (?) C ful G   1048 (22431) o. þ. w. l.] *transp.* E, list **x** F   1049 (22432) sooþsawe] a
þraw E   1050 (22433) þat] þar C   1051 (22434) wele G   1053 (22436) aw] *transp.* G, for
om. C **y**   1055 (22438) to sceu C **y**   1058 (22441) ierome C **y**, sais *add.* C, als þat G, man
wel] *inv.* E   1059 (22442) Sais C, þe *om.* F   1061 (22444) Ouir E Or C **y**, enterwall **x**, þai
E   1062 (22445) nourquare C nauþerquar E   (22443-48) *om.* F   1063 (22446) þof C þoch E
1065 (22448) feloun E   1066 (22449) his *om.* E F, *alt.* F   1067 (22450) nan **x**   1069
(22452) þa E *om.* G *alt* F   1071 (22454) ne *om.* C **y**   1072 (22455) sorful **x** G   1073
(22456) þai] time E þaim G *alt.* F

22459 Þe firste day sal ik of rede,
22460 Ful mikel it es al for to drede,
       For þar sal fall dun fra þe lift   1076
       O blody rayn a drery drift.
       Þe erth schal be al red of hew,
22464 Ne saw man never swilk a dew !
       Childer in moder wambis to lij,   1080
       Wiðin þayr wambes sal þay crij
       Wið heye note and lude steven,
22468 'Mercy, Laverd, king of heven,
       For to be born have we noȝt mint,   1084
       Þu it, lauerd, do vs for to stynt.
       Quarto suld we be born to day,
22472 Quen al þinges sal turn to way?'
       Gretand þay sal call on Ihesu,   1088
       'Laverd, have mercy on all nu.'
       Þe toðer day to bide ywis,
22476 It sal be wele werr þan þis.
       Þe sternes wiþ þayr leme and leven   1092
       Ful radli sal fall duun fra heven,
       Es naan swa wel fest of þaym all
22480 þat it ne sal dun þat day fall;
       And titter sal þay ryn on grund   1096
       Þan firslaȝt dos quen it es stund;
       þay sal on erth ryn her and þar
22484 Wepand als þow þay men war.
       Naa word þowqueðer sal þay sune   1100
       Til þat þey be all fallen dune
       Vnto þabiȝme wiðvten syȝt,
22488 And þar þey sal have tynt þayr lyȝt,
       And worth all black sum any cole,   1104
       Laverd! hu may we þis þole,
       Þat es swa solwed in vr syn,
22492 And als we wonden war þaym in.
       Efter þe twa folwes þe þridd,   1108
       An vncuþ day þan es it kidd
       Þat þe mone þat es sa schene,
22496 Quen in þe waxand it es sene,
       Sal bicum red als any blood   1112
       Þurwȝ drede of him was don on rood;
       On erth dun it sal descend,
22500 Bot þar ne sal it naawyȝt lend,

1074 (22459) first **x y**, i C **y**, of *om*. E   1077 (22462) Of] A C G   1079 (22464) man] i C,
men **y**   1080 (22465) þair *add*. G, mod*er*is E, wamb C G, þar þai li G þat lye F   1084 (22469)
mint] space G, *alt*. F   1085 (22470) þou do it l. C we do us l. G, vs *om*. E, for to stynt] in
þi grace G   1086 (22471) sold E   1087 (22472) þing G, com E, *alt*. F   1089 (22474) Laverd,
laverd E, on all *om*. E   1091 (22476) war C   1092 (22477) bemis E, leman C lemand G
1093 (22478) Ful *om*. E G, Faadeli E saddli C G, sal fall] f. sal þai C fal E, dun] *om*. E, fra
h.] f. þe h. E   1094 (22479) swaa] þat E, fest] f. es E, all] *om*. E   1095 (22480) ne] na E
1096 (22481) sal þay] s. tai E   1099 (22484) *and* wepe F, þow] *om*. **y**   1100 (22485) þ. s.
þay] *transp*. C G   1101 (22486) all] *om*. E G   1103 (22488) have tynt] tine F, miȝt F
1104 (22489) worde E · 1106 (22491) ar F, sulwed C, bunden al wiþ F   1107 (22492) And
þar of wil we neuir blin E   1108 (22493) fules C fulus G   1113 (22498) Þoru **x** For **y**, hem
E   1115 (22500) ne] na E

Bot to þe see þan sal it ryn 1116
And þar sco sal hir hide wiðin
For to flee þe day of aw,
22504 Quen Crist sal cum himself to schaw.
Þe ferðe signe efter þe þre 1120
Sal be ful grijsly on to see,
Þat þe sunn þat es sa bryȝt,
22508 And serves al þis werld o lyȝt,
It sal becum þan ful vnfayr, 1124
Dim and black sum any ayr.
Quen it es fayrest on to look
22512 At midday time, als says þe book,
Blacken it sal þat ilke time 1128
Þat nan þarwiþ sal see a stime.
A! Lauerd! ful waa sal be þat man
22516 Þat hen' sal have na mercy þan.
To þaym þat he his wreeþ sal kith, 1132
Ne sal þay neuer fra þan be blith.
Vglij sal be þe fifte day
22520 Mar þan any tung can say;
All bestes dumb vnder þe lift 1136
Vp þay sal þayr hevedes lift,
Opon vr laverd for to crij
22524 If þay moȝt spek at ask mercij.
Ryȝt to þe erþ þan sal þay ryn 1140
For drednes þar to hide þaym in,
An crijen sal wiþ stijþer steven
22528 Þan nu may do ten or elleven,
Al for drede of his cuming, 1144
Þat dom sal deme of all þing.
Þe sexte day es redd in rune,
22532 Quen al þis werld bath dale and dune
Even ilijke hey sal worþ al, 1148
Þe valis tvprijse, þe fells to fall,
And al þis erth nu vnder heven
22536 Sal be þat day ilijke al even.
For drednes of þat demestere 1152
Þe pes sal al turn into were,
Þe erth sal quake, neuer ar sa fast,
22540 Tur and tun al dun to cast,
Þat es na werc saa strang, or wal, 1156
Þat it ne duun þat day sal fall.
Wodd and wal al duun sal draw
22544 Of demester þat dredful aw.

1117 (22502) sco sal] *transp.* E, *alt.* **y**   1119 (22504) him for E   1120 (22505) ferþ C
feird G firþ F, þride G   1125 (22510) hayr **x y**   1126 (22511) þe *add.* C   1128 (22513)
ilk **x**   1131 (22516) ne] he E, *om.* **y**   1132 (22517) he] þat E   1133 (22518) Ne] Na E
1134 (22519) fift **x** fift þat F   1136 (22521) doun F   1138 (22523) Apon **x y**   1140 (22525)
vnto G, erþ] air C **y**, þan] al C *om.* E   1142 (22527) crijen] cri **x y**, þan *add.* E C *trsp.* E
om. **y**, þer *add* F   1145 (22530) all] alkin C, ting G   1146 (22531) sext **x** F   1147 (22532)
all *om.* E   1148 (22533) he C hit F, wroght G   1149 (22534) Þe *om.* G, wallis E, dals C,
uprise C **y** touris E   1150 (22535) erþ *om.* E   1151 (22536) elike E all like G   1152
(22537) demster **x**   1153 (22538) al turn] *inv.* G   1156 (22541) verc E, ouir E   1159
(22544) demster E, derful E

        Sorwful sal be þe signe sevend   1160
        Mar þan þe sex þat ic have nevend.
        Þe trees forcasten sal þaym payn
22548 For to ryȝt þaym vp ogayn.
        Dun þe crop, vpward þe rote   1164
        Of mirþes þan es nan to mote.
        Vnquemfullij þan sal þay quake,
22552 Þat al þe erth it sal do scake;
        Noȝt a leif on þaym sal lest,   1168
        Quen þat þe gret intwa sal brest.
        Laverd! quar scal we þan rest,
22556 Quan naan schal wite quar þaym to nest?
        All wanes þat time sal vs wan,   1172
        Bot we ne haf þe grace of an.
        Þan behoves al folk to dey
22560 Þurwȝ sorwfulnes þat þey sal drey.
        Þe aȝtande signe it has na make,   1176
        Nan forwiẟ of sa mikel wrake.
        Of hir channel þe see sal rise
22564 To hid it, bot it may na wise,
        It sal bath brest ouer dale and dune   1180
        All kyns þinges for to drun,
        Bot hen' vs fayl þat has it tald
22568 Þat was Moïses þat ald.
        Vp to þe lift rijs sal þe see   1184
        Þarwiþ strengþ to gete entre.
        Þe fisses þat þarin er stadd
22572 Þát we make vs oft of glad,
        Til erẟen way sal þay flee,   1188
        And ween þat God may noȝt þaym see.
        Ogayn þe see þan sal it draw
22576 Duun fra þe lift unto þe law,
        Vntil hir channel sal sco turn,   1192
        And als til þayres ilk a burn.
        Þe nind it sal be cruel and kene
22580 Was nan swilk of þaa forwiþ sene.
        Wiþ speke sal al þing þaym meen   1196
        Als it wiþ mannes muþ had ben.
        I draw to warand saint Awstin
22584 Þat spekes hu þis werld sal fijn.
        Þay sal cry on vr laverd dryȝt   1200

1160 (22545) Sorful **x y**   1161 (22546) þe *om.* C, sexte G, *alt.* F   1163 (22548) again C **y**
1165 (22550) murthes C, þan nan es E nan þan es G nan es þen F   1167 (22552) do] to
x F   1168 (22553) last C **y**   1169 (22554) intwa] of þam C, brast C F   1171 (22556) wet
E, *alt.* F   1172 (22557) sal vs þ. t. G salle we þ. t. F   1173 (22558) ne] na C *om.* F
1175 (22560) Thoru **x y**, sorfulnes **x** G   1176 (22561) havis E   1180 (22565) bath] *om.* G,
ouer *om.* E   1181 (22566) kins *om.* E   1182 (22567) hen fail vs E, hafs E, *alt.* F   1183
(22568) Moses C, selue *add.* G, *alt.* F   1184 (22569) Op E   1185 (22570) strenket E
strenght C F   1186 (22571) es E   1187 (22572) we *om.* E, oft *transp.* G   1188 (22573)
erþerin E erth C erdward G, wai *om.* G   1190 (22575) Again C **y**   1191 (22576) to F,
duun] *transp.* F   1192 (22577) intil G, þan *add.* C (22577-8) *om.* F   1193 (22578) alsua to
C, als tils til E, a *om.* C   1194 (22579) nijnd] neynd E neinind C niend **y**, it *om.* C **y**   1195
(22580) *alt.* F   1196 (22581) speche **x y**   1198 (22583) warant G

'Have mercy on vs for þy myȝt
Laverd God þat lastes ay,
22588 þu sal vs don to wite oway,
To turn ogayn als noȝt ne war;   1204
Lauerd, þu laat vs noȝt forfare,
þe tend vtneem es for to neven
22592 þat es na halwes vnder þe heven
And heven self, ne sal be ferd   1208
Gayn him þat wroȝt þe midelerd,
Als þat vs telles Saint Jerome,
22596 And Gregor þat was pape of Rome.
þe selve angels sal quake vnqueme   1212
For dute of him þat al sal deme
For þan sal quak saint Cherubin
22600 And alswa sal do Seraphin.
Naa creatur sal listen play,   1216
Saint Petre sal be dumb þat day,
þat he a word ne sal dur speke
22604 For dute of demesteris wreke;
For heven he sal see part in sundre,   1220
And he sal her it crij to wondre,
Bath crij and bray for dute and drede
22608 'Have mercij, lauerd, for nu es nede.'   1224
þan sal þai þat in helle er cropen,
Quen lyȝt sal schijn of hevens open,
þa warlawes all sal walken vte,
22612 Saint Pawel says it nes na dute.   1228
Herkens nu quat þay sal say
For dred þai sal haf of þat day:
'Ihesus lauerd þat wroȝt vs aa
22616 In heven, and siðen it took vs fra,   1232
We have it tynt wiþ gret folij,
In þis gret nede we to þe crij,
þin wrecche handewerc in waa
22620 þat þu of fire vs suffres swaa.   1236
Caitiues þat nu sorwes mar
þan ever in helle we won was ar,
þu yeild vs gayn vr hostel nu
22624 þat vs es reft, and wen' waat hu.   1240
We wald it vnderfang ful fayn
If we moȝt have vr erth ogayn.'
þe signes of þe day elleven

1201 (22586) of F   1203 (22588) do C y   1206 (22591) vtenemes C is outane F   1207
(22592) halu G hagie E   1208 (22593) heuen om. E, ne] it x y   1209 (22594) Sain E, made
G, þe om. C G   1210 (22595) sain E   1212 (22597) seluen G   1214 (22599) sant C   1216
(22601) sal þan list C G sal lesten E   1217 (22602) domb E   1218 (22603) he ne a word
dar noht E he a w. dar noȝt F   1219 (22604) doubt E, demester þe C demsteris E, þe mister
þe G   1220 (22605) depart E sonder E   1223 (22608) Ha C   1224 (22609) glopin E   1225
(22610) lyȝt om. C, þe heuennes C heuen E   1226 (22611) walk þan] C y   1227 (22612) it
sais G, ne om. x y   1231 (22616) it om. E, take G   1234 (22619) hanwerc E handwerc C
landwerke G   1235 (22620) vtewandre C in þis fire þou F, þat om. F   1236 (22621) Caitive
E G, alt. F   1237 (22622) we] it C om. G alt. F, wont G   1238 (22623) again E egain G
1241 (22626) might G miht E   1242 (22627) signe C y, elleft x F

22628   It nes na skil þat þay beleven.
       Sar þay sal do for to grise,   1244
       Windes on ilka side sal rise;
       Sa fast gayn oðer sal þay blaw
22632   þat es na þing þat it may schaw.
       þe erth þay sal do for to rift,   1248
       And vp vt of þe stede to lift;
       þe devels vt sal be fordriven
22636   O þat erth þat sal be riven,
       Bers þayr bodys in þat ayr,   1252
       þat syȝt it sal be ful vnfayr!
       þan sal þe raynbow descend,
22640   In hew of gall it sal be kend,
       Wiþ þe windes it sal mell,   1256
       And drive þaym duun all until hell,
       And dint þe devels þiderin
22644   In þayr bale al for to brin,
       And sal þaym bidd to hald þaym þar   1260
       Oboven erth to cum na maar.
       þe term es cumen, have ye sal
22648   þe incume to be in yur bale.
       þan sal þey begin to cri and call: 1264
       'Laverd fader, vr God of all,
       þu lat vs vnder erth be hidd
22652   þat wen' be her na langer kidd.'
       þe twelfde signe es of sorwes sere   1268
       þurwȝ myȝt of him þat al can stere,
       þat es na man in erth wroȝt
22656   þat aw to lat it vt of þoȝt,
       And for to mend his lijf þe mar   1272
       To Ihesu þat vr levedy bar.
       Heven it sal be loken ogayn,
22660   Sal nan be þan þat þayn' sal quayn.
       Hugate her nu may we lend   1276
       Quen al þing draws þus til end,
       þe angels þat in heven sal be,
22664   Sal knele dun for Cristes kne,
       And sal cri merci to þat king,   1280
       þat þay se buun til all þing.
       For þat rethness sal þay be radd,
22668   þey see ouer al þe werld be stadd.
       Quen angels swa sal dred þat pass,   1284

1243 (22628) þay] it **x y**, beleuen] be left **x** F be leuen G   1245 (22630) wind E **y**, ik E ilk
C   1246 (22631) again G, *alt.* F   1247 (22632) tung C G   1248 (22633) þey schal] þan
(þen) sal **y** sal tai E, for *om.* E   1250 (22635) fordreuin E   1251 (22636) out *add.* F, reuen
E   1252 (22637) Ber E **y**   1255 (22640) hu C   1256 (22641) And *add.* E, wind C, þan sal
it C it sal it G   1257 (22642) And *om.* E, all *om.* E into þe E intil G to F   1258 (22643)
dump C dunt E dompit F bete G   1261 (22646) no E   1262 (22647) nu *add.* G, we C
1265 (22650) god, vr fader C, vr *om.* E   1266-7 (22651-2) *om.* E   1268 (22653) tuelft **x y**
1271 (22656) acht E, be *add.* G   1275 (22660) þayn'] taim E   1276 (22661) bend E   1277
(22662) all thinges C alkin thing G, now *add.* E, þus] *om.* E **x** þusga C sal dragh F   1279
(22664) kerel E, don E, befor C **y**   1280 (22665) þair C   1281 (22666) bow E   1282 (22667)
reuthes G drerines F, þay] *transp.* F tai E   1283 (22668) sa] be F *om.* E G   1284 (22669)
angel E, sa E

Of sinful quat sal worth, allas!
þe day þrittend sal be too snell,
22672 Mar þan mannis tung may tell
Of þat sorwful grisly daw   1288
þat Crist sal til his scaftes schaw,
Quen all þe stanes þat er maad
22676 Vndir þe lift in werld braad
Oboven þe erth and bineðen   1292
Ryȝt unto þabime fra heven
Sal smite togedir wiþ sly maȝt
22680 Als þoner dos wiþ fijren slaȝt.
Wiþ hard dintes mun þay kith   1296
þat naan has even to be blith.
Wiþ þrawing sal þay samen þrest
22684 þat all to peces sal þay brest.
þis sal be lastand al a day,   1300
þe signes of þis sorful play.
þe men þat þat day sal ouerbide,
22688 Vnder a fell þay sal þaym hide.
þe day fowrtend sal be ful grill,   1304
Til al þe werld it sal be ill,
A stormy day & streyt of aw
22692 Bath o frost and hayl and snaw;
þan sal þar cum bath þoner and leven   1308
And drove al þat es vnder heven,
þe cludes til þe see sal ryn
22696 For to hiden þaym þarin,
For to flee þat day sa brem   1312
þat vr lauerd sal cum to deme.
Quat sal be þe fiftend day?
22700 Als ik have funden, i sal it say,
Men says and soth it may befall   1316
þat it sal ending be of al.
þis midelerd, ful wayleway,
22704 Al to noȝt sal brin oway,
þe see als þat vmlukes þe land,   1320
And watres all þat rynnes in strand;
Al sal turn ogayn til noȝt,
22708 Als þey war first, ar þay war wroȝt,
Heven and erth to be maad new   1324
þat ever sal be lastand trew.
þan sal be herd þe blast of beme,

1286 (22671) day *om.* C, thretend E   1287 (22672) man wit C, ani **y**   1288 (22673) sorful
x G   1291 (22676) in] on E, word E   1292 (22677) þis erþe E   1293 (22678) into F, heven]
heþen C G   1296 (22681) herd C, mon **x** G, *alt.* F   1297 (22682) havis E, þan *add.* to *om.* E
1298 (22683) strenth þan G, casting F, þrist E, tai E   1299 (22684) brist E   1301 (22686)
sori G   1303 (22688) þaym hide] habide E   1304 (22689) faurtend E   1304-5 (22689-90)
grill : ill *transp.* G   1306 (22691) &] a **x** G   1308 (22693) sal tar E, bath *om.* G   1309
(22694) drone (*print.*) C G droune (*print.*) F   1310 (22695) þe see] þe heuin E   1311 (22696)
hide **x y**, þan *add.* G   1314 (22699) be *om.* C, fiften E   1315 (22700) ik] i C **y**, i] ik E, it]
om. E ȝu G   1316 (22701) it may befall] al be may fall C mai be and fall G, *alt.* F (22701-
2) *inv.* F   1318 (22703) medelerd E, wail C G   1319 (22704) bren F   1320 (22705) als
om. C G   1321 (22706) al þe w. E, rennis G   1322 (22707) torn E   1323 (22708) ar al
was C   1325 (22710) trew] newe E

22712	Þe demester sal cum to deme	
	Þat al þing of standes awe,	1328
	In quatkyns forme i sal yu schaw.	
	We truu and all aw for to truu,	
22716	Bot it be Saraȝin or Iuu,	
	Þat eftir his résurrécciun	1332
	Þe heye day of þassenciun	
	Com Ihesus til his freindes swet	
22720	Þat set war to þayr mete at ete,	
	And þay þat war in drede and dute	1336
	Þarof wiþ truþ he broȝt þaym vt,	
	And siðen vp til heven he stey,	
22724	Many man onstandand sey.	
	His disciples for þis syȝt	1340
	Mikel he did þayr hert to lyȝt;	
	A cluud ogayn him saw þay lyȝt,	
22728	And bar him vp, was wonder bryȝt,	1344
	Verray man and God verray,	
	All for to deme on domesday.	
	Þat ilke forme cum he sal þar	
22732	Þat he in erth his crois bar.	
	Swa sal he cum, bot witt ye þan	1348
	Þat sin þe werld it first began,	
	Was never seen sa sorful tide	
22736	Als þat day sal be for to bide.	
	Quen he com first his cume to kithe	1352
	Wiþ meeknes al he gan it mithe;	
	Þat com was bath derne and hidd	
22740	And noȝt bot quon men to was kidd.	
	His oðer cuming sal he schaw	1356
	Kithly til þis werld to knaw,	
	Bath heven and erth for him sal drede	
22744	Als yee forwiþ has herd me rede.	
	It nes na clerk may wrijt with ink,	1360
	Ne muþ to mele ne hert to þink;	
	Þe hundreth and þe þusand knyȝtes	
22748	Sal folw þat lauerd mikel of myȝtes,	
	Wið him to cum all to þis day.	1364
	Allas! Quat sal þe sinful say?	
	Ungaynand sal be þan his gamen,	
22752	Quen he to brinne sal se all samen,	
	Bath land and lijth and all þinges	1368

1327 (22712) demster E demister G   1329 (22714) quatkin **x y**   1333 (22718) hei **x** G, his G   1335 (22720) and ete G   1337 (22722) trow E trout C trouth G trauth F   1338 (22723) op E, he] him C   1339 (22724) on stad and C constadd and G   1341 (22726) hertis G   1342 (22727) again **x y**   1343 (22728) was] *om.* C   1344 (22729) man godd *transp.* G   1348 (22733) witt ye] witte wel E   1349 (22734) sithen G, it *om.* E   1350 (22735) sua **y**   1352 (22737) he *om.* E   1353 (22738) al *om.* C, he gan] *inv.* G, can C F, it *om.* G   1354 (22739) was] *om.* E, bath] *om.* G   1355 (22740) noȝt bot quon men to was] nobot quon men to C no bit chone men to E bot to fone men was G *alt.* E   1356 (22741) he] be E   1357 (22742) Richli (?) E Rightli G riȝtwis F, al E G, *alt.* F, verd E   1359 (22744) fovit E bifor F *transp.* G, hauis E, haue **y**   1360 (22745) es **x y**   1361 (22746) ne m.] na m. E   1362 (22747) hundret **x**, þe *om.* G   1363 (22748) mikel lord of C F   1367 (22752) bren F   1368 (22753) lijth] see C **y**

þat any werldes hald wið hinges.
Sorful bes þan þe sinful chere,
22756 Quen all þey schal þa trumpes here;
Bifor þe face of þat Kaiser   1372
Angels sal his baner ber,
þat es þe rode he was on spredd
22760 þat he wid vs to lijf has ledd.
Ouercumen þe feind wald al forfare,   1376
Nes na baner he dredes mar.
Was never sunn schijnand sa clere
22764 þe tende part als þat banere!
þe bryȝtnes of þat crois sa scene   1380
Ouer al þe werld it sal be sene.
þus heyly, bot wele heyliker
22768 Sal cum to deme þat demester.
At dome hen' schal noȝt sit allan   1384
Bot felawes oðer many aan.
All þaa þat swa þaymselven buud,
22772 þat werldes worschip al forhuud,
Silver and gold and eyse of lijf,   1388
And taȝt þayr fless for him in strijf,
And travayld þaym on all wijs
22776 To payen him in his servise,
And folwed lelik all his lawes,   1392
þir men sal be als his felawes,
For to deme bath ded and qwick,
22780 Queðersum þay be good or wick.
All þat sal be at þat assise   1396
All haal þaymself þai schal vprise,
In body and sawl al on new wise
22784 Al þurwȝ þe strengþ of þat iustise.
þat ilke fless þat we have nu,   1400
We sal ber þan, sa sal we tru,
And oðer nan we writen find.
22788 þat oðer truus, of truuth er blind;
Of þis truuth hard es truuth to fijnd,   1404
forqui it semis al gayn kind.
þat mannes molten fless and banes
22792 Fra time þat þay be roten anes
Have pijth and lijf, als þay had ar,   1408
It semes swa þat never mar.

1369 (22754) werdische E werlds C   1371 (22756) þay] þan E G   1374 (22759) þat es *om.*
G, his G, þat he was G, sprid E   1375 (22760) he *om.* E, vs will G, havis E   1377 (22762)
ne *om.* **x y**   1379 (22764) tend **x**, tat E   1380 (22765) croice **x y**   1382 (22767) heilik E
1383 (22768) demster E demister G   1384 (22769) ne *om.* C **y**, not C noht E   1385 (22770)
oþer] wiþ him F   1386 (22771) þaimself sua E, bowed E   1388 (22773) es C F esse G
1389 (22774) taȝt] þat E, in *om.* E   1390 (22775) in] C   1391 (22776) pain C G serue F,
him] þaim G crist F, wel *add.* C, his] þaire F   1392 (22777) folud G, leli C **y**, al his] alkin
C   1393 (22778) þer F þaa G, als] *om.* E F þan C   1394 (22779) gode and wick G   1395
(22780) sum *om.* E, ouþer E   1397 (22782) þai *om.* E   1398 (22783) alle of new F   1399
(22784) thoru **x y** strenket E strengh C might G   1400 (22785) ilk **x** F   1401 (22786) we
sal ber þan] þan sal we have G we sal be þan F   1403 (22788) quo F, trous **x** G trawis F,
trouth **x** G trauþ F   1404-5 (22789-90) *om.* G   1405 (22790) agayn **x** G   1407 (22792) ar F
1408 (22793) pijth] lim G   1409 (22794) þat *om.* F

Bot mistruun þat, es na nede,

22796 Herken qui, i sal þe rede.
Quen God wil swa, þat vpbers al,   1412
Þat mannes fless to mold do fall,
Ne moȝt he noȝt wiȝ al his mayn

22800 Þat ilke erth make fless ogayn?
He þat it wroȝt, fordos þe fless,   1416
He makes it eft quen his will es,
He þat dos fless worth into laam,

22804 Of laam may wirk flesslij likame.
A body he may son make of oȝt   1420
Þat al þis werld first made of noȝt,
Forþij es schortly noȝt þat he

22808 Ne may all do his will to be.
Ne duut ryȝt na man in þis dede,   1424
For truuth sal do man best to spede.
Qua dutes he es barn þe mare,

22812 Of truuth allan þis es þe lare.
Al may he do, he þat al weildes,   1428
If þu wil wite hu of þayr eildes
Þat þay schal in þat day vprise,

22816 Saint Pawl vs says on þiskinns wise
Þat litel and mikel, ald and ying   1432
All at þat mikel vprising
Sal be of eild als þay suld here

22820 Have deyed in eild of xxx yeir;
Þat eild þat Crist had at his ded,   1436
Quen he vs broȝt al fra vr quede
And if þat any her lyvand

22824 Was wemmed owȝer on foot or hand,
On heved or back, on brest or side,   1440
Als we se chances oft bitide,
On muþ or nees or ellesquar,

22828 Or boce opon his body bar,
Cripel, crooked, or turnd on baft,   1444
Or limmes maa gayn kindli craft,
Þurwȝ maa or less of lime have last

22832 At þuprising þat sal be last.
All þaa þat God has chosin till his,   1448
For to be broȝt until his bliss,

1410 (22795) mistrou C **y**, it es **y**   1411 (22796) nu *add.* C   1413 (22798) do] to E G se C *om.* F   1414 (22799) Ne] Nan E *om.* F, might G E, noȝt wiȝ] not þam C noght þan G, al] *om.* E **y** *transp.* C   1415 (22800) O þat C, again C **y**   1417 (22802) make C mai it make G, quan G *om.* C   1419 (22804) wirk flesslij] fleis faint E   1420 (22805) noȝt E   1421 (22806) first made] *inv.* G wroht E   1422 (22807) sortli es C schortly es (is F) **y**   1423 (22808) Ne mai his wil al do to be **x** N. m. a. d. h. w. t. b. G   1424 (22809) Na E, duht E   1426 (22811) barn þe] *inv.* C bar þe E   1427 (22812) þis] *om.* F it E   1428 (22813) waldes E   1429 (22814) hu] *om.* E G oȝt F   1431 (22816) vs says *om.* E, þiskinns] þiskin C G suche kin F þis E   1432 (22817) yong E   1433 (22818) All *om.* E G, mikel] fortald G þaire F   1434 (22819) sal be] *transp.* F, suld] sul E   1436 (22821) þat] atte F, hauid E   1439 (22824) was w.] *inv.* G, owȝer] or C *om.* G auþir F, or] or on C   1440 (22825) On h.] Or C, or b.] on E, on b.] or C *om.* G, or s.] on C   1442 (22827) elquare E   1443 (22828) bote (*print.*) **x** F, apon **x y**   1444 (22829) crokil E   1447 (22832) þuprising] þe norising E þis **v.** C   1448 (22833) þaa *om.* E, hauis E   1449 (22834) into C intil E vnto F

Quat sum þay in þis lijf haf ben,
22836   Ne sal na wem on þaym be sen,
Ne sal na þing bot al fayrhede,   1452
Als we in haly scriptur rede;
All sal have ryȝt limmes þar
22840   þey aw to have ne less ne mare.
Bot take tent quat i say to þe   1456
Of fayr stature hu it sal be,
And of þeyr eild of þaym i mele
22844   þat Crist tas for his awen lele,
þaas oðer sal have fayrhed nan   1460
For alkyns welth sal þaym be wan.
Of þaym it es to tell na tale
22848   þat brewes wiðvten bote es bale,
þe childer þat er abortives,   1464
þat es, þat er noȝt born o lives,
Sal rijs in xxx winter eild
22852   To litel bote to þaym or beild.
For þayn' war noȝt baptist ywis   1468
Ne sal þay have na part o blis.
þir mikel maysters says þat þay
22856   May saved be on nankynnes way:
Day sal haf nowðer o wel ne wa,   1472
Bot in mircknes for euer and a.
þe men þat þurwȝ þayr awen gilt,
22860   Wiðs heveding dragged, or hanging spilt,
þurwȝ þayr sinne and þayr felunie   1476
Wiðs hundes eten þe mast partie,
Mauy wenes þat er vnwise
22864   þat tát fless haal suld neuer rise
And tat to wen es bot sothede   1480
Nu i sal þee þe resun rede.
Vt of all skill it es, and ryȝt,
22868   For to mistrun in Godes myȝt,
Quat man may wite, quat man may lere,   1484
Quat eye may see, quat ere may here,
Quat man in erth may þink in þoȝt,
22872   Hu al þis werld vr laverd wroȝt,
Heven and erth al in þayr haldes,   1488
þat myȝty God þat al waldes !

1450 (22835) luf (*print.*) C, has C a F   1452 (22837) Na E, sal] *om.* C y, making thing C
noght G   1454 (22839) lim G   1455 (22840) aw] aght C ah E agh G, to *om.* E   1457
(22842) þair E, hu] quat x F   1458 (22843) ik E   1460 (22845) þa F þar E, faired E   1461
(22846) alkins] al x, alkin y, welth] selcuth G   1463 (22848) brewed w. b. E w. b. brend
G *alt.* F   1465 (22850) þat es] þaa C þaa er G þe quilk F, o] on E with F in G   1467
(22852) To litel] Till G   1468 (22853) þayn'] þaa C þai y   1469 (22854) Na E   1470
(22855) þer F   1471 (22856) nankin E y nakin C   1472-3 (22857-8) *om.* E G of ham to
speke I halde me stille / bot ihesu crist mai do his wille F   1474 (22859) þoru x y   1475
(22860) heuedind E, draght x G slain F   1476 (22861) þoru x y, feloun and þair sine E
1477 (22862) hondis mast parti etine E, þe *om.* F   1479 (22864) hal sal neuer F, sal neuer
hal G   1480 (22865) Nou i sal te resun rede E   1481 (22866) And oute of mistrouning you
lede E, þee] ye C, þe] sum C   1482 (22867) Wit ye wel, it es na r. E   1483 (22868) mistru C
y, cristes G   1484 (22869) man *om.* E, wet E witt G wite F

Qua can say me hu of a sede
22876 He dos an hundreth for to brede?
Þurwȝ his will þat myȝty king   1492
Dos vt of hard tree to spring,
First þe leaf and þan þe flur,
22880 And siðen þe fruit wið his savur,
Ilkynnes fruit in his sesun.   1496
Aw we þer-on to seke resun
Hu he dos al þing to nayt,
22884 Certes, þat war bot surfayt:
Þe mar man swink him þar obute   1500
Fra spede þe ferre he sal ben vute.
A sample sal i scaw yu þarby
22888 Þat i fand o saint Gregory.
Þar he was in a stede sum-quar,   1504
A crafty clerk and wijs of lare
Of askid him a questiun
22892 Of a wolf and a leun,
And of þe þridd þat was a man,   1508
Quarof þe tale he þus began:
"A man welk þurwȝ a wod his way,
22896 Þar ner þe strete a wulf him lay.
Þis wulf it was vnmijser of mete,   1512
Al þis mannis fless he ete.
Als swith als he swa had don,
22900 A hungry leun mett he son,
Vp and dun his pray sekand.   1516
Quen he nan oðer best ne fand,
Þis wulf he feld and ete him al,
22904 Ne left he nowðer gret ne smal.
Þe leun efter deyed in hij,   1520
Ded þar gan his caroigne lij,
And þat was rotin al to noȝt.
22908 Quar nu sal þis man be soȝt?
For ijn' may truu on nankinnes wise   1524
Þat þis man may to lijf vprise,
Sin nan es, als i wen, þat can
22912 Twin þat ert þath com of man
Fra þát erth þat es bredd of best?   1528
Saint Gregor gave answer honest,

1490 (22875) side C   1491 (22876) a h. E G   1492 (22877) myȝty] *transp.* C, will þat] dos *interp.* **x y**   1493 (22878) Dos] *om.* **x y**, þe *add.* C **y**, herd C   1494 (22879) þan] siþen C F   1495 (22880) siðen] þan C   1496 (22881) Ilk E Ilkin C G alkin F   1497 (22882) þarof E þerof F   1498 (22883) al] alkin C   1500 (22885) abouten E   1501 (22886) þe ferre] ferrer C þe ferrer **y**, outer E   1502 (22887) schaw] sceu C scheu **y**, yu] *transp.* **y** *om.* E   1506 (22891) Of] And **x** he F *om.* G, an E   1507 (22892) Of an of wolf E liun E lion G leon C   1509 (22894) Querof C, he *om.* C F, dus G   1510 (22895) wod his] woddes C **y**   1512 (22897) wnmisur E unmessur C unmesur G   1513 (22898) mans C   1514 (22899) als he] he **x** sim he F, hauid E   1515 (22900) An C F   1517 (22902) ne] þar C   1518 (22903) felled E F   1519 (22904) naþer E nauþer F noiþer C   1520 (22905) after C ofter F   1521 (22906) gun C G can F, carsin E carion G coroigne C   1522 (22907) þat] þar **x** þas F   1523 (22908) nu sal] *inv.* E   1524 (22909) on nankin **x y**   1525 (22910) may] *transp.* G   1526 (22911) Siþen G

And to þat man þat was in were
22916 Þe sooþ he schawed him al clere,
And proved him wiþ qwick resun   1532
Þat at þis resurrecciun
Wið alle his limmes hale and fere
22920 Sal cum he for þe demestere.
For þow his body war al brint,   1536
And blawn oueral þe pudre tynt,
Yet may God geder it al ogayn,
22924 And newn it at his will wiþ mayn.
Al þe fless þat was of man   1540
Soþfast sal be raysed þan,
It sal be delt in litel weve
22928 Þat was of best al sal beleve.
Þat bath þe tan and toðer made,   1544
Wel bitwix þaym can he schade.
Swa haaly sal þay risen þar
22932 Þaym sal noȝt want aan hevedes hare
Ne noȝt a nayl of foot ne hand,   1548
Þowqueðer we sal vnderstand
Þat nayl and hare þat has ben schorn
22936 Bes noȝt alquar þay war beforn.
But als potter wiþ pottes dos,   1552
22938 Quen he his new vessel fordos,
22941 He castes eft all in a bal
A better for to make wið-al,
An noȝt he lokes qwilk was qwilk,   1556
22944 Bot makes anoðer of þat ilk,
Wel fayrer þan þe first was wroȝt.
Ryȝt swa sal Crist, ne duut þu noȝt,
He þat es lauerd of erth and heven   1560
22948 May of þat ilke selven even
Þat first was molten into laam
Make a wel fayrer licame,
And if þarof war mare or less   1564
22952 To mesure als his willes es.
On paske day says saintes sum
Þat þe day of dome sal cum,
Þat day he wald himself vprise,   1568
22956 He wil vs rays þat ilke wise.
He sal deme at midward þe nyȝt
Þat ilke time he send his myȝt

1530 (22915) to] of E, o C   1531 (22916) sceud C shewed F   1535 (22920) he for] befor **x**
y   1536 (22921) þof C þou E (!) if F, al war] *inv.* E F   1537 (22922) over *om.* E   1538
(22923) gadir E   1539 (22924) neu him C **y**   1542 (22927) wefe E   1543 (22928) bilefe E
be leue F   1545 (22930) can] þan E   1546 (22931) þan *add.* C G *om.* F   1547 (22932)
þaym] þai G, an] a C **y**   1548 (22933) ne hand] or h. E   1549 (22934) þofqueþir C þohqueþir
E, sal we G   1550 (22935) hauis E, be C   1553 (22938) he *om.* E, new] nu G   (22939-40)
& hit be noȝt vnto his pay, al now he tempris his clay F, *om.* **x** G   1554 (22941) eft all] it
al E al þan C sonc all G, all *om.* F   1556 (22943) An = and] O C of E F *om.* G   1559
(22946) þu] ye C   1561 (22948) ilk **x** F   1564 (22951) war] wanted E   1565 (22952)
To] ga F, hit *add.* F, willis is F will it es G will es C   1566 (22953) þask C, sai C G   1568
(22955) vp *om.* E   1569 (22956) þat ilke] þ. ilk C F on þat E   1571 (22958) ilk **x y**, sent
C G

Vntil Egypt þat folk to quell,   1572
22960 Þat ilke tijme he harwed hell,
Þat ilke time sal cum þat king
His lele until his blis to bring.
Þe stede of dome, quar all sal mete,   1576
22964 Vs telles Joel þe prophet,
And þurwȝ his muþ vs says dryȝtin :
Quen i sal have merci of mijn
Sal breke þayr bandes and þayr lace,   1580
22968 I sal þaym comfort and solace;
In val of Josaphat i sal
Do to be gederd ledes all,
Þar sal i give my dome of drede,   1584
22972 Bot many o man, þow he can rede,
Wat noȝt þis word i forwiþ quaþ
Quat takens val of Iosaphat ;
Omang a hundreth men of wan   1588
22976 Ne vnderstandes it noȝt aan.
Þay wene þat vr laverd dryȝt
Sal cume unto þat dale to lyȝt
Þat Iosaphat es cald ay quar,   1592
22980 Wenis þe dom it sal be þar
Vnder þe munt of Olivet
Als it es nevend of prophet ;
Þey tend allan bot to þe letter   1596
22984 And litel es þaym þar-of þe better.
Josaphat, qwa gives entent,
Betakens Goddis jugement,
Jerom says of þat prophecie   1600
22988 Þat Josaphat may signifie
Vr lauerdes doom, qwa ryȝtlij spelles,
Þat bers þe word and naþing elles.
Bot qwa wil wite þe sooþ and ryȝt,   1604
22992 O saint Pawil saw he myȝt.
He says þat vr lauerd sal lyȝt
Dun to þe cluuds þat er on hyȝt ;
In þ' ayr o loft he sal him scaw   1608
22996 To do his myȝtes for to knaw.
Þar sal we mete wit him to lend
For evermar wiðvten end.
Þe wicked þat dred noȝt his aw   1612
23000 Her dun, þay sal be demed law,
Þey sal na myȝt have vp to win

1573 (22960) ilk C y, herid E y   1574 (22961) ilk C y, þat] þe C   1575 (22962) vnto C G
1578 (22965) þoru x y, said E   1581 (22968) comforth C   1582 (22969) wale x   1583
(22970) alt. F   1584 (22971) give] you E, drede G   1585 (22972) mani mai G, þow] þar E
þat F, he] þai x G   1586 (22973) War E   1587 (22974) bitakens G   1588 (22975) Amang
C y, hundret x hundre F   1589 (22976) Ne] om. F, it om. G, wele add. y   1590 (22977)
þan add. G   1591 (22978) into y, vale G   1592 (22979) siquar G   1593 (22980) wenis] þai
wene G, it om. G   1595 (22982) of] þoru C   1596 (22983) tent x G, alt. F, þarfor E   1599
(22986) godds C   1600 (22987) Ieromie E   1602 (22989) rihti E   1603 (22990) hers C
1604 (22991) wijt C, þe om. F   1605-6 (22992-3) om. E   1605 (22992) paule C y   1606
(22993) vs add. G, ligh C   1607 (22994) ar C F   1608 (22995) In þ'ayr o loft] inv. C, sceu
C   1609 (22996) don E   1613 (23000) dempt C dampned F   1614 (23001) vp] þider C

Swa hevy carked of þayr sin ;
Vp in þe skij þe doom sal be,   1616
23004 Swa truues haly kirk and we.
Bot nes na man sa wijs can tell
Hu lang at dome þat Crist sal dwell ;
Bot þuprising wiðvten hon   1620
23008 Ful swijth ywis it sal be don ;
Bath sal rise in litel way,
Al þat war ded and þat sal dey.
Saint Awstin says onent þat day,   1624
23012 Nes nan can Goddes conseyl say.
Of dom man clepes it þe day,
Queðer þar be ma þan aan or nay.
Vnder þe name of day man sal   1628
23016 Vnderstand þe time þat all
Sal be demd atte dom sa strang.
Quer-sum it last schort quile or lang.
þai þat sal brathly dey þat tide   1632
23020 To bete sal þay na space abide,
Bot þay þat has bot sinnes lyȝt
Sal clenged be al for þe syȝt
O feinds sal to þe dom be ledd ;   1636
23024 For þay for Him schal be swa redd,
He sal have dom sa lath to be
þat saintes þat on Him sal se,
Bath þay dred Him sal and gruu.   1640
23028 Ne þis ne þar na man mistruu
þat þan in sinnes lyȝt war tan
And penance þarof don has nan ;
For penance sal have nan oðer pine   1644
23032 Bot þat dred of þe wiðerwinne.
23035 þat drednes sal be swa vnmete,
þat it may al sli plyȝtes bete ;
þat funden ar þan in dedly sinn   1648
þay weind to pine wiðvten blinn.
At þis dom þat es forwiþ melt
23040 Sal al lede in fowr be delt ;
þe god in twin on his riȝt hand   1652
þe wick in twin on left to stand,
þe formast raw sal stand him nere
23044 Als þaa þat es his duȝty dere

1615 (23002) carkeded E carijd G, *alt.* F   1616 (23003) schi E skew F   1618 (23005) ne *om.* **x y**   1622 (23009) in litel] in a l. E, way] quile G weie E   1624 (23011) onent] enent C G inent E touchand F   1625 (23012) Nes] Es **x y**, godds C   1628 (23015) þe *om.* E   1630 (23017) dempt C demp G dampned F, sua G, atte] at þat **x y**   1632 (23019) brathly deye] *inv.* E   1634 (23021) þay þat] þat þat G, havis E   1635 (23022) clensed F   1636 (23023) O feinds] þe fend E, þe dom] þe day C þat dom E   1637 (23024) Him] þaim G, sua dred G, *alt.* F   1638 (23025) He] þai **y**   1639 (23026) þat] þar E, Him] þaym G   1640 (23027) dred Him] dred in E drede G, *alt.* F   1641 (23028) Ne þ. ne þ.] Na þ. na þ. E And þis (þat F) þar **y**   1642 (23029) *alt.* F, tan] þan C   1643 (23030) þarfor **y**, hafs E   1645 (23032) þe] þat E, *alt.* F   (23033-4) þe drede of ham can na man tel / þai ar sa wikked & sa felle F *om.* **x** G   1647 (23036) swilk E G suche F   1648 (23037) þan *om.* E G *alt.* F   1650 (23039) þat *om.* G   1651 (23040) ledis G   1653 (23042) on left to st.] on his lef hand E þe left to st. C on þe lift to st. F   1655 (23044) þaa *om.* E, es] er C ar F

	þat al þis werldes welth forsok	1656
	And anerli to God þaym tok,	
	þat sinne and sake for him forhuud,	
23048	And body and sawl til him buud,	
	Went þaym into religiun,	1660
	And did þayr bodys in prisun,	
	And swonken þaym bath day and nyȝt	
23052	For to serve vr laverd dryȝt,	
	Gret laverdscip sal þir be lent,	1664
	Forqwi þay sal of nan be demd.	
	All þe haaly men sal cum	
23056	Wiŏ vr lauerd unto þat doom	
	Noȝt to be demd, wel sal þu wite,	1668
	Bot in þayr setles for to sit,	
	For felawscip vr lauerd to bere	
23060	Bath als justijs and demestere.	
	Ihesu Crist es lang ywis	1672
	Sin he þis covenand hyȝt til his.	
	Þe toŏer raw beside sal ben,	
23064	Sal be ful luvely on to sen;	1676
	þat sal ben of god cristen lede	
	þat did in lijf manij god dede,	
	þat þow þay richess had ynouȝ	
23068	Þarfor þey to na treasur drouȝ,	1680
	Bot swilk als þay had in catel,	
	þey did to pover for to dele,	
	And gave þayr hert for luve o mede	
23072	Þe needy for to cleth and fede,	1684
	And willy war to do, and glad	
	þat men of haly kirk þaym badd,	
	And did wele her þayr mis to mend	
23076	Trewly truand at þayr end.	1688
	Swilk men þat swa bar þaym here	
	Of dom bot god þayn' sal noȝt here:	
	Ful lyȝt sal be þayr lot þat day,	
23080	To þaym ful swetly sal he say:	1692
	' Ye blisced folk, bath men and wijves	
	þat me war servand in yur lijves,	
	In mij grevance ye did me god,	
23084	I was hungri, ye gave me fod,	
	Me þristed sare, drink ye me broȝt;	1696

1656 (23045) werld E, welth] werkes E   1657 (23046) vtterli F arlik C   1659 (23048)
al *add.* C   1660 (23049) And *add.* G þat *add.* F, þaim *om.* E F, vnto E   1662 (23051)
suonken þaim] swinkid E trauailled F bath] aboute F   1663 (23052) beserue C   1664
(23053) þir] þar C ham F   1665 (23054) dempt C G shent F   1668 (23057) dempt x G
dampned F, wel sal þou] þat sal þu G þou sal F E   1669 (23058) setes E segis F, sett C
1670 (23059) For *om.* E, to *om.* G   1671 (23060) demster E   1672 (23061) laud E   1673
(23062) Siþen G   1674 (23063) ben] be G   1675 (23064) sen] se G   1676 (23065) þat *om.*
G, ben] be C **y**   1677 (23066) in lijf] in þis l. E   1678 (23067) þof C þouh E, þay] *om.* E,
hauid E, euoh E   1679 (23068) riches E, droh E   1681 (23070) pover for to] pouer men
at G p. men it F   1684 (23073) don E   1687 (23076) Truli C F, trawand F   1688 (23077)
man E, sa E, þaym] *trsp.* E ham F   1689 (29078) þeyn' sal] þaim (*print.*) sal E sal þai C **y**
1691 (23080) Til G   1692 (23081) ȝe blessed F y bliced E   1693 (23082) yor E yur
C G

	Prisund i was, and yee me soȝt ;	
	Quen i in sekenes was sar,	
23088	Ye com to comfort mi care ;	
	Of nakedhed qwen i drouȝ harm,	1700
	Ye gave me clething me to warm ;	
	Quen i was wil and vut o rest	
23092	Godly took ye mee to gest.	
	For yee have served me swa wele,	1704
	To mede ye sal have lastand sele ;	
	þe sele þat ye have soȝt to win	
23096	For euer sal ye leng þarin.'	
	Þan sal þir felawshipes twa	1708
	Led lastand lijf for ever and aa,	
	þat Ihesu Crist mot bring vs to,	
23100	For in þis werld nys bot vnroo.	
	Ful wele es him þat won may þar	1712
	þat kith was never cuþ to care.	
	Þar sal stand on his oðer side	
23104	Wrecches stadd in waa ful wide,	
	And of þaym sal men se alswa	1716
	þayr parti to be delt in twa.	
	Lath and stinkand sal þay be,	
23108	Sary sorful on to see ;	
	þe firste range þe mast stinkand	1720
	Sal be o wrecches mistruand,	
	þat renayd ar, traiturs and fals,	
23112	Murðerers and mansworn als,	
	þat þurwȝ cursing or oðer plyȝt	1724
	Of kirk has tynt þe help wiþ ryȝt.	
	Fra commun vt of cristen men	
23116	þaa careful eeth sal be to ken,	
	þat in þis lijf war won to lij	1728
	In hordom and in leccherie,	
	Folwand al þayr flesses will,	
23120	And mast þaym liked dedes ill ;	
	Wiðvten reuth or will to mend	1732
	Vnschriven war þay at þayr end,	
	Bot deyed in dedly sinn of ded.	
23124	Þir to deem sal be na nede,	
	For þey war demd, ar þey com þar,	1736
	þayr doom opon þaymself þay bar.	
	Þe toðer raw bes ill ynouȝ	
23128	Of cristen fals and ful o wouȝ	
	þat maas þaym cristen men wiþ name,	1740

1698 (23087) i was stadd i. s. s. G stadd *trsp.* F   1699 (23088) to c.] for to c. C G, me of F
1700 (23089) arme C   1701 (23090) claþis F, me to] þat was E wid to G, me for F   1703
(23092) gest] rest E   1706 (23095) sal *add.* E, soȝt] *om.* E   1708 (23097) *alt.* F, felauscip C
1710 (23099) most G   1711 (23100) es C **y**   1714 (23103) his] þis C, left E   1716 (23105)
man C   1717 (23106) to] do F   1720 (23109) first **x y**, rau G   1721 (23110) wriches E
1722 (23111) renaid als traitur E   1725 (23114) has] as E   1726 (23115) of *om.* E.   1727
(23116) eth sal] *inv.* E   1728 (23117) þair **y**, was C F, wont C **y**   1730 (23119) flexli C G
fleis E, *alt.* F   1734 (23123) deadly] *trsp.* (d. d.) E   1735 (23124) þer F   1736 (23125)
demd] *om.* E dempt C G dampnid F   1737 (23126) apon **x y**, þai *om.* E

And vndeserves Godes grame.
Falslike es he cristen cald
23132 þat Cristes lawes wil noȝt hald.
Fals it es þat luve to knaw   1744
þat nowðer wil for luve ne aw
Do þat him suld be to queme
23136 Quarwiþ man myȝt himselven ȝeme.
Bot in pride and treccherie,   1748
In nijth and enst and leccherie,
And in vntelland sinnes fele—
23140 þe hundreth part i may noȝt mele
þat man ryȝt nu his lijf in ledes—   1752
Swa dugeth in þayr wicked hedes
On ilka side þan gadrid þay,
23144 Bot litel bers þe pouer oway,
þat er sa gned þat þayn' may spare   1756
Nowðer to give þaym less ne mare.
þe covaytise, for sooþ to tell,
23148 Has many sawles broȝt to hell.
Bisweld it has þis werld on brede,   1760
Vnneðes sal man find aan in lede
þat wele wil scrive þaym of þis sake
23152 Ne for na conseyl mendes make.
Witt yee for sooth al þat er slike,   1764
þay sal be demd all wiþ þe wicke
To mikel sorwe and sijte to þaym,
23156 þat al þis werld þaym may noȝt raym.
Wiþ mikel wreth and awful chere   1768
Vr lauerd sal say þat þay may here:
'Dos flees heðen, ye maledyȝt,
23160 Vnto mi rijke have yee na ryȝt;
Oft i was wiþ mâlisce met,   1772
Bot for yu was ijn' neuer þe bett;
In hungre and þrist oft saw ye me,
23164 Bot þaarof n'had ye na pitee.
Gaas to þe devel, þar sal ye gaa   1776
For to well wið him in waa,
Euer wiðin his waa to well
23168 Wið him and his þat er in hell.'

1741 (23130) undeserves] vnder seruis E vnder servis C **y**, godds C all goddes G   1742
(23131) Falsli C **y**   1743 (23132) Crist C, wil **x y**   1745 (23134) noþer C nauþer E F, þat
add. E   1746 (23135) him suld be] *inv.* E   1750 (23139) felle E   1751 (23140) hundret **x**
hundre F hundreth G, i mai noȝt] es noȝt to E   1753 (23142) dugid E duked C dogged F
ducke G, wik dedis E wikked d. F   1754 (23143) ilk said C, gad*ir* E gedder F   1755
(23144) bare G   1757 (23146) Nowðer] Noþer C For E nauþer F   1759 (23148) sawles]
sauil E sauls C saule G, browht E, til E   1760 (28149) Bisueled C G begiled F, hauis E,
at weld E   1761 (28150) in eld E   1762 (28151) him E   1763 (28152) tak E   1764
(28153) schilke E   1765 (28154) dempt C demed G dampned F, wike E   1768 (23157)
wret **x** wraþ F   1770 (23159) do E **y**   1773 (23162) was ijn'] ne was E was me C was i **y**
1774 (23163) hung*ir* E hungri F, hung*er* G, and *om.* E F, þrist *om.* E   1775 (23164) Bot]
om. E, ne *om.* C **y**   1777 (23166) wið him in waa] wit i*n* hi*m* wa E þar iu his wa C widin
his wa **y**   1779 (23168) wið him þat er in h.] þarin to dwell C   (23169-23174) wiþ him ȝe serued,
wiþ him ȝe wende / euermare werlde wiþouten ende. / gas wiþ him þat ȝe haue mint. / for
ȝour sorou salle neuer stint. / & þu þat has seruid me. / of þaire ioy salle neu*er* ending be
F *om.* **x** ð

23175   A! Lauerd, quat he war wijs þat moʒt   1780
23176   Stedfast hald þis day in þoʒt,
        To forget þat day neuer mar
        To qwijles þat he livand war;
        For þan mund he make her his way   1784
23180   Fra wrake to wer him o þat day.
        Fra þat day forþ þu aw to min,
        Sal neuer fra body sawil twin.
        For god and ill togedir ar   1788
23184   þey wroʒten, ar þey twinned war,
        Togedir sal þay take alswa
        þayr worthi mede in wel or wa,
        Owðer in heven or helle pijne   1792
23188   Wiþ Satanas, þat wiðerwin;
        þat, fra þe jugement be mad,
        Sal casten be, wiðvten bade,
        In a stinkand stank of fire,   1796
23192   þar sal be yolden hem her hire,
        Als says þe book of privete
        þat to saint Iohn was schawn to see.

1782 (23177) forgied E   1783 (23178) Toquils C   1784 (23179) make her] *inv.* C   1785
(23180) wak E, o] on C G of E F   1786 (23181) yu (*print.*) G   1787 (23182) fra body
sawil] *inv.* G b. þi s. C   1788 (23183) togedirs E, to g. a.] þat þai did are G þai did are F
1789 (23184) þey wroʒten] þai wroʒt C F, *alt.* G   1790 (23185) Togiders E   1792 (23187)
Oþer C auþer E F, heuen pine C hel p. E G   1794 (23189) þe E   1796 (23191) stang C
1797 (23192) hem her] him his x G ham þaire F hem her T   1798 (23193) of] in C   1799
(23194) scawid E scaud C schaud G shewed F

NOTES.

GENERAL REMARKS. As to the various readings, mere orthographic differences are not marked; but there was some difficulty sometimes to decide whether they were important for the dialect of the respective MSS. T is generally disregarded, as it has no superior wording. F is disregarded only when it shows an obvious alteration of *y*, which appeared without consequence.

In the following notes I shall endeavour to justify my readings, supposed to be original with respect to language and dialect. Difficult lines will be elucidated; but I shall generally forbear citing parallel passages from other authors, as I do not want for the present to treat of the matter in every direction. Further studies, I hope, will also enable me to enter upon the theological questions treated in the *Cursor*, for I feel sure that they will give some clue to the life of the author.

It will take some more years' study before I have done working out the whole text critically. Only then shall I be able to give a detailed grammar, and decide upon many questions which must now be left in the dark. I do not think it convenient to point these out at once.

The orthography I have adopted is not consistent everywhere. I thought it necessary to stick to the MSS. as close as possible. There is scarcely a spelling which is not instanced somewhere. Original *e* final has often been kept, though it is silent; but it is then put in italics, and denotes that the vowel of the preceding syllable is rather long. When this vowel is originally long, the final *e* is not kept in the middle of the line, and very seldom in the ryme. I am of opinion that these final *es* which never count in verse die away at the end of the line. Therefore I generally spell þ*ar*, *mar* even in the ryme, but *take*, *make*, *bale*, *tale*, etc.—The letter *y* or *ij* has been used partly to retain an historical spelling, partly to denote an especially open *i*, which is felt much more in a close syllable, *f. i.* before *ȝt*; *y* then marks the rather short, and *ij* the long *i*. Otherwise I do not believe that we should distinguish in M.E. between a close and an open *i*. The English language is altogether strange to a close *i*, such as is in French. Moreover, I have made a difference between þ (sharp) and ð (soft). I find great difficulty in finding the right way. I have spelt ð between vowels, and taken final ð when there was a close connection with the following word beginning with a vowel or semi-vowel in *quaþ* and *wiþ*, because the MSS. readings vary in these words between *th*, *t*, *d*; and the softer pronunciation decidedly suits our dialect. In some words I have adopted *th* from the MSS.

l. 1, *rijmes*] The singular is *rijme*, cf. 14922 (where *rijme* is not plural, as Stratmann makes it). Cf. also Ormin.

l. 2, *romanz*] Cf. ' Havel.' 2327, *romanz* = *romants*. See l. 365, *entens* C, where we may read as well *entenz* = *entents*, and l. 353 *elementz*.

l. 5, *þe strange strijf*] The metre requires *strange*, cf. l. 7, 14, 39, etc. The adjective takes the weak inflection in *e*, when preceded by the definite article, possessive or demonstrative pronoun; f. i. *þis ilke tree* 39, *hir sweete sung* 88, *þe alde lawe* 116, *þe þridde day* 379, *his firste werc* 411, *þat heye curt* 472, *þe lesse werd* 550. But *þe wijsman* 27, *þe ald' lawe* 116.

Substantival adjectives, used as neuter nouns, do not take a final *e*; f. i. *þe good* 566, 665. Substantival adjectives used as masculine nouns drop the final *e*, as *þe wijs* 149, *þe wrang* 29.

l. 6, *þer lijf* C, *þaire* F, *hir* G] The source **w** seems to have had *her*, which was retained by **z**, and has been disregarded by C F. Now *hir* rather appears to be a mistake for *her*, which I have preferred, for a plural would be necessary when *many þusand* is put. I suppose that the *Cursor* reads *hem* beside *þeym* or *þaym*, and consequently *her* beside *þeyr* or *þayr*.

les] is wanted, by the sense and metre, for C's *lesis* is a present.

l. 9, *rike*] I read thus, as the Poet's dialect wants *k*, cf. rike, swike 5168, eke, speke (*sb.*) 18056, ' Havelok' *meke, speke* (*sb.*) 947.

l. 15, *Charles kyng*] Cf. Herod kyng 161.

l. 16, *ne wald*] G's reading *ne wald* permits us to adopt this reading. The negative *ne* is of course often disregarded by our scribes, or is altered into *na*, which Midland scribes again change into *no*.

l. 17, *Ysoud*] C F's *Isot* (*ysote*) must be rejected, as the genuine form is *Ysoud*. The ryme reminds us of Havelok's *troud, god*. As to *d : t*, and Western *t* for *d*, compare the critical part. I wonder why Kölbing (*Sir Tristram*) writes *Ysonde*. The *ns* of the 14th and the 15th century MSS. leave the reader quite at a loss when to read *u* or *n*, so that the MS. is no argument in this respect.

l. 21, *serkyns þinges*] Cf. G 5448.

l. 28, *drawes* or *draus*] The dropping of *e* after diphthongs is quite common; cf. also substantives. C's *draghus* is regular Lancashire dialect.

l. 29, 31, *laþ, leþ*] Such double forms are unquestionable.

l. 32, *werreys*] C's reading suits best in these lines; it is noteworthy that C has retained old *e* in the first syllable, though it generally occurs as *a*.

l. 33, *ilk wijs*] *scilwis* in C appears to be a mistake, and is explained by *scli = slik*.

l. 88, *omang*] There is some difficulty in deciding whether *omang* or *âmang* should be preferred. The MSS. readings *o-mang, a-mang, emang* are not conclusive, for the Western dialect, of course, derives the compound from *on mang*, and *on* and *an* are always confounded. In the East Ormin gives us the form *a mang*, but though he avoids *an* for *on*, we also find *abuten, abufen*, so that there is reason to believe that Ormin lived more to the South (*i. e.* near the Saxon area), and a derivation of *a* from O.I. *â* is forbidden. The *Pricke of Conscience* has the forms *omang, oboven, obout*, but likewise, as we must expect from the scribe, the same compounds with the prefix *a*. I have elsewhere shown that the dialect of the *Cursor* is a stranger to the W.S. prep. *an*, I have good reason to believe that such forms as *omang, obuven, obuuten* must be adopted. It is the same with *ogeyn*, for which the forms *ogain, again, egain* appear in the MSS. In O.E. there are also compounds with *on* and *an*, as *onȝeȝn, onȝên, onȝêan, aȝên, aȝêan*. So Ormin writes *onȝên = O.E. onȝêan*. But the *Cursor* writes *ogeyn = O.E. onȝeȝn*. The various forms with the prefix *a* (short), which appear in the MSS., seem to belong to a later period, for such forms as occur in the *Lazamon, Ancren Riwle, The Owl and Nightingale*, etc., afterwards take their way towards the North. The original Northumbrian form appears to have been formed with the prefix *on*. The *Pricke of Conscience* has, of course, *ogain* and *again;* for towards the middle of the 14th century, *agayn* seems to be quite common in the Northumbrian dialect. It cannot be decided whether the form *ogain* in the Edinburgh MS. is original or taken from its Midland source; E has also *again*. I'll just remark that Koch's *âbufan, âbûtan* (cf. *Gram.* II., § 427 and 431) appear to me wrong, for *a* must be short.

l. 135, *oxspring*] In C's *oxspring, x* represents *sc = sharp s*, as is found elsewhere.

l. 143, *Juus*] I have spelt *Juus* and *Jewës* (cf. l. 146) according to metre. In the Poet's dialect, the different spelling does not imply a different pronunciation of the principal sound; so that *Jewes* is a merely historical spelling.

l. 151, *com*] This form is taken rather on account of the MSS. spellings and the *Ormulum*. Sometimes *cam* is used for *com*, cf. 1205, 2383, etc. The length of *o* cannot be proved anyhow.

l. 154, *saint*] C's general reading cannot be conclusive. Cf. *sent* C 21185, 27187, 21188, 21189, *seint* C 22041, *seint* C 16745, 16858, *sentes* C 18363, 18373, and the peculiar mistake in E *sant es said* = *sum tes said*, cf. G 23405.

l. 160, *presandes*] C F's *presandes* is proved by the ryme *presand, hand* 6652, *brand, presand* 7588, cf. also **x y** 24808.

l. 168, *hoof*] seems to be required by our old dialect and the metre. Cf. F's reading; cf. also 11104.

l. 200, *harwed*] Our dialect seems to prefer *harwe(n)*. Compare *haluin* E, halu C G, while F has *halgh* F 24895.

l. 204, *onstandand sey*] C's reading is not correct in *stad*, but is easily mended, cf. l. 22724 E.

l. 205, *my3tes mast*] C F's *myght es* (*ys*) is, of course, the same, though printed separately.

l. 213, *Antecrist*] I could take the contracted form *Ancrist*, which is not uncommon in M.E., on account of the metre.

l. 308, *hem*] C's reading may, of course, have been taken from a Midland copy; but we can also adopt it for the Poet's dialect.

l. 376, *sunded*] = sounded pp., cf. O.F. *sonder*.

l. 415, *palays*] The first syllable has the stress here. But the form *pales* is not necessary, though allowable. The relative pronoun is retained, so that there is an extra syllable in the cæsura.

l. 417, *creature*] It does office for the plural, which is allowed only on behalf of *twin;* cf. l. 425, 512, but *eyen twinne* 521.

l. 454, *auntur*] I don't prefer G's MS. reading, which in T is rendered by *traitour*. The confusion with *auttur, anttur, antur, auntur* is obvious.

l. 496, *ful harde*] The adverb is meant.

l. 501, *held*] pres. plur. of O.E. *heldan* = 'to incline,' which must not be confounded with O.E. *healdan*, 'to hold.'

l. 560, *an*] The conjunction *and* is meant.

l. 585-6, *eild, weild*] The two forms are sometimes mistaken as to their origin by German scholars. This *elde* can be derived from O.E. *eldo*, while *alde* from O.E. *ealde;* cf. Ormin, who has both forms. M.E. *welde(n)* can be

O.E. *weldan*, and *walde(n)* is O.E. *wealdan*. The subst. *wald* is O.E. *ȝeweald*, and *welde* is O.E. *ȝewild* (st. f., = will or impulse of one's own, arbitrium, O.I. *veldi*; cf. *Beow.*, mid ȝeweoldum 2223). *Ormin* has only the verb *weldenn*, but the substantive *wald*. The *Cursor* has the double forms; as to the meaning of *welde* (sb.) cf. l. 462. These forms are, therefore, scarcely any dialectal criteria. Only the O.E. adjective *eald*, which can be *eld* in the West, and is *ald* in the East and North, is of some consequence.

l. 610, *þe forbod*] The stress on the first syllable is instanced in a good many places.

l. 675-6, *abute : vnderlute*] The MSS. spellings of *vnderlute* are *vnder-lote, vnderloute* 2054, *vnderlute* 3705, *vnderlut* 18206, *vnderlutte* 11190. It rymes with *doute, statute, aboute* in the *Cursor*. The *ū* sound, as appears, cannot be denied, but still it is worth while to consider whether it must be derived from O.I. *lútr*, or can be thought to be the pp. (*vnderlote[n]*) of *vnder-luten*, O.E. *vnderlútan*, used adjectively. It would be necessary to prove the transition of *o* into *u* and *ū*.

l. 826, *blured*] 3 sg. prt. of *blure[n]* = *biluren*, to be sad-visaged, to be aggrieved. Cf. L.G. *láren ; lourin*, 'oboculare, mærere,' *Prompt.* 316; besides cf. *blure* (sb.) (r. w. *cure*), *Townl. Myst.*, p. 310. It must not be confused with *lirten, bilirten*, W.-S. *lurten, bilurten ; lire*, W.-S. *lure* (sb.). C's reading *blurded* appears to be a double formation of the pret., and is not confounded with W.-S. *blurten*, pp. *blurt* (cf. A. R. 280*).

l. 938, *forþij ar*] = lest, cf. Genes. iii. 22.

l. 990, *childer*] = *childre;* cf. *numbre, ordre*, etc.

l. 1002, *o mede*] = *on mede* (= for reward). *on* is used to denote aim and purpose; as in O.E., *mín blôd byð âȝoten on synna forȝifennisse.* As regards the sense, cf. *þat mirthes mettes man to mede* 272.

l. 1087, *way*] O.E. *wǽȝ* = balance, not mentioned in Kaluza's Glossary.

l. 1097, *firslaȝt*] There is no reason to read *flaȝt* for *slaȝt*, as Stratmann (p. 205) does. Cf. O.E. *sleaht* in a compound, as *handslyȝt.*

stund] pp. of O.E. *stunian*, 'percellere, to cast down,' also 'to make senseless' (not mentioned in Kaluza's Glossary). K.'s *stund*[1] (inf.) is mistaken.

l. 1106, *solwed*] pp. of O.E. *solȝan*, 'to soil, stain.'

l. 1125, *ayr*] for *hair* of the MSS. The ryme as well as the sense forbids

---

[1] *d* in *stund* is abundant, as in modern *sound*, etc. The phonetic value of *u* in *stund* (pp.) is proved by the ryme; cf. also *stund* (inf.), r. w. *hund* 7558, so that *stund* has nothing to do with *stunt = stynt.*

me to take *hair* in the meaning of *hair*, as Kaluza does; cf. Gloss. The sense is: 'dim and black as the air when the tempest is drawing near,' cf. 1124-7. Though the *Towneley Mysteries* afford a ryme like *yare, fayre*, the *Cursor* is correct in this respect, and would never allow of such a ryme as *fayr, haar*, for this is the form wanted for modern *hair*. The abundant *h* of the scribes is the well-known cockneyism, as we call it.

l. 1142, *crijen sal*] for *sal cri þan* E, *þan cri sal* C, while *þan* is omitted in **y**; cf. l. 1122.

l. 1166, *lest*] There is no reason to reject *lest* = O.E. lǽstan. But *e* is shortened, like *a* in *last*. As to *lest* (adj.), cf. *geste, leste* 208. This *e* is no characteristic of the South-eastern dialect, as the new editor (Dr. Sarrazin) of *Octavian* wishes to make us believe when he (p. xv) in a most remarkable way refers to *Danker's Laut- und Flexionslehre der mittelkent. Denkm.* (p. 6), and seems to think that M.E. *e* is a development of M.E. *a*, while double forms in ẽ and ã (= O.E. æ or ǽ) are well-known in the earliest M.E. period.

l. 1192, *vntil*] G's reading cannot be preferred. There is no reason to reject *vntil* or *vnto*, cf. § 64. The forms *onto, ontil*, appearing in the 14th century, are developed from *vnto, vntil*,[1] as *op* in E 22548 from *vp;* the transition from *u* into *o* before a nasal sound is very easy, to be sure. Cf. still *vpon, opon, apon* in the MSS. It will be seen in several places how the MSS. have *on* instead of *in*, which seems to have the preference in the Northumbrian dialect.

l. 1194, *þe nijnd*] Cf. nijnd, fijnd 23257.

l. 1206, *vtneem*] = *vt* + O.N. *nœmr;* cf. *fastnœmr, hjartnœmr*, etc., most affecting, heart-touching, and cf. H.Germ. *ausnehmend, ergreifend*, and O.N. *siðnœmr*, well-bred. *nœmr* serves to enlarge the usual extent of an idea; *vtneem*, exceedingly great. The form *vtenemes*, which is followed by *es*, seems to be a mistake here; but cf. *of a well þat es vtneemes, þat vt of ran fowr grete stremes* 1315-16, *vtnem, barntem* 4827-8.

l. 1206-7] The sense is: 'Even saints and Heaven himself shall be afraid,' which is expressed by double negation with the aid of a relative sentence ('There is no . . . but'). There is reason to believe that the Northumbrian scribe omitted original *ne*, cf. § 65.

l. 1242-3, *elleven : beleven*] I think I am right in adopting G's *elleven*

---

[1] Zupitza, cf. *Koch's Gram.* II. 382 rem., connects the first syllable in *vntil, vnto* with the prepos. *on*, because *onto, ontil* occur. The reasoning at least is not conclusive in my opinion.

(final *d* is lost) as an ordinal number, as *þe nijn'* (the ninth part), *mijn* 969-70. *Elleft* is quite strange to our dialect. G's *þat it be leven* shows that it is altered from some other reading found in the source. But it is easy to correct *beleft* into *beleven*, to relinquish, and to avoid G's mistake; cf. E's *signes,* and the plural in l. 1244 (12629).

l. 1247, *þing*] The mistake *tung* may be easily made when the source had *ting* for *þing*.

l. 1254, *þan sal þe raynbow*] As to the double stress in *raynbow,* cf. l. 1990, *sekenes* 23087, *creature* 23413, *forbod* 987, *spusebreke* 185.

l. 1258, *dint*] = thrust. The correct reading has been inferred from E's *dunt,* and its translation *bete* in G, which agrees with the sense.

l. 1275, *quayn*] Cf. O.N. *kveina,* to lament, and O.E. *cvánian.*

l. 1281, *buun*] = inf. of O.E. *búȝan.*

l. 1306, *&*] = and; observe the common mistake *a* in G. I presume on *ā* in the source rather than *a,* so that *strait* is not a substantive here, which, in my opinion, suits better to the preceding *a stormi dai.*

l. 1309, *drove*] = to disturb, to afflict; cf. M.L.G. *dróven* (Stratmann). Halliwell's *droning* is, of course, *droving* = affliction. The printed text of C F G has *drone, droune,* which is a mistake; the MSS. often confound *u* and *n.* 'Thunder and lightning shall disturb their minds,' but not drown them, as Kaluza's Glossary renders the verb.

l. 1311, *hiden þaym þarin*] G's additional *þan* makes me believe that we have to read *hiden,* cf. *hiden* C E 22196.

l. 1339, *onstandand*] Cf. l. 204.

l. 1348, *witt ye*] i. e. *wite,* conj., cf. Orm. *wĭte ȝe, witt tu.*

l. 1355, *noȝt but quon men to was*] I think we must consider G's *was* on account of its position. E C's *no* is a mistake, and *quon* appears to me indeclinable. E's *thone* (thus printed) is misread for *chone* = *quone;* cf. G's *fone.*

l. 1368, *land and lijth*] Cf. Skeat's Gloss. to *Havelok,* s. v. *lith,* p. 132. *lijth* is plur. of *liȝ* = O.N. *liȝ,* 'copiæ, milites.' Cf. also its German translation, '*land und leute.*'

l. 1429, *hu of þayr eildes*] C's reading reminds me of O.E. *hú* c. gen. = at which age. F's *oȝt* can be = anything, anyhow, perhaps. E G appear not to have understood any longer C's Old English way of expression.

l. 1457, *Of fayr stature hu*] E's *þair* is a mistake (cf. l. 22845), which will easily be understood by those who know how *þ* and *f* are so commonly confounded even now-a-days. I need hardly call the reader's attention to Sweet's lucid description of these two sounds (*Handbook of Phonetics*).

l. 1463, *brewes*] G's *brend* must be rejected; cf. ll. 23950, 23951, 24201 (brende F), 24497.

l. 1512, *vnmijser of mete*] The wolf is *vnmiser* = 'not niggard' when eating. It is impossible to think of *unmesure*, as Kaluza does. The rhythm and word-formation forbid any derivation from *mesure*.

l. 1542, *weve*] = waif, Norm. Fr. *weif*, *wef*, Low Lat. *wayfium*, *res vaivœ*, an English law-term, signifying goods found of which the owner is not known (Webster). Not explained in Kaluza's *Glossary*.

l. 1553, *vessel*] Cf. *fetil*, vessel G 20932.

l. 1565, *his willes es*] Cf. E F, and l. 10094 C G.

l. 1584, *give*] There is good reason to believe that E's reading *you* was occasioned by the confusion of *giue* and *giu*, which appears for *you* in the third hand of the MS.

l. 1592, *ay quar*] G's *siquare* makes me suppose that there is some close connection between *siquare* and *sumquare*. It is worthy of notice that F has used *sim* for *sum* 22899, and C *sim* for *sum* 20632. Besides, observe *simquare* (printed *sunquare*) C 1884, and *sequare* G 11199. Now it is remarkable that *siquare* generally denotes 'time'; only in l. 3107 we find the various reading *cuntre* F, and in l. 19852 it might denote *place*. But there is no doubt that *quar* is originally used in the local sense, and indeed, we meet with *sum elles quare* C G 23906, where the reading of E *sum other quare* may at once denote the near relation to 'time.' This meaning is found in *mani quar* x G 21723. As regards *si* in *siquare*, G's *sequare* and C's *simquare* are not without consequence. So that we may presume on some confusion between O.E. *sum* and O.N. *sem*. The double meaning of *place* and *time* is also found in *wai* (*wei*). As regards the meaning 'time', cf. ll. 6141, 12531, 23009. M. Kaluza, in his Glossary, has taken *wai* and *wei* for two distinct words, and has cited there l. 8419 in a wrong place, for *wei* means there O.E. *wiȝa* (= man); cf. § 57, 5.

l. 1624, *onent*] = *onende* = 'opposite, against, with respect to.' The first proper meaning is still known in the modern dialect; f. i. *Hwær art'a b·a·un* (M.E. *bún*) *t'fish? Th·a·u mun goa anent t'pu* (pool). I heard this sentence from a Sheffield man, but I have no doubt that the preposition is still current in the rural dialects of other districts. The Saxon words generally are *an ende, anente, enent, inent*; otherwhere I have found *onent*, which was printed *onence* in Halliwell's *Dict.* and the *Pricke of Conscience*. Cf. § 64.

l. 1689, *þayn'*] E's mistake '*þaim*' is a misreading. The same mistake is found in Kölbing's *Amis and Amiloun*, l. 94, where *þam* is *þain'*, and not the accusative, as the editor states, p. xxxv.

l. 1741, *vndeserves*] The common mistake in **x y** is noteworthy. The meaning of the passage is, 'They are only Christians by name, and do not deserve God's wrath.'

l. 1753, *dugeth*] = O.E. *duȝoð, duȝuð. gader þey* in the following line wants an object. The sense of the passage is: 'They gather riches everywhere, but never give anything to the poor.'

l. 1760, *Bisweld*] cf. *suelud* G, *suelid* C 15383; *bisuelid* G, *bisueld* C 16484, O.E. *svelȝan*. The same double forms in *w* and *ȝ* are found in *harud*, *herid* and *halud*, *halghed* F, *halgied* E.

l. 1767, *raym*] = O.N. *hreima*, sonare, clamare. The diphthong is confirmed by *Kaym*, *raym* E. Tol. 434 (Lüdtke). The W.-Sax. vocabulary appears to have *hrêman*, cf. Stratmann's references.

l. 1773, *þe bett*] = 'eo melius.' Observe also C's *me* for *ine*.

I add a synopsis of common mistakes or alterations in **x y**: *it* for *ne* 22593, *before* for *he* for 22920, *vnder servis* for *vndeserves* 23130; in **x** G: *vnmessur* for *vnmiȝser* 22897, *a* for *and* 22691; or in **x** F: *to* for *do* 22552 (cf. E G 22798), *of* for *an* 22943; in C E (= **x**): *nan* for *man* 22450, *nobot quon* (*nobit chone*) for *noȝt bot quon* 22740, *of* (*o*) for *to* 22915; in E **y**: *richli* (*rightli* G, *riȝtwis* F) for *kithly* 22742.

NOTES ON THE VERSIFICATION.

THE metrical line we have before us is the so-called *Short Metre*, which, as will also be seen from the *Cursor*, has been imitated from the French eight-syllable line.

1. It has no cæsura as a rule, and consists of four lifts or strest syllables, and four beats or unstrest syllables, as,

þer many a þusand les his lijf	6
Adam yode walkand in þat welth	753
Sin nan es, als i wen, þat can	1526
O feinds sal to þe dom be ledd	1636

When there is a kind of cæsura, which is then after the second lift, there may be an extra-syllable, as,

Of Alisander þe Conquerur	
Of July Cesar þe Emperur	3-4
Gaas to þe devel, þar sal ye gaa	1776

There is no need to adopt the elision of *e* in *þe Emperur*, simply on account of the preceding line. After such a kind of cæsura there may also take place a shift of the lift and beat, as,

All bestes dumb under þe lift	1136

Otherwise the lift is shifted only in the beginning of the line, as,

Minning and þat of þinges þrin   561; cf. 267, 920, 1341, etc.

2. The ending of the line is either masculine—*i. e.* the line terminates in the lift or stress—or feminine, *i. e.* the last lift is still followed by an unstrest syllable, as,

O Ionek and of Ysambras	19
Storijs als o serekyns þinges	21
Wið heye note and lude steven	1082

3. The first beat may occasionally be omitted, as,

Sanges sere of selkuþ rime	
Inglis, Frenkis, and Latine	**23-4**

The first beat may also consist of two syllables which are slurred over in one time, as,

Siðen / óf þe dóme yu / sál i sáy   216
Vij máyster stérns er sétt in héven   525

4. The beat can never be dropt, except after the second lift, nor can it consist of two distinct syllables.

Of Brut þat bern bald of hand   7
Wers tre, wers fruit it beres   38
And all þat sek war to leche   176
Of a spusebreke womman   185
Þan sal þe raynbow descend   1254

If two syllables occur forming one beat, they can easily be slurred over in one time, as has been seen in the first beat, as,

For súm o þíjn ful míkel wil þink   975

5. Final *e* is never counted when it is followed by a vowel, and generally not when followed by a semi-vowel (*y*, *w*) or *h*. Of such words beginning with an *h*, note *he*, *him*, *his*, *her*, *hem*, *hu*, *here*, *have*, *had*, or French *honur*, *hure*, *heritage*, *heyr*, and so on. This rule may be exemplified by the following lines—

Þe tende ordre for to fulfil   515
He dos it, for heen' wald ye were   773
And þus he les his grete honur   487
Bot þaarof ne had ye na pitee   1775

6. *Hiatus.* It is generally avoided by way of elision. But we observe—

(*a*) The definitive article þe may stand before a vowel, f. i. *in the alde law* 116, though there are instances enough where þe is apostrophized and joined to the following word, as þangeles 133, 433, þouermaast 395, þuprijsing 1447, 1620, þayr 1608, þaȝtand 1176, þ'haly crois 211.

(*β*) *ne* though generally cut off before such forms of *to be* and *to have* as with a vowel, semi-vowel, or *h*, might be sometimes kept before a semi-vowel or *h*, as *ne have* 1173, *ne wat* 64, *ne harmed* 685. The semi-vowel and *h* then keep their consonantal character.

7. Elision. I have already mentioned that final *e* is silent before a vowel, semi-vowel, or *h*. Of the elision of *e* in þe I refer to 6. Besides, observe *to*, as, *t'vprijse* 1149 ; *ne*, as, *n'es* 1243, *nys* 645, *nart* 654, *ne hadd* 370, 1775, *ne wald* 16, *ne was* 100, *n'vnderstandes* 1589. A kind of elision, to which Ten Brink (*Chaucer*, § 269) gives the happy expression 'synklisis,' takes place in *many es* 930, *a body he* 1420, *body and* 1659, *sundry and* 332, *merci of* 1579. Something like an elision, which is, properly speaking, either an apocope or

an aphæresis, may be called 'enclisis,' as *ín' had* 956, *þaýn' sal* 1275, *hen' schál* 1384, *ijn' may* 1524, *þayn' sál* 1689, *þaýn' may* 1756, *þát es* 427, *hée's* 936, *þayn' war* 1468, *þun' sal* 337. As the MSS. denote the apocope, and the modern usage seems to justify the aphæresis of the other instances, I don't speak of a mere slurring-over.

8. A slurring-over of two syllables in the beat, the first of which belongs to a word in the lift, is made by some sort of syncope, as, *water and* 357, *þowquéðer has* 909, *listen a* 1048, *cruel and* 1194, *héven he* 1220, *éfter his* 1332, *Queðer súm* 1395, *ówðer on fóot* 1439, *Queðer þár* 1627, *Vnder þe náme* 1628, *pénance sal háve* 1644, *nówðer to give* 1757, *énded and* 209, *ángel and man* 424, *maner o scaft* 425, *obúten þe nedes* 192. Observe also this instance in which you have an enclisis and some sort of apocope, as *atte doóm* 1630. I'll also mention under this head such instances as *nímbre þat* 503, *Childer in* 1080, which at first sight exemplify the apocope and the elision.

Syncope. It is generally *e* that is syncopized, as *elementz* 353, *covering* 483, *cómàndmént* 648, 660 (but *commandement* 340), *suffrance* 745, *covenand* 1673; *lauerd* 1205, etc.; *lawed* 249, *heðelike* 449, *vnneeðes* 1761, not to count *luveliest* 1003, for *luve* is always monosyllabic. Then observe the syncope in *over, never, ever, queðer*, as *þouermaast* 395, *ouertakes* 574, *euermaar* 98, *neuermaar* 501, *quer*[1] 1633, besides *pouer* 1755 (but *pover* 1681), *aunters* 12. The syncope of other vowels is to be met with in *heritage* 607, etc. Note also *Ierusalem* passim. Other contractions, so that there is a syncope of a consonant and a synæresis, are *mad, heed*, but also *heved*. In *kidd* 1267, *cledd* 801 (but *cleðed* 798) there is, of course, an assimilation of ð and *d*, and only a syncope of *e*. In *Antecrist* 213 we may presume on the syncope of *e* and even of *t*.

The inflexion furnishes us with many observations on this head.

a. The infinitive has seldom kept its *n*, so that there may be a syncope, *mistruun* 1410 (cf. 15498).

β. Final *es* in the 2. and 3. sg. present, and the plural of substantives, often undergoes the syncope, as *wenes* 289, *standes* 653, *werreys* 32, *multiplijs* 286, *governs* 286, *cums* 308, *haldes* 314, *geetes* 808, *truus* 1058, *behooves* 1174, *saves* 71, *vmluukes* 1320, *tells* 1057, *makes* 1557, *beers* 1603; *laves* 182, *angels* 412 (cf. *angéles* 133, 433), *yates* 590, *elementz* 353, *wijndes* 1245, *felawes* 1392,

---

[1] Compare also spellings like *nerþeless* C 21247, *nourquar* C 23619, *ourquar* C 14570, *ouir*, or 19422, etc.

warlawes 1226, *cluuds* 1607, *days* 214; but *luves* 81, *gruues* 543, *ouertakes* 574, *standes* 901, 1004, *wenes* 769, *telles* 1210, *seemes* 1409, *truues* 1617, *lijkes* 54, *preyes* 108, *menskes* 109, *schijnes* 291, *reyses* 326, *clepes* 604, *neʒes* 1007, *rennes* 1031, *spekes* 1199, *lookes* 1556, *vndeserves* 1741; *þinges* 314, *bernes* 902, *dayes* 921, *treës* 761, *cluudes* 1310, *signës* 1242, *wijndes* 1256, *schaftes* 1289, *presúndes* 160, *clerkes* 356, *leves* 802, *wordes* 888, *flummes* 1032, *limmes* 1445, *huudes* 1477, *sawles* 1759; cf. also *es* in the genitive, as, *doomesday* 1046.

γ. *en* in the participle past shows syncope in *born, schorn, sworn, lorn, lijn, ycorn, slayn, schawn,* but *schawen* 579.

δ. *ed* is treated alike in the preterite and the participle past. The original preterite ending *ede* has found an apocope, and the ending *dẹ* is of rare occurrence, as, *waldẹ* 847. It is, therefore, only the syncope that we are concerned about in the preterite ending *ed.* Observe the following instances, *behoovẹd* 422, *deyẹd* 1520, 1734, *leyẹd* 811, *trávayld* 1390, *purvayd* 284, *órdaynd* 285. Otherwise compare *demd* 186, *fild* 850, etc. There is no syncope in *harmed* 685, *yerned* 786, *schawed* 1531, *proved* 1532, *turned* 180, 929, *heled* 187, *raysed* 194, 1541, *pijned* 198, *harwed* 200, *ended* 209, *hooped* 732, *lijked* 1731. Of syncopized participles past, note *turnd* 1444, *demd* 1630, 1665, *prisúnd* 1697, *besweld* 1760, *truud* 956, *reft* 1239. On the other hand, compare *fúlfild* 422. There is no syncope in *changed* 479, *confermed* 500, *maked* 632, *flemed* 951, *demed* 1613, *carked* 1615, *blessed (blisced)* 197, 1692, *vnsaked* 570, *filed* 880. Observe also the syncope in the adjective *wrecchẹd* 991, but *wrecched* passim. It is not difficult to see that a stem ending in a vowel or diphthong or middle-sound (nasal- m, n) or vibrating-sound (r) or semi-vowel (w, y) facilitates the syncope. Besides, it is by shifting back the word-stress that the syncope becomes necessary, as *órdaind.* Such forms as *kidd, hidd,* show syncope and assimilation, and *maad* has also the guttural syncopized.

10. Diæresis is found in *Ysaÿ* 1057, *Moïses* 143, *Ysaac* 137, *Esaü* 140, *crëaturẹ* 328. The synæresis is a *fait accompli* in such words of French origin as, *seel, veel, preche, emperur.*

11. Shifted word-stress. Observe the following instances of Teutonic and French origin: *godnéss* 97, *wímman* 895, 897, *wimmán* 757, 894, *gódheed* 559, *godhédẹ* 317, *fáyrhed* 666, *feláwes* 1393, *kaisér* 1372, *commándement* 340, *cómandmént* 648, *prophét* 1595, *þe próphet* 704, *súffrance* 745, *channél* 1178, *chánnel* 1192, *tréasur* 1679, *ríchess* 1678, *penánce* 1644, *pénance* 949, 1643, *fántum* 55, *cónseyl* 1625, 1763, *partíes* 344, *párties* 352, *résun* 587,

lécchur 31, *baner* 1377, *báner* 1373, *manére* passim, *máner* 425, *sérmun* 196 ; *Hérod* 161, 172, *Wáwayn* 13. Note also compounds like *ýpbeers* 1415, *fórbod* 610, 872.

Further observe *to cónfund* 728, *cómfort* 1581 ; *commún* 236, 242, *cómmun* 1726 ; *endíng* 668, *winníng* 966, *cursíng* 1724; *gretánd* 1088, *schijnánd* 1378, *lyvánd* 1438, *faránd* 1032, *sekánd* 1516 ; *vglij* 1134, *vnquémfullij* 1166, *flesslij* 1419, *manij* 1677, *breflij* 120, *treystlij* 260, *needfúl* 225, *cáitiues* 1236 ; *swíft-likèr* 341, *héylijkér* 1382, *fayrér* 1563, *luvelièst* 1003, *vnwiliést* 736.

Besides, observe the double stress in trisyllabic verbal nouns, as, *vprijsìng* 202, 1433, 1447, 1620, *bíginnìng* 278, but *bigínning* 269, *báptisìng* 171. In trisyllabic substantives of French origin this double stress is quite common, as *religiún* 1660, *còuaytíse* 1758.

Moreover, observe adverbial compounds, as, *intó* 1772, *intíl* 380, *herbíj* 47, *hérby* 661, *þarfór* 601, *þárfor* 631, *forþíj* 659, *fórþy* 611, *þárwíþ* 917, *tilwárd* 936, *towárd* 1004, *vpwárd* 1164. The regular stress is found in *ínto*, *þarfór*.

12. *Enjambement.* This metrical license, so well known from French verse, is a very good means for making the monotony of the metre less dull. It finds its support by inversion and line-stress. *Ten Brink*, § 317 ff. has given some fine remarks on Chaucer's enjambement. The *Cursor* never has such bold instances as Chaucer's short metre. It will be worth while to give a variety of instances, that the reader may judge for himself.

þat i speke o þis ilke tre	
Betakens man, bath me and þe	39-40
He þat stiþest wenes at stand	
War him his fal is neist at hand	61-2
þat saves me first in erth fra sin	
And heven bliss me helps to win	71-2
Quat bote is to sett travayl	
On þing þat may noȝt avayl	89-90
Quaswa wil of hir fayrnes spell	
Find he sal ynouȝ to tell	95-6
O reuth, o luve, and charite	
Ne was neuer hir make, ne neuer sal be	99-100
Al þis werld, ar þis book blin,	
Wiþ Cristes help i sal ouerrin	121-2
Siðen hit schal be redd yu þan	
Of Ioachim and of saynt Anne	153-4
Hu þat Ihesu Crist himselve	
Ches til him apostels twelve	173-4
Siðen hu þat halij driȝtin	
Turned water into wijn	179-80
Hu vr leveþy ended and yald	
Hir sely sawl, hit sal be tald	209-10

Selden was for any chance
Praysed Inglis tung in France   245-6
Forþij es schortly noȝt þat he
Ne may all do his will to be   1422-3
þis mikel maysters says þat þay
May saved be in nankynnes way   1470-1
O five þusand men þat he
Fedd wiþ five laves and fisses þre   181-2
Nȝ þe neddre was noȝt bitter
þan þow he was ever witter   695-6
' Loo,' he sayd of Adam, ' hu
Lik he's mad tilward vs nu   935-6
A! Lauerd, quat he war wijs þat moȝt
Stedfast hald þis day in poȝt   1780-1

The reader will have seen from these instances that the run-on lines are only allowable when the two separated words bear the line-stress. But these line-stresses must not be confounded with the metrical lifts, four of which are in every line, while the sense generally requires no more than four stresses in two lines. All the metrical lifts, therefore, are not of the same value, and can be distinguished as chief stresses and by-stresses. Now these separated words, which bear the chief stress, are generally disconnected from each other by several other words. When one of the separated words stands at the end of one line, the corresponding word seldom stands at the head of the following line, in order to avoid the close succession of the chief stresses. But there is a good exception to this rule in ll. 935-6, where *huu* and *lijke* bear the chief stress, as would be required in prose. In ll. 1780-1 *þat moȝt*, which is not material to the sense, does not bear the chief stress, though the two words mark the cutting. The lines must be read thus :—

A! Láuerd, quat hé war wijs, þat moȝt
Stédfast hald þis day in poȝt.

Compare also ll. 179-80, where the subject and the object of its activity are emphasized, or ll. 245-6, where the adverb *selden* and the subject are opposed. In ll. 181-2, 1422-3 *he* gets a chief stress because it denotes the Lord, otherwise the stress would be rather weak. In l. 1423 the chief stress lies on *will;* in l. 182 *he* in l. 181 is supported by the two chief stresses at the end of the line. In ll. 695-6 *bitter* and *witter* are opposed to their full effect.

13. As to the ryme I refer to the critical part. The reader will have been persuaded that neither the quantity nor the quality of the ryme is quite correct in the *Cursor*. Nor will the reader wonder at it when he compares other poems by my critical tests.

14. Besides the short metre exemplified by my two specimens of a critical

text, we meet with a 'langer bastune', which I have simply called 'long lines' in my former essay. The line consists of seven lifts, with a cæsura after the fourth lift, so that it is possible to divide it into two parts after the modern way. Inner ryme does not occur except in ll. 17097—17106 G, and in ll. 1795—17100 C, where the first part shows inner rime. In dividing the lines into two parts, I make the same observations as on the short metre, with respect to the omission of the first beat, to the double first beat slurred over in one time, and masculine and feminine endings, etc. The reader may be satisfied with a short specimen of a corrected text (ll. 14937—15040).

Ihésus | went tilward[1] | Ieru|saleem |
Gangand on his fete,
And com he til a litel hill
14940   Man calles munt Olivete.   4
Sex dayes forwiþ paske-day
Wiꝸ his he went þe strete,
Till his disciples þat he ledd
14944   Sli wordes spak he suete: 8
'Wat ye breꝸer quij', he sayd,
'I weind ogayn swa snell?
Herkens nu and vnderstandes
14948   þe sooþ i sal yu tell: 12
Yon Iewes ar, wele waat ye it,
A folk selkuþ fell,
þay wil me never luve, ywis,
14952   For þing i may þaym tell.   16
For luve ne aw ne for na thing
þat i for þaym have wroȝt,
Wiþ many selkuþ, als ye have herd
14956   And wiþ sothfastnes soȝt.   20
Bot al my swinc nu es it swa
Standes me for noȝt,
þe time es nu mannes sun sal dey
14960   And mannes kijnd be boȝt.   24
To yon castel ga yee, he sayd,
Ye se ogayn yu stand,
þar sal ye fijnd an ass best
14964   Wiꝸ hir fole doon in band.   28
Gaas fotte hir me, if any man
Lays vpon yu hand
To lette yuu, ye say ye have
14968   þe lauerd to yur warand.   32

1 (14937) tilward] to F   2 (14938) gaand F, apon G   3 (14939) com he] *inn.* G   4 (14940) clepis G, it *add.* F   5 (14941) niȝtes F, forwit C for wid G before F, pask day C **y**   6 (14942) þe str.] in st. F þat str. G   7 (14943) þat] atte F   8 (14944) suche F   9 (14945) mi breþer G   10 (14946) ogeyn] again C **y**   11 (14947) vnderstande **y**   14 (14950) selcuthli G   17 (14953) ne awe] or agh C, thing] signe **y**   19 (14955) selcouþes F, herd] sene **y**   20 (14956) sothfastnes] softnes þaim (ham) **y**   22 (14958) it *add.* F   23 (14959) man C, *alt.* F   24 (14960) mans C   25 (14961) ga yee, he sayd] *inv.* G   26 (14962) again C **y**   29 (14965) ga F, fet G focche F   30 (14966) yu] hir F, apon C **y**

[1] tilward = toward

	A moder ass ye sal þar find	
	And yee hir sal vndoo	
	Vt of hir band; if any man	
14972	Askes yu quarto,	36
	Ye say to þaym þe laverd has	
	Wiþ þaym for to do.	
	And sal na man yu say bot good;	
14976	Þe stede es yonder, loo!'	40
	Soon þar went disciples twa	
	Vnto þe sayd castel,	
	Bunden þat þay soȝt þis ass	
14980	Þay fand by a postel;	44
	Broȝt þay nouðer on hir bak	
	Ne sadel ne panel	
	To þayr lauerd[1] was nouþer cledd	
14984	Wiþ silk nē sendel.	48
	'My freindes,' sayd he, 'waat ye qui	
	I wend nu to þe tun?	
	Þe sooþ to wite, i sal yu scaw	
14988	Al mij priue resun,	52
	Þe time es cumen nu i sal	
	Suffre mi passiun,	
	Þe fest es nu, mismay yu noȝt,	
14992	Bot maas my riding bun.	56
	Nu,' he sayd, 'sal wommans sune	
	In mannes hand be laȝt;	
	Þay sal him take and deem to ded	
14996	Wiðvten any saȝt,	60
	And wiþ tresun him do on tree	
	Als it es forwiþ taȝt;	
	He sal be ded, bot rijse he sal	
15000	Wiðin þe þridde naȝt.'	64
	Þay kest þayr claðes on þis ass	
	And did him þaron sett;	
	Sone it ras þe word þat he	
15004	Was command bi þe strete.	68
	Þe folk was[1] cumen to þe fest	
	Almast for joy þay grete,	
	Þe simple folk al o þe tun	
15008	Þay went him for to mete.	72
	Wið all þe mirþes þat þay moȝt	
	Derworþly þay him mett,	
	Wið harp and pipe, and horn and trump	
15012	Þe strete þay him vmsett,	76
	Ald and yung, bath less and mare	
	All wið a worde him grett:	

35 (14971) hir *om.* **y**, land F 　　38 (14974) nu *add.* **y**, þeym] hir F 　　40 (14976) stode F 　　42
(14978) into F, þis **y** 　43 (14979) *alt.* G 　　45 (14981) nauþer F 　46 (14982) ne] na C *om.* **y**,
panel] yeit panel **y** 　48 (14984) ne s.] ne yeitt C, in s. ne in s. F 　49 (14985) sayd he] *inv.* **y**
53 nuu i] n. þat i C, þat i **y** 　57 (14993) womman C **y** 　58 (14994) mans C 　63 (14999) bot]
and G 　64 (15000) thrid C **y** 　65 (15001) clothes C 　66 (15002) sett] site F sitte G 　69
(15005) was] þat was C 　70 (15006) grette C 　74 (15010) Darworthli C, gett C mete G
mette T *alt.* F 　75 (15011) and horn] and *om.* G 　76 (15012) wai **y**, þaim G, umbeset F
78 (15014) wit a word all C wid ai w. þai G

[1] rel. pr. nom. omitted.

'Welcum sauveur! lang has þu been,
15016   Al sal þurwȝ þe be bett.'   80
þe lauerdings and þe rike men
  To quijls o-bak þaym drouȝ
And tempred tresun for to tri
15020   To take Ihesum wiȝ wouȝ.   84
þay murned, quijls þe povere men
  And þe childer louȝ,
Befor þayr king þe childer kest
15024   Branches þai brak o bouȝ;   88
And sum þan kest þayr claȝes dun
  In midward þe þrang,
þay spredd þe strete wiþ clath and flur
15028   His ass on for to gang   92
þe folk him folwd and forwiȝ went,
  þay mensked him wiþ sang,
'Osanna, lauerd, welcum þu be,
15032   Quar has þu ben sa lang?'   96
Bot þe childer þat war wayk
  To ga þat pres omang
On walles and on windous, als
15036   þayr hevedes ouer þay hang,   100
Beheild þayr laverd þar he com;
  For-sooþ had þay na wrang,
All þay sang als wiȝ a muþ
15040   þat al þe cite rang.   104

79 (15015) sauuer C   80 (15016) thoru þe sal all G   83 (15019) resun G, trei G, for *om.* G
85 (15021) murn C   86 (15022) loght G   88 (15024) þai *add.* C G, brak *om.* F   89 (15025)
þan] þai C, þayr] þai C, clethes G   91 (15027) cloth C   92 (15028) on for] apon G   96
(15032) sua G   98 (15034) weind y, amang C F emang G   100 (15036) O C ouer F   103
(15039) *alt.* F.

The reader will have observed that this metre appears in stanzas of four lines, but of the same ryme. From l. 15337, however, their length begins to vary between four and ten.—I'll mention from this text two instances of a synizesis: passiun 54, sauveur 79, and one instance of an aphæresis: Osanna 95.

I don't speak of the seven additions which do not belong to the *Cursor.* But I shall treat of them elsewhere, and when opportunity offers, edit them critically.

ADDENDA.

On page 113 (cf. § 1, and see l. 22920), I have to add that the use of *for* in its local sense still occurs in ll. 10497 (C) and 22664 (E).

As to § 2, ll. 20124 and 23087, I'll admit that the reasons given are very weak, and the critical text has abandoned them. As will be found from § 65, the line 20124 must be read:

þat tái ne had óf hìr mistér.

The *Notes on the Versification*, page 254, no. 4, show that a beat may be dropt after the second lift. Now the succession of two lifts (*óf hìr*) seems to avoid any ambiguity as to their disconnection from *mister*. It is the same thing with *sékenès*, which has a double stress. So I might assume that **y**'s readings, as the younger ones, only tried to make up for the want of a beat, which is really done in some other places.

As to ll. 24642 and 24646, I still believe that G shows the correct reading. The mistake of *thogh*, *þoh* for *thoght* is not so uncommon, cf. l. 24537 : *And thoght apon þe* (*þa* E, *þat* C F, *iuus flitt* **y**, where C has *thogh* and E *þoh*). Besides cf. *forþoht* E and *forþou* G 24303. The sense of ll. 22641-3 is : 'I also thought that delay long, and I thought that my misery was entirely repaired by his death : that was my comfort, for then I turned joyful.' E's readings I cannot make out, for I cannot understand how *for grew al þi gle* should suit with *And þoh was þi bal al bet*. Besides, consider the transposition of *þan* in E. It remains now to believe that G's reading is original, and not a correction. Otherwise it would prove that **x** G might share the same mistake of their source, and that E could not be disconnected from C G F. Kaluza fights in the *Englische Studien*, xi. 2, in a peculiar way, only showing his disbelief without giving any reason for his different opinion, and without explaining E's reading, which he is not inclined to reject. The line 24646 '*In langurs all for þe*' is an apposition to *to þi leif*, i. e. 'to your dear who is longing for you.' How could *I languis for þe* be explained, for which E correcting *I* into *In* writes *In languis* (*lagins* print.), thus omitting *n* in *languis*? Should *I languis for þe* be the contents of the *bodeword* or love-message? Such an affected explanation would almost remind me of the coarse remark given by Gierth in the *Englische Studien*, vii. 2, on the relation of the *leuedi* to John. **x**'s reading is, no doubt, a mistake, and is easy to account for by the way of ancient writing.

As to § 3, the reader is, of course, first requested to consider the close agreement of words and rymes between A and **x y** in a good many passages, and the South-Midland character of the MS. (cf. § 41), in order to ascertain for himself that A, which shares North-Midland forms and rymes with **x y**, cannot be derived from a Southern source. I protest against Kaluza's way of fighting in the *Englische Studien*, xii. 3, where he gives the reader a good deal of mere rubbish without facts, taking for granted what never came into my mind, and not caring for whatever reasons I had previously declared were laid down in this publication. Why should he, like an oracle, utter such wayward pretension, without giving facts, or any proof that he knows more about dialects than a young student who always clings to his College notes?

As to § 4, I'll remark that the evidences taken from ll. 20099 and 20113 are not beyond doubt: *þat treulic sal kepen þee* could also be read *þat treúlic sál kèpen þee*, and in *þar scho beleuid al hir liue* the author might likewise have neglected the third beat. But the evidence taken from l. 20118 is undoubted.

As to § 57, 5 (cf. M.E. *i* before *ht* = O.E. *eo, i* and in O.N. slêgð) where *fight* (vb. and sb.) 470, 2233, and *hight* (= O.E. *hehte,* prt.) 442 must be inserted, I have still to add the same forms for *Brunne's Chronicle,* though the Lambeth MS. tries to spell *ei.* Compare, therefore, the following rymes: *fyght* (sb.), r. w. *ryght* 20, r. w. *knyght* 148, r. w. *might* 7826, etc.; *fight* (vb.), r. w. *knyght* 470, 1640, r. w. *myght* 1698, r. w. *tyght* (pp.) 3310, r. w. *on keyghte* 15598, etc. Now consider *sleight,* r. w. *heyght* 5080, r. w. *þe Peyht* 5680, and *sleightes* (pl.), r. w. *feyhtes* (pl. sb.) 7152; *heyyht* (sb.), r. w. *þe Peyht* 5708, 7182, and *Peytes,* r. w. *deseites* 5810, where the Petyt MS. seems to have the original reading *lefe to fehtes.* I do not believe that there is any reason to keep the spelling in *ei,* so that Brunne also has *slight, hight, fight* and *Pyht.* Alter, therefore, in l. 5810 into *leue to fightes.*—*fight* also occurs in *Tristrem,* cf. *fight* (vb.), r. w. *liзt, wiзt, bright, kniзt* 1025, 1001, 1060, 1532, etc. Compare also *Sir Gawayne* 1, 12: *ryзt,* r. w. *fyзt,* r. w. *knyзt* (cf. *Knigge,* etc., p. 23).—The *Bruce* has *myзt* (sb.), r. w. *ficht* (vb.) xvii. 158, though the MS. has a good many forms like *fecht, fechting.* Besides, compare *hight* (height), r. w. *rycht* (sb.) IV. 667, etc. But there is *heycht,* without ryme III. 707.

As to § 60, I'll add a list of occurrences of *þou* in C: *þou* 20083, 21026, 21087, 21168, 24221, (tamen) 10324, *þo* 24692, *þouqueþer* 10895. Besides, consider *þoqueþer* (E G) 22485, þou E 22921, *þar* E (*þof* C þou G *þat* F) 22972, *þan* C (*þoз* E þou G þen F) 19261.

As to § 70, I'll give some further illustrations; f. i. 18359:

it es sene be þe weroni (C).

Weroni = *Veroni* (not mentioned in Kaluza's Glossary) means the image of Christ's face represented in the handkerchief of St. Veronica, who gave it Jesus when he, going to Mount Calvary, broke down under the burden of his cross, and wiped off his sweat on it. This legend seems to have come into existence about the middle of the 13th century.

Then the mention of Raymund (ll. 26904, 28674, 29485) reminds us that in 1238 Raymundus de Pennaforte, the third grand master of the order of the Black Friars (Dominicans), composed by order of Gregory IX. the famous Decretals, and that Pope Innocent (1243—54), who commands priests not to suffer false shrift (l. 26826 ff.), and is called Pater et Organum Veritatis, wrote Commentaries on Gregory's Decretals.

Moreover, I'll give some remarks on lines which contain allusions to the costume of the author's time; f. i. ll. 25463-8 (C):

Nu ask i noþer gra ne grene,
Ne stede scrud ne lorein scene
Ne purperpall, nee pride of pane,

Ne riche robe wit veir and grise—
O werlds aght ask i na pris;
Ne castel mad o lime and stane :

further l. 4387 :   Sco drou his mantel wit þe pan,

and ll. 28010-28021 (C):

And yu leuedis, wit your quite hals,
And sai to yond maidens als,

.   .   .   .

And studis hu your hare to' heu,
Hu to dub and hu to paynt,
And hu to mak yow semle and quaint,
Biletts forbroiden and colers wide,
For to sceu wit your quite hide,
Wit curchefs crisp and bendes bright,

.   .   .   .

Thoru your trail bath wide and side,
Es not at seke to find your pride.

In availing ourselves of the careful illuminations given by Mr. J. R.
Planché, Somerset Herald, in his *History of British Costume*, we may well
presume on the above words describing the costume of the reign of Edward I.
(1272-1307).   In the first citation it is worth while to refer to *ne purperpall,
nee pride of pane*, and to think of the long trailing mantle ornamented with a
pane or border of ermine and other costly furs, as, in contrast with the costume
of the reign of Henry III., will be seen illuminated in a MS. of the reign of
Edward I., in the library of H.R.H. the Duke of Sussex (cf. Planché, p. 110).
Considering the last citation, we may well be reminded of the sarcastic
descriptions in the *Roman de la Rose*, especially in its continuation composed
by Jean de Meun.   Let the reader note that the ladies of this time wear long
robes trailing on the pavement (cf. l. 28020, and see Planché, p. 122, illumina-
tion from Sloane MS. 3983) with wide collars (cf. ll. 28010, 28016, and see
Planché, p. 123, illuminations from Royal MS. 15, D 2), and have their heads
dressed with crisp kerchiefs and bands in variegated colours (cf. l. 28018, and
Planché, p. 123).

As to the Author's religious position, we might infer from his keeping
silent on the immaculate conception of the Virgin when he relates to us the
story of her conception, that he is not an orthodox Franciscan.   The abrupt
conclusion, therefore, of his story of Elsey or the Festival of her Conception,
cf. ll. 24931-34 :

Bot nu es said on oþer wise
Propre of þis fest hali servise
Til ilk man þat will it sai
Redi haf it hali þat dai (C)

will not make us believe that he is a particular friend to the new doctrine
started by the Franciscans, or the new Festival of the Conception of the
Virgin, which was generally celebrated after the 14th century.   So these lines
would not disagree with our supposition that he might have been an inmate of
the Cistercian Abbey of Lindberge.

DR. HUPE'S COMMENTS ON DR. MORRIS'S PREFACE.

No fellow-worker who has for more than four years given his spare time to an Editor, who wanted for his edition of the *Cursor* an inquiry into the MSS., the dialect, and the authorship of the poem, could be more surprised than myself by the Editor's tone in his Preface and Additional Notes to the whole text. The Editor, who saw the proof-sheets of my *Cursor Studies*, and who might have been expected to favour his fellow-workers with support, has been silent these two years without telling me what he thought of the *Cursor Studies.*

This Preface is an unkind answer to the efforts which I made in writing the *Cursor Studies.* From the Notes the Editor has written, it is clear that he cannot have mastered the whole bulk of my studies, for he neglects everything, so far as I can see, and even explains at full length words which I have already explained in the *Cursor Studies.*

As to the short rebuke on p. xvi of the Preface : ' Dr. Hupe thinks that "dight" means "ornamented," and that the first possessor is the author' of the *Cursor*, I refer Dr. Morris to § 59 of my *Cursor Studies*, and I hope the reader will look at the meanings of the O.E. *dihtan*. That Dr. Morris 'speaks somewhat slightingly of my opinion,' will be recognized when he derives the verb *to tift* from the Old French *tiffer*, to trim, though it shares its meanings with *to dight*, O.E. *dihtan*, and has the preterite *tifted !*

Dr. Morris quite mistakes my opinion on *fede* and *quede.* He has not taken the trouble to examine § 60 (gutturals) of the *Cursor Studies.* In line 63 of the Critical Text I have retained ' schaltu,' because the Cursor is not purely Northumbrian. That is the reason why I did not reject ' þei.' In line 176 I left out *e* in *sek*, because it is of no consequence for the metre. See the Notes on Versification. It is just the same with l. 504 *erth*, on which the Doctor should read my Notes on Versification.

Dr. Morris's remark on l. 204 of the Critical Text falls to the ground. For if I take *onstandand* (p. pres.) = standing by, which is supported by F's reading *on-stode* (prt.), I certainly do not refuse to recognize that *stad* is an old participle = O.I. *staddr* (cf. the *Cursor Studies*), but I do not yet know that *onstad* as an intransitive preterite could be a preterite of the transitive *onsteden*, provided that such a verb exists. We have the intransitive verb *bistand* = to stand about, but *bisteden* is transitive. Now I should say, we could think of *to onstand* = to stand by. If *onstad* could be retained, it must be a past participle; but I do not see how I could supply *was*.

As to l. 260, Dr. Morris has misread the Critical Text, which has the reading of C. If Dr. Morris had read the *Cursor Studies* thoroughly, he would not wonder at the change between *ai* and *ei*, and at my orthography, which I adopted on purpose. But it is a trifling matter.

In l. 272 I retain the reading of C, and there is no reason to refuse it on account of G T. I could say as well that Dr. Morris's opinion is here arbitrary. I do not know what the remark on l. 828 of the Critical Text is really meant for. I refer the reader to my remark in the Notes, and will add that G has *lourid*. In l. 22,472 I have preferred *way* = wǣȝ, balance, on account of the verb *turn*. Dr. Morris wonders why I take *solwed* for C's *sulwed*, which is of little consequence. But see the *Cursor Studies* and Stratmann, s. v. *solwen*. *Sulwed* cannot be derived from *sulien*, as Dr. Morris thinks, but it must be referred to *solȝan*. The derivation of *w* and ȝ should be known to Dr. Morris.

In l. 22,510, Dr. Morris is probably of opinion that I did not know the phrase 'blac sum ani hair,' but on considering that *hair* does not suit a diphthong in a rhyme, I thought of *air*. How is it possible that Dr. Morris should make me believe that in my opinion *any air* should be = *any tempest?* The lines run thus:

> It sal becum þan ful unfayr,
> Dim and black sum any ayr,
> When it es fayrest on to look
> At midday time, als says þe book,
> Blacken it sal þat ilke time
> Þat nan þarwiþ sal see a stime.

I really doubt Dr. Morris's suggestion, when we have such an impressive description of the dim atmosphere by which the sun is hidden.

As to l. 22,753/4

> lund and lijth (people) and all þinges
> Þat any werldes hald wiÞ hinges

I am not fully convinced that *see* should be retained, and I still think it may be a mistake owing to the *see* just above in the preceding line. That all the Manuscripts have *see* is not strictly conclusive. In the reading of line 22,897 I willingly agree that I have made a mistake.

Now I ask the reader whether Dr. Morris had a right to give such a verdict on my Critical Text, as he does in his Preface. He has at hand 1799 lines, and criticizes about fifteen lines, of which only three may be admitted to be wrong. Moreover, Dr. Morris knows that the Critical Text is intended to be only an attempt towards finding the original reading, and to be a firmer basis for my Notes on Versification. How conservative the readings should be when only the orthography is concerned, is very difficult to decide upon.

Now I still further ask the reader what the use of Dr. Morris's Notes are, when most of his explanations have been already given in my *Cursor Studies* or in the Glossary? The reader will also often wonder why the others are necessary. But I at once declare that many of them which are meant to correct the statements of his fellow-workers, fail altogether to be right. I shall examine the proof-sheets of the first eleven pages which were sent to me by the Director. The reader can then judge of the other pages by himself.

PAGE 1 OF DR. MORRIS'S NOTES.

Cursor, p. 10, l. 31. There is an explanation of *leth*, which is already given in the Glossary, where it is put beside *lath*, because Dr. Kaluza knows that there are double forms in â and ê in O.E. Instead of this, Dr. Morris compares it with Swed. *leda*, and also gives Swedish etymologies of *wreth* and *breth*. Dr. Morris is wrong in saying that *leth* in l. 23,260 signifies 'comfort,' because T has *ese*, and in deriving it from O.E. *lîŏs*, comfort, pleasure, when we have the common phrase in Southern dialects *wiþouten lothe* (see Stratmann) ; and *leth* is just *leth* = *lath* = O.E. *lêþ*, *lâþ*, injury, aversion. The lines are :

> þat al þair limes are bunden wit
> Wituten leth of ani lith (extreme point of a limb);

so that the *firend brandes* do not consume the limbs, and the pain will be everlasting. What has *lething* 7438 to do here with *leth* 31? *lething* is explained in the Glossary, and every reader will know M.E. *to lethe* = to soothe.

p. 12, l. 63. What is the use of *brathly*, speedily, with various readings, already given in my text, when the Glossary and Stratmann translate *violently*? *speedily* is not the same as *hastily* here.

l. 67. If we prefer 'mer,' it should, of course, be = hindrance.

l. 82. There are the various readings of the line, and the meaning of M.E. *wan*, *woon* is added, though explained in the Glossary.

l. 89. '*hit* as in T seems wanting.' See the Critical Text.

l. 109. '*bald*, sure, confident, not bold.' I should rather say: *bald* has two meanings, as is proved by the O.E. word: bold, confident.

p. 14, l. 124. '*haue in tale*, relate, tell' seems to me an elementary explanation, when the reader will find *tale* = account in the Glossary.

l. 153. 'For *reddynn*, read *redd yuu*.' See my collation of C, which Dr. Morris seems to have neglected.

p. 18, l. 168. '*hoef* = hof (F) baptized, the pret. of hefen,' etc. See Gloss.

l. 185. '*O spousebrek womman*, of the adultery of a woman.' Dr. Morris is wrong to take *spousebrek* as an abstract noun. The word *spousebrek* = adulterer, is known (see Stratmann); besides, a genitive inflection can be omitted only when it precedes the governing noun. The omission of the inflection in the N. dialect is fully explained in the *Cursor Studies*, § 66, so that I think Dr. Morris ought to have worded the following note (l. 190) differently. Other reasons must have led me to adopt the inflectional *s*, which is not omitted as a rule.

Spousebrek in l. 27,322 is an abstract noun, indeed; for *wijf* is an uninflected genitive, as the lines run thus:

> Wif spusebrek sal dern penance
> Do sua wit preist ordinance.

The second line also shows an instance of an uninflected genitive. I therefore think that the Glossary is right to regard *spousebrek* in l. 185 as doing duty for an adjective.

The next three notes are of no consequence.

PAGE 2 OF THE NOTES.

l. 201. '*vnschill* C, written for *unskill*.' See my Critical Text.

l. 202. '*for* is wanted in C, on account of the metre' is of no consequence, for Dr. Morris has overlooked that *vprising* has a double accent. See my Notes on Versification, which Dr. Morris has neglected again. The various readings are in the Critical Text, and I see no reason why they should be rewritten in the Notes, which are meant to be explanatory, otherwise they have to be read in the edited text of the MSS.

The next notes are of no consequence.

l. 256. '*mode* C = mode of life; G's *mede* is evidently wrong.' Why does Dr. Morris repeat what is given in my Critical Text?

l. 257. '*ill-hayl*,' etc. must be known to everybody.

l. 259. '*sum we till heild*' etc. is already explained in the Glossary, and is quite an Anglican phrase, as Dr. Morris could see in the *Cursor Studies*.

The next five notes are of no consequence.

p. 30, l. 376. '*sonded* = *sundered*, divided; see l. 378, where we ought to read *sondird*.' Dr. Morris is altogether wrong. *sonded* refers to the French *sonder* (to measure the depth of; to explore; to examine). The change between *o* and *u* in the Anglo-Norman dialect is known. The text is quite intelligible, as the lines run thus :

> wit water sondird als cristale,
> þat es, þar ouer fra þar under;
> in þ[e]se[1] he sou[n]did al wit wonder.

' The water was explored as being clear like crystal, *i. e.* from the surface down to the ground. He explored everything wonderfully.'

The next four notes are of no consequence.

l. 478. '*ouergart*' is already explained. '*ongard*' is not in l. 7318, but *ougart*, where the sign of abbreviation is wanting. See Gloss.

Page 3 of the Notes.

p. 40, l. 558. '*licam*, body C, is an error for *likness*.' See Critical Text.

l. 564. '*min* C cannot be a passive participle (see l. 718); therefore the reading of G and T is probably to be preferred.' This conclusion is very curious. I cannot understand how *mijn* could be compared to *min* = to remember. I cannot help considering *min* = mine, my own; see Critical Text.

l. 572. '*unsaked*,' etc. and l. 575 '*underfanged*'; see Glossary.

p. 42, l. 610. '*knaulage*,' etc. See *Cursor Studies*, § 74, Remark 1.

l. 621. '*sund*,' etc. ; see Gloss.

l. 641. '*welt(h)ful wan* C G T,' etc. G F T have *of*, which is wanting in C. I prefer the genitive to an apposition, ' a welthful wan.'

p. 46, l. 683. '*samertale*'; see Gloss.

l. 684. '*þar herd* = *hair herd* (flock),' etc. is a doctored text, where Dr.

---

[1] G þis.

Morris has really met a stumbling-stone. 'þar' is the pronoun þair, referred to 'þe bestes'; see Critical Text. The lines show it very distinctly :

> þe bestes self war samertale
> wiþuten hurt þar herd ay hale.

i. e. without any injury their herd (was) always sound.

p. 48, l. 691. '*gripe*, a vulture. Swed. *grip.* Icel. *gripr.*' See Glossary. The etymology is very poor.

l. 698; p. 50, l. 727; ll. 745, 752, 754 are of no consequence. See Critical Text and Glossary.

p. 52, l. 756. '*elth* C = *helth*' cannot be denied.

l. 757. '*a tharu*'; see Critical Text.

ll. 769-70. '*laue;* þe *laue,*' etc. ; see Glossary and Stratmann. I think that its meaning is well known.

The next three notes are of no consequence ; see Gloss.

l. 818. '*bisuak* C, deceived; F *begylet*, G *bigiled*, T *giled*. In l. 819 *suak* C G, *had blent* G T. In l. 2998 all the texts keep *besuik*,' etc. Any reader who had not the text at hand, might think that *besuik* is a preterite ; but it is an infinitive, so that there is no occasion for any note, so far as I understand.

p. 56, l. 825. '*bi-went* gone, departed. The usual meaning of *biwende* in M.E. is, to turn, to turn round.' Well, this meaning also suits here capitally. See : Alkin blis was þan bi-went. *blis* = fortune ; *i. e.* 'fortune is turned round,' viz. the wheel of fortune is originally meant in the metaphor.

Page 4 of the Notes.

l. 916. '*tinsel* C F G = *loos* T, loss'; see Gloss. 'l. 11946, son of tinsel = son of perdition' is well-known; cf. Dr. Furnivall in *Handlyng Synne* (Glossary).

p. 64, l. 980. '*will o wan*, bewildered in thought,' etc. Fully explained in the *Cursor Studies*, § 74, Remark 2.

Page 5 of the Notes.

p. 84, l. 1315. '*vtenemes* C G,' etc. is fully explained in the *Cursor Studies*, p. 249, under l. 1206.

PAGE 6 OF THE NOTES.

p. 168, l. 2807. '*mik or mau* C,' etc. etc. is explained at full length in the *Cursor Studies*, § 80.

PAGE 9 OF THE NOTES.

p. 284, l. 4678. '*ern* C. This plural in *n* shows that the scribe has doctored the original text.' There is no reason to believe that. Had Dr. Morris seen what I have given on Verbs in the *Cursor Studies*, § 67, where we find the plur. pres. *luuen* / 20,375 rhyming, and inflected forms of the infinitive and the preterite, he would have thought otherwise. I am sorry that I am mistaken in my quotation l. 12,106, where the verb is '*wern*' = to deny, to refuse. I cannot now look for such quotations where '*to wer*' = to defend, might occur, and I do not know exactly now whether such plural forms of '*to wer*' exist, since my manuscripts are burnt.

p. 306, l. 5263. '*forhond* C = *forhoud* = *forhuud*, neglected,' etc. I think that Dr. Morris has entirely overlooked my collation of C. Dr. Kaluza could not know it, because he compiled the Glossary before I had collated the MSS. again.

PAGE 10 OF THE NOTES.

p. 310, l. 5314. '*his heued wit hare* C. For C's *wit hare* we ought to read *was hare*, was hoary (grey).' This appears to be a doctored reading, while *hare* is a noun with the meaning of *hoariness*. The omission of 'was,' which stands in the same line, cannot take us by surprise any more than in l. 684.

ll. 5315-6. '*for-liuen* . . . *fordriuen*. Ought we not to read *forleued* . . . *fordreued*? The latter would signify greatly troubled?' Is that possible, when *to dreue* means 'to push forth'? The idea of 'trouble' lies in *many barets*. For 'to trouble' I only know 'to droue.'

I will go no further. The reader may be satisfied with this, and I hope that his mind will have changed now respecting the opinion that Dr. Morris has given on my Critical Text and the *Cursor Studies*, which he can have scarcely read. Dr. Morris quite neglects to see what is most important in my *Cursor Studies*, and has even failed to criticize my Critical Text which was meant to be here of minor consequence.

DR. H. HUPE.

Lubeck, October 18th, 1891.

The manufacturer's authorised representative in the EU for product
safety is Oxford University Press España S.A. of El Parque Empresarial
San Fernando de Henares, Avenida de Castilla, 2 - 28830 Madrid
(www.oup.es/en or product.safety@oup.com). OUP España S.A. also acts
as importer into Spain of products made by the manufacturer.
Printed and bound by CPI Group (UK) Ltd, Croydon, CR0 4YY

05/05/2026
02103007-0005